Lecture Notes in Computer Science 7114

Commenced Publication in 1973
Founding and Former Series Editors:
Gerhard Goos, Juris Hartmanis, and Jan van Leeuwen

Bruce Christianson Bruno Crispo
James Malcolm Frank Stajano (Eds.)

Security Protocols XIX

19th International Workshop
Cambridge, UK, March 28-30, 2011
Revised Selected Papers

Springer

Volume Editors

Bruce Christianson
James Malcolm
University of Hertfordshire
School of Computer Science
Hatfield, AL10 9AB, UK
E-mail: {b.christianson, j.a.malcolm}@herts.ac.uk

Bruno Crispo
University of Trento
Faculty of Mathematical, Physical and Natural Sciences
Via Sommarive 14, 38100 Trento, Italy
E-mail: bruno.crispo@unitn.it

Frank Stajano
University of Cambridge
Computer Laboratory
15 JJ Thomson Avenue, Cambridge, CB3 0FD, UK
E-mail: frank.stajano@cl.cam.ac.uk

ISSN 0302-9743 e-ISSN 1611-3349
ISBN 978-3-642-25866-4 ISBN 978-3-642-25867-1 (eBook)
DOI 10.1007/978-3-642-25867-1
Springer Heidelberg Dordrecht London New York

Library of Congress Control Number: 2011942622

CR Subject Classification (1998): C.2, K.6.5, E.3, D.4.6, H.4, H.3

LNCS Sublibrary: SL 4 – Security and Cryptology

Typesetting: Camera-ready by author, data conversion by Scientific Publishing Services, Chennai, India

Printed on acid-free paper

Springer is part of Springer Science+Business Media (www.springer.com)

Preface

The volume you hold in your hands[1] collects the revised proceedings of the 19th International Security Protocols Workshop, held in Sidney Sussex College, Cambridge, during March 28–30, 2011. The theme of this workshop, "Alice doesn't live here anymore," is developed in the Introduction.

Following the tradition of this workshop series, each paper was revised by the authors to incorporate ideas from the workshop, and is followed in these proceedings by an edited transcription of the presentation and ensuing discussion. The pleasant novelty is that, thanks to the valiant effort of all the workshop participants, this year the proceedings volume is being published in the same year as the workshop, allowing for a more timely dissemination of both the research results themselves and of the debates that they stimulated. Hopefully this will encourage more readers to engage with the authors offline while the ideas that were discussed at the workshop are still topical. Besides, citations to the authors' work will be timestamped with the year in which they were first presented.

Redaction and revision of the transcripts to make them intelligible and coherent is always a labor-intensive and time-consuming operation: after the raw transcription by Lori Klimaszewska (to whom, as always, our heartfelt thanks) the subsequent editing easily takes a day or two per transcript. No surprise that previous volumes had accumulated a backlog, despite the heroic efforts of the editors. For the first time this year we decided to spread the load, in massively parallel fashion, among all the workshop presenters, making each of them responsible for the main editing pass of their transcript. It is thanks to their gratifyingly timely response to this additional request from us, that we were able to put together this volume in just a few months.

Our thanks to Vashek Matyas and Michael Roe for joining us on the Program Committee this year to select the papers that were presented. Thanks also to Microsoft Research for financial support. We hope you find these papers and discussions controversial and thought-provoking, just as we did.

Participation in the Security Protocols Workshop has always been by invitation only. To be invited, you must submit a position paper that is assessed as "interesting," and be willing to present it to a demanding (but supportive) audience. If after reading these proceedings you wish to be considered for an invitation to a future workshop, please contact us and let us know.

September 2011

Bruce Christianson
James Malcolm
Bruno Crispo
Frank Stajano

[1] Or see on your screen.

Previous Proceedings in this Series

The proceedings of previous International Security Protocols Workshops are also published by Springer as *Lecture Notes in Computer Science,* and are occasionally referred to in the text:

18th Workshop (2010)	LNCS 7061	*in preparation*
17th Workshop (2009)	LNCS 7028	*in preparation*
16th Workshop (2008)	LNCS 6615	ISBN 978-3-642-22136-1
15th Workshop (2007)	LNCS 5964	ISBN 978-3-642-17772-9
14th Workshop (2006)	LNCS 5087	ISBN 978-3-642-04903-3
13th Workshop (2005)	LNCS 4631	ISBN 3-540-77155-7
12th Workshop (2004)	LNCS 3957	ISBN 3-540-40925-4
11th Workshop (2003)	LNCS 3364	ISBN 3-540-28389-7
10th Workshop (2002)	LNCS 2845	ISBN 3-540-20830-5
9th Workshop (2001)	LNCS 2467	ISBN 3-540-44263-4
8th Workshop (2000)	LNCS 2133	ISBN 3-540-42566-7
7th Workshop (1999)	LNCS 1796	ISBN 3-540-67381-4
6th Workshop (1998)	LNCS 1550	ISBN 3-540-65663-4
5th Workshop (1997)	LNCS 1361	ISBN 3-540-64040-1
4th Workshop (1996)	LNCS 1189	ISBN 3-540-63494-5

No published proceedings exist for the first three workshops.

Table of Contents

Introduction: Alice Doesn't Live Here Anymore (Transcript)

Bruce Christianson

University of Hertfordshire, Hatfield, UK

Hello everyone and welcome to the 19th Security Protocols Workshop. The theme this year, which it is traditional to mention in the first session (and then never refer to again), is "Alice doesn't live here anymore".

One of the perennial problems in analysing security protocols is how we distinguish Alice from not-Alice[1].

The prevailing wisdom is that Alice possesses something which not-Alice does not. It might be knowledge of something that is used as a key. It might be that Alice possesses some physical characteristic, such as a biometric, or that there is something about the hardware that Alice is running on that is difficult to replicate. Or it might be that Alice possesses exclusive access to the interface to some distinguishing piece of hardware, like a dongle, although such hardware (when we think about it) usually belongs to some other security domain anyway.

This traditional view is unsatisfactory in a large number of respects. It makes it appear that, if Moriarty manages to learn Alice's password or to steal her dongle, then he is now Alice, whereas before he was not-Alice. And conversely, when we want to migrate Alice from one piece of unique hardware to another piece of unique hardware, if the security property is associated with the hardware then it looks as if Alice has become not-Alice, and that's not always what we want either.

It's even more dangerous from a conceptual point of view, because a lot of papers (it's very tempting, we all do it, I've done it myself) assume that the difference between Alice and not-Alice is determined by the protocol that we use to tell the two of them apart. That's fine in the sense that it defines the problem away, but it means we've got no idea of the opportunity cost of using the particular abstractions that we've chosen to use, and no real way of discussing alternatives, because we've agreed that we're aren't going to use any abstraction that allows us to look at the alternatives.

This is particularly bad when one of the characteristics that Alice possesses, and that we use to distinguish her from not-Alice is her location. So we say, for example, that Alice is whoever is plugged into this particular port. The difficulty

[1] Distinguishing Moriarty from not-Moriarty is traditionally regarded as being harder, albeit more interesting. This is true even if we negate the usual assumption that Moriarty and not-Alice overlap.

B. Christianson et al. (Eds.): Security Protocols 2011, LNCS 7114, pp. 1–3, 2011.

then is, how do we know who is really plugged into the port, and what is the location anyway when we have routing attacks[2]?

A second thing that is becoming more worrying is the very large amount of security context that has to be reproduced in order to enable our protocols to function. We design something with nice clean abstractions, and then we discover that there are all these rather ephemeral properties about the way cookies happen to be implemented that you need to get right or the system doesn't actually do what you want. And people are using keys in a way that isn't quite what it says on the box that the algorithm came in, but then the protocols don't work either — not not-work in the sense that the protocol doesn't do what Alice wants it to, but in the sense that the protocol doesn't not do what Alice wants not-Alice not to be able to do.

So the question is, if we de-archive some software in twenty years time, are we actually going to be able to reproduce enough of the context to get it all to work again? Could we de-archive Alice in a state of grace at all, or are we going to need some way of bypassing all of that context to get the archived version to work. And if we're going to archive software and want to talk to it in twenty years time, what's to stop Moriarty from thawing Alice out now and persuading her that she is in *our* future.

Finally, it's often the case that, as computer scientists, we want to use one set of abstractions for modelling one set of properties of a system, and then a different set of abstractions for modelling other properties. Unlike natural scientists, whose instinct when they're given two models covering the same phenomena is always to unify them, computer scientists tend to resist that on the grounds that if they do that they'll end up with something that's more complicated than the system that they're trying to model[3].

So there's a danger that we might switch to using a different set of abstractions and discover that the distinction between Alice and not-Alice has actually disappeared, which means that Alice was never really there in the first place; she was just an artefact of the security model we chose to use. And remember, Moriarty doesn't have to use the same model.

So far as the workshop is concerned, the purpose of the theme is just to let us be a little more open than usual to the possibility that we could use different abstractions to define who is Alice to the ones that we usually use, and to let us at least consider the possibility that when we talk about principals such as Alice and Moriarty we don't actually know quite whom we're talking about.

Now, many of you have been before, but some of you haven't, so I'll just briefly explain the ground rules. This is a workshop and not a conference. It's OK to interrupt the speaker, and if the audience have a view about what would make a more interesting talk than the one that the speaker's trying to give, it's OK to hijack the talk and make it more interesting. Conversely if you're a speaker and

[2] Even quantum ones, e.g. Phil Trans R Soc Lond A (1998), 356, p 1838.

[3] If we don't, then either we forgot to model something important, or else our implementation is unnecessarily complicated, and we should have just animated the model.

you've got something that you really want to say before your talk gets hijacked (or to prevent it from being), then it's a good idea to say it quite early on while you've still got a chance. So, it is OK to express a different point of view, but if you break somebody's protocol you have to help fix it over teatime.

On a building site, it's everybody's job to check that the foreman is wearing her hard hat. Here, everybody please check that the person who is speaking is wearing the microphone and that the red light is on; it won't help you to hear them, but it will certainly help us when we come to do the transcripts later on. And so, without further ado, let us turn the page to our first session.

His Late Master's Voice:* Barking for Location Privacy**

Mike Burmester

Florida State University, Tallahassee, Florida, U.S.A.
burmester@cs.fsu.edu
http://www.cs.fsu.edu/~burmeste

And you all know, security is mortals' chiefest enemy.
Macbeth, III.5.2, W. Shakespeare

Abstract. Bob died suddenly leaving his treasure to sister Alice. Moriarty will do anything to get it, so Alice hides the treasure together with Nipper, and promptly departs. Nipper is a low-cost RFID device that responds *only* to Alice's calls—making it possible for Alice to locate the hidden treasure later (she is quite forgetful) when Moriarty is not around. We study the design of Nipper, the cryptographic mechanisms that support its functionality and the security of the application.

Keywords: RFID, localization privacy, location privacy, device discovery.

1 Introduction

Radio Frequency Identification (RFID) is a promising new technology widely deployed for supply-chain and inventory management, retail operations and more generally, automatic identification. The advantage of RFID over barcode technology is that it does not require line-of-sight reading. Furthermore RFID readers can interrogate RFID tags (devices) at greater distances, faster and concurrently. One of the most important advantages of RFID technology is that tags have read/write capability, allowing stored information to be altered dynamically.

In this paper we focus on *passive* RFID devices that are battery-less and harvest power from RFID readers. Some passive RFID devices such as WISP (Wireless Identification and Sensing Platform) [21] developed by Intel Labs, have additional features such as a real-time clock (that relies on harvested power) and a 3D-accelerometer, while others are more basic. EPCGlobal [8] recently ratified the EPC Class 1 Gen 2 (EPCGen2) standard for passive RFID deployments

* The HMV trademark comes from a painting by Francis Barraud who inherited from his late brother Mark a fox terrier, Nipper, a cylinder phonograph and a number of Mark's recordings [11]. The painting portrays Nipper listening to the sound emanating from the trumpet of the phonograph.

** This material is based upon work supported by the National Science Foundation under Grant No. 1027217.

B. Christianson et al. (Eds.): Security Protocols 2011, LNCS 7114, pp. 4–14, 2011.

which defines a platform for RFID protocol interoperability. This supports basic reliability guarantees and is designed to strike a balance between cost and functionality. EPCGen2 operates in the 860-960 MHz band for which the effective broadcast range is rather restricted—typically less than $10m$. RFID systems that broadcast at GHz frequencies, such as those used with automatic toll collection systems, have a larger range, typically $100m$.

Several RFID protocols that address security issues for passive devices have been proposed in the literature. We refer the reader to a comprehensive repository available online at [1]. Most RFID protocols use hash functions [19,16,10,2,7,15]. Some protocols use pseudo-random functions [5,20,3], or pseudo-random number generators. Recently a lightweight RFID protocol was proposed [4] that is based on loosely synchronized pseudo-random number generators.

Our contribution in this article is to study a novel application of RFID in which tags will only "backscatter" a signal if this is authentic. Authentication is the primary goal for RFID deployments, however it is important that the process used to support it does not have a negative impact on other security goals, such as privacy. If an RFID tag has to reveal its identity to get authenticated, then an eavesdropper can track its movement in the supply chain. For some applications *linkability* is a serious privacy threat. To deal with such threats one typically uses pseudonyms. However this still will not prevent the adversary from detecting the *presence* of responding tags. The location of a transmitting device can be determined by analyzing its radio signals. For outdoor applications the signal strength and/or direction are used (with triangulation protocols (see e.g., [17]); for indoor applications one may have two antennas on each tag and analyze the phase difference of their signals (to deal with multi-path effects, see e.g., [9]).

Localization privacy requires that an RFID tag will only respond to a challenge from an RFID reader if it can first ascertain that the challenge is authentic and fresh (current).[1] In particular, that it is not replayed. Since the range of RFID readers is rather short, replay attacks are a major threat for RFID deployments—in the scenario discussed in the abstract, Moriarty may find the treasure by replaying Alice's call to Nipper, if Moriarty happens to be close to the treasure and Alice is out-of-range.

Localization privacy captures a novel aspect of privacy extending the traditional privacy notions of anonymity and unlinkability to devise discovery. Anonymity and unlinkability (see e.g., [6,14]) are slightly weaker notions: even though the adversary may not be able to recognize a tag, or link its interrogation sessions, knowing its location will identify that tag to some degree, particularly if the tag is static and there are only a few tags in the range of an RFID reader—see Section 2.1, Application 1. Localization privacy is essentially a steganographic attribute. The goal of steganography is to hide data in such a way that the adversary cannot detect its existence, while the goal of localization privacy is to hide a device in such a way that its presence cannot be detected.

[1] The title of this paper: "Nipper barks for location privacy", captures this functionality.

Our Contribution. RFID localization techniques enable applications that reveal the location of tags. In this paper we consider the problem of protecting the privacy of localization. We show that:

- If temporal and location mechanisms are available then location privacy can be achieved for one-time interrogation applications in the presence of a ubiquitous adversary. For applications requiring multiple tag interrogations we only get weak localization privacy.
- If only location mechanisms are available then localization privacy can be achieved for one-time tag interrogations in the presence of a ubiquitous adversary. For applications requiring multiple tag interrogations we only get weak localization privacy.
- If only temporal mechanisms are available then we cannot achieve localization privacy for ubiquitous adversaries (unless the reader and tags have highly synchronized clocks); however we do get weak localization privacy.
- If neither temporal nor location mechanisms are available then we cannot achieve any kind of localization privacy.

2 RFID Tags Know the Current Time and Their Location

To motivate our application we start with the case when RFID tags have clocks and know their location.

In our first protocol (and the following) the RFID reader shares with each tag a unique secret key k. Let $time_r$ be the time the reader sends its challenge and loc_r the location of the reader (as measured by the reader); and let $time_t$ be the time the challenge was received by the tag and loc_t its location (as measured by the tag).

Protocol 1

Step 1. The RFID reader sends to the tag the challenge:

$$time_r,\ loc_r,\ x = MAC_k(time_r, loc_r).$$

where MAC_k a keyed message authentication code (*e.g.*, OMAC [12]).

Step 2. The tag checks the challenge. If the authenticator x is valid, $|time_t - time_r| < \delta_{time}$ and $dist(loc_r, loc_t) < \delta_{range}$, where $\delta_{time} > 0$, $\delta_{range} > 0$ are appropriate bounds, then the tag responds with

$$y = MAC_k(x).$$

Step 3. The RFID reader checks the response y. If this is valid it accepts the tag (as authentic).

Step 1 of this protocol authenticates the RFID reader to the tag, and can be thought of as the response to a "time and location" query from the environment (a trusted entity that is not under the control of the adversary). The tag only responds if the time the challenge was sent and the location of the reader are within acceptable ranges related to its own time reading and location. This assures localization privacy. Replay attacks beyond the range of the reader are thwarted by having the location of the reader included in the challenge; replay attacks in the range of the reader (at a later time) are thwarted by having the time the challenge was sent included in the challenge.

The actual location of the tag is determined by using a localizing algorithm. Such algorithms determine the source of a transmission by analyzing the RF waveform of it signals, *e.g.,* by using the signal strength and/or direction (multilateration algorithms [17]), or the phase difference [9]. More than one reader will be needed but only one reader needs to broadcast the challenge.

The tag's response authenticates the tag to the reader, so we have mutual authentication. In Section 6 we shall show that this protocol provides mutual authentication with localization privacy for device discovery against ubiquitous adversaries (as defined in Section 2.2).

2.1 Applications

There are several applications for localization privacy. In this paper we consider two such applications for static tags:

1. *Device discovery.* This involves one-time tag interrogations: when the device is discovered it is recovered and the task for that device terminates. An example of such an application involves the deployment of tagged plastic mines. More generally, applications in which objects are hidden so that they can only be recovered later by authorized agents. For such applications, for each object, localization privacy lasts for only one interrogation.
2. *Sensor deployments in hostile territory.* Tagged sensors can be deployed by casting them from aircraft over hostile territory. The sensors are used for monitoring the deployment area but are not networked for localization privacy. Instead an armored RFID reader traverses the deployment area interrogating those tags on its route that are in range (the route must go though every cell of the sensor range grid). For this application localization privacy should endure for several interrogations.

2.2 Threat Model

Our threat model is based on a Byzantine adversary that can eavesdrop on, and schedule, all communication channels, adapted for the wireless medium to allow for: (*i*) *localization (or surveillance) technologies* that analyze radio signals (based on the strength and/or direction of the signal, phase differences, etc) and (*ii*) *radio jamming technologies* that override signals emitted by devices.

We distinguish two types of adversary: (*i*) *ubiquitous*, that can access all deployed tags,[2] and (*ii*) *local*, whose wireless range is approximately that of

[2] This can be achieved in several ways, *e.g.*, by using a hidden network of listening devices—although setting up such a network may be perilous in a plastic mine deployment.

authorized RFID readers. Local adversaries are restricted by their broadcast range: protection against such adversaries assures only weak localization privacy. In our threat model for localization privacy we constrain the impact of localization and signal jamming technologies by assuming that:

1. The adversary *cannot* localize a non-active tag by using a non-linear junction detector, or more generally a device that floods a target area with an RF signal and analyzes the reflected signal.[3]
2. The adversary must eavesdrop on *at least one* complete tag response to localize the tag.
3. The adversary *cannot* localize a tag during an authorized interrogation if the tag's response is too weak to be received by the RFID reader.[4] Similarly, the adversary *cannot* localize a tag during an interrogation by jamming its response (to prevent the reader from getting it).[5]
4. A local adversary *cannot* localize a tag from its response while it is interrogated by an authorized reader.[4]

Assumption 4 highlights the weakness of local adversaries. It is partly justified by noting that the tag's response (a modulated backscatter) is much weaker than the reader's challenge, and attenuates as the inverse fourth power of traveled distance. Without it we cannot have localization privacy with multiple tag interrogations since the location of the tag would be revealed the first time it responds to an authorized challenge.

From Assumption 3 we either have:

4. *Reliability.* If a tag is in the range of an authorized RFID reader that interrogates it, then the interrogation will be completed,

or we have a DoS-deadlock between the authorized reader and the adversary. We shall assume that in the second case, the authorized reader always wins—the intruder is located and destroyed.

Remark 1. A ubiquitous adversary can eavesdrop on all communication channels, and therefore can also localize any tag that is interrogated by an authorized RFID reader, *after* the reader has localized it (by Assumption 2; disruption attacks are restricted by Assumption 3). For such adversaries localization is restricted to one-time tag interrogations. After the tag is localized it is inactivated/killed. We have:

5. *One-time tag interrogation.* A ubiquitous adversary *cannot* localize (discover) a tag that has already been located by an authorized reader.

---

[3] Non-linear junction detectors operate at (very) close proximity to target devices. If there are privacy concerns with particular implementations then the IC circuit of RFID devices should be shielded.

[4] The tag will only respond to the reader's signal if this is sufficiently strong.

[5] The reader will either identify, locate and destroy the intruder or refrain from interrogating the tag.

The scope of replay attacks against localization privacy with one-time tag interrogations applications (*e.g.*, device discovery), is restricted to replaying reader challenges beyond the range of the reader (by Assumptions 3 and 5, since a tag will only respond once, when the challenge is authentic.

Remark 2. In Protocol 1 the RFID reader must send a different challenge to each tag (using the shared key k). If the number of tags is large and the reader does not know the approximate location of each tag (as possibly in the sensor deployment discussed in Section 2.1) then tag interrogation can be time consuming—the protocol is not scalable. For such applications we may use Public Key Cryptography: the RFID reader authenticates the time and its location with an Elliptic Curve Cryptography (ECC) signature [13]: $sig_{\mathrm{SK}_r}(time_r, loc_r)$, instead of the message authentication code $MAC_k(time_r, loc_r)$. Here SK_r is the private key of the RFID reader. The tag can verify this using the public key PK_r of the RFID reader. However verifying ECC signatures can be computationally expensive.[6]

Remark 3. In both applications discussed in Section 2.1 only the RFID reader is mobile, while the location of the RFID tag is fixed for the lifetime of the system. Consequently if a Global Positioning System (GPS) is used, this is activated only once. It follows that the tag can be equipped with a small battery and a GPS used to establish its position on deployment. Several hybrid RFID solutions are currently available (see *e.g.*, [18]).

3 RFID Tags Know Their Location

In our second protocol the RFID reader shares with each tag a secret key k as well as a counter ct which is updated with each interrogation. The reader stores in a database for each tag a pair (k, ct) containing the key and the current value of the counter. The tag stores in non-volatile memory a list (k, ct^{old}, ct^{cur}) containing an old value and the current value of its counter. The stored values at the reader and tag are updated by: $ct \leftarrow next(ct)$ and $ct^{old} \leftarrow ct^{cur}$, $ct^{cur} \leftarrow next(ct^{cur})$, respectively, with the tag's update made only if the value of the received counter ct is the same as the stored value of ct^{cur}, where the operator $next(\cdot)$ gives the next value of the counter. At all times at least one of the two values of the counter of the tag is the same as that stored at the reader. Initially $ct = ct^{old} = ct^{cur}$.

Protocol 2

Step 1. The RFID reader sends to the tag the challenge:

$$ct, loc_r, x = MAC_k(ct, loc_r).$$

[6] If the tag responds with the message authentication code $MAC_k(time_r, loc_r)$, then we still have a scalability issue (but this time on the search time rather than the number of broadcast challenges): the reader must check the response for all keys k in its database. For one-time interrogation applications, the tag can include its tag ID, or a preassigned pseudonym.

Step 2. The tag checks the challenge. If $dist(loc_r, loc_t) < \delta_{range}$, where $\delta_{range} > 0$ is an appropriate parameter, and if x is valid for either $ct = ct^{old}$ or $ct = ct^{cur}$ then it responds with:

$$y = MAC_k(x),$$

and if $ct = ct^{cur}$ the tag sets: $ct^{old} \leftarrow ct^{cur}$ and $ct^{cur} \leftarrow next(ct^{cur})$.

Step 3. The reader checks the response y. If this is valid then it updates its counter $ct \leftarrow next(ct)$ and accepts the tag (as authentic).

In this protocol the RFID reader updates its counter after receiving a response from the tag (Step 3). If a response is not received, then the same value of the counter is used the next time. This is why the tag must keep the old value of the counter ct^{old}. This value will only be updated when the interrogation is completed. It follows that at all times, at least one of the values of the counters of the tag is the same as that of the counter of the reader.

In Section 6 we shall show that Protocol 2 provides mutual authentication with localization privacy for one-time tinterrogation applications. For applications where a tag can be interrogated several times we only get weak localization privacy. This is because even though a local adversary cannot discover a tag while it is interrogated by an authorized reader (Assumption 4), it can eavesdrop on the interrogation and later replay the reader's challenge (in the same location) and use a localization algorithm to locate the tag.

Remark 4. In Protocol 2, loosely synchronized counters partly capture the functionality of loosely synchronized clocks in Protocol 1. However there is a subtle difference between these protocols. If the adversary in Protocol 2 is allowed to prevent the reader from receiving the tag's response in Step 2 (Byzantine adversaries schedule communication channels) then the reader will abort the session without updating its counter. The adversary may later replay the reader's challenge to localize the tag: since the counter was not updated the tag will respond. This attack is prevented by Assumptions 3,4. Protocol 1 is not subject to this weakness.

4 RFID Tags Know the Current Time

In our third protocol the RFID reader shares with each tag a secret key and the reader and tags have loosely synchronized clocks.

Protocol 3

Step 1. The RFID reader sends to the tag the challenge:

$$time_r\ ,\ x = MAC_k(time_r).$$

Step 2. The tag checks the challenge. If $|time_t - time_r| < \delta_{time}$, where $\delta_{time} > 0$ is an appropriate parameter, and if x is valid then it responds with:

$$y = MAC_k(x).$$

Step 3. The RFID reader checks y. If it is valid then it accepts the tag (as authentic).

This protocol does not provide (strong) localization privacy. A ubiquitous adversary can use an online man in the middle attack to relay the flows of the RFID reader to the tag, when the tag is not in range of an authorized reader—unless the tag and reader have highly synchronized clocks. In Section 6 we shall show that Protocol 3 provides mutual authentication with weak localization privacy.

Remark 5. Observe that the temporal mechanism in Protocol 3 cannot replace the location mechanism of Protocol 2. The reason is that online man in the middle attacks on location mechanisms are constrained by the broadcast range of RFID readers (tags can determine their location in this range), while such attacks on temporal mechanisms are constrained by the speed of light (tags can only detect such attacks if they, and the reader, have highly synchronized clocks).

5 RFID Tags Do Not Know the Time or Location

Theorem 1. *Localization privacy cannot be achieved when the tags are static if neither temporal nor location information is available to the tags.*

Proof. The proof is by contradiction. Suppose that neither temporal nor location information is available. First consider a ubiquitous adversary. If a tag is not in range of the RFID reader that challenges it, then the adversary can use an online man-in-the-middle relay attack to forward the reader's challenge to another area of the deployment zone were the tag may be. The tag has no way of checking that the challenge was sent from far away and/or much earlier. So it will respond. This violates localization privacy.

Next consider a local adversary. In this case suppose that the tag is not present during the interrogation. Then the adversary may record the challenge of the RFID reader and replay the challenge later (an offline man in the middle attack). Again the tag has no way of detecting that the challenge was sent from another location earlier, and will respond. □

6 Proofs for Protocols 2, 3 and 4

We now sketch the security proofs for the protocols presented in this paper. Proofs in a strong security framework will be given in the full version of the paper.

Theorem 2. *Protocol 1 provides implicit mutual authentication with localization privacy for one-time tag interrogation applications against ubiquitous adversaries. For applications where tags may be interrogated several times we only get weak localization privacy.*

Proof. (Sketch) First consider a ubiquitous adversary with one-time tag interrogations. By Assumptions 5 the adversary cannot discover a tag that is already discovered (interrogated). Also, the adversary gains no advantage when the interrogation fails by Assumption 3. If the tag is not present while it is interrogated then the adversary can replay the reader's challenge to other areas where the tag may be. This is thwarted because the challenge contains location information. The only remaining attack is to forge the keyed message authentication code: if a cryptographic hash function is used this is not feasible.

Next consider applications where tags can be interrogated several times, with a local adversary. By Assumption 4 the adversary cannot localize a tag while it is interrogated. However it can replay the challenge of the reader in the same place at a later time: this attack is thwarted because the challenge contains temporal information. If the tag is not in the range of the RFID reader when it is challenged, then the adversary can replay the challenge to other places where the tag may be. This attack is thwarted because the challenge contains location information. Finally forging the message authentication code is not feasible as observed earlier.

We get mutual authentication because the RFID reader is authenticated to the tag in Step 1 and the tag is authenticated to the reader in Step 2. The authentication is only *implicit* because the tag does not receive confirmation from the RFID reader. □

Theorem 3. *Protocol 2 provides implicit mutual authentication with localization privacy for one-time tag interrogation applications against ubiquitous adversaries. For applications where tags may be interrogated several times we only get weak localization privacy.*

Proof. (Sketch) As in Theorem 2, a ubiquitous adversary will not succeed while the tag is interrogated, and will not succeed by replaying the reader's challenge to some other areas when the tag is not present during an interrogation, because the challenge contains location and information. Also forging the message authentication code is not feasible. The only remaining attack is to de-synchronize the counters of the reader and the tag. This is not possible because that tag always keeps an old value of the counter, and the counters are only updated when the interrogation is completed.

Next consider applications where tags are interrogated several times and the adversary is local. Again the adversary cannot localize a tag which is interrogated, but can replay the challenge either in the same location (later) or other locations. The first attack is thwarted because the reader and tag have updated their counters; the second because the challenge contains location information. Finally forgery and de-synchronization attacks fail as in the ubiquitous adversary case. The proof for implicit mutual authentication is as in Theorem 2. □

Theorem 4. *Protocol 3 provides only implicit mutual authentication with weak localization privacy, unless highly synchronized clocks are available.*

Proof. (Sketch) As observed in Section 4, a ubiquitous adversary can use an online man in the middle attack to relay the flows of the RFID reader to the tag, when the tag is not in range of an authorized reader—unless the tag and reader use highly synchronized clocks (which is not practical for lightweight applications). The tag will then accept the reader's challenge and respond. So we cannot have localization privacy.

Next consider applications where tags are interrogated several times with a local adversary. Again the adversary cannot localize a tag while it is interrogated by an authorized reader. However it can replay the challenge, later. Replaying it will not succeed because the challenge contains temporal information (this is an offline man in the middle attack, so the difference between the send and receive time will be greater than δ_{time}). Finally as in Theorem 3 forgery and de-synchronization attacks will fail and we have mutual authentication. □

Acknowledgement. The author would like to thank Xiuwen Liu and Zhenghao Zhang for helpful discussions on accurate localization technologies and security issues; Jorge Munilla for helpful comments on th6e protocols and localization; and all those present at the SPW 2011 presentation of this paper for helpful suggestions; finally Oakland.

References

1. Avoine, G.: RFID Security and Privacy Lounge (2010), `http://www.avoine.net/rfid/`
2. Avoine, G., Oechslin, P.: A scalable and provably secure hash-based RFID protocol. In: PERCOMW 2005: Proceedings of the Third IEEE International Conference on Pervasive Computing and Communications Workshops, pp. 110–114. IEEE Computer Society, Washington, DC, USA (2005)
3. Burmester, M., de Medeiros, B.: The Security of EPC Gen2 Compliant RFID Protocols. In: Bellovin, S.M., Gennaro, R., Keromytis, A.D., Yung, M. (eds.) ACNS 2008. LNCS, vol. 5037, pp. 490–506. Springer, Heidelberg (2008)
4. Burmester, M., Munilla, J.: Flyweight authentication with forward and backward security. ACM Trans. Inf. Syst. Secur. 12 (2011), `http://www.cs.fsu.edu/~burmeste/103.pdf` (accepted August 27, 2010)
5. Burmester, M., van Le, T., de Medeiros, B.: Provably secure ubiquitous systems: Universally composable RFID authentication protocols. In: Proceedings of the 2nd IEEE/CreateNet International Conference on Security and Privacy in Communication Networks (SECURECOMM 2006). IEEE Press (2006)
6. Danezis, G., Lewis, S., Anderson, R.: How Much is Location Privacy Worth? In: Fourth Workshop on the Economics of Information Security (WEIS 2005), June 2-3. Harvard University (2005)
7. Dimitriou, T.: A secure and efficient RFID protocol that can make big brother obsolete. In: Proc. Intern. Conf. on Pervasive Computing and Communications (PerCom 2006). IEEE Press (2006)
8. EPC Global. EPC tag data standards, vs. 1.3, `http://www.epcglobalinc.org/standards/EPCglobal_Tag_Data_Standard_Version_1.3.pdf`
9. Hekimian-Williams, C., Grant, B., Liu, X., Zhang, Z., Kumar, P.: Accurate localization of rfid tags using phase difference. In: IEEE International Conference on RFID (RFID 2010), pp. 89–96. IEEE (2010)

10. Henrici, D., Müller, P.M.: Hash-based enhancement of location privacy for radio-frequency identification devices using varying identifiers. In: Proc. IEEE Intern. Conf. on Pervasive Computing and Communications, pp. 149–153 (2004)
11. His Master's Voice, http://en.wikipedia.org/wiki/HisMaster'sVoice
12. Iwata, T., Kurosawa, K.: OMAC: One-key CBC MAC. In: Johansson, T. (ed.) FSE 2003. LNCS, vol. 2887, pp. 129–153. Springer, Heidelberg (2003)
13. Lee, Y.K., Batina, L., Singelee, D., Preneel, B., Verbauwhede, I.: Anti-counterfeiting, Untraceability and Other Security Challenges for RFID Systems: Public-Key-Based Protocols and Hardware. In: Sadeghi, A.-R., Naccache, D. (eds.) Towards Hardware-Intrinsic Security, Information Security and Cryptography – THIS 2010, pp. 237–257. Springer, Heidelberg (2010)
14. Liu, L.: From data privacy to location privacy: models and algorithms. In: Proceedings of the 33rd International Conference on Very Large Data Bases, VLDB 2007, pp. 1429–1430. VLDB Endowment (2007)
15. Molnar, D., Soppera, A., Wagner, D.: A Scalable, Delegatable Pseudonym Protocol Enabling Ownership Transfer of RFID Tags. In: Preneel, B., Tavares, S. (eds.) SAC 2005. LNCS, vol. 3897, pp. 276–290. Springer, Heidelberg (2006)
16. Ohkubo, M., Suzuki, K., Kinoshita, S.: Cryptographic approach to "privacy-friendly" tags. In: Proc. RFID Privacy Workshop (2003)
17. Poirot, J., Mcwilliams, G.: Navigation by back triangulation. IEEE Transactions on Aerospace and Electronic Systems AES-12(2), 270–274 (1976)
18. RFIDNews. EarthSearch launches GPS-RFID hybrid solution, http://www.rfidnews.org/2009/03/16/earthsearch-launches-gps-rfid-hybrid-solution
19. Sharma, S.E., Weiss, S.A., Engels, D.W.: RFID Systems and Security and Privacy Implications. In: Kaliski Jr., B.S., Koç, Ç.K., Paar, C. (eds.) CHES 2002. LNCS, vol. 2523, pp. 454–469. Springer, Heidelberg (2003)
20. van Le, T., Burmester, M., de Medeiros, B.: Universally Composable and Forward-Secure RFID Authentication and Authenticated Key Exchange. In: Proc. of the ACM Symp. on Information, Computer, and Communications Security (ASIACCS 2007), pp. 242–252. ACM Press (2007)
21. WISP. Wireless Identification and Sensing Platform, Intel Labs, Seattle, http://seattle.intel-research.net/wisp/

His Late Master's Voice
(Transcript of Discussion)

Mike Burmester

Florida State University, Tallahassee, FL, USA

My name is Mike Burmester and I will be talking about *localization* privacy, which I will distinguish from *location* privacy. First I will try to motivate the topic—this is a novel application. Then I will explain the title of this talk: "His Late Master's Voice", and I will say something about RFID technologies, which I will be using.

I will present three protocols: the idea is to try to capture the essence of this distinctive steganographic attribute which is *localization*. I will talk about the adversarial model towards the end; clearly this is not the way to design good (secure) protocols, but because my application is novel I will break the rules.

I will start talking about how to solve the private localization problem without telling you exactly what the adversary can do, but I will hint at the different kind of adversarial threats. This is a wireless application, so the adversary can do nasty things. I will come up with a sort of negative conclusion. Sometimes when we design protocols, knowing that something cannot be done is as important as knowing that it can be done. I will show that, without some kind of special approach that involves either time or location (or equivalent information), private localization cannot be achieved.

I will try to explain the problems involved, and motivate the discussion: this is a security workshop, so if you have any comments you are welcome to make them while I am discussing issues. This work was started when I first was told about this workshop. I thought it would be interesting to motivate the discussion with a famous painting by Francis Barraud in which a dog is listening to his (late) Master's Voice through the horn of a phonograph. But, before that, let me discuss two motivating examples.

The first one has to do with a sensor deployment in an area that is hostile, controlled by the enemy (the adversary). A large number sensors are deployed by casting them from a plane (so only their *approximate* location may be known), or in some other way (in which case their *exact* location may be known). The sensors are used for passive monitoring. If a wireless sensor network used in a hostile territory, then the moment the sensors start talking to each other, you are finished—the adversary will locate the sensors and destroy them. So I will assume that the sensors are not linked, but that each has an attached RFID that is used as a radio communication interface.

The problem is how to protect the transmissions of the tags. Imagine an armored vehicle that traverses the territory, collecting monitored information. If the lifetime of the system is ten years then, provided the batteries of the RFIDs will not run out during that time, the armored vehicle can collect sensor

B. Christianson et al. (Eds.): Security Protocols 2011, LNCS 7114, pp. 15–24, 2011.

information. Ideally one should use battery-free (Class 2) RFIDs, or battery-assisted RFIDs. The challenge is to secure this application: the tags should not respond to adversarial challenges, otherwise they will get located. That's the first application.

The second application is *device discovery*. You can think of the devices as plastic mines, or a treasure chest. The devices have an attached RFID tag which is the communication interface with an RFID reader (device locator). The devices are hidden—the person who puts them there may not be available and, for security, no location map is kept. The devices can be found later by using this new approach (localization privacy). Of course the adversary will also want to find them, and the adversary can do whatever the authorized RFID reader can do: call (challenge) the RFID tags. The tags should only answer if an authorized reader challenges them. This uses a new technology and involves *fine grain localization*. Fine grain localization, as opposed to regular RFID technology, is quite a useful technology: for example, if you want to find a book on a shelf and the book has an attached RFID tag, then RFID technology may tell you that the book is on a particular shelf, but it won't tell you that two books are placed in the wrong order on that shelf. You want millimeter accuracy for that: that involves *fine grain localization*. There are technologies that can do this and I will talk about them later.

Back to the title of my talk. In 1897 Francis Barraud, a painter, inherited from his late brother, a dog, a cylinder phonograph, and some cylinder recordings of his brother's voice (phonographs didn't use discs but cylinders). You might notice that the device in this famous HMV painting is a gramophone and not a phonograph, but the original scene involved a phonograph. The dog in the painting—called Nipper—was very depressed after its master died. Francis noticed that, if he played a recording of his brother's voice, Nipper would listen to it very attentively, as if he recognized his master. In the painting Francis tried to capture the dog's expression—an explicit recognition of his master's voice.

This prompts the following motivating paradigm. Bob dies suddenly, leaving his treasure to his sister Alice. However Eve wants the treasure as well and she will do anything to get it, so Alice buries the treasure together with Nipper, and leaves promptly—Nipper of course isn't the dog anymore, but an RFID device which will behave in the same way as the dog; more specifically, Nipper will only respond to Alice's calls.

So the RFID tags must only respond to authorized readers. The typical way of authenticating RFID tags is to use a three-pass protocol: you have a challenge, a response, and finally a confirmation. In our case the tag should only respond if it is certain that the challenge is authentic. So the RFID reader must be authenticated with the challenge, and you cannot have a third pass to complete the authentication. That is very hard. Authentication protocols typically have a third pass in which the response of the tag is combined with the challenge.

The point is that localization privacy is a steganographic attribute. One is not merely trying to obfuscate signals so that an attacker can't read them, but actually hiding the presence of the tag. The moment a tag responds to a challenge, even if it doesn't reveal any information about its identity (or other private information), it has already given away its location (it can be found by using a localization algorithm). So it must keep quiet—in the HMV painting the dog should only bark if it is one hundred percent certain that the challenger is Alice. And that distinguishes it from a normal cryptographic (authentication) application.

So, because localization privacy has steganographic aspects, we have to use application layer information, either temporal information (it may not be exactly clocks), and/or location information. RFID technology, since tags are cheap and reliable (particularly if they don't have a battery), is ideally suited for such applications.

Localization comes in different flavors. Outdoor localization is much easier to achieve because we don't have multipath reflections, which can make it harder to localize objects. Typically signal strength or signal direction is used, and triangulation protocols are used. For indoors localization one has to deal with multipaths. In this case the transmitted RF signal is reconstructed: typically two signals are used and the phase difference is computed, or something similar to this. The equations involved are very complex. There are some clever technologies which try to approximate solutions by linearizing equations, and they're quite accurate.

My first protocol is basic and a motivating one. Before describing it I must discuss some technical aspects of RFID systems. One of the problems with RFID protocols is that the range of an RFID reader is rather short. An RFID reader is only aware of what happens in its range. If the range of the reader is say 100 meters (or something similar) and if the deployment area is say 10 kilometers, then the reader cannot pick up signals from one kilometer away. Whereas a ubiquitous adversary can wire up the whole deployment area with (hidden) listening devices, and eavesdrop on all communications.

So the adversary can be more powerful than the authorized RFID readers—the bad guys have more power than the good guys. Normally we can bound the power of the adversary, but now the wireless aspect takes over, and the bad guys have control of areas that the good guys don't.

What may happen is: because the signal of a responding RFID tag can be used to determine its location, if that tag is not in the range of the broadcasting RFID reader but is in the range of the adversary, then the adversary can relay the authorized challenge and localize the tag from its response. For example, the adversary can take a valid signal challenge (an authorized signal) from the RFID reader, and replay it to some other area of the deployment, say two kilometers away; if the tag is in that area then it will accept the challenge because it's the right signal. The only way that the tag can recognize that the signal was sent two kilometers away, or that the signal was sent some time ago, say yesterday and not today, is if the signal contains some location or temporal information.

So the idea is that the sender (RFID reader) includes its local time and its location in the challenge as well as a MAC with a key it shares with the tag. Then the tag checks that the location of the reader is within an acceptable bound from its own location, that the time is within an acceptable bound from its own time, and that the MAC is correct. This authenticates the reader. The tag then sends its response, which also includes a MAC. So we have a two pass mutual authentication protocol. There is a virtual pass, which is not here. If you think of Nature as a third party (or the Environment), which is honest and trusted (not controlled by the adversary), then in this pass Nature gives the RFID reader and the tag their location and the time.

Matt Blaze: So, in other words, the reader is trusted?

Reply: The reader, yes, of course is trusted. The trust is based on sharing a key with a tag. But the environment is also trusted to maintain the time—the exact time is controlled by the environment.

Matt Blaze: So we need to trust the environment's ability to enforce that?

Reply: Indeed, we need accurate clocks, which are provided by the environment, and we also the location, so we also need GPS devices (or something similar) which can give us the location. These are controlled by the environment.

Frank Stajano: So basically when you are deploying the sensor system you have to tell it "I have placed you here"?

Reply: Not necessarily: sensors could have their own location devices. I was talking about the reader.

Frank Stajano: I'm talking about the sensors because, when you drop the RFID tags from an aeroplane...

Reply: ...you can give them their approximate location, or you can give them their actual location.

Omar Choudary: Or you could put a GPS.

Reply: Yes, there are various ways of doing it.

Frank Stajano: In that case it cannot be a sub-dollar sticker-type RFID, if it has to have a GPS.

Reply: A good point, this issue is not a simple one, but I'm breaking away from my contention that RFID tags cost ten cents. The moment you have an RFID tag which has a clock the cost goes up. WISP tags are quite cheap and scavenge energy from the surrounding environment.

Sandy Clark: But this clock doesn't need a battery?

Reply: It can scavenge energy for its clock: you need very little energy to run a primitive clock.

Omar Choudary: Here is an idea: if you want to avoid using GPS with tags, you input the location where you throw them from the plane, which is much less expensive, and then you know roughly where it landed.

Reply: If it is thrown from a plane, yes I agree.

Omar Choudary: There is still a problem here though, you don't have a nonce, which means that I can replay; if I have a sensor close to you, and I'm recording your challenge now, and you said that the tag will accept it. If the tag is within a time-frame...

Reply: So I need loose synchronization, which will bound the time-frame. What happens is as follows. If, while a tag is interrogated by an authorized reader, the adversary is present, and the adversary partly jams the tag's response, or does something similar in order to discover the tag before the reader does, then the adversary should fail. In the paper I say that, if the bad guy is present and active during an authorized interrogation, then the good guy will kill him, destroy him, or won't initiate the protocol.

Feng Hao: So for the location data the tag actually verifies that the location is accurate?

Reply: Yes, in the protocol [speaker pointing to the second pass].

Feng Hao: But that's computational power for the tag.

Reply: There is some power needed to do this computation; but remember: with RFID tags, there's a transfer of power from the reader. So the protocol starts with the RFID reader powering-up the tag. I will come back to this because there's a point here: because the tag does some internal calculations to check whether the challenge is authentic, *before* it broadcasts its reply it may leak some information. Can I come back to this later? This is an issue which has to be addressed, but I will address it in a different place.

Sjouke Mauw: I have one more question: it seems that all tags share this key k?

Reply: No, that's my next slide, thank you for prompting me. There is a problem when using symmetric keys, it's a scalability problem. Each tag has its own key, so which key should the reader use in its challenge? The tag could be, say, 100 meters away from the reader, which may be beyond the range of the reader. EPCGen2 specifies a broadcast range much shorter than than 100 m, but for our application we use a different transmission frequency, as high as you can go, for which the range is at least 100 m. Then the question would be, if the reader doesn't know which tag is in its range, it won't know which key it has to use, so it will have to broadcast challenges for all tags. If there are a thousand tags, then it will have to broadcast all one thousand challenges every time, and that is why we have a scalability issue.

A way around this is for the reader to have some rough information about the location of the tags. So if its range is, say, a kilometer, then it would only broadcast challenges with the keys of those tags which are expected to be in that range, maybe say one hundred tags, and only the ones that are actually there will respond. But this, the symmetric key issue, is a problem.

Matt Blaze: How big a scalability problem is that? How much bandwidth do you have? It seems that there's no core problem since the reader is powering the sensors.

Reply: The sensor will never respond to a challenge it does not recognize.

Matt Blaze: Right, but we don't really care about wasting sensor energy.

Reply: Yes, there are no power concerns.

Matt Blaze: Right, so it's a bandwidth issue.

Reply: It's a bandwidth issue, and it's a time issue, because if there are ten thousand tags, you may have to send ten thousand challenges.

Matt Blaze: So how long does it take to send a challenge?

Reply: Oh milliseconds, probably less, but once we start using specialized devices then we go to more expensive tags. In this case public key cryptography would do it better.

Bruce Christianson: How does public key cryptography help?

Reply: I haven't thought this one out! I have something here, let me see...

Bruce Christianson: The reader could sign the challenge with a private key.

Reply: Indeed, and then the tags can verify with the public key. Yes that would work. So the tag authenticates a digital signature.

Matt Blaze: But then, if an adversary intercepts that, it can use that for a replay attack.

Reply: That is correct, and that is why the reader has to sign the time and location. If that information is not correct, the challenge is not accepted.

Ross Anderson: The value of such protocols is that you can just use them to stop attacks scaling hugely. There are a lot of attacks you don't care about if they happen on a thousand phones, but you care very much if they can hack a hundred million phones. So this kind of thing could be implemented by saying that in order to do X you need to get three other mobile phones to swear that they have seen you on Bluetooth within ten kilometers of some place or another. And, OK, that can be attacked, but it can't be attacked economically on a planetary scale.

Reply: I agree with you. So if you go out of the area you can support, if you bring in other sort of dimensions to the problem, you can address the issues and make it much simpler. I was trying just to stick to this basic application, but I agree that if you can support security by using information from other areas then you can simplify the protocol.

This first protocol is a motivational example, so now I will try to simplify it and get rid of various things. The first one is time. The same approach can be used in the second protocol: I put in the time, and authenticate the time but not the location. This would offer some protection but not total protection. An online relay attack would actually kill it. What would happen is this: unless the clock of the tag and the clock of the reader are highly synchronized (not just loosely synchronized), the adversary could send this challenge from one area to another area a few kilometers away, which the authorized reader is not monitoring. Then, if the tag happens to be there, it will accept the challenge and respond. Of course the unauthorized (attacking) reader would never succeed in completing the protocol, because it won't be able to do mutual authentication; but the attacker will succeed in localizing the tag using a localization algorithm.

So this won't do what I want: it will only work for a weak adversary with a broadcast range similar to that of authorized readers, so now I have to discuss the adversarial scenario. What kind of adversaries do I have? Do I have *ubiquitous* adversaries or *local* adversaries? But let me first discuss the third protocol.

For this third protocol the tags only know their location. This is a little bit better. This protocol uses a concept from another RFID protocol: it uses counters, but loosely synchronized counters. So I am replacing time by a counter, a counter which the sender and the receiver share. Instead of having a clock and looking up the time, you look up the value of the counter. And the counter is updated each time, but this has to be done in a careful way. In this case the counter will actually deal with time issues, and the location will deal with location issues, so this can be shown to be secure. For this we need a third pass in which the reader updates its counter. This works for ubiquitous adversaries, so now I'm gradually coming to the time when I can discuss my adversarial threat model.

Ubiquitous adversaries are adversaries that can eavesdrop on all communications, over the whole deployment area. Local adversaries have restricted eavesdropping power, they can only eavesdrop in an area, similar to the range of authorized readers.

Now I will show that, if the tags do not know their approximate location or the approximate time, then we cannot get localization privacy. Here is a sketch of a proof that localization privacy doesn't work. There are two parts. The first one involves a man-in-the middle attack and exploits the fact that tags do not know their location: so the adversary relays to some other part of the deployment area the challenge of an authorized reader. If the tag happens to be there, it will respond—it has no way of checking that the location of the authorized reader is far away. The tag's response (just the raw signal) reveals the position of the tag to the attacker who uses a localization algorithm. That is the first part. The second one involves a replay attack and exploits the fact that the tags do not know the time. Since tags do not know the time, replaying an earlier challenge at the same location will be accepted as valid. Again the tag will respond thus revealing its location. So, if you don't have both location *and* time information, you cannot have localization privacy.

Finally, back to the adversary. Security in the presence of a local adversary is not very satisfactory. You want to be secure against an adversary who can eavesdrop on all communication. What happens in this scenario is that the good guys (authorized readers and tags) have a restricted range while the bad guys (the adversary) have wired up the whole deployment area. The adversary also can schedule the communication—the Byzantine threat model, but you have to adapt it to allow for the wireless medium and jamming technologies. The adversary only wins if he can succeed in localizing a tag. For this we assume that a complete response from a tag is needed. This also means that the response must not be too long.

Frank Stajano: If the adversary can eavesdrop on everything, it looks like it can always exploit the reader's challenges to localize the tags, no? Because he can always listen on the answer.

Reply: Indeed, so I have to put some constraints. If the attacker happens to be in the area where the authorized reader is, and is present and active during a tag interrogation, then in the threat model we assume that he *loses*: the attacker is captured by the authorized reader.

Frank Stajano: So it looks a bit too powerful compared to what you're doing, because if the attacker can eavesdrop on everything, then for a succesful attack it suffices for the reader to do a correct interrogation, and then the adversary to overhear it?

Reply: That's right: essentially the attacker needs only one response to an interrogation to discover the tag. For such a powerful adversary, the good guys win only once, so you can locate the tag only the first time. This is a one-time interrogation application; the authorized reader wins the first time because it find the treasure first. But then the adversary knows its location and, unless it is removed, he gets it.

Frank Stajano: But there's no guarantee that you (good guy) will know the tag's location before them: indeed you will know it at exactly the same time as them.

Reply: Yes. But in our model we assume that the first one that gets the response is the one who wins. Even if the adversary knows where it is, he cannot use that information: if he does, he will be captured.

Essentially you can only have ubiquitous adversaries if you assume that the one who finds the sensor first is the winner. However, after discovering it, the sensor is exposed—the adversary may have eavesdropped on the interrogation, so it must be removed. So you can only have one-time applications, which is the case with Bob's treasure; when Alice finds it, she must take it.

Matt Blaze: Whether I believe that the second part of your adversary model is practical depends on whether the range of an RFID type exciter and interrogator is significantly greater than the range of other kinds of electronic location technologies, like non-linear junction detectors.

Reply: The signal strength, if you use battery assisted tags, should be sufficient to guarantee a range of approximately 100 m. These are extremely weak signals.

Matt Blaze: Right, but there are technologies for locating electronic devices. All our RFID gear should fall into the category of devices that can easily be located by throwing RF at them and just looking for the harmonic response.

Reply: But they will not respond, they will not backscatter a signal. If you have a metal detector...

Matt Blaze: No, not as a metal detector. They don't respond with an RFID signal, but they respond because there are silicon junctions in there.

Reply: The computation that the tag does can be quite simple if we use some tricks, so the leaked signal should be minimal.

Matt Blaze: No, you're not detecting the radiation of the computation...

[Speaking together]

Reply: It shouldn't radiate anything, because otherwise it would be detected.

Matt Blaze: It's not clear to me that it's possible to design a device (that has an antenna) that is not susceptible to techniques like that.

Reply: It may be that with such technologies as non-linear junction detectors you have to be very close to a device to locate it.

Matt Blaze: I think the range is smaller than the range required to excite an RFID, which I think may be the saving grace of that, but I think that's what it depends on.

Joseph Bonneau: Also, couldn't you drop a lot of null tags that wouldn't respond to the same thing, but wouldn't do the crypto computation here?

Reply: The adversary?

Joseph Bonneau: No, the good guys!

Bruce Christianson: Alice can simply spread a whole load of RFID tags.

Reply: So you can hide in the crowd.

Joseph Bonneau: Yes.

[Many speaking together]

Reply: You can have a ubiquitous adversary and a local adversary. Most of the results are for local adversaries, which have restricted power. For any cryptographer the idea of an adversary who is limited is not very satisfactory, but this is a compromise solution.

Bruce Christianson: But Ross is quite right: a major feature of a good protocol is that it forces the adversary to become ubiquitous. Something that forces the attacker to do a wholesale attack rather than a retail attack.

Reply: Essentially when we say that the attacker must work much harder than the good guy to win, that is a weaker model from the traditional one where the adversary is polynomially bounded or has unlimited computational power. So, essentially, secure localization can be done using traditional methods, but this does not take into account physical (steganographic) aspects, and therefore may be vulnerable to physical attacks.

To conclude, let me recap. I have discussed localization privacy, a steganographic application that tries to hide the presence of devices, rather than to obfuscate signals. This means that it it is much harder to prove robustness, because what you are really asking for is much more than cryptographic security. For localization privacy you need location information and temporal information.

Thank you for all your comments!

Can We Fix the Security Economics of Federated Authentication?

Ross Anderson

Computer Laboratory
University of Cambridge, Cambridge, UK

There has been much academic discussion of federated authentication, and quite some political manoeuvring about 'e-ID'. The grand vision, which has been around for years in various forms but was recently articulated in the US National Strategy for Trustworthy Identities in Cyberspace (NSTIC), is that a single logon should work everywhere [1]. You should be able to use your identity provider of choice to log on anywhere; so you might use your driver's license to log on to Gmail, or use your Facebook logon to file your tax return. More restricted versions include the vision of governments of places like Estonia and Germany (and until May 2010 the UK) that a government-issued identity card should serve as a universal logon. Yet few systems have been fielded at any scale.

In this paper I will briefly discuss the four existing examples we have of federated authentication, and then go on to discuss a much larger, looming problem. If the world embraces the Apple vision of your mobile phone becoming your universal authentication device—so that your phone contains half-a dozen credit cards, a couple of gift cards, a dozen coupons and vouchers, your AA card, your student card and your driving license, how will we manage all this? A useful topic for initial discussion, I argue, is revocation. Such a phone will become a target for bad guys, both old and new. What happens when someone takes your phone off you at knifepoint, or when it gets infested with malware? Who do you call, and what will they do to make the world right once more?

Case 1 — SSO

Perhaps the oldest fielded example of federated authentication is corporate single sign-on. The goal of such systems is to enable a company's employees to log on to a diversity of internal applications with one password or token. I have been wrestling with such systems at various employers and consultancy clients since the 1980s. Even before the minicomputer ended the dominance of the corporate mainframe, employees faced multiple logons; a bank might have its branch accounting system running on top of MVS while its treasury systems ran on DB2 and its internal HR on top of something else again. The proliferation of Unix, Windows and Cloud systems has made life ever harder.

The main lesson is that even where all the users are the staff of a single company, which has unity of purpose, and the systems are purchased and maintained

B. Christianson et al. (Eds.): Security Protocols 2011, LNCS 7114, pp. 25–32, 2011.

by a single IT organisation that tries hard to manage complexity in order to control costs, the battle for single sign-on is never won. There are always systems that just don't fit. Even in young high-tech firms with everyone trying to pull in the same direction—in short, where there are no security-economics issues of strategic or adversarial behaviour between firms—there are always new apps for which the business case is so strong that exceptions are made to the rules. This should warn us of the inherent limits of any vision of a universal logon working for all people across all systems everywhere.

Case 2 — SSL

The second cautionary tale comes from the proliferation of certification authorities (CAs). After SSL was adopted as the default mechanism for web authentication in the mid-1990s, and a handful of firms like Verisign and Baltimore cornered the market, people rightly objected. Things have since gone to the other extreme with hundreds of CAs having their certificates embedded in common browsers; and as Chris Soghoian has documented, many of these appear to have no function beyond enabling various police and intelligence services to perform silent man-in-the-middle attacks on SSL sessions, and to covertly install surveillance software on people's machines [2].

Might this be fixed? At the authentication workshop following FC2011 I asked a panelist from the Mozilla Foundation why, when I updated Firefox the previous day, it had put back a certificate I'd previously deleted, from an organisation associated with the Turkish military and intelligence services. The Firefox spokesman said that I couldn't remove certificates—I had to leave them in but edit them to remove their capabilities—while an outraged Turkish delegate claimed that the body in question was merely a 'research organisation'. The Firefox guy then asked what sort of protocol might be appropriate for denying access to the certificate store in an open product; surely every organisation that meets publicly-stated norms should get in. They'd have to observe something bad happening before they yank a cert (though observing bad things is hard). This exchange shows how intractable the problem of global 'identity' provision has become. Perhaps it nudges us towards the relative naming in SPKI/SDSI [3], where there is no confusion between 'What Verisign calls Gmail' and 'What Tubitak calls Gmail'.

At least until then, global single sign-on will be made hazardous by government coercion. I may trust Google to be robust in resisting government attempts to read my Gmail, in that they will contest warrants presented by the police forces of countries in which I am neither resident nor located; but if Facebook and the people who issue driving licenses can also log me on to Gmail (and might thus be coerced to log on to Gmail as me), I have to think about their policies too.

Case 3 — 3DS

The third case study is 3D Secure, branded as MasterCard SecureCode and Verified by VISA, which enables you to use a password with your credit card to authenticate a payment at merchant websites. This was the banks' answer to the surge in cardholder-not-present fraud that followed the introduction of EMV payment cards in Europe.

We documented in [4] how 3DS has become the most widely-deployed single sign-on protocol in the world; despite having poor technical security, poor security usability and poor privacy, it has strong incentives for adoption—merchants who use it get their transactions treated as if the cardholder were present. This means lower interchange fees and less liability for chargebacks in the event of disputes; in effect, liability is passed to the cardholder. This is a good example of how bad engineering with strong adoption incentives can trump good engineering without them. (It may also be worth noting that the hard issues such as enrolment and lost passwords are handled in 3DS by the card-issuing banks and their contractors.)

Case 4 — OpenID

The fourth case to consider is OpenID. After earlier attempts to set up proprietary global schemes (such as Microsoft Passport), a number of firms got together in 2007 to create a scheme under which each user chooses an 'identity service provider', and relying parties will redirect them to their chosen provider in order to authenticate them. Yet the uptake of this has been disappointingly slow. Kosta Beznosov and colleagues identify the problem as a lack of incentives for hosting and service companies, and a lack of demand from users [5]. Thus although there are over a billion OpenID-enabled accounts at large providers, there are few relying parties. His studies indicate that users are concerned about phishing; a quarter of them about single points of failure; that 40% are hesitant to consent to release of personal info when signing up with a relying party (which is actually the work of a separate protocol, OAuth, that's often bundled with OpenID to help websites collect personal information); and 36% said they wouldn't use single sign-on for critical sites like banking, or for valuable personal information, or on sites they did not believe to be trustworthy. In view of the above discussion, users are being rational in avoiding OpenID (and OAuth), as are many websites.

Mobile Wallets

The application that motivates this paper is the mobile wallet. In Apple's vision of the future, your iPhone is not just a phone, address book, calendar, mail client and mobile browser, but also a wallet containing credit cards, store loyalty cards, gift cards, vouchers, your AA card and maybe even your driving license. The other smartphone technology companies—Microsoft, Google, and Blackberry—will no doubt follow suit, and we'll see wallets from other suppliers too.

The mobile wallet may become the new battlefield of information security. Until now, most malware has been written for Windows, and the bad guys monetise infected machines by selling them to botmasters. But price competition has been fierce; machines in the USA and Europe now sell for 13 c each, while machines in Asia can be had for 3 c. Mobile phones already offer a monetisation path through apps that silently call premium-rate lines, and we're beginning to see the malware industry producing a lot of these. Once phones contain wallets and malware can steal real money, the incentives will become stronger still. We may predict that whichever platform wins the current smartphone market race will become a major malware target—and perhaps even overtake Windows as *the* major malware target.

Also, once the average person's phone contains their money and all the other keys to their life, thefts of phones will become more common, and lost phones will become more serious. At present, about 2% of phones are lost or stolen each year; if at equilibrium we have a billion smartphone users (plus another two billion using less sophisticated phones, many in less developed countries) then every year twenty million people will suffer the inconvenience and even anguish of having their digital lives lost or stolen. (We may also have to cope with a similar number of phones infected with malware, but in what follows I'll mostly discuss the lost-or-stolen case, as it's simpler.)

The trust architecture of a typical mobile wallet will have about four layers.

1. A secure element (SE), which is a smartcard chip, packaged along with the near-field communications (NFC) chip and mounted either on the phone's motherboard or (for older phones) as a plug-in accessory. The SE is available from several vendors; it contains implementations of payment protocols such as PayPass and EMV as well as Java Card, and will have one or more control applets as well as an applet implementing each credit card that the user loads on it.
2. The mobile phone itself, whether running Android, iOS or Windows, will have a wallet application that talks to the SE and which may in turn be called by other apps on the phone. With luck the wallet will provide a trustworthy user interface.
3. There will be an online service with which the wallet communicates and which provides logging, backup and other facilities. The mobile phone also goes online for similar services. However, while the online service provider may synchronise address-book data with the phone in the clear, it will not store clear values of the cryptographic keys that credit cards use to authenticate purchases. These keys will be encrypted in the SE for online backup.
4. Keys will be managed by a third party called a trust services manager (TSM), the online equivalent of the personalisation houses that at present contract with banks to issue EMV smartcards. Indeed the TSMs are likely to be the existing personalisation firms: their hardware security modules (HSMs) contain the key material needed to initialise cards, verify PINs, set up keys

so that they or their customer banks can check the message authentication codes with which transactions are authorised, and so on.

When the user wants to install a credit card on her phone, she will call her bank which will identify her by whatever protocol it is comfortable with (which might range from asking her mother's maiden name, through sending a magic number in the post, to asking her to attend at a branch with her passport) and then authorise the TSM to load the payment card into the SE of her phone. (The SE comes pre-loaded with ignition key material that is available to the TSM, and that bootstraps this protocol.)

When she wishes to make a purchase, the SE talks to the merchant terminal via the NFC interface and the merchant then talks via its acquiring bank to the issuing bank. The phone might not be online—reception in stores can be poor, and the merchant terminal may be online only intermittently. But the phone will go online eventually once reception is restored, and then it can synchronise its transaction record with the cloud.

The final ingredient in the problem is that businesses naturally try as hard as they can to externalise costs by 'leveraging' the services of others. Online businesses find the cost of call centres onerous; one online bank, for example, has 3000 call centre staff but only 400 'proper' staff (of whom 150 are IT people), while a phone company reckons that each call to its call centre costs $20. In the UK, call centres employ 3.5% of the workforce—over a million people—and there are still more in India [6]. So online businesses design their systems to minimise call-centre use. Each customer must typically designate an email address to be used to recover a lost password; and the large email service providers such as Gmail, Hotmail and Yahoo ask for a mobile phone number. But this game of pass-the-parcel has to end somewhere, and the problem becomes acute with mobile wallets: a mugger who steals my wallet thereby gets my phone, my email account and my money. When that happens, who am I to call?

A Security-Economics Proposal

While the cost of call centres can be reduced by usable system design, it is unlikely that we can ever reduce customer contact to zero. Passing the cost (and liability) on like a hot potato to whoever will catch it cannot be the answer. Instead we should design the ecosystem so that each customer contact can be handled by whichever firm has the most to gain, or the most to lose.

If a mobile wallet is stolen, the parties with the most to lose are not the phone companies (to whom the marginal cost of minutes is near zero) but the banks. It is therefore rational for the customer to contact one her banks to cancel the credit cards in her mobile wallet. At present, if my physical wallet is stolen, I have to call all my banks one after the other, unless I am pre-registered with a card protection service. For example, one of my banks (Lloyds TSB) offers premium customers a free plan to notify all our card issuers following one phone call (less wealthy customers must pay £39.95 a year for the service). Mobile wallets allow such a service to be provided more cheaply: rather than notifying several other banks who then block payments through the interbank system, the contact bank can disable all the cards in the wallet at once by locking the SE. This is a better control point than doing something on the phone, in the cloud or in the bank transaction processing system. (It also helps in the case of phone malware—which is still rare, but is bound to increase, especially if careless phone vendors design wallets from which malware can easily steal money.)

Which bank should I call? The first part of my proposal is this. With a mobile wallet, unlike a leather wallet, the designer has to provide for a single credit or debit card to be the default. Wallets will no doubt have interfaces that allow the user to select the card of her choice for an in-store transaction, but for rapid transactions—tapping a subway turnstile or a parking meter—one card will be on top. And the privilege of being on top is immensely valuable. For example, there has been a long tussle between the US retail and banking industries over the approximately 1% higher charges levied for credit cards versus debit cards. Walmart would dearly love its debit card to be the default, while your bank would greatly prefer its credit card to be in that position. The natural way to align the incentives is for the default card issuer to be the firm you call to report a loss or theft.

Of course, a wallet provider cannot give a 'revoke' button to just anyone, because of the risk of abuse. The firm that wants its card on top will have to indemnify other card providers, and the phone company, against the consequences of improper revocation. But the industry is used to this; my bank's scheme insures £1500 up till reporting and £75000 thereafter so long as the loss is reported within 24 hours.

Now revocation is the easy part; the harder part is 'reprovisioning' the cards into the new phone I buy the day after the mugging. If a bad man can cancel my wallet, that's a nuisance; if he can social-engineer a call centre into transferring my credit cards to a phone he controls, that's serious.

Here the phone company definitely does have an incentive to cooperate. In the typical case I will go into a shop operated by one of its partners and select a new phone. I then have to show ID, perhaps pass a credit check if I'm extending a contract, and wait while the sales clerk goes online to link my new phone and new SIM card to my old phone number. There is an interesting control point here: if I'm switching from one phone company to another, I typically have to go to the old company and get a code to release my phone number. This adds a few days' delay to the process; the switching cost thus introduced increases the phone company's lockin enough to be of value (while not so much as to seriously impair competition). Economic theory predicts that in service industries the value of a firm is equal to the total lockin of all the customers [7].

So my second suggestion is that we make social-engineering attacks harder and simultaneously reward phone companies that agree to participate fully in the system as follows. If the customer wishes to switch away from a participating phone company, then the scheme operator (whether the wallet provider or the TSM) should send her an unlock code by physical mail at her registered address. However a participating company should be able to reprovision its own customer on the spot (subject to joint approval by the relevant bank). Card portability, like number portability, should add just enough lockin for the phone companies to participate, but not so much as to strangle competition.

It would probably be unreasonable to let a phone company reprovision credit cards to a new phone on its own. The sales clerk's commission provides a perverse incentive; the phone company won't want all the liability; and in any case, when the customer buys a new phone for the first time, she has to interact with her bank (or at least with a TSM acting on its behalf) in order to load her first credit card. So here the proposal is that the bank that wants its card to be the default on the new phone must interact with the customer (or pay a TSM to do so).

The final missing piece in the puzzle is what incentive the other card providers might have to allow their own cards to be reissued by the lead bank. I suggest that there might be an industry scheme with uniform and non-discriminatory rules, perhaps to the effect that when the phone company and the lead bank authorise the reprovisioning of a phone, then all cards issued by members of the scheme should be re-enabled together. It could be both complex and invidious if the lead bank could selectively disable the cards of other banks that it considered to be acute competitors. There should also be an agreed level of indemnity and compensation in the event of reprovisioning errors.

Commercial terms are clearly for industry negotiation; but the wallet suppliers have a strong interest in encouraging agreement, and governments seeking to solve the problem of 'e-ID' may also have a role to play in bringing the various stakeholders to the table.

Conclusion

Federated authentication has mostly failed to work because the incentives were wrong. Identity providers assumed no liability and were open to traceless coercion; relying parties gained little benefit and had to cope with increased complexity; users rightly feared single points of failure.

Mobile wallets are both a problem and an opportunity. In the one market where NFC payments have already been deployed—Japan—things are somewhat fragmented. Not all customers can remotely disable lost or stolen phones; those who can't, have to call all their card providers, who have widely varying provisions for blocking and recovery. As a result, NFC payments there are largely limited to low-value prepaid cards. It is in the interests of all stakeholders to get a better outcome as NFC is deployed globally.

In this paper I argue that while wallets make the revocation part of federated authentication much more important, they may also make it more solvable—because the incentives of banks and phone companies are reasonably well aligned with the underlying customer contact problem. Banks do indeed wish to revoke their customers' compromised payment credentials, while phone companies for their part do indeed wish to sell new phones to customers whose phones have been lost or stolen.

With only a modest amount of tinkering and tweaking, the wallet providers who set the rules for this ecology may be able to ensure that the existing call-centre and know-your-customer resources of the banks and phone companies are deployed constructively to solve the problem. The key, I suggest, is that the bank or other card issuer which values the customer relationship the most should have its card set to be the default, as a reward for being the first port of call; that switching away from a participating phone company should become slightly harder; and that banks which fail to participate will lose market share when their cards are no longer re-provisioned automatically.

Finally, a robust mobile payment ecosystem with serious incentives to keep phone credentials bound to the people authorised to use them can provide a firmer platform for all sorts of other authentication services. I predict that in five years' time we will no longer think of recovering from a stolen phone by using the email account attached to it; we'll think instead of the wallet as the source of ground truth to recover credentials for other systems. It's the one thing everyone's got a real incentive to defend. Perhaps even the ambitions of the German government will fade away—and a stolen Personalausweis will be recovered using the citizen's mobile wallet, rather than vice versa.

Indeed, rather than being monopoly providers of 'identity', the proper role of government should be to set the rules within which a market for federated authentication services can flourish.

Acknowledgement. Many of the ideas in this paper were developed while I was on sabbatical and working for Google in January–February 2011. I'm grateful for discussions there with Rob von Behren, Jason Waddle, Justin Brickell, Mark Andrews, Kosuke Suzuki, Vinay Rao, Ken Thompson, Mike Burrows, Rich Cannings, Ben Laurie and Alma Whitten. Others who have given useful feedback include Johann Bezuidenhoudt, Don Norman, Joe Bonneau, Shailendra Fuloria and Hyoungshick Kim. Needless to say the opinions expressed herein are mine rather than Google's.

References

1. National Strategy for Trusted Identities in Cyberspace, `http://www.nist.gov/nstic`
2. Soghoian, C.: Caught in the Cloud: Privacy, Encryption, and Government Back Doors in the Web 2.0 Era. 8 J. on Telecomm. and High Tech. L. 359, `http://papers.ssrn.com/sol3/papers.cfm?abstract_id=1421553`
3. SPKI/SDSI Certificates, `http://world.std.com/~cme/html/spki.html`
4. Anderson, R., Murdoch, S.: Verified by Visa and MasterCard SecureCode—or, How Not to Design Authentication. Financial Cryptography (2010), `http://www.cl.cam.ac.uk/~rja14/Papers/fc10vbvsecurecode.pdf`
5. Sun, S.-T., Boshmaf, Y., Hawkey, K., Beznosov, K.: A Billion Keys, but Few Locks: The Crisis of Web Single Sign-On. LERSSE-RefConfPaper-2010-006, `http://lersse-dl.ece.ubc.ca/record/244`
6. Hudson, A.: Are Call Centres the Factories of the 21st Century? BBC News (March 10, 2011), `http://www.bbc.co.uk/news/magazine-12691704`
7. Shapiro, C., Varian, H.: Information Rules. Harvard Business School Press (1998)

Can We Fix the Security Economics of Federated Authentication? (Transcript of Discussion)

Ross Anderson

University of Cambridge, Cambridge, UK

OK, so the talk that I've got today is entitled "Can We Fix the Security Economics of Federated Authentication?" and some of this is stuff that I did while I was at Google in January and February. I'm on sabbatical this year and so I'm visiting various places, and doing various things that I don't normally do.

Let's go back 25 years. When I was a youngster working in industry the sort of problem that you got if you were working with a bank was this. People joined and had to be indoctrinated into four or five systems and get four or five different passwords. You might find that your branch banking system ran under MVS, so you needed a RACF password; your general ledger ran under DB2, so you needed a DB2 password – and that was a different lady in a different building – and if you became the branch's foreign exchange deputy clerk then you needed a SWIFT password, which was yet another administrative function in yet another building. And of course this played havoc with usability: post-it notes with passwords are a natural reaction to having to remember six of them. And if you tell your staff to change passwords every month, of course they'll just rotate them.

You've got all these problems, so the big vision then was single sign-on. Can you build a widget which will automagically sign everybody on to all systems at once? An awful lot of programmer time was expended on this in the 80s. Even those firms who threw serious money at it and gave shedloads to people like CA, who have suites of products that kind of plugged into everything and all talk to each other, found that they could only get about 80% of their apps to fit.

Why? Because even in a single organisation there are conflicting incentives. The IT shop wants to keep its systems clean, but the mortgage people really need to introduce this new system next month. And of course when you've got multiple systems, nowadays you put stuff in the cloud; you put stuff on your legacy mainframe; you've got stuff sitting on server farms in Linux, or whatever – it's even harder. So we must be realistic about how much we can do with federated authentication. But there are still things that can be done and will be.

Going back to fifteen years ago, public key crypto started poking its head up and being actually deployed. Protocols such as SET and SSL got designed and started being promoted. The idea there was that you would fix the whole problem by giving every service a certificate saying what it was, and you'd give every user a certificate saying who he was, and this at least would make the authentication stuff easy. Of course you've still got the admin stuff saying that

B. Christianson et al. (Eds.): Security Protocols 2011, LNCS 7114, pp. 33–48, 2011.

'Joe is a teller at grade 3 at Barclays Bank and is therefore entitled to use the following 53 systems', but at least some part of the system engineering might be done in a uniform and global way.

But of course this hasn't worked for a number of reasons. Heavyweight protocols like SET didn't get chosen because of the admin overhead. The lightweight protocol we have – SSL/TLS – is one-sided by default, which means that we don't have client certs issued at any scale. And then there's the issue of certification authorities. If we go back ten years the near-monopoly of Verisign was just cracking; both Verisign and Baltimore had enormous market caps and were just starting to crumble. Now how many certs do we have this week in the Microsoft CAPI – 247, 250, do I hear any advance? It's an awful lot, and some of them are actually rather dodgy.

I had an interesting interaction three weeks ago at the Financial Cryptography Workshop. We had the Mozilla guy on a panel, and that morning as it happens I had upgraded Firefox. Firefox thoughtfully put back a certificate that I had removed, for Tubitak, which is an organisation associated with the Turkish intelligence services. So I asked the chap from the Mozilla Foundation why they thought it essential that they should replace a removed Turkish Intelligence Service certificate on my computer. This led to an interesting conversation with a Turkish gentleman from the floor saying "How dare you insult our country!" and "Tubitak is simply a research organisation!" and the guy from Mozilla wringing his hands and saying, "Well, you know, I can't think of what procedures should be followed to take out certificates."

This rather illustrated to me the difficulty of trying to do any centralised authentication at scale. Because if you say "We'll have the Greek certificates in but not the Turkish certificates", well you've now got a war in the Aegean on your hands. (Laughter.) If you accept the Turkish certificates but won't allow in the Kurdish certificates – oh dear, there's going to be an uprising in the mountains. And if you allow in the Kurdish certificates now the Turks will say "The Kurds don't exist, they're just mountain Turks!"

And this is fundamentally an insoluble problem, because if you try and do things in a centralised way that's open to coercion – or at least buy-in – by national governments, then you encapsulate in every system every single lost long running-sore dispute, civil-war, grumble, in the whole of the diplomatic world, and that's not good. So governments are dysfunctional, not just because they can't write code – they're dysfunctional because of all the disputes that you import.

Now in 2010 we see another attempt, a slightly more lightweight attempt by governments that get involved in this. The US National Strategy for Trustworthy Identities in Cyberspace, if you download it to look at it, has visions that in future you should be able to use your driving licence, as identity cards have to be called in the States, to logon to Gmail; or your Facebook account to file your tax return; or anything to logon on to anything else. In theory this might seem a good idea until you start thinking about incentives and liability and so on. Now we've got mechanisms, technical mechanisms – OpenID and OAuth and so on – but they're not getting used. There's over a billion OpenID-enabled accounts but there are very few relying parties. That's where you sign into Gmail or Facebook, and then use that to access an account somewhere else.

There was an interesting talk by Kosta Beznosov at Financial Cryptography about why this doesn't work. He went and did some research, and it turned out that hosting companies don't like OpenID because of a lack of incentive; basically the people who do the authentication won't accept any liability if things go wrong, and users distrust single sign-on for perfectly rational reasons. First, they're not prepared to use single sign-on for high value sites like banking; and second, for sites that they think are untrustworthy like porn sites (and again the WEIS paper last year on the porn industry showed that people are quite right to not trust porn sites because there's a lot of pay-per-install working there). People also won't trust single sign-on for sites that handle their sensitive personal information, and again, they're being perfectly reasonable in this. And so because there's no particular reason that you should trust a third party if that third party is not prepared to be liable to you when they do something wrong, this whole thing is not working.

One exception though, which we talked about last year, is the whole Verified-by-VISA and MasterCard SecureCode protocol suite, which is poor engineering but has become the world's most widely-used single sign-on protocol – simply because it gives very strong incentives for adoption. If you're a merchant operating a shopping website and you don't use Verified-by-VISA, you will be offered a cardholder-not-present rates, and you will be almost completely liable in the event of a dispute. But if you do use Verified-by-VISA then you get cardholder present rates, which means that you pay a smaller discount to the bank, you get more money in other words, and it becomes much more difficult for customers to dispute liability for payments too. So incentives appear to be the key to getting any kind of federated authentication to work.

Now let's look at the reality of how things work outside the Verified-by-VISA world, that is the world of financial transactions. And it's a game of pass the parcel. If you forget your password for your social networking site, they say "press the button!" and they send a new password to your email account. Now if your bank account somehow goes wrong, that's a little bit more heavyweight: they'll send you something in your email, and quite possibly send you a text to your mobile phone, and then they'll also ask you your mother's maiden-name, or some other information that can be found from your entry in Who's Who, or Facebook, or whatever, and then they will restore your bank account privileges. But most of the world is much less formal than this. You recover your Gmail password, for example, which gives you access to almost everything else, from your mobile phone.

And now here's a question. Suppose you had a wallet in your mobile phone, suppose you could do payments, how would you recover that? From your Gmail account? You see we're beginning to see a circularity in the graph here. And the problem is that everyone wants to free-ride off of everybody else. Everybody wants to benefit from everybody else's call centre without the cost of running one themselves. And no-one really wants to answer the phone. Why? Because it costs money.

Now my feeling is that this is all about to come to a head, and in a very interesting way. 2011 is the year in which almost everybody is going to launch some kind of electronic wallet that will live in your mobile phone. There have already been announcements of various kinds. Nokia's made an announcement, Blackberry has made an announcement, Eric Schmidt at Google has said various things. And what a wallet application on your mobile phone will look like is actually fairly straightforward. It's a piece of software that will enable you to pay stuff, so you will be able to thumb through my MasterCard, my VISA card, my AA card, and so on and so forth. If it's using the NFC protocol, well there are four vendors of the chips for that, and you can go and speak to them at any exhibition and see demonstrations and draft specs. Basically there's a piece of epoxy that has in it an NFC chip that does radio, and a secure element that is essentially an EMV smartcard with a Java card in it. The two are wired together so you've got a hardware trusted path from the payment element to the antenna, and there are various ways in which that can interact with the CPU in the phone.

If you're a sensible designer you will design your wallet so that it interacts with online services for things like logging and backup and so on. And you will do all those things that you can do to minimise the likelihood that people's phones will be taken over by malware, because once the bad guys can steal money from a phone by writing malware, then they will stop writing malware for Windows and they will write it instead for Android, and Blackberry, and Nokia, and so on.

And then there is another trusted third party in here of the old type: TSMs as they're called – Trust Services Managers. These are companies which will provide to you over the air crypto keys, virtual credit cards, and so on. These will almost certainly be the same kind of companies who at present run personalisation bureaus for the banks. They are specialist IT firms; they have licensed bonded staff; they have racks of hardware security modules; they know your bank's PIN key; so they can manufacture your physical debit card; and they can emboss it and mail it to you. And in the future they will be able to send a bundle of bits to your mobile phone over the air when the bank tells them to.

So where's this heading? By 2015 I reckon your phone might have five credit cards, and ten coupons, a gift card, an AA card, and the people at Apple and so on are starting to talk about putting people's car keys in there as well. No doubt, if this all flies, then all sorts of stuff will appear in your phone. And this of course starts to tell us that there's going to be a huge cross-domain trust issue here. If somebody who steals your phone can also steal your car, then that's not just of interest to Mr Apple, but also of interest to Mr Mercedes. And there are many interesting issues around here.

Now given what we're talking about in this workshop, let's look at revocation. Because lots of people lose their phones or have them stolen – at least two percent a year, maybe more than that. What happens if your phone is infected? Well let's forget about that for now because it's a more complex case. But if you believe that one to five percent of PCs are infected, then you can assume that the bad guys will start infecting the phones in the league of something like that, once they can actually steal money.

So let's just concentrate on the case of two percent lost or stolen per year, as the best case that we can imagine – and most future realities are likely to be worse than that. The one place that we can look to see this stuff fielded is Japan, where there are half a dozen different services selling NFC payments. There, there hasn't been any coordination, and as a result it's pretty chaotic. A couple of the services link NFC payments to an existing debit or credit card, but the rest of them are essentially prepaid. What happens if your phone is lost or stolen is that for some of them it's tough luck; with others of them you can phone up and revoke the NFC payment element, or indeed the whole phone. With some of them they will do the revocation instantly; with others they will perhaps revoke it after two or three days, and maybe give you some money back if you're lucky. As a result NFC payments tend to be limited to small amounts, and in fact current UK banking rules say that this sort of payment shouldn't be for more than £15.

There is an interesting subtext here in that the protocols that VISA and MasterCard have approved for contactless payments don't deal with PINs. This is simply because of the fight between VISA and Walmart in the USA, because at present Walmart does about $200bn a year of credit card transactions. Walmart would deeply love to make those into PIN debit transactions so they would pay one percent per annum less to the banks, and the banks are very, very concerned that Walmart should not be able to get away with that. So we find that we've got an EMV contactless protocol that won't do encrypted PIN debit. That's a side issue that hopefully may get resolved sometime over the next year or two. Certainly there's nothing in theory to stop banks using NFC tap-and-pay along with existing PIN pads which would use legacy methods to authenticate PINs.

Anyway, assuming we could coordinate the thing, suppose that we had a thousand million smartphones in use in developed countries. That's 20 million thefts a year, and if each of these is going to cost $20 of call centre time, that's basically 20 minutes to the call centre of your local phone company, that's $400m. But if things are not coordinated, so you have to phone every single credit card and debit card issuer, and the AA, and you know, call John Lewis to get your gift card back, and so on and so forth, then it could be ten times as much. This is beginning to be serious money.

In fact when you look up the numbers it turns out that call centres are now employing over three percent of the UK workforce, and this is growing all the time. So it's perfectly understandable that people try and dump costs, but if everybody tries to dump costs then the industry as a whole ends up paying ten times as much money. So there's got to be some way to make it work – or at least we hope that there's some way to make it work.

Now the key technical fact here is that once you have got all this stuff residing in a secure element in your mobile phone in the smartcard chip, then someone possessed of the appropriate crypto key can say to the smartcard chip "Die

O Chip!" And it will immediately kill itself, and will no longer be any use to anybody. This is much more controllable and much more final because of the tamper resistance than simply remotely locking or remotely bricking the phone. So as a real sanction to use against people who steal phones you could make the payment part of it permanently and irrevocably dead. Yes?

Alf Zugenmaier: I've got an economics problem. What is the incentive for someone who gives out gift cards or pre-paid cards to refund the money?

Reply: This is a big problem and I'm coming to it in three slides' time.

Mike Burmester: What about the guy who steals it somehow it can prevent the owner from revoking.

Reply: There's a hard answer to that, but it depends on design details, some of which may be NDA. Believe me, that's not a problem. You can see to it that the SC is involved in all transactions, just that you can see to it that your smartcard in your pay TV set-top box is involved in producing all control words for your descrambler.

Mike Burmester: It's not the owner, it's the thief – the person who's stolen it, who wants to prevent attacks.

Reply: In order for the thing to be usable as a payment instrument you can see to it that the secure element is online regularly.

Mike Burmester: So the other side, the purchaser

Reply: So the bank who owns the backend servers in the cloud can put the SC on the die list and next time that chip that is allowed to go online by the wallet software it will die.

Mike Burmester: And if it doesn't go on he knows that he is prevented from all transactions.

Reply: Well again, that's a parameter you can tweak.

Mike Burmester: Maybe he just challenges, or maybe he can get confirmation.

Reply: If you decide that you'll allow people to do up to three offline transactions for up to \$100 before they must go online, that's your exposure. It's controlled, it's not an issue. But the simple fact is that once you have got the secure element synced up with the servers in the cloud, whether it's at the banks' trusted third party, or whether it's with the mobile phone maker's cloud service, or whether it's your telco's cloud service, once you've got that synced up you have got the ability to reprovision all the keys at once.

So you can not only nuke the secure element, you can cause all the keys to come back as one encrypted blob – so that suddenly all these credit cards, affiliation cards, gift cards, everything, all appear in the one instance on the new phone that the customer has bought. That means that you can bypass the cost of having the customer call up ten different call centres inflicting a \$20 plus cost on each of them, and also inflicting an unacceptable user experience on the customer.

The fact that you have got this central control over the secure element and the link to the cloud is maybe the key enabling factor, because it's a control point which you can use to create a regulated environment in which a market for authentication might take place.

So how can we make this market work? Well here's a couple of suggestions. The first is that when you have a mobile wallet, one of the things you figure you have to engineer first is a default card. Because although the punter may take out his phone and say "I'll use my VISA" – or my MasterCard, or my Discover, or any other card – when he's buying a TV, if you're just going to pay $4 for a parking meter you don't want to be bothered with that. So there's got to be a default card on top that just works when you just go "bing" to a parking meter. And the banks are really, really keen for their cards to be on top, so there the banker earns the eight cents when somebody goes "bing" for $4.

So the first proposal is that to be the default card issuing bank a card issuer should sign up to our revocation and reprovisioning scheme. In other words, they should be able to use a standard set of protocols within a standard set of contracts to firstly provide a customer with a protocol when they've just been mugged and had their phone taken off of them.

Right, this is going to be very, very serious stuff! If you're walking through Oakland after the Oakland Conference one year and a nice gentleman with a shotgun says "May I have your card sir?" You say, "Certainly!" "And what is your password sir?" and you tell him. "Thank you sir, have a nice day!" And you run in a state of great shock back to the Claremont and you say to the receptionist "I've just been mugged! Somebody's taken my phone!" You'll be able to hear a pin drop...

Matt Blaze: What do you want to do, you're in Oakland.

Reply: In 2015 your phone will be your life. Somebody has just taken your life away. So the concierge at the Claremont says "Well would you care to use my phone and make a call?" then where are you going to call? This is the big question!

One possible answer to this is that you phone Citibank, or whichever bank is the default card in your wallet. Another would be that you phone AT&T, or whoever is your phone provider. But what you do not want to do is to have to phone 15 people one after another. So if Citibank is the bank that's providing the 24/7 call centre for stolen cards, as they do already for people who have their leather wallet stolen when they go into Oakland, then we make the world easier for them – nice interface, press the button, do it.

In order for this to work though you have to get the bank to indemnify all the other card issuers against negligence or abuse. If they are careless and allow people to revoke other people's phones when they shouldn't, that's got a cost attached to it and they've got to pick that up. But the banks do this already. I checked out my own – well one of the banks that I use, Lloyds TSB. And they have this service, one phone call to zap all your cards. If you have a Gold Card or up then it's free, and if you're poor then it costs you £40 a year. That's perhaps a signal for services the banks don't really want to supply, but they think they should anyway, at least for good customers – where the price discrimination is the wrong way round, but hey. With wallets you can make that easier because everything is in the same place.

The next question to ask is what the phone companies want – how can we persuade phone companies to participate in such a scheme? Well what the phone companies most want is that when your phone is lost or stolen they want you to buy a new one from them rather than from a competitor. So if you're Vodafone Android is stolen in Oakland they want you to buy a new Android from someone in that system, Vodafone, AT&T, or whoever, they don't want you to go and buy an iPhone.

So here's the second proposal, which is that although revocation can be done by one party, reprovisioning is a two-factor sort of thing. It's bad enough that someone can revoke my cards or my phone by pretending to be me, but if he can cause them to reappear in a phone that he controls, that's serious bad stuff. So mere prudence suggests that we get both the bank and the phone company involved in this. And if someone decides that they wish to change their phone company at the same time as they're buying a new phone then they've got a problem in that does the new phone company really know them?

Now from the phone company's point of view, what it wants to do is to make it slightly more difficult for repeatedly the customer to depart. And so the proposal here is that if you're a Vodafone customer, for example, and you want to get a new handset from Vodafone, then the chap in the Vodafone shop can just press the button, and assuming that you make a phone call to the person at Barclays and convince them that you are who you are, your phone will come alive with all its cards back in it.

However, if you decide to walk across Lion Yard and get an iPhone instead, then the TSM will send you at your home address a letter saying "Dear Matt, the unlock code for your mobile wallet is blah." When you receive that in the post you can then walk around to the Apple Store and get a new iPhone. So this imposes a delay of two or three days. And again, the precedent is the transfer of mobile numbers that we have at present. If you want to move your number from Vodafone to Apple, for example, you wait, and you get an unlock code, and a few days later you can go and do the transaction. So the trick I suspect is to increase the lock-in just enough that the phone companies will play ball, but not so much that you hose competition in the market.

There's a lot of details that we need to figure out. People may want to do their revocation and replenishment where they're comfortable. I asked my wife where she'd like to deal with a problem like this and she said "Well John Lewis, you know, the service department is reasonably friendly." And that's OK because John Lewis issue credit cards and they also sell mobile phones.

That may bring in further issues because if you're got someone who's a card issuer and also a phone sales outlet – another example being Tesco. Then what about the dual control aspects? And then again, there are other industry issues where you've got some card issuers are proper banks, and others are banks and also retailers, and some are banks plus retailers who are turning into banks like Tesco Bank, and you need some reasonably fair and transparent rules that can apply to all of them. The edge case, which somebody mentioned already, is what happens with gift cards. A gift card is typically implemented nowadays, and certainly in a system like this, as a one-time credit card. So although you don't realise it, it's a MasterCard, and it's got a limit of fifty bucks, and it cannot be replenished. And the banks absolutely love these because a significant proportion of them are never redeemed.

So once you start making the recovery of gift cards automatic, there are some losers, even in the absence of phone thefts. What's more, once you start letting people deal with coupons on their phones, then that's going to be a shock to the system, because at present most people don't bother to collect and redeem coupons. They're used by the industry as a means of price discrimination between people who will spend more money to save time, and people who will spend more time to save money. But once you make it completely easy and frictionless to redeem coupons then very many more people will redeem them.

Joseph Bonneau: So they actually did that last year, the Groupon people, and it's turned into a billion dollar company, and it could be destroying the whole coupon concept.

Reply: Well hey! So when you bring in a new platform you can turn businesses upside down, and that's often good because they've become all crufty and tiresome. When you bring in a platform like this, when you bring in a platform of mobile wallets, you will destroy all sorts of businesses – and that's good, that's creating disruption, that's progress. But if those businesses are about to be destroyed understand quickly enough that they're going to be destroyed, they might not participate and this might make progress a bit hard.

Now from the point of view of the protocols community the interesting thing is that we may be turning the problem round, because in the old days we assumed that trust had to be rooted in some third party, because this is how people talked about from day one. In the New Directions paper, Whit Diffie and Marty Hellman said, you will of course put your public key in the phonebook. Oh good, said the telcos, and they invent this thing called X.509 which has got basically a worldwide phonebook implementing and distributing various certificates. Then governments thought that they might jump on the bandwagon and build little empires. And we got variants on that here and there. But by and large the thinking has always been: you've got a central authority – be it a government, be it a bank, be it a TSM, or whoever – who says what people are.

However, once we all have mobile wallets they're something that we've all got a really good incentive to defend. It's not like a throw-away webmail account; it's not like a mobile phone, where if you start getting spam messages from an ex girlfriend or boyfriend you just toss the thing in the skip and go and buy another prepay from Tescos for £40. A lot of young people nowadays treat electronics accounts and devices as throwaway, but that may change, just as Facebook is beginning to create online identities they can't really throw away, so the mobile wallet can do the same thing for devices that we carry. And if we can line up the incentives right to get the banks and phone companies working together over this, then we will have robust revocation mechanisms that will be well tested out in practice. Because the bad guys will come – the guys with shotguns will put them up your nostril and say "Give us your phone!" Wicked hackers will write bad code that will do remote middleperson attacks on mobile wallets if the people who design the architecture are dumb enough to permit that. It is going to happen. But because it will be costing real people real money on an industrial scale, it will be fixed if the technology persists.

Matt Blaze: Do you have some slide coming up where you're not going to suggest putting like my two favourite kinds of organisations together to make them more powerful?

Reply: The point, Matt, is that we unfortunately have to have your two favourite kinds of organisations in the game in order to make you more powerful – right? Because they are the only people who have hundreds of thousands of guys answering the phone, right? If you imagine there's a billion, half a billion Androids in the world, do you really think that Larry and Sergei are going to want to hire another fifty thousand people to manage the system for you and do all revocation for the central point? I can't see anybody in Google making that sale. But Citibank have got thirty thousand people in their call centre, and so do each of the big eight banks in the USA, and we know the phone companies also have call centre personnel on that kind of scale. Worldwide there are probably over a million people working in call centres for banks and phone companies. They are the people who have got the actual muscle for the weeping, crying customers to turn to. The tech companies can't realistically to do that.

And in fact there are many organisations, both banks and phone companies, that actively don't like the idea of tech companies knowing their customers' names and addresses. There were two times in the last ten years when people tried to create links between phone makers and customers. Firstly when people came up with the idea of a phone with two SIM card slots in it about ten years ago, Vodafone just told them "Guys, we're not letting this on our network so forget it!" And then in 2005 when Nokia came up with its second generation DRM, again Vodaphone and the other big phone companies said "Guys, you are not going to field a technology that lets you know our customers names and addresses. Go away!"

So even if Larry and Sergei, and Steve Jobs, and the other tech company bosses were prepared to go and hire tens of thousands of people to answer the phones, the phone companies wouldn't let them – and the banks wouldn't be too keen either. So one way or another the bullet's got to be bitten.

Matt Blaze: Well thanks for depressing me before lunch.

Jonathan Anderson: So the John Lewis thing is interesting because their company, you know, they're neither a telephone nor a bank, but they have every incentive to get you to come in, chat with their customer service people, get more fuzzies about John Lewis, and then on your way out pass the appliances, right?

Robert Watson: Great opportunity for them to ruin their brand by tying themselves to online theft.

Jonathan Anderson: Well there's also that I suppose.

Matt Blaze: They also resell HSBC products.

Reply: Yes, so they do their credit card. Tesco similarly have got their own bank, they're just now becoming a proper bank because it used to be a front for Royal Bank, but Royal Bank was a little bit short of cash, so Tesco bought out their share and is now busy building its own spanking new systems from scratch. So that's a really interesting case because it's an entire bank without any legacy IT.

Jonathan Anderson: But there might be other people who have customer services people already, not even necessarily in call centres, who are happy to, who are big enough to do the kind of the liability stuff that you need to to deal with other players in the game. And even if they're not the default card in your wallet, they still might be happy to make you feel nice about them because they're saving you from the bad guys.

Reply: Well another interesting thing about this is that presumably you end up with some kind of industry framework agreement, and as it's going to have to involve, I would suspect, the mobile phone industry and the banking industry, which culturally are very, very different. It's going to be interesting to see how that gets negotiated. There isn't, you know, an international mafia of phone companies incorporated with which VISA and MasterCard can sit down and see people round the table. It might take some time and a bit of pounding to get it sorted out. But my point is that there are great potential gains for everybody, you know – billions of dollars in saved call centre costs, and so there's everything to work for.

Alf Zugenmaier: As a customer actually I would prefer to have lots of different cards of which I can leave half of them at home, the other half I take on a conference, and only one I take with me when I go wandering through the streets of Oakland. So I actually have this feeling that what we are doing is putting all eggs into a basket, and maybe that's not exactly what I want to do in order to minimise my personal risk. Revocation is nice, but how about I just take my prepaid credit with me when I wander around the streets while I have to expect someone with a shotgun.

Frank Stajano: Yes, in fact in the thing I'm going to talk about after lunch, one suggestion I had, if you have some high-value things put them on a separate device.

Joseph Bonneau: Two things. First, having grown up in Oakland I'm a little bit concerned about that, writing an entire security model around the threats of Oakland.

Frank Stajano: Are you carrying a shotgun? (laughing audience)?

Joseph Bonneau: But I was wondering about the assumption that the value of being the default card is enough to cover the entire price of doing the revocation and covering the liability for every other card in the wallet, it seems like maybe that's true but it's not necessarily stable, and it could be undermined by some card which refuses to be the default but offers really good airline miles or something, and gets a lot of people to use it instead of the defaults. So I guess I'm concerned that that seems like a core assumption for this whole thing, and I'm not sure if will always be true.

Reply: Well if you're the director in charge of a wallet say at Apple, under what circumstances would you allow a bank to have access to the revoke button? What would you make them sign? Would you make them sign up to a standard industry agreement, or do you haggle bank by bank by bank? How many hours do you have in a year?

Robert Watson: Well it sounds like we'll end up being like Apple – they will enlist certain banks who play by Apple's rules.

Reply: And they might end up being different between different wallet users. I mean, Nokia has a long history of signing up deals with big banks for phone payments. They've just signed up Union bank in India, which they hope will be enormous with hundreds of millions of accounts, and they may not wish to take part in any further schemes, well at least while they build market share. Apple might decide that "we will play with the top eight banks and the rest can go hang". Android being an open platform might not even think of that as an option to begin with. Blackberry is already involved in a huge big fight with phone companies, and so maybe they're not thinking carefully enough about how they can circumvent that by building alliances with the banks. And so on. It's not clear that you will end up with one standard industry solution. It might very well be in the interests of regulators – perhaps in the USA where they're a little bit better informed and a little bit more muscular than here – to try and bring the banks and the phone companies round the table in order to make things happen more quickly.

Joseph Bonneau: So I guess my concern is if the bankers don't think that being a default card is worth that much then they may refuse to sign up to this scheme and say, "We don't want to be the one who has to do revocation even if we get to be the default card because we don't care enough about that". And then it seems that you have to weaken the amount of liability they take on doing the revocation process to get them interested again.

Reply: Well in that case the option available to the wallet maker might be to say that unless the bank certificate has bit C set for cooperation then the user physically cannot make it the default card unless he roots the phone – and if you root the phone all bets are off. Liability is a new power on the banks, even in those countries where the banks carry it. That may be the sort of arrangement that sorts it. But then would the aggressive salesy bank litigate about that, would the other banks call it into a room and say "Oi, you're out of line!" or would they all rush for the bottom? All these behaviours are possible in terms of conceivable business negotiations. What's new about this is that you have got a new control point, namely that you have got approximately four vendors of mobile phone platforms who have got significant power, at least initially, about the way in which they nudge the phone companies and the banks towards agreements on these rules. If agreement can't be reached on the rules then the phone companies and banks will end up paying a hell of a lot more money.

Alf Zugenmaier: Just a point that for a bank, it may not be enough that a certificate can default provider because how do you ensure that this really means default, how do you ensure that there is usage action not some robot system without even rooting the thing that will automatically select whenever you make a payment, automatically select the other card that gives you more mileage or so. So in fact what is happening is that there's a local decision about default, and there's within your agreement a side who is going to be the main revocation provider, and you would have to make a strong link between those two and enforce that one otherwise you will have to push the cost of being default revocation provider to the user. Then of course the default revocation provider may, let's say John Lewis, decide, "There's enough value for us to be cheap as a revocation provider." That would be a completely different business model.

Reply: Yes, you could maybe explore these sort of lines. However I would imagine this is that those banks which behave themselves, who have signed up, would then have their cards presented to the user and he would decide which was to be the default. Do you wish to have your Barclaycard, or your Tesco card, or your Lloyds card as the default? But if you try and make your Bank of Cocaine and Crooks International card your default, it won't let you because it doesn't have the C bit set. So you've got user choice plus higher filtering in the same model.

Now if you want the banks to compete on the cost of security, I think that would be hard, because banks don't want to make security – and the probabilistic eventual certainty of phone loss or theft – salient to the user at the time of signing. But it could be packaged in other ways. "Let us be your bank of choice and for every year that you make us your bank of choice we will give you an extra 300 air miles. " Whatever, the game's open. But what we want to do is come up with a series of rules, which will cause it to converge at a reasonable place, where revocation will be robust. Now we're just talking here about the case of loss of theft, and of course malware infection is even more nasty, and that becomes a separate conversation – in which of necessity the tech suppliers are more closely involved, because if you're iPhone gets rooted then Mr Apple is in a much better position to detect that and do something about it than Mr Barclays. And in the end this may give more power to the phone platforms, because although initially your two percent annual losses might be almost all loss or theft, by 2015 you might start seeing malware being a significant part of that.

Anyway, so what we might get to is a place where rather than recovering your stolen wallet using your Gmail or your passport, which are roughly speaking the current electronic and physical world ways of doing things, you do it the other way round. You recover your passport or your Gmail account using your wallet.

It would be a particular problem in Germany where the federal government's vision is that your Personalausweis will be the root of trust for the online world, and if turns out to be the wallet – so that your Ausweis is stolen you then do something on your phone, and the Bundesdruckerei sends you a new Ausweis – well hey, that might be logical. Would it be politically acceptable?

But if it can be made to work a lot of interesting things happen. Now at Financial Cryptography Omar presented a paper that was done with Frank, and Steven, and Mike Bond and me, showing how you could use EMV cards as they already exist to do digital signatures on arbitrary data. There are some ifs and buts on that which we can essentially remove in the world of wallet thanks to the way the chips are made. If you for example bought an airline ticket using your VISA card, then right now it would be possible for the boarding pass dispensing machines at Heathrow to get to your EMV card to sign a random challenge to prove that you are you before they actually dispense the boarding card.

And this may have a significant role when it comes to the purchase of online goods. You do a transaction to buy membership in an online computer game for example, and your mobile wallet then acts as an authentication device to log you on to the game. This can all happen more or less seamlessly. The chip is a Java card, so you can sign arbitrary stuff. There are issues about various keys and personas that you have in the card, and banks might not wish you to use your VISA card as a generic logon device – except perhaps for those devices that you have bought with your VISA card. Or they might want you to do an initial transaction with your VISA card to set up a logon to a computer game which then uses a different key in the card, and so on and so forth. So there's a whole bunch of protocol work to be done in there as to how you manage hierarchies of trust, and that are run out of people's mobile wallets, and how you write all the Java applets and stuff that will do that.

But more generically we're then moving to a world where you put a signature creation device in every phone, and if you've got robust "R and R" – Revocation and Reprovisioning – and if you've got robust login in the cloud, so that you can get some help resolving disputes, and if, as Mike was saying earlier, you've got GPS – you can imagine protocols where you verify your GPS by getting testimony from nearby phones – then that could be useful in seeing to it that the sort of attacks that at the present time can scale globally, can't in the future scale.

Suppose, for example, it turned out that there was some kind of middleperson attack on the secure element on a mobile phone. The way that you might catch that is by linking transactions of payments to physical location in a way that wouldn't scale. And once you have got programmability and upgradability, and once you have cloud service surveillance so that you can see the patterns of what's going on, then there's a very much larger and richer toolkit available to defend us than was the case before.

Now the interesting thing is that this is the very opposite of just about, well just about everything from when X.509 was planned. Their plan was that you have Sam, Sam the omniscient sitting in his bunker at MIT or whatever, handing out the certificates. Instead we've got a world where we've got ultimately billions of mobile phones, each with a bundle of private keys, and some kind of trust engine – GPS, WiFi, Bluetooth, etc. What sort of stuff can you build on top of that?

We have perhaps one small insight into that with the web of trust because that never really got anywhere; it wasn't really used for much, what sort of killer apps can we find for a world in which there are billions of devices that are trustworthy most of the time? Now of course any individual phone can be stolen or rooted by malware, but assuming you can manage the ecology so that stolen phones undergo "R and R" within a day in most cases, and phones that become identified as infected because they misbehave are similarly dealt with, then you end up with a world with billions of principals that are trustworthy most of the time.

So that's what may be the new take on single sign-on. People have been working on it for thirty years or so, and it basically doesn't work very well. Initially the problems were complexity inside firms, and in the last 15 years it's complexity of incentives between firms. And the possibility is that mobile wallets change all this. Why? Because you have to defend them, once your money is in there. Sure, malware can be written. Sure, shotguns can be put in people's nostrils. But the point is that it can't be happening most of the time! If the world is going to keep on turning, then most mobile wallets have got to be actually under the control of their users 99% of the time. That perhaps gives us a different, and more resilient, and more optimistic view of the world of trust.

Matt Blaze: How do you design a small, general purpose computer that's under the control of the user, especially when it has communication capability?

Reply: You arrange the world so that it is not under the control of the user, he finds out soon enough.

Matt Blaze: Well we've never built one that's always under the control of the user, even if I, it might be under my physical control on the outside of the box, but it's a computer, and bad guys can send bits at it.

Reply: You have to trust to some extent the people who made the hardware and the people who made the software, but ARM's reputation is worth something to them, and Apple's reputation and Google's reputation are worth something to them.

Matt Blaze: But their reputation doesn't seem to suffer when their products are crap from a security point of view.

Reply: It takes time, but if you look at the decline in market share of Microsoft, for example, that talks. If you go to a conference nowadays, computer scientists or rich business types or whatever, more and more people have Apples. It takes years, but eventually trust does count.

Matt Blaze: But not as many bad bits are being thrown at the Apples.

Reply: And believe me, once everybody's money is kept in their mobile wallet, there will be lots of people trying to throw bad bits at mobile wallets. Either the technology will succeed or it will fail, and if the malware writers get the upper hand, and mobile wallets become a cesspit like Citizens Band Radio did, or Usenet, or whatever, then it will be "Nice try, try something else." But there may just about be enough money in this, and enough clever people who are determined to make that money, that it's possible to make it work.

Bruce Christianson: The banks have almost been reluctant to compete overtly on security, is the same kind of reluctance apparent in the mobile companies, or are they going to be up for it?

Reply: I've no idea. At present security isn't particularly salient for the mobile phone companies because we don't yet see large amounts of malware. But believe me, the amounts are racking up very, very quickly indeed, with more and more people who are working on this problem. We have seen occasional scares in the UK about kids being mugged for mobile phones but that's a phenomenon of the Daily Mail newsdesk rather than any underlying physical reality.

Bruce Christianson: Thanks very much Ross. Now the lunch.

Pico: No More Passwords!*

Frank Stajano

University of Cambridge Computer Laboratory,
Cambridge, UK

Abstract. From a usability viewpoint, passwords and PINs have reached the end of their useful life. Even though they are convenient for implementers, for users they are increasingly unmanageable. The demands placed on users (passwords that are unguessable, all different, regularly changed and never written down) are no longer reasonable now that each person has to manage dozens of passwords. Yet we can't abandon passwords until we come up with an alternative method of user authentication that is both usable and secure.

We present an alternative design based on a hardware token called Pico that relieves the user from having to remember passwords and PINs. Unlike most alternatives, Pico doesn't merely address the case of *web* passwords: it also applies to all the other contexts in which users must at present remember passwords, passphrases and PINs. Besides relieving the user from memorization efforts, the Pico solution scales to thousands of credentials, provides "continuous authentication" and is resistant to brute force guessing, dictionary attacks, phishing and keylogging.

1 Why Users Are Right to Be Fed Up

Remembering an unguessable and un-brute-force-able password was a manageable task twenty or thirty years ago, when each of us had to use only one or two. Since then, though, two trends in computing have made this endeavour much harder. First, computing power has grown by several orders of magnitude: once upon a time, eight characters were considered safe from brute force[1]; nowadays, passwords that are truly safe from brute force and from advanced guessing attacks[2] typically exceed the ability of ordinary users to remember

* It's OK to skip all these gazillions of footnotes.

[1] The traditional DES-based `crypt(3)` didn't even *allow* a longer password.

[2] Thus, respectively, `long&Full^Of_$ymbo£$`, or even meaningless: `u4Hs9D6GdCVi`.

B. Christianson et al. (Eds.): Security Protocols 2011, LNCS 7114, pp. 49–81, 2011.

them[3,4]. Second, and most important, the number of computer-based services with which we interact has grown steadily, while our biological memory capacity has not increased: we no longer have just a single login password to remember but those for several computers, email accounts, dozens of web sites, encrypted files and various other services, not to mention a variety of PINs for our bank cards, phones, burglar alarms and so on.

Let's henceforth refer to all such password-requesting applications and services as "apps"[5]. For the implementer of a new app (say a new web site), passwords are the easiest and cheapest way of authenticating the user. And, since the password method is universally understood and used everywhere else, there is no apparent reason not to continue to use it[6].

This approach doesn't scale to the tens of passwords, passphrases and PINs each of us must use today. Users frequently complain that they can't stand passwords any longer. And they are right: the requests of computer security people have indeed become unreasonable, as highlighted by Adams and Sasse back in 1999 [1]. Users are told never to write down their passwords but they know they will face substantial hassle or embarrassment, if not total loss of their data or other assets, if they ever forget them: availability is often worth much more to them than confidentiality [3]. If they comply with the request not to write down their passwords, they'll want to choose something memorable. But, they're told, it must also be hard to guess[7]. Once they find a strong, memorable yet hard to guess password, the annoying computer security people also dictate that they can't reuse it anywhere else. It's hard to find several dozen different passwords that are all memorable and yet not guessable by someone who knows a little about the user. To add insult to injury, the next security request is that the passwords also be *changed* on a regular basis, to reduce exposure in case of

---

[3] Bruce Schneier, 1999: "Password crackers can now break anything that you can reasonably expect a user to memorize".
`http://www.schneier.com/crypto-gram-9910.html#KeyLengthandSecurity`

[4] It is in theory possible to mitigate the brute-forcing threat of ever-increasing attacker power by regularly increasing the number of rounds of hashing applied to the password before using the verification value. For other uses of passwords, such as file encryption, a similar countermeasure involves the use of a highly iterated key derivation function. Online systems could rate-limit the password guessing attempts, regardless of attacker power, as appropriately argued by Florêncio et al [12]. But experience (cfr. Sklyarov's brilliant presentation at Passwords^11) shows that many widely deployed systems are still open to brute-force password cracking attacks that get more powerful with every new generation of CPUs—and now GPUs. We agree with Florêncio and Herley [11] that, for online systems, requiring users to adopt stronger passwords is an arrogant and counterproductive excuse for not adequately protecting the hashed password file.

[5] There is no connection between our "apps" and smartphone applications.

[6] As also observed by Bonneau and Preibusch [4], this situation is what economists call a *tragedy of the commons*: "What harm could my site cause by requesting a password, since everyone else's also does?" And yet, since everyone does, the burden collectively placed on users becomes unmanageable.

[7] Despite the easily retrieved digital footprints we all leave behind online.

compromise. Fat chance of ever remembering them all, then! Not to mention the difficulty of typing a complex password correctly, or of fixing a minor typo in it, without visual feedback ("****************").

Users are more than justified in being fed up. If the rules imposed by the computer security people are mutually incompatible, users cannot possibly follow them all, even when they are genuinely cooperative and willing to comply[8].

Imagine we could afford to start again from scratch, without concerns for backwards compatibility, and that our primary directive were to invent a user authentication method that no longer relied on users having to remember unguessable secrets. At a minimum, the new method would have to do better than passwords under at least three respects (refer to Table 1 on page 54 for a concise summary):

Memoryless: Users should not have to memorize any secrets[9].

Scalable: The effectiveness of the method should not be degraded even if the user had to authenticate to dozens or even thousands of different apps.

Secure: The alternative should be at least secure as passwords[10].

The design proposed in this paper meets these requirements. It is based on a token that remembers the user's authentication credentials. Any token-based alternative to passwords, however, should also address two additional concerns:

Loss-Resistant: If the token is lost or destroyed, the user must be able to regain access to the services.

Theft-Resistant: If the token is stolen, the thief must not be able to impersonate the user—even assuming that the thief can tamper with the token and access its insides.

---

[8] According to the insightful model of Beautement et al [3], users have a finite "compliance budget"—there's only so much hassle they'll take from the rule-makers before they'll stop complying. What we are saying here is that our password rules are contradictory and impossible to follow all at once, even for fully cooperating users who have not yet exhausted their compliance budget. Even the people who *issue* those rules cannot possibly come up with fifty different strong passwords, never write them down anywhere, change them every month and remember them and type them out without errors whenever needed. These rules are mutually incompatible. Some of them *will* be broken. Which ones? Maybe the passwords will be reused. Maybe they will be written down. Maybe they will be changed and then changed back. By imposing an unsatisfiable set of rules, you can't anticipate *which* rules will be violated. But some of them definitely will.

[9] Some will argue that this requirement is not strictly a necessity and that it would be acceptable, for example, to rely on a single master passphrase. I shall call this inferior alternative **Quasi-Memoryless**. But the original motivation for my work on Pico is specifically to relieve users from having to remember *any* secrets.

[10] We actually mean: as secure as passwords would be *if* users were able to follow all those implausible and contradictory rules. Too easy otherwise.

The proposed design also meets these additional requirements. Its main disadvantage, aside from the obvious fact of having to carry a token[11], is that it requires changes to the verifying apps, which will be a barrier to deployment. For this reason, after describing the clean-slate design, in section 5 we evaluate possible variations aimed at trading off some security in order to increase convenience, backwards compatibility or market acceptance.

2 Pico: A Usable and Secure Memory Prosthesis

This section gives an overview of the proposed system, Pico, and of all the benefits it claims to provide, besides the ones listed as mandatory in the previous section. Once again, a concise reference summary is in Table 1 on page 54. Benefits are typeset in boldface when first introduced. Refer to section 6 for related work.

The user has a trustworthy device called a Pico[12] that acts as a memory prosthesis and takes on the burden of remembering authentication credentials, transforming them from "something you know" to "something you have".

This shift addresses the first and fundamental requirement (MEMORYLESS) of no longer having to remember passwords. We could have trivially addressed it simply by writing the passwords down on a piece of paper; the solution, however, would fail the THEFT-RESISTANT requirement. Storing the passwords in encrypted form in a "password wallet" on a PDA or smart phone comes one step closer to the idea of the Pico. In section 4.1 we explain how the Pico offers the THEFT-RESISTANT benefit thanks to its Picosiblings.

The first few additional benefits are usability-related: let's review them.

A number of ingenious systems have been proposed to solve the problems of *web* passwords, from Single Sign-On (SSO, surveyed by Pashalidis and Mitchell [29]) to in-browser or in-cloud password wallets. However, even if they worked perfectly, solving the problem only for web passwords would still not satisfy users: if passwords and PINs are a nuisance, they are a nuisance everywhere, not just on the web. For the user, a password is a password, and it's annoying whether on the web or elsewhere. We must provide a comprehensive solution: **WORKS-FOR-ALL**. Pico replaces all passwords, not just web ones, including screen saver passwords, passphrases to unlock files on your local computer and the PINs of standalone devices such as your car stereo, burglar alarm, phone or smart cards.

[11] As Laurie and Singer [22] observe for their Neb: "users already carry [security tokens such as] keys and credit cards; the open question is how to persuade them that to view [this gadget] in the same class as the things they already carry".

[12] After Giovanni Pico della Mirandola, an Italian 15th century philosopher known for his prodigious memory. About twenty years ago, at my old workplace ORL, for a short while we used the abbreviation PiCO (note lowercase "i") to mean "Personal interactive Computing Objects" [40]; despite the striking similarities there is no intended connection between that name and this, and my Pico is an eponym rather than an abbreviation. Finally, Pico is also totally unrelated to the 10^{-12} SI prefix—and to the other thing they use that word for in Chile.

In-browser and in-OS password wallets alleviate many burdens but are only available from the local host on which the credentials are kept. Pico, instead, like SSO and in-cloud wallets, works **From-Anywhere**.

Even if a system remembers passwords on behalf of the user, like a password wallet does, if there are many of them (and we promised with the Scalable benefit that there could be thousands) then the user faces the secondary problem[13] of selecting the appropriate credential for the circumstance. Pico's **No-Search** benefit means that the appropriate credentials are selected automatically when the user wishes to interact with an app[14].

But offering the correct password to the user isn't enough. If the password is strong (long, mixed-case and unpronounceable), even if I am no longer forced to remember that the password was `u4Hs9DB66Ab18GIUdCVi`, it is still rather tedious and error-prone to have to transcribe it[15]. With Pico, therefore, **No-Typing**: the user no longer has to type the damn password[16].

A rarely discussed problem of traditional password-based authentication is that, if a session lasts several hours[17], the app has no way of telling whether the prover is still present—it only knows that the prover was there at the start of the session. Repeatedly requesting the password after every few minutes of inactivity is hardly acceptable from a usability perspective, so the app must live with a window of vulnerability during which access is granted even though the principal interacting with the app may have changed. How much nicer it would be if the app could sense the presence of the authenticated principal continuously throughout the session, but without imposing an additional burden on the user![18] Pico uses short-range radio to offer the **Continuous** benefit: the user is authenticated to the app continuously throughout the session, not just at the beginning. In the course of the session, the app can lock and unlock itself automatically depending on the presence of the user's Pico (section 4.2).

Next to these usability benefits, Pico also offers several security benefits over passwords. Firstly, by letting the Pico, rather than the user, randomly[19] choose strong credentials for each account, we solve two typical problems of passwords: it is not possible for a careless user to choose a weak (brute-forceable or guessable) password (**No-Weak**); and it is not possible for a user to reuse the same credential with different apps (**No-Reuse**). Therefore it is not possible for a malicious verifier to impersonate the user elsewhere, or for a careless verifier (whose verification database gets compromised) to cause the user to be impersonated elsewhere.

---

[13] With both usability and security implications.

[14] But see footnote 34.

[15] Thus by using passwords we impose at least three distinct usability burdens on the user: burden of **remembering**, burden of **selecting**, burden of **typing**. Pico avoids each of them with, respectively, Memoryless, No-Search and No-Typing.

[16] In fact the password isn't even there any more, but that's an aside.

[17] Sometimes even weeks, in the case of persistent login cookies.

[18] Section 6 discusses relevant prior art [40,20,21,6,25].

[19] Pico will need a good quality source of random numbers.

Table 1. Summary of desirable properties of password replacement systems. In the text, benefits are listed in boldface where first defined.

My minimum requirements for a password replacement system:	
MEMORYLESS	Users should not have to memorize any secrets
SCALABLE	Scalable to thousands of apps
SECURE	At least as secure as passwords
Additional requirements if token-based:	
LOSS-RESISTANT	If token lost, user can regain access to services
THEFT-RESISTANT	If token stolen, thief can't impersonate user
Benefits promised by Pico in addition to the above:	
(Usability-related)	
WORKS-FOR-ALL	Works for *all* credentials, not just web passwords
FROM-ANYWHERE	The user can authenticate from any client
NO-SEARCH	The user doesn't have to select the correct credentials
NO-TYPING	The user no longer has to *type* the damn password
CONTINUOUS	Authentication is continuous, not just at session start
(Security-related)	
NO-WEAK	The user cannot choose a weak password
NO-REUSE	The user cannot reuse credentials with different apps
NO-PHISHING	Phishing (app impersonation) is impossible
NO-EAVESDROPPING	Network eavesdropping is impossible
NO-KEYLOGGING	Keylogging is impossible
NO-SURFING	Shoulder surfing is impossible
NO-LINKAGE	Different credentials from same user can't be linked
Additional desirable properties that are not goals for Pico:	
NO-COST	As cheap to deploy as passwords
NO-APP-CHANGES	Deployable without changes to existing apps
NO-CLI-CHANGES	Deployable without changes to existing clients
Also worth considering for a fair comparison:	
IMPLEMENTED	This system was built, rather than just described
OPEN	The code and design are available as open-source
WIDELY-USED	Has been used by over a million individuals
NO-CARRY	Does not require the user to carry anything
NO-TTP	No reliance on a TTP who knows your credentials

Another problem is that a malicious app could masquerade as the genuine app and trick the user into revealing the password. With web sites this is commonly indicated as *phishing*, but an equivalent attack could also occur locally, for example with a Trojan application displaying a fake login screen on your computer. To prevent this, Pico authenticates the app before supplying the user's credentials, thus offering **NO-PHISHING**: it is not possible for a malicious app to steal the user's credentials by impersonating the app to which the user wanted to authenticate. The machinery for such authentication is available to web sites in the form of Secure Sockets Layer (SSL) but, given our pledge to WORKS-FOR-ALL, we want NO-PHISHING to apply in all other cases too.

SSL also offers an additional protection: an encrypted channel that prevents network eavesdroppers from overhearing the password to reuse it later. Pico, too, offers the **No-Eavesdropping** benefit: it is impossible to extract any usable credentials by listening in (at any stage) between the Pico and the app.

Even with SSL, though, a keylogger may steal the password before it enters the encrypted pipe: maybe because the victim's machine has been compromised by malware or because it's not even theirs (cybercafé) and they don't know what's installed on it. With Pico, therefore, we offer **No-Keylogging**—a major benefit over passwords, meaning that your credentials cannot be stolen even if your local endpoint machine is compromised[20]. The low-tech equivalent of keylogging is shoulder-surfing, which passwords only partially avoid[21] by not echoing the typed characters, at the expense of usability. Pico, instead, as a consequence of No-Typing, also fully offers **No-Surfing**.

For privacy, we design the Pico so that an app (or even several colluding apps) cannot link the different credentials used by a Pico user: **No-Linkage**.

We also explicitly list some non-goals: Pico does *not* attempt to be as cheap to deploy as passwords (**No-Cost**), nor to be deployable without modifications—whether to verifiers (**No-App-Changes**) or to provers (**No-Cli-Changes**).

Finally, since we might wish to use the list of benefits in table 1 as column headings for a matrix comparing competing alternatives[22], it is only fair to list other benefits that Pico currently does not offer, much as it hopes to in the future—such as having actually been built (**Implemented**), having its design blueprint and source code published as open source (**Open**), having been used by over a million people (**Widely-Used**)—as well as other benefits that passwords themselves already offer but that some of their replacements don't, such as the usability benefit of not requiring users to carry anything (**No-Carry**, which Pico can't possibly offer) or the security benefit of not relying on a Trusted Third Party not controlled by the user (**No-TTP**, a benefit that Pico offers but which is violated by some in-cloud SSO password management schemes that deposit the passwords with an entity that then issues them to apps on your behalf).

---

[20] So long as the Pico itself isn't, that is. Conceptually, one might object, we have only moved the endpoint one level back. But it still makes a major difference in practice, particularly because the Pico is not a general-purpose computer running user-installable code, and therefore the task of securing it against malware is not as hopeless as it would be for the actual machine. Laurie and Singer [22] have a related discussion about their Neb.

[21] The finger movements can still be observed by a skilled operator. Not as scalable as keylogging, though, as it requires a human attacker.

[22] We fully agree with Herley and van Oorschot [16] that, to find suitable replacements for passwords, we need to specify the requirements clearly and then compare competing alternatives against these requirements. Cfr. footnote 74.

3 User Authentication with the Pico

3.1 Core Design of the Pico

The Pico is a small, portable, dedicated device, intended to be carried along all the time, just like your watch or home keys. It has two important buttons called "main" and "pairing"[23], a small display, a camera suitable for the acquisition of 2D visual codes and a short-range bidirectional radio interface. It could be shaped like a smart phone but also like a watch, a key fob, a bracelet or an item of jewellery.

Internally, the Pico's permanent memory (which is encrypted) contains thousands of slots, one for each pairing between the Pico and an app. Each slot contains the Pico's credential (a private key) for that particular pairing and whatever else is necessary for mutual authentication.

Each app, whether local or remote across the network, has its own public-private key pair. The Pico talks to the app over radio (either directly or through intermediaries) by sending an encrypted message to the app's public key (NO-EAVESDROPPING). The Pico's message contains an ephemeral public key generated by the Pico, which the app can use to reply over radio[24]. The Pico remembers the public key of the app when it first pairs with it (section 3.3), thus defeating phishers and other men in the middle in subsequent interactions. This is conceptually similar to the Pico doing some kind of SSL with the app, but without a PKI to certify the app's key[25].

This arrangement gives us bidirectional encrypted wireless communication between the Pico and the app, but so far only the app endpoint has been authenticated. To authenticate the Pico to the app, the Pico proves ownership of the credential established during pairing (section 3.3) (NO-TYPING).

The general model of the app is that it requires a *(userid, credential)* pair, which it verifies against its stored validation data in order to authenticate the user. This suits most cases, including some in which the userid is implicit. There

---

[23] Plus possibly other controls—maybe "soft" buttons based on a touch screen—to scroll the display etc. If we can get away without them, so much the better. The goal is for the UI to be minimal but without becoming frustratingly unusable; whether any given design achieves this goal can only be validated through user studies.

[24] The reason for using an ephemeral key rather than the Pico's long term credential for that app is to protect the user's privacy and prevent tracking: the user's identity is only revealed to the app *after* the app's identity has been verified by the user's Pico. When the Pico first talks to the app, by encrypting its message to the public key whose hash is in the chosen visual code, the app has not yet proved possession of the corresponding private key, so it could still be an attacker impersonating the app.

[25] But without a PKI, couldn't a malicious app impersonate the genuine one from the first time onwards? Yes, in the sense that the attacker could fool the Pico into believing that her fake app is the genuine one. No, in the sense that if the victim already has a relationship with the genuine app (e.g. has a deposit account at that bank) then the middleperson attacker won't be able to access those assets with the credentials fraudulently established between the fake app and the victim's Pico. This is because the visual code authenticator provided by the app out of band in that case (see section 3.3) is tied to the real app's public key (NO-PHISHING).

are, however, cases that this model does not represent well and that we must treat differently, as discussed at the end of section 3.4.

The opening screen where the app would normally display a "userid/password" request is now augmented with a 2D visual code (using the technique pioneered by McCune, Perrig and Reiter [24]) that encodes a hash of the app's self-signed certificate, containing among other things the app's human-readable name[26] and public key. Whenever that screen is visible, the user can initiate one of two actions by acquiring the 2D visual code by pointing the Pico's camera at it and pressing either of the Pico's buttons: the main button to send pre-established credentials to the app (as if typing a password), or the pairing button to establish a new pairing (as if creating a new account).

Transmitting the hash over the visual channel and the rest over radio constitutes a multi-channel security protocol [41]: most of the protocol takes place over a main bidirectional channel, namely radio, that is convenient to use and has good capacity and latency; but one message instead goes over an auxiliary channel that (despite being only unidirectional, requiring manual acquisition and being of limited capacity and latency) offers data origin authenticity and forces the user to actively designate the intended app.

3.2 Main Button: Offer Credentials

Pressing the main button of the Pico is the equivalent of typing the password. Which one? There is no password as such, but the Pico automatically selects the appropriate credential based on the visually acquired hash for the app (NO-SEARCH, but see footnote 34). If the app's public key is not among the ones stored in any of the Pico's slots, the process stops[27]. Assuming the Pico had not already been fooled during pairing, phishing is impossible (NO-PHISHING).

If the Pico recognizes the app, it talks to the app's public key over radio and sends it an ephemeral public key to reply to. The Pico challenges the app to prove ownership of the app's private key. Once the app does, the Pico sends its long-term public key for that pairing, thus identifying itself to the app, and then, as challenged by the app, proves ownership of the corresponding private key (for example by signing a specially-formatted message containing a challenge defined by the app), thus authenticating itself to the app.

Unlike a password, that can be keylogged when it is typed, here the credential is a secret key that never leaves the Pico[28]. The use of challenge-response,

[26] To have something to call it by on the Pico when necessary.

[27] Possibly with a phishing warning, as the user's intention suggests a belief that an account has already been set up with that app. Various heuristics could be used to assess the likelihood of the current app being a phish, including whether its human-readable name (or even page layout and colour palette) is similar to the one of any app registered in the Pico's slot (as in: did the user click the Main button without meaning to, or because she genuinely thought this was the banking site for which she already has a registration?).

[28] The Pico is not a general purpose computer, does not accept external code and could even include a small hardware security module for its key storage.

instead of merely exhibiting the raw credential, is how the Pico provides No-Keylogging.

Now the Pico and the app have mutually authenticated: they can set up a session key and proceed with continuous authentication (section 4.2).

Note that, despite the use of the visual channel, this authentication procedure is still vulnerable to a relay attack. Adding a nonce to the visual code, while useful, does not stop the attack because the "unique" visual code could be relayed as well[29,30]. Stajano et al [39] discuss fancier and less practical multichannel protocols specifically aimed at thwarting relay attacks, but this isn't one of them. The quest for a reliable solution against relay attacks must continue[31].

3.3 Pairing Button: Initial Pairing

Pressing the pairing button is the equivalent of creating a new account.

We must distinguish two cases: pairing with an app that has no prior relationship with the user (as when creating a new account with a free webmail provider) or pairing with an app whose back-end already has some relationship with the user (as when signing up for online banking with a bank where you have already deposited some money).

---

[29] Norbert Schmitz pointed out to me at Passwords^11, commenting on the case in which the Pico's radio talked to the local computer rather than directly to the app, that an attacker could visit the app's login page, show the victim the visual code of that app on a fake page, let the victim acquire it and unsuspectingly perform the radio part of the protocol with the real app on the attacker's computer nearby. At that point the attacker, sitting in front of the app's real page, would find himself logged in with the credentials of the victim. Quite right. As a countermeasure, Norbert suggested that the app embed a nonce in the visual code. This turns out to be necessary anyway if we let the Pico talk to the app without going through the local computer (e.g. via the cellphone network or wifi), if nothing else in order to distinguish concurrent login sessions from each other (see footnote 37); but it is insufficient to stop the relay attack, because the attacker could still relay the visual code with the genuine nonce too.

[30] Dirk Balfanz also pointed out the same attack at Usenix Security 2011 and showed me how Google addresses the same problem in their similar (experimental) system: the cellphone acting as the Pico shows an interstitial page asking the user to confirm that they really meant to log into Google. This solution works, but suffers from the well-known security-usability problem whereby a proportion of users will just become accustomed to clicking OK without really checking.

[31] In this context, distance bounding protocols based on timing of a speed-of-light message exchange (such as the Hancke-Kuhn [13] that we envisage using for the Picosiblings in section 4.1) cannot be used on the end-to-end link between Pico and app (which may go across the Internet and/or the cellphone network). Conversely, bounding the distance between the Pico and the terminal, rather than between the Pico and the app, would be hard, because the terminal is untrusted and shares no secrets with either the Pico or the app; but more importantly it would be pointless, as the terminal itself could be one half of a relaying attacker.

In the first case, since we work without a PKI, a malicious app could in theory masquerade as the app that the user intends to pair with[32]. In the second case, at the time the "prior relationship" is established between app and user before the Pico first sees the app's "userid/password" screen, the app's back-end must give the user some special codes that will allow the user's Pico to recognize the app when it first sees that screen. One code will be the normal visual code of the app, encoding the hash of the certificate that contains the app's public key; another code will be a nonce, signed by the app, that identifies the user to the app, so that any resources (e.g. the money deposited by the user) can be associated with the user's Pico once that Pico presents that signed nonce during initial pairing. The Pico must thus have a procedure[33] for acquiring the signed nonce *in conjunction* with the app's visual code, with the semantics that the nonce must be sent only to that app, only during the initial pairing with that app. In either the first or the second case, once the initial pairing has taken place, the Pico will only ever send its credentials for that pairing to the app it originally paired with. This is how the Pico bootstraps its NO-PHISHING property.

Back to what happens when the Pico acquires the visual code of the app when the user presses the pairing button. If the Pico already knows that app (i.e. it has that app's public key in a slot), it may issue a warning: "you already have a pairing with this app, do you really want to establish another one?" But it would only be a warning, not a veto, because the user is still free to, say, open several webmail accounts under different names[34]. Assuming the user does wish

[32] But philosophically, even if we had a PKI, all the PKI could do would be to ensure that the public key of the app matched its human-readable name. It could still not guarantee that the user is really pairing with the intended app, as opposed to being fooled into pairing with an app with a similar-sounding name. From a theoretical viewpoint, the user needs *some* relationship with the app (even just knowing its correct name); otherwise she can't be fooled into pairing with the wrong app because there can be no right or wrong app by definition—no way to tell them apart. Reversing the argument, if we accept that the user needs initially to acquire an identifier for the app through some other trustworthy means, we might as well say she ought to use that unspecified trustworthy means to acquire the app's visual code (or the public key itself) with her Pico that first time—and thus we fall into the second case, which is safe.

[33] Possibly involving a third button. This is preferable over relying on tagging information in the visual code for the signed nonce, because otherwise an attacker could perhaps social-engineer the user into feeding a signed nonce to her Pico without realizing it, thinking she is just pairing with a new app.

[34] If the user maintains several distinct pairings with the same app, though, when pressing the Main button the Pico will not fully be able to honour NO-SEARCH and will have to ask the user, with some appropriate UI, to select the intended persona for that app. This is unavoidable, whatever the design, and not a failure of the Pico—it is not possible to select the userid and credential automatically and yet give the user the freedom to maintain several independent pairings with the same app. Note also that the Pico's design, without PKI and with independent user credentials for each pairing (as opposed to, say, using a global key pair for the Pico), protects the user's privacy with respect to the app. Even several userids of the same Pico with the same app will appear to the app as totally independent, offering NO-LINKAGE.

to proceed with pairing, the Pico gets the full public key of the app via radio, checks that the key matches the acquired visual code, possibly caches it in the Pico and, if all is well, responds with an ephemeral public key. As before, the Pico first requests proof that the app knows the private key matching the public key in the visual code before telling the app the Pico's own long-term public key for that account[35].

If the user had a "prior relationship" with the app then, now that a bidirectional encrypted channel has been established, the Pico sends the app the signed nonce, so that the app can associate the newly received credential with the already-existing back-end account. If appropriate, a userid is also defined on the app using the traditional procedure (on the host computer, not on the Pico) and sent back from the app to the Pico to be stored in the relevant slot[36].

3.4 Replacing All Passwords

Web apps. The case that has received the most attention, both in the literature and in actual implementations, is that of authenticating a user to a web app. Partly because it's web apps that are primarily responsible for today's proliferation of passwords and partly because the uniform interface offered by the web makes this case easier to address, for example by augmenting the browser or by using a proxy. However, as we said, our aim with Pico is to get rid of all passwords, not just web ones, so we should be more general in our design. The app requires the ability to talk to the Pico over the two channels (radio and visual) of our multi-channel protocol, but these channels don't necessarily have to go through the browser. While it is easy for the visual channel to go through the browser (it's just a matter of rendering a bitmap as part of the web page), the other channel could be implemented as radio only from the Pico to a piece of middleware on the local computer, and from there turn into IP packets and reach the relevant app across the Internet without even touching the browser[37]. It would even be conceivable for the Pico to talk to the app via an external radio access point rather than via the computer on which the app's visual code is displayed.

Other remote apps—perhaps non-graphical. Having factored out the browser, there are no major architectural differences between the case of web apps and that of other remote apps (mail and various forms of network login). The only notable point is that some apps (e.g. ssh) are text-based and it might be difficult

[35] Which may have been precomputed, to save time during pairing.

[36] This userid is presented by the Pico to the user when, for example, on pressing the Main button, the Pico asks the user which of several accounts with this app should be used to log in.

[37] If the web app added a nonce to each rendering of the visual code and asked the Pico to sign and return it in the rest of the protocol, it would know which "page impression" triggered which instance of the radio subprotocol, even if it didn't arrive from within the browser.

or impossible for them to display a visual code[38] at the time of requesting the "password". In such cases, so long as an alternative pairing procedure can be set up (for example using a web client) in which the app's back-end can securely communicate the app's public key to the Pico, then subsequent authentications will still be protected from phishing. The user interaction flow will have to be designed carefully, though, because there will be no visual code to acquire when pressing the Main button. The app's public key will be available over the radio channel, but so would several others, potentially. In absence of the visual channel, the Pico will have to ask its user to confirm which of the recognized public keys (if any) it wishes to send credentials to, thus partially reneging on No-Search.

Local apps—and protection of app secrets. As far as Pico-based authentication is concerned, there are also no major differences between remote apps and those running locally, such as logging into a local account on your computer, running an application that requires administrator privileges, switching to another user, unlocking the screen saver or entering the restricted section of the BIOS configuration utility[39]. The main difference is that the app's secret must be stored on the local computer.

On the back-end side, whether local or remote, apps using passwords can be attacked, depending on the strategy they use to store the verification credentials. If passwords are stored in cleartext[40] then a breach into the back-end exposes them wholesale, regardless of their strength. If they are stored in hashed form[41], a breach into the back-end exposes them to brute-force and dictionary attacks, which can be mitigated by increasing the number of rounds of hashing (to counter Moore's Law) and by salting (to thwart precomputation). But stolen passwords are only valuable if they were common to several accounts and thus can be reused elsewhere, or if the site owners don't notice the breach and revoke them[42]. With Pico, credentials are never reused across accounts (No-Reuse) and stealing the verification data (the Pico's public key for that account) only allows the attacker to talk to the Pico and verify signatures made by the Pico, not to impersonate the Pico—not even to the app from which the verification data was stolen[43]. What *could* be stolen is the secret keys of the app (rather than of the

[38] In theory we might try to provide an alternative implementation of the visual channel by creating an ASCII marker (with suitable redundancy) and performing OCR on it. In practice such a solution is unlikely to match the robustness and capacity of regular 2D visual codes.

[39] Note that the last two typically don't require a userid.

[40] Irresponsibly careless but not unheard of—cfr. RockYou, December 2009.

[41] But perhaps unsalted, as still happens in Microsoft's NT LAN Manager (NTLM, still widely deployed in 2011, even on new systems, for compatibility reasons), thus opening the door to precomputed brute-force attacks such as Rainbow tables.

[42] And, in the latter case, the attackers have already broken into the back-end to steal the passwords, so how plausible is it to assume that they cannot also directly steal the assets that these credentials are meant to protect?

[43] If the attackers who can steal the credentials can also rewrite them, they might be able to substitute their own public key to that of the victim in order to access the victim's account; but the comment in footnote 42 applies.

various Pico clients who authenticated to the app), which could then be used to mount phishing attacks against any users of the app, indirectly defeating the NO-PHISHING claim. One possible defense against that threat, if warranted by the value of what the credentials protect, is to store the app's secret key in a Hardware Security Module (HSM) on the verifying host[44]. This countermeasure can be applied to both local and remote hosts.

Non-computer apps. Authenticating to a non-computer app covers such cases as having to type an unlocking PIN into a car stereo, a burglar alarm, a cash dispenser, an electronic safe and so forth.

Under the assumption that some form of bidirectional channel is available between the app and the Pico[45], this case is not substantially different from the one already seen for non-graphical apps. An alternative pairing procedure is needed whereby the public key of the app can be securely transferred to the Pico. Of course, if the device has a graphical display, as more and more will, it can instead show its visual code just like a computer-based app.

The case of the cash dispenser is interesting: if the PIN is used to authenticate to the bank, as in the case of magstripe cards, the app is either the ATM (if the PIN check is local) or the issuing bank (if the PIN check is done at that bank). But if the PIN authenticates the user to a chip in the smart card, it's that chip itself that is the app, and the ATM is only its display[46] and radio interface. In any case, since the Pico system architecture is end-to-end between the Pico and app, we don't really care that much about how many intermediaries we have.

Passwords not used for authentication. Consider the case of a program that performs symmetric encryption and decryption on files. For sure it requests you to remember and type a password (potentially a different one for every file) and as such it must be catered for by the Pico, otherwise we'd be failing to offer the WORKS-FOR-ALL benefit.

But it is difficult to model it as a login-style app requesting userid/password, as we have done so far. Would every file be a different app? Or would the encryption program be the app, and every file a different userid? What if I wanted to encrypt the same file under five different keys, to give it to five different recipients—should the userid be my own annotation, such as "file X that I'm sending to recipient Y"?

And a more fundamental problem: even if my Pico successfully proved ownership of the correct credential for the chosen file, how would the app decrypt the file for me? Would it authorize use of a decryption key stored next to the verification data for my credential? This additional indirection is architecturally wrong because then the app holds the key to my file. My file is no longer protected by encryption but by the (probably much weaker) mechanism through

[44] And, once its secret key is safe, the app can sign the public keys of all the Pico clients it pairs with before storing them, to preserve their integrity.

[45] Via local short-range radio or perhaps a radio-to-IP access point if the app already has IP connectivity.

[46] But note how the visual code for the card's chip could even be printed on the card.

which the app protects that key. If the app is compromised, my file is no longer secure. That's not how things should work.

There is indeed a crucial conceptual difference between this case and the previous ones: the file encryption application, even though it asks for a password like all the others, is not *authenticating* the user, nor is it *verifying* any credentials whatsoever: it is just *accepting* a passphrase from the user and deriving from it a cryptographic key with which to decrypt the selected file. This app, unlike the others, shouldn't even *know* how to unlock the user's assets (i.e. the encrypted file) without the user-supplied string—it's not the case that the app has access to the data but won't grant it to others until they prove they're worth it. And it's crucial that the app *not* be able to decrypt—the information necessary from decryption must be supplied by the user, not remembered by the app. It's a subtle but significant distinction[47].

For this kind of application, the proper thing for the Pico to do is to use the previously-described machinery just to establish a secure channel with the app (to ensure No-Eavesdropping and especially No-Keylogging), but to then transmit a strong encryption key to the app over that channel. Some additional user interface elements on the Pico beyond the Main and Pairing buttons will have to be involved, and some careful thought will have to go into the design of the user interaction flow. As a first sketch: the user starts by authenticating to the encryption app using the Pico; then the UI of the app is used to select a file and the operation (encryption or decryption) to be performed on it. For encryption, the Pico creates a random bit string of the appropriate length and sends it to the app as the key to be used. For decryption, the user selects the file using the app's UI and the Pico provides the correct decryption key for it[48].

The case of passwords not used for authentication is somewhat annoying because it requires special treatment, but it is also the most intellectually stimulating. The open question is whether there are any further uses of passwords that are not yet captured by any of the interaction models described above.

4 Details of Pico Operation

4.1 Locking and Unlocking the Pico with the Picosiblings

In any token-based authentication system, all the verifier can do is to check for the presence of the token; from that, it is a leap of faith to infer the presence and consent of the actual user.

[47] Especially if you think about the one-time pad where different decryption keys yield different plaintexts for the same ciphertext, all equally valid a priori.

[48] This problem is not trivial, and as yet unsolved, if we are also to provide the No-Search benefit of not requiring the user to pick the appropriate credential on the Pico itself. Using the file name to identify the password is ambiguous—the user might have several files by that name, in different places or at different times, to be encrypted with different keys. Using the hash of the encrypted file is only appropriate if the file is immutable once encrypted; otherwise, if the file is updated and re-encrypted, its key would change, causing trouble if we ever had to access previous versions (e.g. when restoring from a backup).

Many token-based systems quickly dismiss this problem, either by equating it to that of your physical home keys (i.e. by doing nothing and just hoping you won't lose the token) or by simply protecting the token with a short PIN. A PIN with an HSM-enforced rate limit after three wrong guesses might appear to offer reasonable security; but that's before taking several factors into account: people's tendency for choosing easily guessed PINs (violating NO-WEAK) and/or the same PIN as for other apps (violating NO-REUSE), the cost of providing a PIN pad on the token[49], the burden and security risk of having to type the PIN into the token (violating NO-TYPING and NO-SURFING) and of course the burden of having to remember a PIN in the first place (violating MEMORYLESS).

Then there is the window of vulnerability from time of check to time of use, now shifted one level from authentication of the token to the app to authentication of the user to the token: user types PIN in the morning, unlocking token for the day, then loses token at lunchtime, allowing finder to use it in the afternoon. Requesting the PIN more frequently has a high usability cost.

For all these reasons, the Pico uses its own method (the Picosiblings, described next) for locking and unlocking. The rest of this section (4.1) can be considered conceptually separate from the core design of the Pico described in section 3.1 but the discussion above shows how many of the benefits promised by the Pico (MEMORYLESS, NO-TYPING, CONTINUOUS, NO-WEAK, NO-REUSE, NO-PHISHING, NO-EAVESDROPPING, NO-KEYLOGGING, NO-SURFING) also crucially depend on the way in which the token itself is locked.

As already mentioned, the secrets of the Pico are themselves encrypted[50]. They are unlocked by the Pico Master Key, which is reconstructed using k-out-of-n secret sharing [35]. The shares are held by other entities known as the **Picosiblings**. The idea, which we first mentioned in 2000 as "family feelings for the Resurrecting Duckling" [36] and that was also independently suggested in 2001 by Desmedt et al [7], is that the Pico will "feel safe" and unlock itself when in the company of its Picosiblings; and defensively lock itself up otherwise.

The shares, except for the two special ones described next, are held by the Picosiblings, which are small objects chosen for the property that the user will wear them practically all the time: glasses, belt, wallet, various items of jewellery—even piercings, wigs, dentures and subcutaneous implants. In daily usage, the user interacts with them in no other way than by wearing them: they talk to the Pico with short-range radio and they don't require much of a user interface.

With an appropriate initialization protocol based on the Resurrecting Duckling [38], each Picosibling is securely paired to the Pico. From then on it responds to the radio enquiries of its master Pico using a "Picosibling ping" protocol with the following properties:

[49] Or, if the PIN pad is provided externally, as in EMV payment cards, the possibility that an attacker might intercept the traffic from the keypad to the token, or insert malware on the keypad itself (violating combinations of NO-EAVESDROPPING, NO-KEYLOGGING, NO-PHISHING) [9,2,5].

[50] With the equivalent of "full disk encryption" or perhaps even with an internal HSM.

- The Pico can ascertain the presence of any of its Picosiblings in the vicinity.
- The Picosibling responds to its master Pico but not to any other Pico.
- At each ping, the Picosibling sends its k-out-of-n share to the Pico, in a way that does not reveal it to eavesdroppers.
- An eavesdropper can detect the bidirectional communications between Pico and Picosiblings but not infer identities or long-term pseudonyms.
- The Pico can detect and ignore old replayed messages.
- The Pico can detect and ignore relay attacks (e.g. with Hancke-Kuhn [13]).

Internally, the Pico keeps an array with a slot for each paired Picosibling. Each slot contains, among other things, a decay (countdown) timer and some space for the key share contributed by the Picosibling. At each valid ping response from a Picosibling, the corresponding decay timer is refilled with the starting value (e.g. 1 min) and starts counting down immediately; the Picosibling's share is refreshed and, if appropriate, the k-out-of-n secret is reconstructed. Whenever a decay timer expires, the corresponding share is wiped; the k-out-of-n secret is also wiped and, if possible, reconstructed from the other shares.

When the shared secret is not available, the Pico's credentials are inaccessible and so the Pico doesn't work. If the Pico fails to reacquire k shares within a set timeout (e.g. 5 min), it switches itself off, thus forgetting *all* shares, and must be explicitly turned on and unlocked before it will work again[51].

Two of the shares are special[52] and have a much longer timeout (e.g. a day). One of the special shares is derived from a biometric measurement[53], with suitable error correction [14]. The purpose of this share is to ensure that, even if an attacker gains control of enough Picosiblings (for example by raiding the user's swimming pool locker), a lost Pico will eventually switch itself off if it is away from its owner.

The other special share is obtained from a remote server (conceptually belonging to the user) through a network connection. It has a dual purpose: auditing the reactivations (the server keeps a log of where and to which address it sent out its share) and allowing remote disabling of the Pico (the user who loses control of the Pico can tell the server not to send out the share any more[54]).

---

51 The user may of course also switch off the Pico intentionally even while all the Picosiblings are in range.

52 Depending on the chosen policy, they might even weigh more than "1" in the k-out-of-n budget. Their presence might be required regardless of that of any others.

53 The biometric as an additional authentication factor has the advantage of usability (and few of the privacy concerns normally associated with biometric authentication, because the verifier is your own Pico rather than Big Brother) but won't be as strong as the published statistics on biometric authentication reliability might suggest because here the verification is not supervised by a human verifier suspicious of the prover. The verification process thus isn't resistant to an adversary who has control of the Pico and feeds it iris photographs or gummy fingers [23]. The process should still make at least a basic attempt at verifying that the biometric is live.

54 Ironically, the user will need a way to issue this order without her Pico. One solution, inspired by the work of Schechter et al. [34], might be to control the remote server with the secret-sharing-based consent of a few trusted friends.

How does the user manage her Picosiblings? Aside from the two special shares, handled separately, let's say that the security policy of our user requires proximity of three other Picosiblings to unlock the Pico, for example two earrings and a pair of glasses. Even though only three items are necessary, the user ought to register several pairs of earrings and several pairs of glasses[55] and perhaps also other items for good measure, such as a bracelet, a belt, a medal, a smart card and so on[56]. The n in k-out-of-n secret sharing says how many Picosiblings are registered with this Pico; it can be much greater than k, which says how many Picosiblings the Pico must sense to unlock. All the unworn $n - k$ Picosiblings must be kept in a safe place. Defining a new set of n Picosiblings, as well as changing n and k, is conceptually an atomic operation (see section 4.3).

4.2 Continuous Authentication

A major advantage of Pico is its CONTINUOUS benefit: once you have "logged in" by acquiring the app's visual code and letting the Pico do its stuff over the radio, the app can continue to ping the Pico over their confidentiality- and integrity-protected channel and use that to confirm that you and your Pico are still around. As soon as you are not, the app can block access[57]; and, what's even better, if your Pico reappears before a set timeout expires, the app can grant access again without even asking you to reacquire the visual code.

One potential threat in this situation is the relay attack, which an adversary could use to make it look as if you were still close to the computer even after you left. Guarding against relay attacks at the level between Pico and app is harder than at the level between Pico and Picosiblings because the link may have unpredictable latency, possibly even going through the Internet, and thus distance-bounding methods won't work reliably.

Further engineering details to be addressed include state preservation (things must work like an automatic suspend/resume where you still find everything just as you left it, not like an automatic logout/login where all open programs get closed) and the nesting of app sessions (one of the apps may be your actual login session on the local computer and another might be your webmail session within your web browser; each with its own key pairs and so on; the suspend and resume pairs must nest in the correct order).

4.3 Backup

To protect the user from permanent loss of access if the Pico is destroyed or lost (LOSS-RESISTANT), regular backups must be taken—but actual users never

[55] So that she can still use her Pico whatever earrings she chooses to wear today.

[56] So that she can use other items on days when she wants to wear no earrings, or non-Picosibling earrings. And also so that she has enough extras that, even after losing today's earrings and glasses or having them stolen, she can still unlock her Pico, or her backups (see section 4.3) if she also lost her Pico.

[57] Like a locked screen saver that came on *only* when you left, not merely when you stopped typing for a while; and *as soon* as you left, not merely half an hour later.

do backups. We therefore introduce what Norman [26] calls a forcing function: the Pico's docking station recharges your Pico (as you do with your phone) and automatically takes a backup every time you dock. Since the storage of the Pico is encrypted, the backup is too, automatically. The docking station works as a standalone device, writing the backup to a memory card (and possibly also storing the last few internally)[58] but it can also be connected to a computer to provide a user interface. An encrypted backup can be restored onto a virgin Pico, but it only becomes accessible by unlocking the Pico as usual through its Picosiblings (section 4.1).

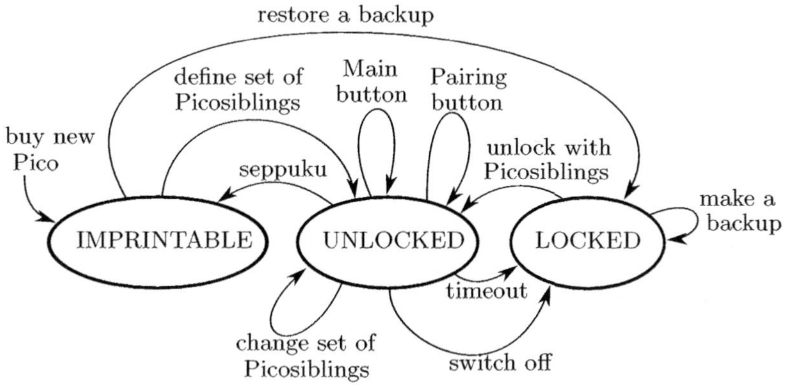

Fig. 1. State diagram of Pico, based on Resurrecting Duckling

More formally, the model for the Pico is derived from the Resurrecting Duckling [37,38]. With reference to the state diagram in figure 1, a brand new Pico is in the "imprintable" state and contains no credentials. The other two states, "unlocked" and "locked", both count as imprinted. From "imprintable" you can either restore an existing backup, thus taking the Pico to the "locked" state, or define a new set of Picosiblings and pair them with the Pico[59], taking the Pico to the "unlocked" state.

The "unlocked" state is the one in which the Main and Pairing buttons work. From there, you move into the "locked" state by timeout or by explicitly switching

[58] The docking station contains no secrets and is not paired with the Pico or Picosiblings. Even so, since it contains the backups, it is prudent to leave one's docking station at home ("safe place") and use a different one for trips, not for confidentiality but for availability, i.e. so as not to lose the only copy of the backups. It would in theory be possible to use the same docking station everywhere if one religiously extracted the backups and stored them elsewhere, but Murphy says it's unwise to rely on this happening.

[59] This is a complex subprotocol in which a random master key for the Pico is generated and then split into shares, and the shares distributed to the imprintable Picosiblings.

off the Pico. From the "unlocked" state you can change the set of Picosiblings[60]. You may also order seppuku (suicide), thus wiping all stored credentials and returning both the Pico and all its paired Picosiblings to the "imprintable" state.

The "locked" state is the one in which the Pico remembers credentials but won't let anyone use them. From this state you can take a backup (remaining in this state) and you can get back to "unlocked" with the cooperation of enough Picosiblings.

This model allows the possibility of having different Pico instances containing the same credentials—if they were all restored from a common backup. They might then go out of sync if credentials are added to one and not the other. Additional protocols might be defined to keep such instances in sync or to kill off all but one of them, relying on a hardware serial number and on the fact that all these Pico instances talk back to the network server that holds one of the special Picosibling shares (section 4.1).

It is also in theory possible to extend this model by allowing users to select and export individual credentials from one Pico to another. So long as this is done securely and the interaction is designed without excessively complicating the management interface, this feature might be useful to implement *selective delegation* ("I give you a copy of the key to my filing cabinet, but not a copy of my front door key"). It is architecturally cleaner to support this function at the verifier's end instead ("henceforth, Bob's key too will open Alice's filing cabinet"), but transferring the credential provides *plausible deniability* (now nobody can tell whether the filing cabinet was opened by Alice or by Bob)—which, depending on circumstances, might be a bug or a feature.

To recover after losing the Pico, the user obtains a new imprintable Pico[61], restores the backup onto it (bringing it to the "locked" state), then unlocks it with the Picosiblings. In the unlucky case that the user also lost the Picosiblings, she must unlock the backup using the spare Picosibling she wisely stored in her safe deposit box[62] when she defined the original set of Picosiblings. Once her restored Pico is unlocked, it would be a good idea for her to define a new set of Picosiblings, including some new ones to replace[63] the ones she lost, and then take a new backup.

4.4 Escrow

The Pico model is quite flexible and covers a wide spectrum of requirements, from those of the individual to those of the corporate user. It is possible, though

---

60 This is another complex subprotocol in which existing Picosiblings are returned to the imprintable state, a new Pico master key is generated and the Pico is reencrypted under it, then the new master key is split among a new set of imprintable Picosiblings and the shares distributed to them; all somehow atomically, so that you can't lock yourself out of your Pico if something goes wrong halfway through.

61 We can buy pay-as-you-go cellphones for less than \$10 nowadays, so imagine that to be the price of the Pico once everybody has one. People might even keep a blank imprintable Pico at home, and another at work, "just in case".

62 Or gave to non-colluding friends, since Picosiblings naturally support secret sharing.

63 And thereby implicitly revoke.

by no means mandatory, to register additional Picosiblings and leave them in escrow with the company to allow access to the resources protected by the Pico if the employee is run over by a bus. Similarly, it is possible for an individual to register additional Picosiblings and leave them in escrow with a spouse, a trusted friend or a notary as a kind of "digital will".

It is also possible for a single user to operate more than one Pico[64], for example one for corporate secrets and one for private ones, so as not to have to place one's private secrets in escrow with the company.

4.5 Coercion Resistance

The paranoid threat model for passwords is that you may be kidnapped by the mafia or the secret police and tortured in a dark basement until you reveal them. If you succeed in destroying your Pico before capture, then all your credentials become inaccessible and Pico removes the rational incentive[65] for torturing you.

If you are James Bond on a special mission and suspect that you might be captured[66], you might wish to trade off some availability in exchange for security and disable the remote server, after setting the timeout of the remote share to the duration of your trip. You won't be able to reactivate your Pico until you get back home if it ever goes off, but neither will your captors. Now all you need to do while being captured is to switch off the Pico, not even to destroy it.

The assumption is that your backups (and spare Picosiblings, and network server) are in the proverbial "safe place" and that if the bad guys allow you to go back to your safe place to get them, then they can't force you to come out of it. The bad guys could however force you to ask someone else to get the backups out of the safe place in your stead while you are still in their hands.

Nothing in this subsection is to be taken as much more than poor cryptogeek humour[67], but the semi-serious point is that it is possible to make the Pico a coercion-resistant system *if* you are prepared not to be able to recover its secrets yourself. If there is a way for you to recover from the destruction of your Pico, they might be able to force you to use it. But if you destroy the Pico and have

[64] Though they might each require their own cloud of Picosiblings. Since each Picosibling can only be paired to one Pico at a time, this puts a practical limit on the number of Pico per person, which is just as well to avoid the "I won't have the right Pico when I need it" problem.

[65] Of course they might still torture you out of revenge, or just because they like doing it—no guarantee they'll be rational about it.

[66] Or, more mundanely, if you are on a trip away from home and think there's a higher than usual risk that you might lose your Pico.

[67] The *Akevitt* Attack, suggested by Erlend Dyrnes, is more effective and less violent: generously offer victim twenty shots of said Norwegian liquor; then, once victim under table, grab and use their still-unlocked Pico and Picosiblings. Perhaps one of the Picosiblings should include a mercury switch and stop working when the user is horizontal—but this would not suit Cory Doctorow who wants to websurf in bed.

no backups, they can torture you all they want but won't be able to recover your secrets[68], even with your full cooperation. You can't claim that for passwords.

Another practical strategy for protecting especially precious credentials (and for being able to deny that they even exist) is to dedicate a separate Pico just to them. Your ordinary Pico would hold your day-to-day credentials; then another special Pico (that nobody would know about, kept in a safe place and less likely to be misplaced or stolen) would hold the more serious and rarely accessed stuff. The caveat in footnote 64 against Pico proliferation applies, but having a separate "travel" Pico still sounds like a sensible precaution.

4.6 Revocation

To complete the Pico design we need appropriate facilities for revoking key pairs, both on the Pico side and on the app side since the authentication is mutual. We may well adopt the standard technique (used, among others, by PGP) of keeping in a safe place a revocation request signed with the private key to be revoked; but we'll have to address the standard problem of the intended party not hearing about this revocation in a timely fashion, especially in our decentralized non-PKI-based environment.

5 Optimizations (As Roger Needham Would Call Them)

"Optimization", Roger Needham famously remarked, "is the process of taking something that works and replacing it with something that almost works, but costs less". There are various ways in which we could "optimize" the design of the Pico in an attempt to bootstrap its acceptance and market penetration[69].

5.1 Using a Smart Phone as the Pico

One of the "costs" of the Pico for the user, besides the price tag, is the burden of having to carry yet another gadget. To counter that and offer QUASI-NO-CARRY, some will want to implement the Pico as software for a smartphone, which already has a good display, a visual-code-compatible camera, a radio interface and, above all, is a device that users already carry spontaneously. But the smartphone is a general-purpose networked device and thus a great ecosystem for viruses, worms, trojans and other malware. I, for one, would not feel comfortable holding all my password replacements there. I also doubt that a smartphone program

68 The main difficulty will be convincing them that that's the case before they start. "Read this before torturing me" might not work—especially with a paper this long.

69 Once a critical mass of users is reached, these "optimizations" should be rolled back. The next concern will then be our ability to use Pico in absolutely all situations, including by users with disabilities (at this stage Pico seems to be doing fine, but this would have to be assessed more carefully) and in locations that disallow the use of a camera, such as certain military or industrial facilities (it's debatable whether we should change the Pico or choose not to support these cases).

would be granted enough low level control of the machine by the OS to be able to encrypt all of its data without inadvertently leaving parts of it in places that an attacker with physical control of the device could re-read.

A halfway-house between an insecure smartphone and a secure piece of dedicated hardware and software might be to use your old smartphone as your Pico[70] and your new one as your regular phone. Not as secure as a purpose-made Pico, and it would fail to offer No-Carry, but it would be a cheaper way to prototype and field-test the Pico without building custom hardware.

5.2 Typing Passwords

The most significant "cost" of the Pico is undoubtedly the fact that it requires changes to the apps; next to that is the cost of the changes (hardware and software) on the local computer. A way of eliminating these costs and thus achieving No-App-Changes and No-Cli-Changes is to drop public keys and visual codes and to make the Pico just remember straightforward passwords. With a USB connector the Pico could emulate a keyboard and type the password for you, honouring the No-Typing benefit[71].

The ways in which this optimization works only "almost" are unfortunately many. Giving up the SSL-like operation opens the door to app impersonation, losing No-Phishing. Because the app no longer has a visual code or public key, the Pico can't select the appropriate credentials, losing No-Search. Because the app can no longer ping the Pico, we lose Continuous. Passwords typed by the Pico can be intercepted, losing No-Keylogging. All we retain, provided that we manage the passwords sensibly, are Memoryless, No-Weak, No-Reuse, No-Typing and Quasi-Works-For-All[72].

An even more radical cost saving measure would drop the USB connector, forcing the user to transcribe the passwords manually and essentially bringing us back to the PDA with password wallet software. Neither option is recommended.

5.3 Removing Fancy Features

Further savings could be obtained by dispensing with some of the Pico's special features: by not bothering with the Picosiblings (section 4.1), perhaps replacing them with a master PIN; by dropping proper mass storage encryption (section 4.1); or by not implementing the automatic backup from the docking station (section 4.3). We noted at the start of section 4.1 the disadvantages of securing the Pico with a master PIN; and not performing backups automatically would be a *really* bad idea. On the other hand, future user studies might tell us that managing the Picosiblings is found to be as complicated as having to remember and juggle dozens of strong passwords. We need prototypes and impartial user

---

[70] Wiping it of any other apps and restricting network functionality to getting the special share from the remote server as described in section 4.1.

[71] Some commercial devices already do that—see footnote 83.

[72] If we claim No-Cli-Changes we must exclude the situations, like ATMs and burglar alarms, that don't already support external USB keyboards.

studies to understand whether this is so. Picosiblings are just *one possible way* of locking and unlocking the Pico and as such they are the feature subset that one could most easily remove. Perhaps the first simplification might be to remove the special Picosibling share of the network server, which carries its own management burden; and then to remove the other special share (biometric). A more drastic alternative might be to omit the Picosiblings altogether.

5.4 Gradual Adoption

Some users might welcome the convenience of the Pico but not trust it for absolutely everything: they might feel safer remembering one or two strong passwords for their highest security accounts and using the Pico for everything else. This is fine: until the THEFT-RESISTANT and LOSS-RESISTANT claims of the Pico have been validated beyond reasonable doubt by hostile review, we would consider this trade-off[73] a prudent diversification strategy.

6 Related Work

Replacing passwords is an extremely crowded research area and any survey, however long, will necessarily be incomplete; for more references than we discuss here, start with the extensive bibliography in Bonneau and Preibusch [4]. We mentioned in the introduction Adams and Sasse's classic study on password usability problems [1], but in this section we focus instead on alternatives and solutions, highlighting how they score against the criteria set out in Table 1[74].

How do ordinary people cope with password overload? Following a long-established tradition many of them, having exhausted what Beautement et al. [3] would call their compliance budget, achieve benefits MEMORYLESS and WORKS-FOR-ALL simply by writing their passwords down; some even keep them in a file on their computer, to allow cut and paste and thus enjoy NO-TYPING. A negligible minority of crypto-geeks do the same but also encrypt the file, thus degrading to QUASI-MEMORYLESS but additionally achieving SECURE and THEFT-RESISTANT[75]. This rather sensible approach was at some point embodied into stand-alone "password wallet" applications, of which one of the earliest was Schneier's Password Safe (1999). Password wallets running on PDAs rather than on the user's main computer were less at risk from malware, especially if the PDA wasn't network-capable, but gave up on NO-TYPING. Some of these programs also offered NO-WEAK and NO-REUSE, to the extent that the program

[73] The price to pay for not putting all the eggs in one basket is not just the downgrade from MEMORYLESS to QUASI-MEMORYLESS but also the loss of all the Pico's usability *and* security benefits over passwords for those high security accounts, including protection against keylogging and phishing.

[74] For reasons of space we only present significant highlights, rather than a complete (products $\times$ benefits) matrix, as some cells would require extensive discussion. But we might one day extend this section into a full stand-alone comparative survey.

[75] Plus LOSS-RESISTANT if they back up the file.

could, on request, generate a random password. A significant advance in this direction became the integration of the encrypted password wallet within the web browser—one of the first examples being the Netscape/Mozilla family (1999?). This solution added NO-SEARCH to NO-TYPING, with a marked improvement in usability, but obviously gave up on WORKS-FOR-ALL because it only worked with web apps. The latest versions of such browser-based password wallets offer the option of storing the passwords in the cloud[76] and of synchronizing them among different browsers, to offer FROM-ANYWHERE; but some of these implementations are less convincing than others with respect to the trust that the user must place in the wallet provider. There exist also versions of password wallets integrated in the operating system rather than in the browser, such as OS X's Keychain. While they still fail to provide WORKS-FOR-ALL, they handle additional passwords not managed by the in-browser wallet, such as the ones for WiFi. Note how most of these systems only provide QUASI-MEMORYLESS rather than MEMORYLESS, because they require a (keyloggable) master password.

A conceptually related approach (having a single password that unlocks your other passwords that are then supplied automatically to the relevant apps) is the WIDELY-USED Single Sign-On (SSO). The useful taxonomy of Pashalidis and Mitchell [29] classifies SSO systems along two dimensions: local vs proxy (does the entity to which the user authenticates, known as the Authentication Service Provider or ASP, reside on the local computer or in the network?) and true vs pseudo (is SSO supported by design or just by transparent simulation of pre-existing authentication methods?). According to this taxonomy we might describe password wallets as local[77] pseudo-SSO systems. SSO systems may offer NO-PHISHING, NO-EAVESDROPPING and even, depending on the mechanism chosen for authenticating to the ASP, NO-KEYLOGGING (cfr. the IMPLEMENTED, OPEN "Impostor" [30], which uses a primitive challenge-response; its IMPLEMENTED successor "KYPS" [28] and the independently IMPLEMENTED "URRSA" [10], which use one-time passwords). Pseudo SSO systems even offer NO-APP-CHANGES: the apps don't even know that the user is logging in through an ASP rather than directly. True SSO systems effectively get rid of passwords with respect to the downstream apps, thus offering NO-WEAK and NO-REUSE and, with a proper protocol, NO-PHISHING, NO-EAVESDROPPING, NO-KEYLOGGING and NO-SURFING over the connection from ASP to app; but they might offer only "quasi" versions of these benefits if the user still authenticates to the ASP with a password. One further dimension that could be added to the Pashalidis-Mitchell taxonomy would distinguish between an ASP under

---

76 An interesting twist is a wallet that *generates* your passwords rather than storing them: `www.passwordsitter.de` derives your passwords by encrypting the app's name and other details with your master password, therefore weak and reused passwords are replaced by app-dependent hashes. It can work as an in-cloud wallet or as an offline one. However, while it's true that "your passwords are not stored", you aren't much better off than if they had been stored encrypted because, for your convenience, their server stores a file with your app names and the other relevant details—so your only protection is still the (keyloggable and potentially guessable) master password.

77 Or proxy for in-cloud ones.

the control of the user ("privacy-protecting"), which would also offer NO-TTP, and one run by a third party ("privacy-invading", because the ASP would get to know about every app you visit)[78]. Both Pico (seen, at a stretch, as a kind of "local, true" SSO) and Impostor [30] (a "proxy, pseudo" SSO) would count as "privacy-protecting", whereas systems such as Facebook Connect or OpenID would be "privacy-invading". In this sense KYPS is "privacy-invading" but, in a strange combination, offers NO-TTP because even physically capturing the server does not yield the stored credentials, which are reconstructed on access by XORing them with the OTPs.

One advantage of the Pico over SSO systems is CONTINUOUS, of which the Active Badge IMPLEMENTED by Want and Hopper [40] offered an early glimpse as far back as 1992: it would lock the workstation's screen as soon as the user left. A more security-conscious approach to the problem came in 1997 when Landwehr [20] proposed, patented (with Latham [21]) and IMPLEMENTED a system that would continuously monitor the presence of an RFID token worn by the user and, in its absence, disconnect the keyboard and monitor from the computer. To address the fact that a physical attacker could still access the raw disk, in 2002 Corner and Noble [6] presented (and later refined with Nicholson [25]) "Zero-Interaction Authentication", a well-engineered IMPLEMENTED system in which proximity of the token would unlock the keys of the laptop's cryptographic file system[79]. Absence of the token would flush the decrypted files from the cache and wipe their decryption keys.

An in-browser system designed to offer NO-APP-CHANGES, NO-REUSE and NO-PHISHING is the IMPLEMENTED, OPEN and deployed PwdHash [33]: when the user enters a web password, PwdHash replaces it with a hash of the original password and domain name. Even if the same password is used at several sites, each site sees a different version; in particular, the passwords seen by the phishing and phished site are different. Weak passwords are still vulnerable to dictionary attacks but the benefits above are provided at QUASI-NO-COST.

An important precursor of the Pico is the "Phoolproof Phishing Protection" system by Parno, Cuo and Perrig [27]. Their objective is not to eliminate passwords (which they still use) but to prevent phishing. Yet their system, whose archetypal function is to protect online banking accounts, introduces many architectural features that Pico also adopts: it involves a cellphone interacting via Bluetooth with the local computer, a web browser plugin to talk to the radio and a full SSL interaction, with mutual authentication, with the remote web server. This IMPLEMENTED system offers NO-PHISHING, NO-EAVESDROPPING, NO-KEYLOGGING and FROM-ANYWHERE. Contrary to Pico, Phoolproof is much closer to a drop-in replacement: it requires only minor modifications to web apps, which already have SSL, and users already have suitable cellphones; it thus

[78] LPWA [19], an early (1997) IMPLEMENTED "proxy, pseudo" SSO, despite being "privacy-invading" by our definition because the server was under the control of Lucent, offered an insightful discussion of web privacy and introduced a variety of useful mechanisms to protect it (auto-generated aliases, per-site email addresses etc).

[79] Though note that the token itself had to be activated once a day with a PIN.

arguably offers QUASI-NO-COST, QUASI-NO-APP-CHANGES, QUASI-NO-CLI-CHANGES. By design, it does not offer NO-SEARCH, because the authors want the user to select the app from a "secure bookmark" on the trusted device[80]. Pico takes a different approach (thus providing SCALABLE and NO-SEARCH) because the "secure bookmark" strategy only works when the request to supply the credentials can be initiated from the token; this would not usually be the case for non-web apps (e.g. a desktop application requests the root password because it needs system privileges to run the function you invoked).

The specific problem of online banking authentication has attracted anti-phishing solutions from industry and academia. The system IMPLEMENTED and sold by Cronto[81] to banks to protect online transactions is not intended as a password replacement but it is perhaps the first commercial system to use a visual code and a multi-channel protocol to protect against phishing. Johnson and Moore [18] IMPLEMENTED an anti-phishing device based on a USB dongle with display and buttons, robust against malware having compromised the local computer. The device was also designed to provide audit logs suitable for hostile cross-examination in case of dispute.

The Yubico[82] Yubikey (IMPLEMENTED) is a very low-cost USB token without moving parts, with one capacitive "button" and no display[83]; at every button press it "types" a one-time password which, in conjunction with a password typed by the user, implements a two-factor authentication system. No changes are required at the prover side (NO-CLI-CHANGES), since the Yubikey just looks like a keyboard, but the verifier side needs to know the next OTP to expect. In order not to require the user to carry one Yubikey per app, the apps may outsource their verification procedure to a common authentication server run by one of them or by a third party (possibly Yubico), thus implementing a kind of "proxy, true, privacy-invading" SSO. This easy to use and QUASI-MEMORYLESS system offers QUASI-WORKS-FOR-ALL[84], FROM-ANYWHERE, NO-SEARCH, NO-REUSE, NO-SURFING and NO-KEYLOGGING[85] but is still vulnerable to phishing.

The market-leading RSA SecurID[86] (IMPLEMENTED, WIDELY-USED), a small device whose display offers a new "pseudo one-time" password every minute or

[80] One might argue—we do, and so do Laurie and Singer [22] cited further down—about the wisdom of rating the smartphone a trustworthy device; but, in fairness, Parno et al. have IMPLEMENTED a working prototype before publishing their paper, which can't be said of the Pico or the Neb. The first prototype of the Pico might one day be implemented on a smartphone too, before moving to more secure hardware.

[81] `http://www.cronto.com`

[82] `http://www.yubico.com`

[83] The sCrib (`http://www.smartarchitects.co.uk/`) is similar: it types out passwords while offering NO-CLI-CHANGES and NO-APP-CHANGES.

[84] Like any "true" SSO, it can work with any app whose back-end can be connected to the ASP, and thus it is not limited to web apps.

[85] The password typed by the user can be keylogged but the OTP ensures that, without the token, this captured password is insufficient on its own.

[86] `http://www.rsa.com/node.aspx?id=1156`

so, is meant to strengthen authentication using two factors, rather than replacing passwords or improving usability. The two factors together, though they cannot prevent phishing, offer at least NO-WEAK, NO-REUSE and NO-KEYLOGGING. But the devastating March 2011 compromise of RSA's database, which forced the recall and reissue of 40 million tokens[87], highlights the dangers of a system without NO-TTP.

In an entertaining position paper, Laurie and Singer [22] describe yet another security token. Since a general-purpose OS cannot be secured, they offer a *trusted path* to the user via a stripped-down, single-purpose device (the Neb) that can be made sufficiently simple as to be trustworthy. The Neb is not merely a password replacement: details are sketchy but a crucial part of the proposal appears to be trusted-path validation of the operations performed on the general purpose system (e.g. don't just authenticate user Neo to the blogging site, but display his edits on the Neb to get him to approve them). The Neb would certainly provide at least FROM-ANYWHERE, NO-PHISHING and NO-KEYLOGGING, but it is unclear how user Neo authenticates himself to his Neb, casting doubts over it being LOSS-RESISTANT and THEFT-RESISTANT. Indeed, no solution is offered for loss of the device other than "centralized revocation and reissue".

On a different note we cannot fail to mention biometrics, which are certainly MEMORYLESS and (beating Pico) NO-CARRY; they are also potentially SCALABLE but perhaps not entirely SECURE, LOSS-RESISTANT or THEFT-RESISTANT. They offer all the usability benefits of Pico except CONTINUOUS[88] but, as for security, they fail to offer NO-PHISHING, NO-REUSE and especially NO-LINKAGE. For privacy, this last point is quite serious: if apps collude, all your authentication acts can be tracked across them, without plausible deniability; and you can't revoke your biometrics and get new ones to regain some privacy.

Concerning Picosiblings, as we mentioned in section 4.1, we first wrote up the idea in 2000 as "family feelings for the Resurrecting Duckling" [36], based on a suggestion from Markus Kuhn. In 2001, Desmedt, Burmester, Safavi-Naini and Wang [7] independently proposed a similar system that featured a threshold scheme. The issue of resharing a shared secret (e.g., for Pico, to change the set of Picosiblings) had been discussed by various authors in other contexts [8,42] but, with specific reference to a quorum of ubicomp devices, Peeters, Kohlweiss and Preneel [31] devised a protocol to *authorize* resharing (in order to prevent an attacker from breaking the scheme by altering the set of devices holding shares) and, with Sulmon [32], also investigated its usability.

In closing we note that several other approaches to the problems of passwords we highlighted in the introduction still ask users to remember something. We won't discuss the many proposals that involve remembering secrets other than passwords (images, gestures, paths ...), as they still all go against what we

[87] `http://arstechnica.com/security/news/2011/06/rsa-finally-comes-clean-securid-is-compromised.ars`

[88] Though you might imagine a camera that...

initially listed as our primary requirement, namely a MEMORYLESS solution[89]; but there are still a few papers we wish to mention.

Jakobsson and Akavipat [17] IMPLEMENTED Fastwords, which are passphrases with special properties, made of several dictionary words. The authors argue that Fastwords are easier to remember, easier to type (especially on smartphones, thanks to auto-completion) and yet of higher entropy than the average password. Like all solutions that involve memorizing and then retyping secrets, Fastwords can't offer MEMORYLESS, SCALABLE, NO-PHISHING, NO-TYPING or NO-KEYLOGGING. They do, however, work with existing smartphones (NO-CLI-CHANGES) and thus, in the context of web apps, can be deployed unilaterally by upgrading only the servers: a major advantage that breaks the vicious circle faced instead by Pico.

A different viewpoint is that passwords are still OK and that it's just the password rules that are unreasonable. In a provocative and stimulating paper, Herley and van Oorschot [16] observe that no other technology offers a comparable combination of cost, immediacy and convenience and that the often-repeated statement that passwords are dead has proved "spectacularly incorrect". The well-argued thesis that Herley, Florêncio et al. develop over several papers [12,15,11] is that we should alleviate the users' memory burden by allowing them to use simpler passwords—because policies requiring stronger passwords impose a definite usability cost without returning a matching security improvement. While we agree that password policies are unreasonably complex, we are not convinced that allowing users to adopt less complex passwords will be sufficient to solve, rather than just temporarily mitigate, the usability problems of passwords, especially if the number of necessary passwords continues to grow. We'd much prefer a MEMORYLESS solution potentially SCALABLE to thousands of credentials. Besides, remembering the passwords is not the only usability problem—that's why we also sought NO-TYPING. And, besides usability, as these authors are first to acknowledge, passwords still suffer from phishing and keylogging.

7 Conclusions

It is no longer reasonable for computer security people to impose on users such a self-contradictory and unsatisfiable set of password management requirements. Besides, there are too many passwords per user, and it's only going to get worse.

Pico is perhaps the first proposal of an alternative that would eliminate passwords altogether, not just for web sites. It is presented as a clean-slate solution,

[89] We do not believe that any of the "remember this other thing instead of a password" methods can possibly offer a long term solution to the fact that users must now remember many secrets, all different, all unguessable, and change them every so often. Systems based on human memory can't scale to hundreds of accounts unless they turn into SSO variants where the user effectively only remembers one secret (and then it's the SSO that's really solving the problem, not the "remember a non-password" method). And that's before considering their sometimes dubious claims about usability and memorability, and their susceptibility to smart guessing attacks that anticipate the way in which users choose their memorable secrets.

without regard for backwards compatibility, to explore not the relatively crowded design space of "what can we do to ease today's password pain a little?" but the more speculative one of "what's the best we could do if we didn't have the excuse that we have to support existing systems?". You may use Pico as a springboard to explore the question: "if this isn't the best alternative, why isn't it, and how could we do better?".

There is no expectation that Pico will replace passwords overnight. Even after Pico is debugged security-wise and is ready for prime time usability-wise[90], the success of its deployment will crucially depend on its ability to reach a critical mass of users, capable of self-sustaining a chain reaction of growth[91].

Many password replacement solutions trade off some security to offer greater usability—or vice versa. With Pico, instead, we move to a different curve: more usability *and* more security at the same time. It's not a trade-off, it's a trade-up! It will be hard to break the compatibility shackles, but non-geek users deserve a better deal than we have been offering them until now with passwords[92].

To encourage and facilitate widespread adoption, I have decided not to patent any aspect of the Pico design. If you wish to improve it, build it, sell it, get rich and so forth, be my guest. No royalties due. Just give credit by citing this paper.

Acknowledgements. I am indebted and grateful to Virgil Gligor and Adrian Perrig for their generous and intellectually stimulating hospitality, as the first draft of this paper (repeatedly rewritten since then) originated while I was on sabbatical at Carnegie Mellon's Cylab in 2010. I am grateful to Markus Jakobsson, Joe Bonneau, Attilio Stajano, Omar Choudary, Angela Sasse, Ben Laurie, Matt Blaze, Alf Zugenmaier, "Handslive", "Richard", Paul van Oorschot, Norbert Schmitz, Eirik Schwenke, James Nobis, Per Thorsheim, Erlend Dyrnes, Kirsi Helkala, Cormac Herley, Virgil Gligor, Adrian Perrig, Paul Syverson, Sid Stamm, Andreas Pashalidis, Mark Corner, Bart Preneel, Dirk Balfanz and Carl Landwehr for insightful comments and additional references, as well as to all the other attendees of the Security Protocols Workshop 2011 in Cambridge, UK (whose comments appear in the proceedings), those of the ISSA conference 2011 in Dublin, Ireland, of the Passwords^11 conference in Bergen, Norway, of the Security and Human Behaviour 2011 workshop in Pittsburgh, PA, USA, of the Usenix Security 2011 conference in San Francisco, CA, USA and of the IEEE RTCSA 2011 conference in Toyama, Japan for providing stimulating feedback and probing questions as I presented an evolving version of this work.

---

[90] One of the most interesting questions, to be answered through user studies with real prototypes, will be whether managing a family of Picosiblings is felt to be less complicated than managing a collection of passwords.

[91] As Per Thorsheim commented at Passwords^11: "Just get Facebook to adopt it!".

[92] We reiterate what we said in the introduction: passwords may be seen as cheap, easy and convenient for those who deploy them, but they are not for those who have to use them (subject to mutually incompatible constraints) and who have no way of pushing back. App providers may just think "Why should my password be a problem if users are already managing passwords for every other app?", but that's just a *tragedy of the commons*.

References

1. Adams, A., Angela Sasse, M.: Users are not the enemy. Communications of the ACM 42(12), 40–46 (1999), http://hornbeam.cs.ucl.ac.uk/hcs/people/documents/Angela%20Publications/1999/p40-adams.pdf
2. Anderson, R., Bond, M.: The Man-in-the-Middle Defence. In: Christianson, B., Crispo, B., Malcolm, J.A., Roe, M. (eds.) Security Protocols. LNCS, vol. 5087, pp. 153–156. Springer, Heidelberg (2009), http://www.cl.cam.ac.uk/~mkb23/research/Man-in-the-Middle-Defence.pdf
3. Beautement, A., Angela Sasse, M., Wonham, M.: The compliance budget: managing security behaviour in organisation. In: Proc. New Security Paradigms Workshop 2008, pp. 47–58. ACM (2008), http://hornbeam.cs.ucl.ac.uk/hcs/people/documents/Adam%27s%20Publications/Compliance%20Budget%20final.pdf
4. Bonneau, J., Preibusch, S.: The password thicket: technical and market failures in human authentication on the web. In: Proc. 9th Workshop on the Economics of Information Security (June 2010), http://preibusch.de/publications/Bonneau_Preibusch__password_thicket.pdf
5. Choudary, O.: The Smart Card Detective: a hand-held EMV interceptor. Master's thesis, University of Cambridge (2010), http://www.cl.cam.ac.uk/~osc22/docs/mphil_acs_osc22.pdf
6. Corner, M.D., Noble, B.D.: Zero-interaction authentication. In: Proc. ACM MobiCom 2002, pp. 1–11 (2002), http://www.sigmobile.org/awards/mobicom2002-student.pdf
7. Desmedt, Y., Burmester, M., Safavi-Naini, R., Wang, H.: Threshold Things That Think (T4): Security Requirements to Cope with Theft of Handheld/Handless Internet Devices. In: Proc. Symposium on Requirements Engineering for Information Security (2001)
8. Desmedt, Y., Jajodia, S.: Redistributing Secret Shares to New Access Structures and Its Applications. Tech. Rep. ISSE-TR-97-01, George Mason University (July 1997), ftp://isse.gmu.edu/pub/techrep/9701jajodia.ps.gz
9. Drimer, S., Murdoch, S.J.: Keep your enemies close: distance bounding against smartcard relay attacks. In: Proc. USENIX Security Symposium, pp. 87–102 (August 2007), http://www.cl.cam.ac.uk/~sd410/papers/sc_relay.pdf
10. Florêncio, D., Herley, C.: One-Time Password Access to Any Server without Changing the Server. In: Wu, T.-C., Lei, C.-L., Rijmen, V., Lee, D.-T. (eds.) ISC 2008. LNCS, vol. 5222, pp. 401–420. Springer, Heidelberg (2008), http://research.microsoft.com/~cormac/Papers/otpaccessanyserv%er.pdf
11. Florêncio, D., Herley, C.: Where do security policies come from? In: Proc. SOUPS 2010, pp. 10:1–10:14. ACM (2010), http://research.microsoft.com/pubs/132623/WhereDoSecurityPoliciesComeFrom.pdf
12. Florêncio, D., Herley, C., Coskun, B.: Do strong web passwords accomplish anything? In: Proc. USENIX HOTSEC 2007, pp. 10:1–10:6 (2007), http://research.microsoft.com/pubs/74162/hotsec07.pdf
13. Hancke, G.P., Kuhn, M.G.: An RFID Distance Bounding Protocol. In: Proc. IEEE SECURECOMM 2005, pp. 67–73 (2005), http://www.cl.cam.ac.uk/~mgk25/sc2005-distance.pdf
14. Hao, F., Anderson, R., Daugman, J.: Combining Crypto with Biometrics Effectively. IEEE Transactions on Computers 55(9), 1081–1088 (2006), http://sites.google.com/site/haofeng662/biocrypt_TC.pdf

15. Herley, C.: So Long, and No Thanks for the Externalities: the Rational Rejection of Security Advice by Users. In: Proc. New Security Paradigms Workshop 2009. ACM (2009), http://research.microsoft.com/users/cormac/papers/2009/SoLongAndNoThanks.pdf
16. Herley, C., van Oorschot, P.C.: A Research Agenda Acknowledging the Persistence of Passwords (in submission, 2011)
17. Jakobsson, M., Akavipat, R.: Rethinking Passwords to Adapt to Constrained Keyboards (2011) (in submission), http://www.markus-jakobsson.com/fastwords.pdf
18. Johnson, M., Moore, S.: A New Approach to E-Banking. In: Erlingsson, Ú., et al. (eds.) Proc. 12th Nordic Workshop on Secure IT Systems (NORDSEC 2007), pp. 127–138 (October 2007), http://www.matthew.ath.cx/publications/2007-Johnson-ebanking.pdf
19. Kristol, D.M., Gabber, E., Gibbons, P.B., Matias, Y., Mayer, A.: Design and implementation of the Lucent Personalized Web Assistant (LPWA). Tech. rep., Bell Labs (1998)
20. Landwehr, C.E.: Protecting unattended computers without software. In: Proceedings of the 13th Annual Computer Security Applications Conference, pp. 274–283. IEEE Computer Society, Washington, DC, USA (December 1997), ISBN 0-8186-8274-4, http://www.dtic.mil/cgi-bin/GetTRDoc?Location=U2&doc=GetTRDoc.pdf&AD=ADA465472
21. Landwehr, C.E., Latham, D.L.: Secure Identification System. US Patent 5,892,901, filed 1997-06-10, granted 1999-04-06 (1999)
22. Laurie, B., Singer, A.: Choose the red pill and the blue pill: a position paper. In: Proc. New Security Paradigms Workshop 2008, pp. 127–133. ACM (2008), http://www.links.org/files/nspw36.pdf
23. Matsumoto, T., Matsumoto, H., Yamada, K., Hoshino, S.: Impact of Artificial Gummy Fingers on Fingerprint Systems. In: Proc. SPIE, Optical Security and Counterfeit Deterrence Techniques IV, vol. 4677 (2002), http://cryptome.org/gummy.htm
24. McCune, J.M., Perrig, A., Reiter, M.K.: Seeing-Is-Believing: Using Camera Phones for Human-Verifiable Authentication. In: Proc. IEEE Symposium on Security and Privacy 2005, pp. 110–124 (2005), http://sparrow.ece.cmu.edu/group/pub/mccunej_believing.pdf; updated version in Int. J. Security and Networks 4(1-2), 43–56 (2009), http://sparrow.ece.cmu.edu/group/pub/mccunej_ijsn4_1-2_2009.pdf
25. Nicholson, A., Corner, M.D., Noble, B.D.: Mobile Device Security using Transient Authentication. IEEE Transactions on Mobile Computing 5(11), 1489–1502 (2006), http://prisms.cs.umass.edu/mcorner/papers/tmc_2005.pdf
26. Norman, D.A.: The Psychology of Everyday Things. Basic Books (1988) ISBN 0-385-26774-6, also published as The Design of Everyday Things (paperback)
27. Parno, B., Kuo, C., Perrig, A.: Phoolproof Phishing Prevention. In: Di Crescenzo, G., Rubin, A. (eds.) FC 2006. LNCS, vol. 4107, pp. 1–19. Springer, Heidelberg (2006), http://sparrow.ece.cmu.edu/group/pub/parno_kuo_perrig_phoolproof.pdf
28. Pashalidis, A.: Accessing Password-Protected Resources without the Password. In: Burgin, M., et al. (eds.) Proc. CSIE 2009, pp. 66–70. IEEE Computer Society (2009), http://kyps.net/xrtc/cv/kyps.pdf
29. Pashalidis, A., Mitchell, C.J.: A Taxonomy of Single Sign-On Systems. In: Safavi-Naini, R., Seberry, J., et al. (eds.) ACISP 2003. LNCS, vol. 2727, pp. 249–264. Springer, Heidelberg (2003), http://www.isg.rhul.ac.uk/cjm/atosso.pdf

30. Pashalidis, A., Mitchell, C.J.: Impostor: a single sign-on system for use from untrusted devices. In: Proc. IEEE GLOBECOM 2004, vol. 4, pp. 2191–2195 (2004), http://www.isg.rhul.ac.uk/cjm/iassos2.pdf
31. Peeters, R., Kohlweiss, M., Preneel, B.: Threshold Things That Think: Authorisation for Resharing. In: Camenisch, J., Kesdogan, D. (eds.) iNetSec 2009. IFIP AICT, vol. 309, pp. 111–124. Springer, Heidelberg (2009), http://www.cosic.esat.kuleuven.be/publications/article-1223.pdf
32. Peeters, R., Kohlweiss, M., Preneel, B., Sulmon, N.: Threshold things that think: usable authorization for resharing. In: Proceedings of the 5th Symposium on Usable Privacy and Security, SOUPS 2009, p. 18:1. ACM, New York (2009) ISBN 978-1-60558-736-3, http://cups.cs.cmu.edu/soups/2009/posters/p1-peeters.pdf
33. Ross, B., Jackson, C., Miyake, N., Boneh, D., Mitchell, J.C.: Stronger Password Authentication Using Browser Extensions. In: Proc. Usenix Security, pp. 17–32 (2005), http://crypto.stanford.edu/PwdHash/pwdhash.pdf
34. Schechter, S., Egelman, S., Reeder, R.W.: It's not what you know, but who you know: a social approach to last-resort authentication. In: Proc. CHI 2009, pp. 1983–1992 (2009),http://research.microsoft.com/pubs/79349/paper1459-schechter.pdf
35. Shamir, A.: How to Share a Secret. Communications of the ACM 22(11), 612–613 (1979), http://securespeech.cs.cmu.edu/reports/shamirturing.pdf
36. Stajano, F.: The Resurrecting Duckling – What Next?. In: Christianson, B., Crispo, B., Malcolm, J.A., Roe, M. (eds.) Security Protocols 2000. LNCS, vol. 2133, pp. 204–214. Springer, Heidelberg (2001), http://www.cl.cam.ac.uk/~fms27/papers/2000-Stajano-duckling.pdf
37. Stajano, F.: Security for Ubiquitous Computing. Wiley (2002) ISBN 0-470-84493-0, Contains the most complete treatment of the Resurrecting Duckling [38]
38. Stajano, F., Anderson, R.: The Resurrecting Duckling: Security Issues in Ad-Hoc Wireless Networks. In: Malcolm, J.A., Christianson, B., Crispo, B., Roe, M. (eds.) Security Protocols 1999. LNCS, vol. 1796, pp. 172–182. Springer, Heidelberg (2000), http://www.cl.cam.ac.uk/~fms27/papers/1999-StajanoAnd-duckling.pdf
39. Stajano, F., Wong, F.-L., Christianson, B.: Multichannel Protocols to Prevent Relay Attacks. In: Sion, R. (ed.) FC 2010. LNCS, vol. 6052, pp. 4–19. Springer, Heidelberg (2010), http://www.cl.cam.ac.uk/~fms27/papers/2009-StajanoWonChr-relay.pdf
40. Want, R., Hopper, A.: Active Badges and Personal Interactive Computing Objects. IEEE Transactions on Consumer Electronics 38(1), 10–20 (1992), http://nano.xerox.com/want/papers/pico-itce92.pdf
41. Wong, F.-L., Stajano, F.: Multi-channel protocols. In: Christianson, B., Crispo, B., Malcolm, J.A., Roe, M. (eds.) Security Protocols 2005. LNCS, vol. 4631, pp. 112–127. Springer, Heidelberg (2007), http://www.cl.cam.ac.uk/~fms27/papers/2005-WongSta-multichannel.pdf; updated version in IEEE Pervasive Computing 6(4), 31–39 (2007), http://www.cl.cam.ac.uk/~fms27/papers/2007-WongSta-multichannel.pdf
42. Wong, T.M., Wang, C., Wing, J.M.: Verifiable Secret Redistribution for Archive System. In: IEEE Security in Storage Workshop 2002, pp. 94–105 (2002), http://www.cs.cmu.edu/~wing/publications/Wong-Winga02.pdf

Pico: No More Passwords!
(Transcript of Discussion)

Frank Stajano

University of Cambridge, Cambridge, UK

Virgil Gligor (session chair): We have a session about passwords and you will hear at least two different points of view—possibly even two contradictory points of view, which is par for the course for this workshop. Our first speaker is Frank Stajano who argues that there should be no more passwords.

Frank Stajano: My title should give you a hint about my position towards this problem. What's a password? A password is a way to drive users crazy!

Passwords were not so bad when you had only one or two of them, and when a password of eight or nine characters was considered a safe password. Nowadays computers have grown so powerful that ten character passwords can be brute-forced with the kind of computer you buy in the supermarket next to your groceries. And you don't just have one or two passwords: you have dozens of them, because there are so many more services that now require you to have a password.

If you, poor user, listen to the computer security people, they will say that your passwords must be unguessable, otherwise attackers with figure out what they are; they must be impossible to brute-force, therefore you must fill them up with special symbols, and a strong mix of upper and lower case, and put in numbers as well; and you must not write them down, so you must make sure that you don't forget the complicated passwords that you make up; and, however many passwords you have, they must all be different. This set of requirements is a problem.

If you look at what people who develop websites think, for them the password is very convenient, because every user knows how to authenticate by password, so no training is needed; it's very cheap, because you don't need any equipment at the prover end; and it's very easy to implement, because there are standard library functions for computing the hash and so on. For software developers, the password is an easy way to do user authentication. But if you ask users, then passwords are a real pain. While each developer individually thinks it's OK to use a password ("well, everybody else also requests a password, so what's wrong if I do too?"), users, instead, end up with so many passwords that remembering them all is an unmanageable problem. That's what we call the tragedy of the commons.

If you look at these requirements that we (the unreasonable computer security people) inflict on regular users, it's obvious that there's an empty intersection between them: no passwords will satisfy all of these constraints, so users are quite fed up with passwords, and rightly so. I haven't done a proper user study but I have acted (as I'm sure every one of you has too) as the informal help

B. Christianson et al. (Eds.): Security Protocols 2011, LNCS 7114, pp. 82–97, 2011.

desk for all my relatives and friends who are not into computers. And one of the first things they mention is: "How can I do all of these stupid things with passwords?" (All different, complicated, never written down etc.) I sympathize with their sentiment that the requirements they get from the computer people are contradictory, and that it's unfair for us to ask that they follow all these constraints that can't be satisfied simultaneously.

Alf Zugenmaier: This last constraint, that passwords cannot be written down: why is that? There seems to be some computer security folklore that says "you must not write down passwords"; but why?

Reply: Several pieces of advice are now folklore, as you rightly mention, including others such as "you must change your passwords every month". Despite the fact that this advice is not necessarily rational, it is still being given to users[1] and users still believe they have to comply with it.

If we could start again from zero, and if we could forget about passwords, and find another way of dealing with user authentication, what would it be? There have been a number of interesting proposals in the literature for fixing parts of this problem, web authentication in particular, and I understand that the following talk in this session is essentially about that. But I argue that that's no longer enough, because for a user a password is a password, whether it's used for web authentication or for any other purpose; and if you get users fed up with passwords, they will be fed up with *all* passwords, not just web passwords; so we should solve the problem globally, not just for the web or for online systems. I want to get rid of all passwords, and the way I want to do this is by going from "something you know" to "something you have". I propose a device that acts like a memory prosthesis that frees up the part of your brain that is now devoted to remembering passwords.

What minimum requirements would a password replacement system have to offer? First of all, on the usability side, users should not have to remember passwords: that's the whole point of the exercise. And, as far as security goes, the new method should be at least as secure as passwords (if it were possible to comply with all these contradictory requirements). Then, scalability: the new method should work even if you start having thousands of entities that request a password from you. By the way, let me call "apps" these entities that act as the verifiers of your passwords (not to be confused with cell phone apps). If we are shifting from passwords to tokens, then the new system must also offer availability: if you lose the token then it must be possible for you to regain access to the apps that were protected by those credentials. And the fact of having physical control of the token should not be enough to allow anyone to impersonate you: your token, even if stolen, should not be usable by anyone other than you. These are my baseline requirements.

Now I'm going to stick my neck out and explicitly list the benefits that my system promises to provide; then you can check against the rest of what I say

[1] Or even enforced by some operating systems, in the case of password expiration.

and see if that's true[2]. My system is called Pico, because there was a guy called Pico della Mirandola a long time ago who had a very good memory, so Pico can take care of the memory effort in your stead. The first thing Pico promises to do is to relieve the user from having to remember passwords. Another problem with passwords is that users will choose a password that is weak, easy to guess or easy to brute-force: that is not possible with Pico. Another problem is that users will recycle passwords between different apps, and then if one of the apps is malicious it can impersonate the users with the other apps; or if one of the apps is careless and has its password database stolen and cracked then, even if that app was not malicious, the user who recycled the password can now be impersonated everywhere else; again, this is not possible with Pico.

The NO-TYPING benefit is going to be satisfying for many users: regardless of whether you can remember it, you won't have to type the password any more. The NO-PHISHING benefit is a slightly subtler point: you could be persuaded to type your password into the wrong app, and that would then allow a malicious attacker to reuse your password with the real app, either in an online man-in-the-middle attack, or just offline to screw you later; but the Pico offers facilities that prevent apps from impersonating other apps.

An important point is that Pico works not just for web authentication, but for relieving your memory of *all* passwords, passphrases and PINs, even the one for your burglar alarm. Another point is that, if you have dozens or hundreds of different apps and your token has the credentials for all of them, it becomes tiresome to have to scroll through menus to get to the right one to select which credential to give to the current app. With the Pico you don't have to go through menus to decide which credentials to send to which app.

Matt Blaze: Conspicuously absent from your list[3] is the requirement that apps be allowed to work as if Pico didn't exist.

Reply: Right. I am starting from a clean slate and therefore I won't worry about backwards compatibility, at least until later.

Matt Blaze: OK, so this is not an entirely client-side design?

Reply: No, not at all: it requires changes to the apps to provide all these benefits. Besides, these are just the benefits I claim to provide, and I don't actually provide the benefit that you mention. This one here is not a list of requirements but a list of promises.

Matt Blaze: OK, so the price of your benefits is that the apps have to change?

---

[2] In the pre-proceedings presentation the benefits were numbered. In the following rewrites, as I kept rearranging and expanding the set, I decided instead to give them short mnemonic names. I have now translated these names in the transcript, which now reads "NO-TYPING" where I said "Benefit 4".

[3] The list on the slide had only the promised benefits of the Pico. Following Matt's comment, I explicitly added the "non-goals" section to the table in the paper.

Reply: The price is that apps have to change, and more; but down here, CONTINUOUS, is an additional benefit I will give you for changing your apps. With passwords, you type in your password, then you have an interaction; or maybe (after you typed the password) someone else has an interaction, and the app is not really sure whether *you* are still in front of the app. Maybe you've left it, you have gone to the toilet for a minute and someone from the desk near you is using your computer, or something like that. With the Pico the authentication is continuous, it's not just a point in time, it happens all along, and therefore the app knows that you are there for all the time that you are there. So you don't have a session that is started with you there and then lasts for two hours; or, as Joe pointed out to me, you login to a website and then you have a persistent cookie for two weeks, and it's assumed that you're still the same guy who authenticated two weeks ago; with Pico, this doesn't happen. Extra benefit.

The physical design of the Pico is that of a small device that has a wireless connection to your main computer, has a camera, has some buttons and a display. It's natural to think about it in the form factor of a smartphone, which already has all these things, but Pico doesn't have to be shaped like a smartphone, nor does it have to be an application on your smartphone; it could be something small, it could be a tiny square touch-screen gadget like the latest generation iPod, very cute, or maybe something I could attach to my keychain like this key fob; or maybe a watch, an item of jewellery, or whatever. You may visualize it as a smartphone if you wish but it doesn't have to be shaped like that.

Each app will have a public and private key, and will have a visual code that is basically a certificate for the public key, a certified graphical version of the public key that can be acquired by the camera. We can thus build a multichannel protocol around the process of selecting the app. I point the Pico at the app I want, acquiring the app's code, and then the app sends its public key to the Pico over radio, because a public key is probably too big to fit inside a visual code. So there are two channels: the camera, to acquire the visual code, and the radio, which is bidirectional, to exchange more bits and do everything else that's required in the protocol.

This part will look a bit like SSL: the app, which is a bit like a website, offers a public key; and the client, which is the Pico, recognises that it is the right one, although without using a PKI. Then enough stuff goes on that they achieve mutual authentication and set up a session key (shared secret) to protect the confidentiality and integrity of the rest of their interaction.

The app will always show a kind of front page which displays the visual code: that's equivalent to having the fields where you type in your username and password. At that stage, the Pico can do two things. One is the equivalent of typing in the password, and the other one is registering with that app for the first time; one or the other happens depending on which of two main buttons you press on your Pico. So the two principal actions on the Pico are: "offer credentials", which is like typing in your password, or "initial pairing", which is like creating a new account.

Later I will mention systems that already do a number of things that the Pico does, but none of them does the same subset. One of them is the password manager that Firefox has. You visit a website, you type in your password, it offers to remember it and then pre-types it for you when you next visit that same site (with everything encrypted under a master password). Firefox is second-guessing what you're doing and sometimes it gets confused, for example on some occasions where you have to define your password on a different page from the one where you enter it later (or when you change passwords). With the Pico system it's very clear that there is just one place, the place where the visual code of the app is displayed, where you can do both of these actions.

I'm now going to describe those two actions, "initial pairing" and "offer credentials". The first one is done only once per application, while the second one is done much more frequently, at each authentication. First, the user points the Pico at the chosen app, to acquire the visual code of the app. This is how the user communicates her intent of interacting with that particular app, without the Pico getting confused by other apps nearby that might advertise their public key over the radio at the same time. This is initial pairing so we expect that the app might be new to the Pico; but there's actually a subtlety because you might register with the same app again if you want to have another identity, such as when you open a second Gmail account. For that reason you are still allowed to do an initial pairing with an app that is already registered in your Pico, and you would get a different account for it. Conversely, if the app is not already known to the Pico, then the other button for "offer credentials" won't work; in fact, instead of working, it might give you a warning that you're probably facing a phishing attack because, if you have never paired with that app, it would make no sense for you to log into it.

The Pico gets the public key of the app through the radio channel and checks that it matches the acquired visual code, because otherwise it could be some other malicious app that is sending the public key instead of the one that you want to interact with. Then the Pico talks to this app by encrypting messages to the app's public key: the Pico sends the app an ephemeral public key, one that's just made up for this temporary interaction, and it does so to preserve the user's privacy in case that the app is fake. If the app cannot prove that it owns the secret key matching the public key in the visual code, then there is no reason for Pico to disclose the identity of the user to that app. Therefore, only after the Pico is convinced that the app knows the secret key of its public key will the Pico give the app its permanent public key for that account. Inside, the Pico has a different key pair for every account.

Bruce Christianson: Is that limited to asymmetric keys or may it just be a symmetric key at this stage?

Reply: Admittedly, there aren't that many advantages in using the public key crypto for the client side. You do need the public key crypto for the app side, but on the client side you could do almost exactly the same stuff just by having some secret bit string that is then transferred through the channel that you have established with the app's public key[4]. And in fact this is one getaway trick that I can use later for saying, in cases where I need to be more backwards compatible, then I will have the Pico just remember a secret string and send it to the app that way. Note that, if I take this route, I still have to change the app so that it can receive something over the public-key-protected channel; but, compared to just typing in the password, I avoid all the attacks of eavesdropping, keylogging, hijacking, phishing and so forth.

The username (which identifies the user to the app) is defined on the application itself and is then sent back to the Pico. There is little point in sending this username to the Pico because, to the app, the ultimate identifier of the user is its public key; however, it's nice to have some human-readable name just for the benefit of the human user, to browse accounts in the Pico, when he has to select which account to activate of the several that he has with that particular app: if I have three Gmail accounts and I want to send my credentials, I have to say which ones in that case.

If we are talking of initial pairing with something like a Gmail account, where anyone can get a new account whenever they like, then there's not much else that the app needs to do. But if this initial pairing connects to some resources that already belong to the human user, even before doing the pairing (as in the case where I register for online banking and my existing bank account needs to be attached to this online persona that I am making now), then in that case the app at the back-end needs to check that the user who's registering is the one linked to whatever resources are available (in this case the bank account) before doing this linking. And so, offline, before any of this interaction starts, the back-end will send the user a letter containing two visual codes: one is the visual code of the app, the same one that the app will present on its start page; and another one is a visual code that encodes some authenticator that says "OK, you are the Pico public key that is going to be linked to the resources of your bank account". The Pico acquires these two codes from the letter, and its behaviour will be: "I will only spit back this authenticator to the app whose public key matches the other visual code I acquired in this atomic transaction". And then, as part of the "initial pairing" protocol, the Pico sends that authenticator to the app, and the app checks that it's the right one, and then it links that newly created account to those existing resources.

What happens during "offer credentials", the normal day-to-day interaction where I would usually type the password? The beginning of the operation is practically the same as initial pairing: the Pico requires the visual code of the app the user wants to interact with, but then finds this time that it has a public key memorized for it. (As I said before, if the app was not known then you cannot offer credentials but maybe there's a flag that says "you are perhaps being phished".) An ephemeral public key is sent by the Pico as before and, once the Pico is happy that that app really knows its secret key, then it sends

[4] The pre-proceedings version of the paper discussed the trade-offs betwee symmetric and asymmetric cryptography in greater detail but this was dropped from the final paper for brevity, having decided not to offer symmetric keys as a variant.

its long-term public key which can be challenged by the app—and that's the part where, after authenticating the app to the user, we authenticate the user to the app. Then they do whatever else they would normally do after verifying passwords. Except that, as I anticipated, the Pico system offers the possibility for the app to keep checking whether the user is still there throughout the session, instead of just during the verification at the beginning.

Alf Zugenmaier: You mean that the app can check if the *device* is still there?

Reply: Good point. Indeed the app can only check through radio whether the Pico is still there, and the question is: how does it know that the Pico is still attached to the user as opposed to having been left on the desk? Let me jump ahead and talk about that right now, even though it was going to come a few slides later. This is the topic of Pico locking and unlocking.

As I said earlier, it's not appropriate for a token to be available to anyone who holds it: your token should only work when it's in *your* possession. The token will thus have a locked mode and an unlocked mode, and when it's in locked mode then you cannot use it, you cannot retrieve its credentials or operate with it in any other way. This implies some kind of tamper protection of the device, which is very important, but at this stage is still just an engineering detail. The whole contents of the Pico should be encrypted all the time.

But the more difficult question is: when is a good time to unlock the Pico? I have been working on authentication throughout my computer security career; regulars of this workshop will remember that, the first time I was here, I talked about the Resurrecting Duckling for pairing up two devices. The following year my talk also had to do with the Resurrecting Duckling and one thing came up in that discussion which I am re-using now: using family feelings between various ubiquitous computing devices to decide whether they are in a safe situation or whether they have been kidnapped. We thus have some Picosiblings, which are siblings of the Pico, and they could be your glasses, your watch, your keyring, your belt, things that you tend to have with you all the time. They also talk through radio; when the Pico is within range of all these Picosiblings it feels safe, but if it's left on the desk because you go to the toilet, then it's not with its Picosiblings any more, and from that it deduces that it is no longer with the user. Besides these we have two special items, which I will describe in a moment, but let's just stick with the standard Picosiblings for now. Each sibling holds a share, and all these shares together[5] make the key that unlocks the Pico. These shares are pinged periodically by the Pico. There is a decay counter for each share, which is refreshed (topped up) every time you find the share in these pings; if shares are missing or expire, they cannot be used to reconstruct the full key that unlocks the Pico, so the Pico is unusable. That way, if you leave your Pico on the desk and go to the toilet, it cannot authenticate. If you come back from the toilet before another timeout, the Pico will find the Picosiblings at the next ping and it will work again. If that longer, second timeout is also exceeded,

[5] The design proposed in the pre-proceedings version was based on n-out-of-n secret sharing, later changed into k-out-of-n for greater flexibility and usability.

then the Pico will switch itself off and you will have to restart from zero with all the shares present.

Alf Zugenmaier: What is my incentive not to leave all Picosiblings in one big pile on the desk?

Reply: Your incentive is so that you don't lose all your keys.

Alf Zugenmaier: I could have one Pico on my person all the time, or I could put all the Picosiblings on one keyring.

Reply: You could.

Alf Zugenmaier: And then, if I leave, the Pico and all the Picosiblings are still together and it all looks the same to them. What's the incentive for me? What benefit do I get out of not putting all my Picosiblings on the same keyring such that, if I lose it, I lose all of them?

Reply: Well, the benefit is exactly what you're saying!

Alf Zugenmaier: No, I am not talking of security benefits now: outside of this room, nobody cares.

Bruce Christianson: Security benefits are not real!

Reply: The reason for having Picosiblings like your glasses, your watch or your earrings is precisely because they will be "attached to you" without you even thinking about it. The Pico can sense the presence of other devices that are even more closely attached to you than the Pico itself: some people find it fashionable to wear a piece of hardware attached to their nose—it could well be a Picosibling for them, and it's unlikely that they would undo it and leave it on the desk when they go to the toilet.

Ross Anderson: Then the gentleman in Oakland with the shotgun, instead of saying "please give me your phone", will say "please give me your Picosiblings, and here I have a pair of bolt cutters to assist you with removing your nose jewellery".

Reply: This is the reason why, besides the Picosiblings, I have two other items, one of which is the biometric (which might be a liability if it means the Oakland gentleman will want to chop off your finger).

Bruce Christianson: A link to your Pico-pacemaker will probably be OK.

Alf Zugenmaier: But then why do you have any siblings? I mean, you could stick everything into one, especially if they work with an n-out-of-n secret sharing scheme and thus you need to have all of them together. It's not like, if you forget your watch, your glasses will do as well; it's instead, if you forget one of these things, you are out of luck, nothing will work! Then why don't you just have it as one piece, and that can be your pacemaker, or your nostril jewellery, or whatever?

Reply: It's rather harder to have a sensible user interface on your pacemaker or your nostril jewellery than on a handheld Pico, so I think it's better if you have the Picosiblings just as a proof that you are there, and have something else as a user interaction device.

Bruce Christianson: Well, it would seem sensible to have a Pico and to have something that it has to be in the proximity of.

Reply: Exactly.

Bruce Christianson: But then they're kind of not siblings, it's a different sort of relationship.

Reply: You mean there is a hierarchy between them?

Matt Blaze: I don't want to give people an incentive to steal my pacemaker.

Bruce Christianson: They'll just wait till you go swimming.

Omar Choudary: I think in the Oakland scenario the guy comes over and demands all of them.

Reply: I have a later slide about coercion resistance, so let me show it to you now. First, when you see that Oakland guy with the shotgun, you take your nostril jewellery and you just destroy it, or even throw it far away so that it loses contact with the Pico, and then the Pico after a while switches off. But I have an additional protection against that attack: one further share comes from a network server. (It's somewhat debatable whether you do want your Pico to be re-enabled only after talking to a network server.) The biometric share and the network server share have a much longer timeout than the others: the latter may be of the order of minutes while the former may be of the order of hours or even a day, which means that once a day you have to show your eye to the Pico, and once a day the Pico has to talk to a network server.

The nice thing about a network server (your own network server) is that, if someone has stolen all these Picosiblings from you because you were in the swimming pool and they were all in your locker (even your glasses, though perhaps not your pacemaker), then you still have a chance, after having lost everything, to login to your network server and say "don't give out your share any more"; so, from tomorrow, it would no longer be possible for anybody to use your Pico.

Jonathan Anderson: Can you login to your network server though?

Ross Anderson: The point is that the semantics of the network server may be quite different. The network server is your R&R (Revoke and Re-provision) facility. If it's also vulnerable to legal coercion, and that's not just coercion by the government, but also coercion by you, then if all else fails you can go to the county court, pay the £30, and get your life back.

Reply: I like two things about the network server: first of all, it gives me the ability of revoking the Pico after I have lost control of it. It's easy to say "when you see the guy with the shotgun approach, just break your Pico, you can recover it later from the backup"; but you can't do that if he mugs you before you realise you're being mugged. If you can revoke the Pico after he's left, and he cannot coerce you on the spot, that's more secure. The other nice thing is that the network server will keep an audit trail of any shares that it sends out, so you can see all the instances in which your Pico has been woken up from a switched-off state.

If you are worried about the paranoid threat model that, if you know the password to something very valuable, they could kidnap and torture you until you tell them the password, then with a Pico you are in a better situation because there's nothing you know or have that can help them. And if you just break the Pico, or break the connection between Pico and Picosiblings so that the Pico becomes unusable, then there's nothing you can do to let them re-enable it which they cannot already do themselves.

Jonathan Anderson: I'd rather be on the other side of this debate. If I suspect that a man is going to walk up to me in Oakland with a shotgun, I want to be in a position where I can help him, and make him feel good and go away! I don't want to be the guy who says "oh sorry, I've just broken the thing that would let you have my money" and now he's in a bad mood! I like the revoke-after-he's-taken-my-stuff story, but in fact I'm quite happy for him to take the Pico and go away.

Joseph Bonneau: I'm not sure about that.

Reply: There's a series of answers to this one, some of which I have already written up in the pre-proceedings. First of all is that (as I said when we were discussing the previous talk, in fact), if I have something that's really valuable, when I'm going to somewhere dodgy like Oakland or Afghanistan...

Matt Blaze: Can I please speak for the dangerousness of Philadelphia?

Reply: We can have an auction!

Bruce Christianson: That's W C Fields's epitaph.

Reply: If you're planning a trip to Oakland, or Afghanistan, or Philadelphia, or other similar places, you might decide *not* to take the Pico that has all your most valuable passwords. Nothing prevents you from having two or three Picos, and there's one where you just have the stuff that you plan to use on that trip, and then another one you just leave at home in your safe.

Alf Zugenmaier: You aren't allowed to write down your Picos either?

Reply: What do you mean, write them down?

Alf Zugenmaier: This way you'll get to the 37 Picos situation eventually, and then I think we are not much better off than with written down passwords.

Bruce Christianson: (You could write on each Pico which one it was!)

Reply: I don't quite buy that argument. This is just like having two security levels, with different classes of accounts in them.

Sandy Clark: But I'd argue that the common people can't really function that way: they're going to put them all together into one for convenience. It's only paranoid people like us that think about having more than one.

Reply: Well, whenever I travel I never take all my home keys. It's like Alf: if the hotel wants me to have a credit card I carry a credit card, and I will take one key just to get back home, but I'm definitely not going to take all my other keys because I'm scared of losing them.

Omar Choudary: I disagree with the claim that ordinary people are not as paranoid as us. I am not as paranoid as my father, for instance, who is a mathematician, but he will never type the number on his credit card: he's very careful about this kind of things.

Sandy Clark: Mr and Mrs Average Citizen are not bad.

Jonathan Anderson: If Mr and Mrs Average Citizen don't have anything more valuable to steal than banking credentials, well, who cares! Because they can get that back if they talk to their bank within 48 hours or so.

Ross Anderson: ...if they're in North America.

Reply: So Sandy, what is your recommendation that would suit the average citizen?

Sandy Clark: I don't have a solution for this. I was imagining combining your idea with Bruce's and having an embedded system that was actually physically embedded, so you'd have one wallet that is your Pico that is embedded with you and you carry it around all the time. And then are you going to lose appendages every time you get attacked?

Ross Anderson: There might be something to be said, in the case of an organisation like Cambridge University, for having a Pico, perhaps an iPad with our bank authorisation software on it, bolted into a half-a-ton slab of concrete in the Old Schools, so it can only function in one precise physical location. Or perhaps we could do a better implementation than half a ton of concrete.

Reply: One of the things I rely on is the existence of a secure location for you. You can assume you're not going to be in trouble in that place: it could be your home, it could be the headquarters of the spy centre if you're a spy, or something like that. There's a place you can go back to and do things safely: that's where you do your backups, that's where you have your revocation server, all this stuff.

Joseph Bonneau: If you assume that, then you assume the attacker won't say "don't go home and disable the Pico or else I'll do <whatever bad thing> to you".

Reply: That's why I said that, before I go to Oakland, I can set the decay time for that share of the network server to be long enough to cover my trip; but if

I ever switch off the Pico, that's it, I won't be able to authenticate to anything during that trip because I won't have a second chance. And that's the price I pay: availability. In exchange, if someone mugs me, then they're stuffed, they can do nothing with it, it's as if I didn't have the Pico with me.

Mike Burmester: Did you say that, if it's physically separated from you, after an hour or so it will just die? It needs your warmth, your presence?

Reply: Yes.

Mike Burmester: So if I steal it from you, take it from you, it will die?

Reply: Yes, that's it.

Mike Burmester: A natural death?

Reply: That's part of the design, but I can revive it by having all the other Picosiblings there and by reactivating the network server.

Mike Burmester: Then it is a threat to the system because I will force you to take me to the other places.

Reply: Yes, and that is why I said: if I expect to be under that coercion threat, then I will make it impossible for me to revive it after it switches off. But in normal circumstances, when it switches off, I just have to pay the small penalty of doing some authentication dance that includes contacting the server, iris scan, Picosiblings and so on.

Mike Burmester: So how do you control the separation? What does "separation from your body" mean for Pico? What would trigger the break?

Reply: Separated would mean out of radio range of the Picosiblings, which you can define from signal strength—or, to be fancy and more secure, through distance bounding.

Ross Anderson: One of the things that I was thinking about when thinking about revocation was how does the upper class do it, because often you design services well by looking at the services that you get if you are a software billionaire or a duke, and then seeing whether we can do 90% of that for 10% of the cash. Now if you're a billionaire you'll have an account at somewhere like Coutts (there are branches here in Cambridge for the software billionaires) and you will have a young man, let's call him Rupert, who knows you by name and does your banking. Rupert knows your dogs' names and your kids' birthdays, and stuff. Now, if you get mugged in Oakland and you're a Coutts customer, it's no problem: you phone Rupert and Rupert makes the world right! Rupert will helicopter a new mobile phone, Rupert will send a messenger round from the nearest bank with $2000 in cash to tide you over, Rupert will fix your bill at the Claremont, Rupert will pick up your medical bill at the Alto Medical Centre. How close can we get to that and still make it economical?

Sandy Clark: But at that level you're not carrying any money anyway. you're relying on someone else to do all the paying.

Reply: Perhaps, if you are that rich, you wouldn't even have the Pico: Rupert would have your Pico and would do all of this kind of low level authentication for you.

Ross Anderson: Yes, but Rupert is sitting in Cambridge, you're in Oakland, you've been mugged, all you have to do is phone Rupert.

Bruce Christianson: Rupert is a server somewhere and you just have to get some message to Rupert and that's going to download all the stuff you need into some other Pico.

Reply: I think the practical issue is that, if you are at that galactic level of wealth, then you just have other minions do things for you anyway. But the philosophical problem, which is interesting, is how do you authenticate to Rupert? Because you're falling back on human authentication anyway, which of course is the thing that always works.

Ross Anderson: But you know Rupert, he comes to your parties, he buys presents for your children.

Reply: Yes, that's human authentication!

Bruce Christianson: We share the password.

Reply: I mean, it would be good if we could implement something as good as humans recognising each other in a way that worked for all this other stuff.

Ross Anderson: An interesting thing about this is if Pico can somehow recognise you, or if a Pico can be conjured into existence that would recognise you, even in a strange place. That can be a sort of Pico Rupert.

Reply: There is the old David Wheeler quote: "every computer science problem can be solved with another level of indirection". And here we're basically taking one extra step away: authentication is not between me and the app, it's between my Pico and the app; and then I have to authenticate to the Pico, and I do that through the Picosiblings and so on. And if there's Rupert, then there's yet another layer: Rupert authenticates to my Pico, I authenticate to Rupert and so on.

Jonathan Anderson: But the thing that Rupert gives you is that he is sitting in the city of London somewhere and a mugger in Oakland has absolutely no sway over him.

Bruce Christianson: No chance of getting to him at all.

Jonathan Anderson: And it's like a time-locked vault, and you tell the bank robbers: "sorry, there's nothing I can do".

Reply: Indeed. Without that extra level of Rupert, that's the whole point of my network server construction: nobody can mess with the network server, even when they're in front of me with a shotgun.

Ross Anderson: Now let me give you another example of a threat model. In São Paulo and Rio de Janeiro, if you look too rich and you go out in a bad street, then somebody will kidnap you and take to a favela, where you will be milked. They will sit you down at a PC and get you to transfer all your money to them; they'll take you around ATMs at gunpoint and get you to empty your accounts; and the police don't go there except with military backup.

Reply: Then the Pico is perfect for this. When you are getting kidnapped you destroy one of your Picosiblings: you just let it fall out of the window when they get you. And then you go there and you say "oh shit, it doesn't work, there's nothing I can do".

Ross Anderson: Boom.

Bruce Christianson: You want it to work a bit.

Reply: In your dying breath you will tell them: "you don't understand how this works!"

Bruce Christianson: In really dangerous places like New York I understand you're supposed to carry two wallets, one in your hip pocket for when you get mugged, and one somewhere else.

Alf Zugenmaier: And of course the crooks know that as well.

Bruce Christianson: Yes, but it's a social convention, there's a convention about how much it's polite to have in the hip pocket wallet.

Sandy Clark: How civilised!

Bruce Christianson: If the protocols involve the identity for the particular Pico that's being used, you could revoke from another Pico. The second Pico could just say to everyone you did business with: "if Pico number 37 comes online to you, please just give it these digits"—digits that mean to Pico number 37 "switch yourself off forever"[6].

Sandy Clark: Couldn't it incorporate the two wallet idea and have just two levels, where one set of digits gives them a little bit of money, and the rest gives you access to the remainder?

Ross Anderson: But there's a problem with that: how can you convince them that you've given them all the digits that are available? How do you get them to stop torturing you?

Matt Blaze: Fundamentally, it seems that this system works well if I can create the impression that the Pico is necessary, but in fact the Pico isn't necessary.

[6] These digits would have to be signed to prevent crippling denial of service attacks.

If I really want to get the money, I want to be able to get it, I just don't want anybody to know that I can get it.

Reply: The point is that, in order to really get the money if I don't have the Pico, I may have to go to the secure place in person, which may not be done with the kidnapper holding me at gunpoint, because when he takes me to the headquarters of the spy centre with a gun he will be stopped by people with many more guns.

Alf Zugenmaier: That's why you don't give them to your wife and children. I think for coercion resistance, you may want to have it as a limited risk, like cash: you get asked for money, you hand it over and that's it, you walk away.

Omar Choudary: You might make two sets of passwords with this website, let's say the bank website; once you get just $n-1$ of the Picosisters, your Pico issues the password for the low level, where you can get at most £100; with all n you give the other password that gives access to all.

Reply: Similar to Sandy's suggestion. I guess that the danger with all these tricks is that, if you make the solutions too institutionalised, then the bad guy will know; then, as Ross said, they'll say: "OK, that was the first level; now open up the second level or I keep on torturing you".

Ross Anderson: But institutions sometimes help. There's no point in you demanding my house at gunpoint because surely you would have to sign the transfer document as well, and the social conventions are that you have estate agents, and searches, and you can't even sell a house nowadays without an energy certificate. I can't lawfully sell you my house even if Shireen and I both wanted to, until you've got some geezer crawl over it and count the radiators. Does that not add some value?

Reply: Isn't that in the same spirit as having that server in a bunker somewhere that nobody can mess with?

Matt Blaze: But Ross, I can hold you at gunpoint until you give me as much money as your house is worth.

Ross Anderson: Then I would have to raise a mortgage against it which would require Shireen to attend at the Cambridge Building Society and sign various documents.

Matt Blaze: Well I'm sure there are phone calls that you can make that would persuade Shireen to do this. Like: "help, I'm being held at gunpoint!"

Bruce Christianson: But one of the effects of protocols is just to slow things down.

Jonathan Anderson: I just worry that (aside from the property of not having to type passwords any more) strengthening the coercion resistance properties of the Pico to this degree is only useful against attackers who are already so committed that they'll do whatever it takes to get around even this level of coercion resistance.

Joseph Bonneau: I think we're imagining attackers that are much more powerful than actually exists in Oakland. Or Planet Earth.

Bruce Christianson: I think alien abduction is the real threat.

Sandy Clark: The probes will find out where your Pico is.

Joseph Bonneau: Criminals aren't stupid and they know the difference between the charges that they'll take for different attempted crimes. Mugging won't get them nearly as much as going to your house with a gun and kidnapping somebody. And we have to push them into things they don't want to be doing.

Jonathan Anderson: Against mugging, you don't need an n-out-of-n threshold sharing scheme blah, blah, blah; all you need is: it times out.

Bruce Christianson: Joe's is a very good point, and it's the same one Ross made this morning: a good countermeasure is to raise the stakes for the attacker.

Ross Anderson: So we bring in the death penalty for muggers.

Bruce Christianson: Yeah!

Jonathan Anderson: Well no, because then you have the perverse incentive that there used to be: if you're going to steal bread, you might as well kill people, because the penalty is the same.

Bruce Christianson: But there's also going to be the death penalty for littering. So, as soon as you drop that earring out of the taxicab, you're gone!

Virgil Gligor: OK; on that note, perhaps we should go on to the second talk.

Getting Web Authentication Right

A Best-Case Protocol for the Remaining Life of Passwords

Joseph Bonneau

University of Cambridge, Cambridge, UK
jcb82@cl.cam.ac.uk

Abstract. We outline an end-to-end password authentication protocol for the web designed to be stateless and as secure as possible given legacy limitations of the web browser and performance constraints of commercial web servers. Our scheme is secure against very strong but passive attackers able to observe both network traffic and the server's database state. At the same time, our scheme is simple for web servers to implement and requires no changes to modern, HTML5-compliant browsers. We assume TLS is available for initial login and no other public-key cryptographic operations, but successfully defend against cookie-stealing and cookie-forging attackers and provide strong resistance to password guessing attacks.

1 Introduction

The vast majority of large websites rely on passwords for user authentication [3]. Due to the originally stateless nature of HTTP and the extremely low adoption of HTTP Digest Authentication, nearly all websites using password authentication rely on HTTP cookies to cache authentication decisions. Creating and validating session cookies securely has historically been a major source of bugs, with many websites implementing ad-hoc protocols with basic cryptographic flaws [4].

However, the precise practice of verify user passwords and managing secure sessions over the existing technology stack of HTTP/TLS with HTML and JavaScript has attracted relatively little attention from the cryptography and security research communities. Instead the focus has largely been on whole-sale replacements for the current architecture, requiring either vastly different user behavior, new client-side software, or significantly re-designed servers, and often all three. While we would agree that such fundamental changes are needed, we expect that web authentication will continue to operate using the current technology only for at least five to ten years. It is worthwhile to get authentication right in the current framework, even while the research community is actively seeking its replacement.

In this work we seek to outline a complete protocol for secure web sessions which is:

- As secure as possible using already-deployed technology
- As simple and efficient as possible given the first goal

B. Christianson et al. (Eds.): Security Protocols 2011, LNCS 7114, pp. 98–104, 2011.

For the first goal, we specifically rule out any solution which requires changes in user behavior or new software to be installed, including updates to current-generation browsers. Our proposal is not fundamentally new in that many elements of it are either directly analogous to elements in other proposals, or are straightforward constructions to those familiar with cryptographic literature. However, we do not believe any currently deployed web servers deploy the complete defense-in-depth we propose, including in-browser password hashing to prevent against buggy server software, storage of credentials in a server-side database to limit the damage from database compromise, cookie creation which is not possible with read-only database access, and active computation of a MAC with each web request to prevent cookie-theft.

2 Previous Work

Fu et al. proposed a basic scheme in 2001 to remedy the problems they observed in a survey of common implementations, namely:

$$\text{auth\_cookie} \quad = \quad \text{time\_stamp } t||\text{user\_data } u||\mathbf{MAC}_k(t, u)$$

This basic framework has the advantages of being stateless on the server side and secure against a passive network observer. It represents a reasonable basic password implementations and most carefully-designed web servers implement a close variation of it.[1] However, this scheme is completely vulnerable to an attacker who captures the cookie, either through cross-site scripting or over an unprotected wireless network. It is also vulnerable to an attacker who gains read access to the server's databases, for example via SQL injection.

Murdoch proposed a hardened version of this scheme [10] designed to protect against an attacker with read-only database (which can occur as a result of SQL injection). This is achieved by using a pre-image of the stored password hash which can be checked against the final password hash stored in the database with each request. However, this scheme is still vulnerable to cookie theft, and allows an attacker with databases access to indefinitely extend the validity of a stolen cookie.

In a different vein, Adida proposed a scheme called SessionLock [1] to protect specifically against cookie theft by storing a session identifier in the browser's fragment identifier. The fragment identifier is never transmitted to the server, protecting against cookie-theft on an insecure network, or "sidejacking," but not protecting against cross-site scripting attacks. However, SessionLock is stateful on the server side and many important password-management details are left out of the scheme.

Finally, there are a number of more complicated proposals [7,6,9,13], all of which require either modifications to existing browsers or public-key operations performed outside the scope of the TLS protocol, both of which we consider to be too heavy-weight to gain widespread adoption. Additionally, few of these proposals take an

[1] Many minor tweaks with no security relevance, such as splitting the fields up into multiple cookies, are commonly seen in practice.

integrated approach to password authentication, incorporating difficult issues such as preventing guessing attacks [11] and user-probing attacks [3].

3 Our Proposal

3.1 Notation

We assume cryptographic primitives for semantically symmetric encryption, message authentication codes (MAC), and collision-resistance hashing. We denote $\mathbf{AE}_k(m)$ to be the authenticated encryption[2] of plaintext m under key k and $\mathbf{AE}_k^{-1}(m)$ to be the verified decryption of m under key k.

We assume a primitive hash function $\mathbf{H}$, and denote

$$\mathbf{H}^k(x) = \mathbf{H}(k||x)$$

allowing us to easily come up with different random functions with equivalent security to $\mathbf{H}$. We further denote $\mathbf{H}_n^k(x)$ to be an iterated hash,[3] specifically:

$$\mathbf{H}_1^k = \mathbf{H}^k(1||x)$$
$$\mathbf{H}_n^k = \mathbf{H}^k\left(n||x||\mathbf{H}_{n-1}^k(x)\right)$$

3.2 Enrolment

Our scheme is designed so that the user never submits a password in the clear to the server, not even over an encrypted TLS session. We consider this to be prudent practice to protect against server mistakes[4] which may leak the plaintext password. We take the further unusual step of not storing usernames in the clear on the server, making it more difficult for a user compromising the database to export the list of usernames.

To enrol with username u and password p with server[5] s, a user computes via JavaScript:[6]

[2] Authenticated encryption can be implemented as encrypt-then-MAC, or a combined mode such as EAX or GCM.

[3] The iterated hash is used purely to increase the difficulty of brute-force attacks. The purpose of folding the hashed data x and round number n in before each hash iteration is to prevent pre-computation of any long sequences of $\mathbf{H}^k$ from being useful.

[4] Hashing the password in-browser also makes insider attacks more difficult, as they require modifying the JavaScript on the login pages, instead of modifying any servers behind the SSL gateway.

[5] The inclusion of s prevents collisions between multiple sites implementing the same scheme. It could be either the domain name, or a 128-bit site-specific random number to allow the possibility of domain name changes.

[6] Our preliminary experiments indicate that iterated hasing using SHA-256 is feasible in modern browsers. We were able to hash at a rate of $\sim$ 50 kHz on desktop PCs, and $\sim$ 1 kHz on mobile devices. Since this calculation is only performed during log-in we consider a 1 s delay to be acceptable, which will allow for at least 1,000 iterations.

$$x = \mathbf{H}^{\mathrm{X}}_{\ell_1}(u||p||s)$$

and sends x along with u to the server, with ℓ_1 a configurable security parameter.[7] The server then stores the following values in its databse:

$$y = \mathbf{H}^{\mathrm{Y}}_{\ell_2}(u) \qquad z = \mathbf{H}^{\mathrm{Z}}(u||x)$$

The advantage of this formulation is that usernames are not stored in the clear in the server's database, preventing a database compromise from leaking the entire list of usernames.[8] For practical reasons including keeping a count of password attempts and password recovery, it is necessary to include a hash of u, slightly limiting the privacy provided if the adversary has a large set of candidate email addresses to test. However, by using a relatively high security parameter ℓ_2 which is only computed on enrolment, incorrect log-in, or password recovery, this search can be made more difficult.[9] In ordinary use, the user's entry can be looked up by the second column, $\mathbf{H}^{\mathrm{Z}}(u||x)$ if a database index is maintained for this column as well.

On first glance, this scheme seems to violate common practice by storing $\mathbf{H}^{\mathrm{Z}}(u||x)$ which is derived from the user's password with no random salt. However, this hash incorporates both the username and the site-specific string s. As long as the site-specific identifier is unique and the site doesn't allow multiple accounts with the same username, this will mean that the hash function applied to the password p is in fact unique, eliminating the need for a salt.

3.3 Login

For normal login, the user's browser collects u and p, re-computes $x = \mathbf{H}^{\mathrm{X}}_{\ell_1}(u||p||s)$, and sends x and u to the server over a secure TLS session. The server then re-computes $z = \mathbf{H}^{\mathrm{Z}}(u||x)$ and checks for its existence in the database. With a collision-resistant hash function, it is impossible for this value to exist in more than one row, so a simple existence check is sufficient. It is not useful to submit a value of x stolen from another user, since u is included in the hash to bind the result to the correct user.

If the calculated z is found in the database, the server returns to the user a fresh random encryption key K_u and an authentication token:

$$a = \mathbf{AE}_{K_{\mathrm{S}}}(K_u, u, x, t, d)$$

where K_{S} is a secret key for the server, t is an expiration time, and d is any additional data associated with the session. Critically, we assume that the

---

[7] Common practice would be to pick the hash iteration count $\ell_1 \approx 1,000$. Our scheme has the advantage that this computation is performed in-browser, the server never needs to compute iterated hashes.

[8] In practice, usernames are often email-addresses and it is important to prevent adversaries from easily determining if an email address is registered with the website.

[9] It can also be offloaded to the client, as with the iterated hash of the password.

authenticated and encrypted token a is stored as an `HTTP-only` cookie, while K_u is stored in HTML5 local storage.[10]

3.4 Site Interaction

After successful login, all future requests to the site are MAC'ed with K_u. It is assumed that the majority of site interaction will not take place over TLS, making this MAC the only verification of the user's intentions. This requires a small JavaScript routine to dynamically add to all HTTP and AJAX requests a MAC parameter $\mathbf{MAC}_{K_u}(p)$ on all request parameters p, a technique originally proposed in the SessionLock protocol [1]. This MAC is sufficient to ensure the integrity of any request, but to prevent relay attacks it is also necessary to include a per-request timestamp parameter.

In addition to the request-specific MAC, the authentication token a is sent as a cookie in the normal way. In fact, because it was declared `HTTP-only`, this is the only way a can be sent, it is not accessible by the in-page JavaScript. Given a cookie a, the server computes $\mathbf{AE}_{K_S}^{-1}(a)$, checks the expiration time t, and then accepts the request as authenticated. It can then check its access-control lists to verify the request using the username u, the session-data d and the request-specific parameters p.

3.5 Optimisations

The server can also optionally re-compute $z = \mathbf{H}^Z(u||x)$ with the values of u, x recovered from a and verify that there is a row in the database with z. This optional check prevents specifically against an attacker who has has read-only database access and has stolen K_S. Such an attacker will be unable to forge cookies with the proper x unless they know the user's password. The fact that such a check is optional in our system means security and performance can be more finely tuned. In the Murdoch scheme [10], this check is required with every access, limiting the appeal of the protocol as a "stateless" web protocol. However, our system allows the check to be skipped with some high probability, or perhaps only checked before extremely sensitive actions are performed.

A second optimisation is to include an extended-validity authentication cookie $a^* = \mathbf{AE}_{K_S}(K_u, u, x, t^*, d)$, with $t^* > t$, and mark this cookie both `HTTP-only` and `secure`. The `secure` flag means this cookie will only be be sent over TLS, making it significantly harder for an adversary to steal. Of course, since we have assumed the majority of site interaction will not take place over TLS, a^* will not be sent by default. If a user sends an authentication cookie a with an expired timestamp t, however, the server can re-direct them to a special TLS server which can receive and verify a^* and then re-issue a with an extended timestamp. This

[10] It is also possible to "store" K_u in the fragment identifier, which was a significant part of the complexity in [1]. We assume that a sufficient super-majority of today's browsers implement HTML5 local storage that this technique is now obsolete. We have omitted the details, but this technique can still be implemented to deal with legacy browsers.

process can be done with no user interaction, saving the difficulty and risk of re-typing a password. A practical set-up might be to have a^* last for several weeks, as current persistent log-in cookies frequently do, and to have a expire after ten minutes or one hour. This technique can greatly reduce the vulnerability of a sidejacked cookie, while still limiting the frequency of TLS connections to a very low number, and to a singled dedicated server.

3.6 Password Recovery

We have so far ignored the difficult but important procedure of recovering user passwords when they are forgotten. The simplest procedure for achieving this is by sending a one-time reset link over email [5]. This process fits naturally with our scheme and should be sufficient for most purposes.

4 Security Properties

As mentioned, our scheme makes it difficult for an attacker to retrieve usernames from the database. It also requires per-user brute-force for each password in the database, as hashed passwords always include a username in the hash. Our cookies only contain a hash of the user's password, but this is encrypted with the server key K_S. If an attacker has stolen this, they have likely stolen the account database as well, allowing them to brute-force values of z stored in the database.

Cookie forgery is prevented by the requirement of knowing $x = \mathbf{H}^{X}_{\ell_1}(u||p||s)$ and K_S to compute a valid cookie. This means that an attacker must gain both read-access to the database and the user's password in order to forge a cookie.

The scheme also offers very strong protection against cookie theft, similar to SessionLock. The storage of K_u in local storage means it is never transmitted. It can be stolen using cross-site scripting, however the authentication token a is marked as an `HTTP-only` cookie, meaning it cannot be accessed via JavaScript. Thus, to steal credentials in our system an attacker must both steal a by "side-jacking" the cookie from an unprotected access point, and also steal K_u via cross-site scripting. Even if credentials are stolen in this way, the expiration date cannot be changed. This is a very high barrier to credential theft, than that enabled by previous systems that don't require changes to the browser.

References

1. Adida, B.: Sessionlock: securing web sessions against eavesdropping. In: Proceeding of the 17th International Conference on World Wide Web, WWW 2008, pp. 517–524. ACM, New York (2008)
2. Blundo, C., Cimato, S., De Prisco, R.: A Lightweight Approach to Authenticated Web Caching. In: Proceedings of the The 2005 Symposium on Applications and the Internet, pp. 157–163. IEEE Computer Society, Washington, DC, USA (2005)

3. Bonneau, J., Preibusch, S.: The password thicket: technical and market failures in human authentication on the web. In: WEIS 2010: Proceedings of the Ninth Workshop on the Economics of Information Security (June 2010)
4. Fu, K., Sit, E., Smith, K., Feamster, N.: Dos and don'ts of client authentication on the web. In: Proceedings of the 10th Conference on USENIX Security Symposium, SSYM 2001, vol. 10, p. 19. USENIX Association, Berkeley, CA, USA (2001)
5. Garfinkel, S.L.: Email-Based Identification and Authentication: An Alternative to PKI? IEEE Security and Privacy 1(6), 20–26 (2003)
6. Gouda, M.G., Liu, A.X., Leung, L.M., Alam, M.A.: SPP: An anti-phishing single password protocol. Computer Networks 51(13), 3715–3726 (2007)
7. Juels, A., Jakobsson, M., Stamm, S.: Active cookies for browser authentication. In: 14th Annual Network and Distributed System Security Symposium (NDSS 2007) (2007)
8. Liu, A.X., Kovacs, J.M., Huang, C.-T., Gouda, M.G.: A secure cookie protocol. In: 14th International Conference on Computer Communications and Networks (2005)
9. Masone, C., Baek, K.-H., Smith, S.: WSKE: Web Server Key Enabled Cookies. In: Dietrich, S., Dhamija, R. (eds.) FC 2007 and USEC 2007. LNCS, vol. 4886, pp. 294–306. Springer, Heidelberg (2007)
10. Murdoch, S.J.: Hardened Stateless Session Cookies. In: Christianson, B., Malcolm, J.A., Matyas, V., Roe, M. (eds.) Security Protocols 2008. LNCS, vol. 6615, pp. 93–101. Springer, Heidelberg (2011)
11. Pinkas, B., Sander, T.: Securing passwords against dictionary attacks. In: Proceedings of the 9th ACM Conference on Computer and Communications Security, CCS 2002, pp. 161–170. ACM, New York (2002)
12. Pujolle, G., Serhrouchni, A., Ayadi, I.: Secure session management with cookies. In: Proceedings of the 7th International Conference on Information, Communications and Signal Processing, ICICS 2009, pp. 689–694. IEEE Press, Piscataway, NJ, USA (2009)
13. van der Horst, T.: pwdArmor: Protecting Conventional Password-Based Authentications. In: Annual Computer Security Applications Conference (2008)

Getting Web Authentication Right
(Transcript of Discussion)

Joseph Bonneau

University of Cambridge, Cambridge, UK

What an honour to be the person not talking about how to replace passwords [laughter]. I was struggling to come up with a metaphor for why I'm giving this talk after Frank's talk, this was the best I could do. Does anybody know why I chose this?

Jonathan Anderson: Is that the fighter they had at the end of the war?

Reply: It is, yes. Towards the end of World War 2, the Americans started putting Merlin engines on to the P-51, which is still the most popular propeller plane for hobby pilots trying to acquire, and produced essentially the highest-performance propeller plane ever built[1] This was in 1943, and it was the only time that we really perfected the art of getting a piston engine to make a plane go very, very fast. The Germans hadn't invested in making a fighter of this generation because they were so caught up in making jet fighters, which you see coming down in flames in the background[2]. By this point in history designers knew that propeller planes would be gone within ten years and jets would replace them for all the reasons that we use jets now, but in that window propeller planes were still a lot better: there were huge reliability problems and other issues with jets, and they couldn't quite get to the performance that the best propeller planes had.

So I do think while we have jet engines coming in the authentication space, like Frank has been talking about, I think we've actually been in this window for probably 15 years now. Here is a screenshot of the Wall Street Journal's web site from fifteen years ago compared with today and it basically hasn't changed at all in terms of what a password is on the web.

Bruce Christianson: Passwords are shorter now.

Reply: True. The instructions have also gotten shorter because they assume that people know what a password is, but it's basically the same implementation. I've looked at password implementations at big sites a lot the last year, I did a big survey for WEIS last year where I looked at 150 different websites. Recently I've been auditing web development frameworks and seeing what they do with passwords. The technology has not moved very far on the server side in this entire time. And I think a big part of that is that we've been waiting to replace

[1] Editors' Note: Although the De Havilland 103 Hornet, first assembled in 1944 on what is now the De Havilland site of Hertfordshire University, was over 30 mph faster.

[2] By the time they realised their mistake, and built the Dornier 335, the war was over.

B. Christianson et al. (Eds.): Security Protocols 2011, LNCS 7114, pp. 105–114, 2011.

passwords for so long there has been very little academic work on just getting the current generation of technology right. So in some ways I could have been doing a lot of this talk years ago, although I'm going to mention a couple of things that are only available now, that I think help a lot with passwords. But I'm trying to argue here that I think we're still going to have websites collecting passwords for at least five years as a very conservative estimate, and it will probably last longer than that before something like Pico comes along, so there is real value in getting the details right based on what I've actually found in practice.

Since I spend so much time writing papers decrying how poorly people do passwords, how I don't think people do it right, and there are all of these security holes, this talk is basically my exposition of how I would like to see it done. I'm going to present about three pages of protocol and that's it, and try to show how we can do the P-51 of password implementations with only the current technology.

When I say, as simple as possible, I think that the two most important things are: no technology is going to be deployed that's not already in browsers, so I'm not going to assume any new technology, and I also don't think the user experience can change at all. I'm actually fairly convinced by the argument that passwords at this point fulfil a psychological role more than anything else, users are reassured by the act of typing in a password, and even if you have something like the Pico, which may be much, much better when talked about in this room, if it makes people uncomfortable that would be a huge disincentive to adopting it.

OK, now I'll talk about the limits of this, what sorts of problems we will never be able to solve in the current generation, we will have to wait for the Pico to fly in as the jet engine technology. I tried, as someone said this morning, to have a threat model at the beginning of my protocols workshop talk. This is the best I could do in talking with Richard Clayton, who I think is the resident authority on wickedness on the web. And also when giving interviews, I've tried to come up with a list of, when somebody's password gets stolen, what the most likely culprits are. I think they're roughly in this order. At the top are things that I'm going to completely punt on, and I'll get more realistic answers as we go down.

OK, so this is slide one of my actual protocol, I think I have the whole thing on two slides. So to register with the site, the user will hash their password in their browser. I have a security parameter for how many times you want to iterate the hash, standard stuff. And then what I'm doing, which is a little untraditional, I've never seen it done before, I'm going to completely forget the use of salts, and instead use the username and the site in place of the salts. I've had some objections to this, but the whole point of salt is to make the hash that you're using unique to each user so that you can't use any sort of pre-computed data structure like a rainbow table, and an attacker has to focus their effort per user. Username and site should be completely unique in the world, so it can serve that purpose just fine. And the nice thing about this is that all of the hashing now gets done in the browser, so the plaintext password never has to get sent to the site, we've eliminated any risk of insider attack at the sites, or just poor handling, the password getting caught in the log somewhere.

Unknown: So the browser makes sure that the site identifier is correct and not changed?

Reply: Yes. So obviously when I say in the browser this is not by modifying the browser, this is all JavaScript that the site sends to be run in the browser. And critically this part needs to be actually encrypted in TLS, I'll talk a little bit more about that.

Bruce Christianson: Just remind us what the L1 and L2 subscripts are.

Reply: That's just a security parameter for the iteration of the hash, to strengthen it and make it more difficult to do exhaustive search.

Frank Stajano: So correct me, the thing that is sent to the other site is the hash after the local machine has computed it?

Reply: Yes.

Frank Stajano: So how is it different from just a password?

Reply: In a sense it's not, I mean, it won't be useful at any other site for one thing, but it is going to get hashed first.

Frank Stajano: So it's still just a bit string that you send you could replace, it's not like a password?

Reply: Yes, it is, it's vulnerable to replay attacks subject to the fact that this part is done in TLS. Anyway, this top part is computed in JavaScript in the browser, and then on the server side we store a hash of the username, and we hash one more time the already-hashed password that the user sends with the username. So another curious thing I decided to do is not store the usernames in plaintext. The reason to do that is to make it more difficult to find the complete list of people who are registered at the site, which is a fairly minor risk but it's easy to do.

OK, so that was the registration, which is done through TLS. At login time obviously you're going to compute the same hash of your password, your username, and the site. You have to do the iterated hash in the browser, I'll talk a little bit more about the performance of that later. And then the only thing the site has to do is just verify that the hash they get exists in the database. The more clever part of this is what gets returned. You get two things, a session key and a session cookie, the session key will be randomly generated, and the cookie will be an authenticated encryption, so it's encrypted and it's MACed, and it's going to include the session key, the username and timestamp, additional data if needed, and the hashed password that was previously sent, which is the pre-image of the thing that is stored. This is actually a trick that I think Steven Murdoch introduced at the Protocols Workshop four years ago[3], and this

[3] LNCS 6615, 93–106

defends against an attacker who gets read-only access to the database on the server, and wants to forge cookies, and this actually makes it impossible to do that because they won't have the pre-image for the hash in the database even if they discover the hash.

Notice that to register and login you have to connect over TLS, but for all the rest of the interaction with the site I'm assuming we don't use TLS and we have to do everything over HTTP. This is a point of controversy, I mean, there's been a big stink in the last year, people encouraging Gmail on Facebook, and others try and do TLS for everything, and there's been arguments back and forth about whether or not that's really practical, whether the sites are just saying it's not practical because they don't care and don't want to do it. I've come to believe it's not, I think most sites could do it if they want but most sites aren't going to do it because they think it requires too many changes, and it's not in their interest to do it. So I tried to design to avoid something that sites have demonstrated for ten years that they don't want to do. Anyway so we're now doing just our regular interaction.

Sjouke Mauw: But they had to do TLS before?

Reply: Yes. So this section is very, very common, and most sites collect your password over TLS, and then they just return a cookie, which you send back and forth, not over TLS.

Ross Anderson: Why don't you hash the initial authenticator as well to stop people doing rainbow table lookup?

Reply: What?

Ross Anderson: $y = H^y(u)$ can become H^y of u and a salt s.

Reply: OK, what do you want to stick where?

Ross Anderson: Salt both of the questions on the top line, because many people choose human readable and human guessable user ids. And if you want to deny easy wins to people who have temporary read access to the server database then you should logically salt the hashed username as well as the password.

Frank Stajano: Where is this salt from?

Reply: Yes, where would the salt come from I guess is the question.

Jonathan Anderson: The site name is the same as the password thing.

Reply: Are you proposing using a random salt that's different from the username inside it?

Ross Anderson: Well what you could do is have per-user random salts that are kept in the file.

Reply: Kept on the server side? OK, but then if I want to attack your account ...

Ross Anderson: Then you have to do a brute-force search for each user name, not for a whole dictionary of user names.

Reply: Yes, well I have that here, you already have to do it per user, if you add a random salt to this you'd be able to query the random salts for whoever you want to target by just going to the login page of the website, and they would have to send the salts to your lookup up in the database, so I can get your salts either way. So that was why I didn't add anything.

Jonathan Anderson: But wouldn't adding the site identifier in there with the hash stop the attacker from building a big rainbow table of hashed usernames, hashed email addresses in fact.

Reply: Yes, it's there though, that's what s, s is site.

Jonathan Anderson: But isn't $y = H^y(u)$ stored?

Reply: Ah, OK, I'll just bring this slide up.

Ross Anderson: So what we might also do is customise the hash for each site somehow.

Reply: It is customised for each site, I have the site name added into the salt. Sorry I screwed this up, I can see how that made nonsense of what I was just saying. x is supposed to be equal to this hash, and y is supposed to be equal to this hash, so the thing that is the authenticator doesn't include the site name and the username, which I think is the point you were making.

Sjouke Mauw: So $x =$ and $y =$ is respective?

Reply: Yes, and then it's in everything works.

Bruce Christianson: Just there, does z include p and s?

Reply: It does because it's a hash of s which included them.

Bruce Christianson: Oh, x is the right hand side, got it.

Reply: Yes.

Unknown: So what's the benefit of using hash of the username rather than store username in plaintext?

Reply: Because then you don't have a list of usernames stored in plaintext at the site.

Unknown: But you still have a hash?

Reply: Yes, so you can still look them up. I wanted to get rid of that, the only reason you can't do that is because then password recovery becomes impossible.

Omar Choudary: OK, so you don't want the list of usernames to leak?

Reply: Yes, although this is a fairly minor security point, and it's probably not worth focusing on. The most interesting thing I think about what I'm proposing is how to be as secure when you're working over plain HTTP, and this is done using new web technology of the last few years, which already exists in almost everybody's browser. So two things, so we have a session cookie and a session key. The cookie is just transmitted like any other cookie, and this is basically a certificate saying that, you're logged in as this user with this session key, it's valid to this time, there's possibly some additional data. And then the session key is actually going to be used in JavaScript, every time you either send AJAX data to the server, or if you make another request, you can map all the parameters using the session key and send those along. So the new tricks that have come out recently, there's a special syntax for cookies, that they can be marked HTTP only, which means that they're not readable by JavaScript, which is really nice because this means that this cookie now can't be stolen by a cross-site scripting, and with HTML5 we can store the session key in local storage, which means that it won't be transmitted as a cookie. Previously this would have had to have been stored as a cookie, which meant it would be transmitted over the air, and it could be stolen over an insecure access point.

The upshot of this is that to get both the key and the cookie you have to do cross-site scripting to steal the key, because any JavaScript you inject can view the key, and you have to sniff packets on an unsecured connection in order to get the cookie. Doing the two of those simultaneously I think is actually a pretty high bar for an attacker. And then, as I mentioned before, there's special protection against an attacker who has read-only access to the database, and I'll talk about that in a second.

Another small wrinkle that's possible to add to this is that you can have a longer-lived cookie that's only sent over a secured connection. So this is another new bit of HTTP, which has come out only in the last year, but it's now on all the browsers, you can mark cookies as being secure, and this means that they'll only be transmitted over TLS. And so you can have a longer-lived cookie with a later expiration date, if you're worried that your cookie might get stolen if it exists for say two weeks, you can have the secure cookie live for two weeks, then you can have the short-lived cookie live for only a couple of hours, and if the site receives the short-lived cookie that's expired, it can redirect you to a secure page which will then receive the secure long-term cookie, and it can re-issue automatically a new short-term cookie that can then be sent on unsecured connections to do all your regular site interaction. So this is basically automatic updating of a potentially insecure cookie, without having to go through sending your password again.

So it's pretty obvious what the server does with all this based on what I've said. You get the cookie, the cookie lets you verify that this user is using this key, which is valid until this time. You then use the key to verify the data they sent, you check the timestamp, and you check basically with the user id and what they're trying to do, and that it fits with all the access control that you have. And then the optional step, based on the fact that we've sent this pre-image as something that's stored in the database, you can opt to look that up in the database, so you hash it and look it up and see if it's there, and that will protect against an attacker forging cookies if they have read-only access to the database. So this is something that the site could choose to do either with every connection, or every so often, or maybe only when you're doing an especially secure action with the site.

So that's the summary of how I think it should be done. The questions I sort of punted on are password recovery, which is more just opinion, but having seen it done poorly all over the web I think the best solution I've seen is that after you have exceeded the incorrect guess limit on internet passwords the server will force you to reset the password via email. Since we have to have password reset anyway, and most sites offer a fairly low bar there, it doesn't make it any less secure to force a password reset in that situation.

OK, so how much performance overhead did I add? I was trying to keep it very close to zero so I could argue that it's not hurting us that much. During the login the server just has to compute one hash, one authenticating encryption, one lookup in the database, that's pretty standard, any scheme you will have to at least go to the database. We've only added one hash, so the browser has actually done the iterated hashing, and I've been doing experiments in the last couple of weeks about how efficient doing hashing in the browser is, and this is encouraging. It's actually surprisingly good in modern browsers. The benchmark I did was a thousand iterations of SHA-256, and basically all of the PC browsers that I tried could do that in less than a hundred milliseconds. The iPhone and my Android phone could do it in about a second, which is not great, but a second delay before logging into a site is probably OK.

To actually interact with the site with every packet that you send, there are two authenticated encryptions on each end, that's nothing for the server, it is an optional database to lookup that you don't have to do with every request if you don't want to. On the browser side the overhead of doing the encryptions on a PC is almost zero, ten milliseconds I think is enough to keep the site fairly lively, more like a tenth of a second on a phone, which could be a problem for some sites, but most phone internet connections are so slow that I think that that would be OK.

Omar Choudary: You said on your previous slide that you have some parameters on the number of iterations you can do for encrypting the security, so I see the parameter there about one second for the iterated hashing with the mobile phones, and it says one iterated hash, how many iterations do you think you would need for security?

Reply: When I said one iterated hash, I should have made clear that's a thousand iterations, so a thousand iterations took one second on a phone, so it's one kilohertz capacity if you like.

Bruce Christianson: The reason for the iterations is just to drive the attacker's cost up.

Reply: Yes, you have to iterate the hash in case the database is ever compromised to make it more difficult to extract all the passwords from it.

Omar Choudary: Besides doing a hash from mobile phone, can it do a hash in encryption operations like doing a authenticated encryption and so on?

Reply: I haven't built this yet, I mean, the next goal is to actually build this into probably something that's a drop-in plugin to a common web development framework. I've tested the pieces in isolation and they seem extremely fast.

Omar Choudary: I'm asking because I was working with someone from NEC I think it was, and she was saying that she doesn't believe that cryptography is very adequate yet on mobile phones, I mean, in order to do all the public key stuff she said that even the smartphones are not up to it.

Reply: Yes, there's no public key cryptography here, except the TLS connection, which you have to do anyway. Smartphones do symmetric key crypto OK. I've only tested on very recent generation, like iPhone 3G and the most recent Android phones, I'm sure it's worse for older phones, but it should be getting more and more practical.

Jonathan Anderson: But this is all implemented in JavaScript too, right?

Reply: Yes.

Jonathan Anderson: Like if this became popular then there could be a JavaScript library that just plugged into the native side.

Reply: Right, but (it's maybe the first time you'll ever hear this) I don't want this scheme to become popular to the point that we're building extra software for it. Remember, there are much better things to replace passwords, there are jet engines, so optimising around this has no long-term future. What I've done here is, this is my best effort at duct-taping onto what we currently have. If we're going to have a custom implementation we could do a lot better, and we would do Gmail and other things.

Jonathan Anderson: Well I guess a generic optimised JavaScript crypto library would be useful?

Reply: It would be really nice if JavaScript had you know, SHA and AES primitives, that were accelerated.

Bruce Christianson: There's an argument that if you forced the JavaScript support to include additional primitives that would be useful for jet engines as well, then you're doing everyone a favour.

Frank Stajano: At the moment have you implemented the hash yourself in JavaScript?

Reply: No, I used the most popular JavaScript crypto library out there, which may be the only JavaScript crypto library, the one that actually gets used and stuff.

Sandy Clark: You said which that you thought separating the cookie from the JavaScript was a sufficiently high bar, but I don't know a single black hat or grey hat, or even like our penetration testers who are running Firesheep, who are not also running Wireshark, so they are sniffing the network at the same time they are capturing cookies.

Reply: Yes, but that captures a cookie, that doesn't get the session key which requires JavaScript. Firesheep doesn't magically gives you script injection into the application that they're running.

Sandy Clark: No, sorry, I've got the wrong app. But basically if they're attacking at the whole system at once maybe they can do both?

Reply: Maybe, but cross-site scripting vulnerabilities pop up all the time but they don't last forever. The threat there is that if you have one that you can do as a really scalable attack, maybe for a day, until it gets patched the next day, this makes that a lot harder, because you then also have to be in physical proximity with all the people you're attacking.

Bruce Christianson: It means the attack would have to globalise in order to be credible, which pushes the odds up.

Reply: I think to close I'll just skip a couple of slides. And in terms of whether or not I think sites would actually do this, these were some of the highlights of the big paper I wrote about how passwords actually get implemented in practice. Given some of these findings I'm hard-pressed to believe that people will get excited about this. I don't think for a second that people who develop newyorktimes.com and others that have all of these basic problems despite being websites that get in the tens of millions of hits per day, I don't think that they're going to read any sort of paper or guide and actually re-implement the way they do things. I think a lot of websites despite being really being popular are completely stuck in the mud.

Ross Anderson: Well the one thing that will shift them, in America at least, is the cost of insuring against the risk of having to contact thirty five million customers at a cost of $10 a customer following a privacy compromise, that is the thing that will shift this, and if you can persuade the US insurance industry to implement, and to insist on having usernames hashed in JavaScript, and TLS turned on, then they'll do it, otherwise they won't.

Unknown: Where do you get the 29%–50% number?

Reply: The 29% were websites that must have stored passwords in cleartext, because they emailed them to me in the clear when I tried to reset them the week after I registered them. The 50% is that plus all of the sites that had very suspicious rules like, the password couldn't contain quotation marks or less than signs, or a very low arbitrary limit like password can't be more than 12 characters, those are normally indications that the site isn't hashing passwords but is storing them directly in a database table.

Matt Blaze: The password cannot contain the sub-string drop tables.

Reply: Yes, and it's possible that some websites just think you shouldn't have more than 12 characters even though they do hash it, but it seems extremely unlikely. Anyway, I guess the last think I'll say is Oakland.

Unknown: Is that going to be followed by, it's not so bad?

Reply: No, I thought I'd just say Oakland because every other speaker has said it.

When Context Is Better Than Identity: Authentication by Context Using Empirical Channels

Bangdao Chen, Long Hoang Nguyen, and Andrew William Roscoe

Oxford University Computer Science Department, Oxford, UK
{Bangdao.Chen,Long.Nguyen,Bill.Roscoe}@cs.ox.ac.uk

Abstract. In mobile computing applications the traditional name-based concept of identity is both difficult to support and frequently inappropriate. The natural alternative is to use the context in which parties sit to identify them. We discuss this issue and the ways in which Human Interactive Security Protocols (HISPs) can play a role in enabling this.

1 Introduction

Context arises in an application when one or more entities are acting in a certain situation. For example, one of the most significant types of context is location, which can influence a wide range of decisions about who to connect to across many applications.

We notice that context serves better than identity in some cases. For example, a customer C wants to pay a shop S. In this scenario, C knows he is in *this* shop and wants to pay it, even though he does not know its identity in a conventional sense.

To understand this better, think of the scenarios in which you would be willing to hand over cash: you might trust a merchant by experience or reputation, you may choose to trust him by context, or you may "trust" him to receive payment because you have already received goods or services from him. Note that there is a weaker need for trust if, as with handing over cash, you know that the damage that can be caused by an abuse of trust is strictly limited (i.e. to losing a defined amount of cash).

Therefore we conclude that when it is difficult for ordinary users to correctly verify the identity of whom they pay, context may be better than identity to be used to help users to authenticate the payment. The difficulties of users may consist of two parts:

A. Users lack the necessary knowledge to correctly verify identity;
B. Users can be lazy, especially when the amount of payment is small.

We investigate how the payer (human) can authenticate that his device (typically mobile phone) is connected to the intended payer. This authentication both provides assurance directly to the human and opportunities for improved transaction security such as better authentication of the human's identity.

B. Christianson et al. (Eds.): Security Protocols 2011, LNCS 7114, pp. 115–125, 2011.

We assume that there is a low-bandwidth empirical channel from the payee to the human that is not fakeable. This enables the human to play his part in the protocols in Section 3. This is straightforward when the two are in the same place and various ad hoc solutions also work in remote contexts, such as e-commerce. More discussion about defining proper context is made in Section 2.

We note that the payee and the payer usually both require authentication of the other. The payer needs typically to know he is paying the right entity for the transaction he is trying to complete. The payee, or more accurately, the infrastructure supporting payment (such as the banking system) needs to know that the payer is who he claims to be and that he is entitled to make the payment. As we have already noted, the first of these is frequently best attached to context. The latter on the other hand, is a much more typical process and we note that much technology has been developed for this. It is also worth noticing that in most cases the payee itself does not need to have the payer's identity information, rather the assurance of its bank that it will make (or has already made). Therefore the payee, in authenticating the payer, is acting as a proxy for the bank. Current technology typically gives the payee all information such as the credit card number, password/PIN, or at least makes it easy for this to be obtained. *This is undesirable as it offers opportunity for abuses.*

Similar situations can be found in access control examples: in order to pass a check-point CP of building B, user C must submit his credentials (stored on his own device) to CP. In order to protect C's credentials, C needs to authenticate CP. In other words he needs to know that his device is giving information to precisely this CP. But C does not know the identity of the person who stands in front of CP or there are no personnel at all. Therefore only context that C can draw from the situation can help authenticate CP, for example, the location of CP (given there is no other check-points standing there), the logo of CP, C's recognition of CP based on previous experiences, or somebody else C trusts tells C that this is the correct CP. In this case, there is only context rather than actual identity.

Another example can be found in social networks. Social networks are constantly changing our social styles and habits, and they are often considered to be our virtual presences on the Internet. Although different people may have the same name, but the photos they share, the activities they join, the friends they have, and the profiles they present, provide a sophisticated body of context which can allow people to authenticate "who's who". We will investigate in details of how to properly adapt security to the impact of social networks in our demonstrations.

We can further observe that when context is better than identity, authentication by context brings more security than authentication by identity. To fulfil this requirement, we need to firstly obtain all the required contexts which would introduce the following three challenges:

1. It is difficult to define what proper context is or what is context after all.
2. Quite a few contexts cannot be automatically sensed by machines.
3. Some contexts can be easily forged.

The objective of this paper is to clarify the sort of situation in which context-based authentication is most appropriate, as well as giving examples and one technical solution for achieving it. We will be able to demonstrate various implementations and applications of these ideas.

2 Defining Proper Context

We borrow the definition of context from [5], as we think this best describes the meaning of context in the above cases:

> Context is any information that can be used to characterize the situation of an entity. An entity is a person, place, or object that is considered relevant to the interaction between a user and an application, including the user and application themselves.

However, this definition does not outline what is proper context that can be used in a specific application, because the scenarios of applications differ in both the nature of applications and the environments of applications.

While context-aware applications are now widely available, we notice that some contexts, for example, logos, images, biometrics like faces, voices cannot be easily recognized by machines (it may require special hardware support as well as large amount of computation); and some contexts just simply cannot be sensed by machines at all, for example, human trust.

This creates a gap between a system and a human in terms of contribution to the process of bootstrapping security. We are looking for a method of authentication that can capture the properties of the process when we try to establish our trust in daily activities as described in Section 1. Such an authentication may be required in two different sorts of situation: remote authentication and on-site authentication. On-site authentication is the most natural way of allowing humans to make their own judgements: humans can see, hear and touch. While remote authentication, can also provide humans an interface to sense if there is a proper proxy, for example, a phone call with a known individual, a PC and an *https* session, or a known social network web-page protected by *https*[1].

Such a method should be resistent to attacks using fake contexts. For example, locations, which usually appear in the form of addresses or GPS data (longitude, latitude, altitude), can be easily forged by presenting the false data; names, logos, photos can be easily forged as well. In order to achieve more pervasiveness, we do not rely on specific hardware or infrastructure support to solve this problem, instead, we assume that humans, with or without enough knowledge, can make a choice between genuine context and false context on behalf of their own risks.

The authors of [8] give an example of using telephone line to authenticate location. Given that a telephone is located in a place where the user is, a phone call can be made to send a challenge to the user, and the user will send back

[1] By the time we were writing this paper, Facebook had just released its *https* service on 26th Jan, 2011[1].

the challenge together with other information back to the service provider via another electronic connection. Such practices are common in financial services, for example, banks or credit card companies make phone calls to verify suspicious card transactions, and we have to answer a few secret authentication questions to get authenticated. We are interested to notice that even though we do not know the caller's phone number, we are still willing to give our secrets to the caller who claimed to be the bank or the credit card company. The context of when and where we receive this phone call, or the fact that the caller knows our names and the transactions we made or being made, persuades us into believing that this call is authentic, even though it is subject to a man-in-the-middle attack.

The discussion of security of hardware and software is beyond this paper. Our focus is that in either remote or on-site authentication, humans are able to find or create an empirical channel which is resistant to man-in-the-middle attacks. The question of whether we trust a telephone line to provide a good empirical channel is clearly open to different answers depending on the nature of threat and risk.

Before introducing our solution, we firstly assume that in any application that has human presence, humans are capable of evaluating their own risks based on the context and then making their own judgements. Such context can be sensed either by human recognition or sensors.

In this way, the problem of defining what is proper context for each application and the problem of sensing contexts can be generalised as the user's choice of whether or not to trust the data received from the empirical channel. By incorporating humans into the design of protocol, we can avoid the difficulties of defining specific scenarios and provide a homogeneous way of incorporating trust into our protocols. In addition, the process of human interaction can be regulated by the design of implementation in order to eliminate unexpected human errors.

3 Authentication by Context

The ease of on-site authentication has already been recognised and supported by various technologies, for example, the development of NFC interface on mobile phones provides users a convenient method to create their "bond of trust". A user can touch his mobile phone to a touch pad to complete an authentication: the proximity is used to create such a bond which is similar to the cash payment scenario described in Section 1.

Remote authentication is made by using a proxy, or a "referee". It is a common practice in our daily life that when P_1 meets an important person P_2, presenting a reference letter from a person P_3 that P_2 knows can effectively earn P_2's trust. Therefore the trust from P_2 between P_3 can be used to bootstrap trust between P_2 and P_1 even if P_2 has never met P_1 before. The creation and delivery of such a reference letter is essentially the communication via an empirical channel. For example, Bob makes a phone call to Alice, by recognizing the caller's phone number or his voice, Alice knows that she is communicating with Bob. In this case, the telephone is a proxy between Bob and Alice. However, the assumption of knowing the caller's phone number or recognizing his voice does not stand in ad-hoc scenarios.

The difficulty of remote authentication arises when two parties can not easily "find" each other, for example, Bob may not know the phone number of Alice, or Alice can not recognise Bob's phone number. In order to solve this problem, we introduce the idea of using social networks[2] which provides a platform where Bob and Alice both know how to "find" each other.

3.1 The Impact of Social Networks

Social networks are being integrated into every aspect of our daily life, for example, nearly every major news web-site has one or more social network plug-ins to allow readers sharing with their friends, many commercial products or services are using them to promote their business, and many people are using them as their main social communication tools. One significant move for social networks is the integration on mobile phones. For example, today the messages sent via Facebook[3] work exactly the same as SMSs. Such a movement facilitates the online communication and attracts more and more people to join. In the future, we could see that all communications are carried out within social networks, for example, our contact-list may be replaced by the social network friend-list, our SMS service may be replaced by the social network messages, and our phone calls will be or could be linked directly to our social network accounts.

The growing pervasiveness and importance of social networks allows us to make the following assumption: in the near future, most people will have an active social network account, which serves as his or her web-presence in the virtual world. And because of the rich context maintained on social networks, we can search a "friend" by name, email address, phone number, location, school name, company name and other context information on social networks. Therefore we further assume that one can easily find one another via social networks.

The Quantified-I. The strength of social networks can be further enhanced by integrating sensor technology. For example, by using a set of on-body sensors, one can display his or her physical conditions on social networks. In this way, a human can become quantifiable online: one social network account may consist of a large amount of sensory data from which one's social patterns or identity can be deducted. This can be exploited to provide more convenient and robust authentication services in security applications.

3.2 Authenticating Online Identities

The basic question that needs to be asked when using social network web-pages as empirical channels is "how do I know that what I am seeing on the page comes from the person or other entity that I think".

---

[2] Unless otherwise stated social networks discussed in this paper all refer to semantic web-based social networks.

[3] Users can activate this service on their Facebook.

This divides into two sub-questions: how do I know the (e.g. Facebook) page I am seeing is authentic within the social network, and how do I know it belongs to the person I think it does. The first of these problems can be solved by conventional computer security, for example, the *https* service on social networks. The second of these can be solved by answering the question: is this an established friend for which you are certain of the link between page and person. If so, then a secure access to that page is clearly a good empirical channel. More speculation is the idea that we might use "crowd knowledge" about a web-page that we do not have experience of. We give a solution of how to authenticate the instance found on the social network in the following sections.

3.3 Ratings on Social Networks

An empirical channel can be established by using a "trusted" proxy, which can refer trust between two parties. But it is difficult in practice that two parties can find such a proxy they both trust. We can, however, to create a general proxy to allow humans to determine the extent of trust between each other. In order to achieve this, we assume a rating system virtually exists, and for each session created for bootstrapping security has a minimum requirement of a trust rating. For example, if we have ratings from 1 to 10 (10 means absolute and complete trust), then a user with rating 3 should not be allowed to join in a session with rating 5.

Rating by trust is a common practice in social network researches. The authors in [7] describe a semantic web-based social network, and they developed algorithms to rate the inferred reputation of a node. In their model, a user can rate each others' trustworthiness in general or with respect to a given topic on a 1-10 scale.

Based on the "6-degree of separation" theory proposed by sociologist Stanley Milgram (similar theories of online society can be found in [2,3]), given the situation in which a vast majority of people have established their online relationships via social networks, there is always a route from person P_a to person P_b via $P_i ... P_{i+j}$, in which P_i is a friend of P_a and P_{i+j} is a friend of P_b. Therefore two strangers can also view each other's rating. Theoretically a person's rating will be more accurate when the number of his or her friends increases.

3.4 The Evaluation of Risks and Trust

In practice, the concept of trust may vary, for example, in a payment scenario, when Bob needs to pay Alice, Bob will make a payment only if he is sure that the one he is paying is the correct instance of Alice, and the credibility of Alice is ignored in this case. Note this is a distinct difference to the ratings on ebay, where ratings indicate the credibility of the seller. Therefore the trust here is binary: true or false. For example, this is the answer to the second sub-question in Section 3.1. We call it "binary trust".

The term "binary trust" reflects the process of human evaluation of risks and trust of context, which is the essence of authentication by context. In the following section we will discuss how to formally convert the human evaluation of context into security by using Human Interactive Security Protocols (HISPs).

Note the empirical channels we are discussing in this paper all assume "binary trust". Because the protocol we will introduce does not include the decision making process of why to make the payment or proceed with action. However, in practice, especially in group (size > 2) authentication scenarios, HISPs can be extended by allowing more sophisticated ratings in order to reduce conflicts and speed up the human evaluation process. We will discuss this issue in Section 6.

Is trust transitive? Christianson and Harbison argued in [4] that trust may not be transitive in many aspects, for example, when trust transitivity is happened unintentionally. However, the improved transparency as well as the extended boundary of trust on social networks gives users more convenience and confidence in determining whether trust is transitive, for example, one can explicitly choose to trust information from one another in respect of a certain property.

4 Human Interactive Security Protocols

A new family of authentication protocols that are based on human trust and interaction have been introduced over the past few years. These protocols are often referred to as HISPs. They use a non-fakeable Short Authentication String (SAS) exchanged over a low bandwidth empirical channel (denoted $\longrightarrow_E$) to supplement a normal insecure communications medium, usually a high bandwidth channel (denoted $\longrightarrow_N$) subject to the Dolev-Yao attack model [6].

Those protocols satisfy the requirement that we have laid out in Section 1 and 2, which allow humans to receive, check and compare an SAS over an empirical channel. And the information received from an insecure high bandwidth channel will be authenticated based on the result of human interaction. [9,10,11,12] are good examples of HISP.

To demonstrate the use of such protocols in real life, we have selected two distinct scenarios to discuss in details: one is mobile payment; the other is registration of on-body medical sensors, in which a patient wants to register his newly purchased on-body medical sensors to a doctor in a remote hospital.

The following symmetric protocol is modified from a group authentication protocol originally described in [9] in order to adapt the above two scenarios. S and R means the sender (the customer or the patient) and the receiver (the merchant or the doctor). In general, we need to authenticate each party in the first place, which is achieved by using an SAS over $\longrightarrow_E$; and to provide security to protect private data, which is achieved by establishing a symmetric key using an uncertified public key pk_R transferred over $\longrightarrow_N$.

1. $S \longrightarrow_N R: ID_S, INFO_S, hash(hk_S, ID_S)$
2. $R \longrightarrow_N S: ID_R, INFO_R, pk_R, hash(hk_R, ID_R)$
3. $S \longrightarrow_N R: hk_S, \{k\}_{pk_R}$
4. $R \longrightarrow_N S: hk_R$

5a. $R \longleftrightarrow_E S: digest(hk_S \oplus hk_R, ID_S, ID_R, INFO_S, INFO_R, pk_R, k)$
5b. S and R compares the *digest value* with its own version.

digest value represents the SAS that is manually compared by humans. pk_R is later authenticated in step 5b, and if successful, S and R is both assured of the authenticity as well as the security of the symmetric key k. $INFO_S$ and $INFO_R$ includes details of contexts[4] of S and R respectively, for example, a logo, a picture, a recording of voice or film, a name, the amount of a payment, an account number or a few words of description. $INFO_S$ and $INFO_R$ can be displayed together with an input field of digest value, in a way that S and R can verify these details before entering the digest value. Therefore, a successful comparison of digest values allows the conclusion that the identities and the required contexts of S and R are mutually authenticated. $INFO_S$ and $INFO_R$ can then be used in the rest of the application as authenticated data. For details of the security analysis of the protocol please refer to [9].

5 Using a HISP

The requirement of using a HISP is simple: we need to establish two communication channels and use a certain amount of cryptography. The mobile phone is a good platform which provides well developed human interfaces and powerful connectivity as well as computing power. The first communication channel is a relatively high speed but insecure electronic connection, for example, Bluetooth, WiFi, GPRS or 3G. The establishment of the second communication channel depends on specific scenarios. We discuss two scenarios in the following sections.

5.1 Mobile Payment

The use of a HISP in mobile payment is appropriate because scenarios of mobile payment are typically much more "ad-hoc" than other kinds of e-payment. The mobile phone in this scenario is used as a "trusted device" which can carry payment account details, for example, we can integrate our bank cards onto mobile phones.

In collocated mobile payment, where two parties are close to each other and authentication is on-site, the empirical channel is the direct interactions by or between human(s). We notice those physical contacts or the physical presence can effectively allow symmetric authentication: if I can see you, then you can see me. And the protocol can run exactly as the one presented in Section 4.

In remote mobile payment the two parties can be connected via Internet, for example, a mobile phone can connect to the Internet via GPRS/3G, WiFi or any possible medium. We suggest using an *https*[5] web-page to construct the empirical channel in remote mobile payment. This is because it is common in practice that the payer knows the payee's web-site or web-page and it is in accordance to the

[4] Usually the contexts included in $INFO_S$ and $INFO_R$ can not be easily sensed by machines.

[5] We are aware of various attacks against *https* or the web-browser, but as long as it is being used as the security solution in current payment systems, using it does not increase the risks in our proposal.

principles we laid out in Section 1. Telephony can be used only if the payer knows the phone number of the payee.

If the payee is a merchant, we can trust the message displayed on its *https* website because *https* authenticates the payee (the merchant) to the payer. In case of a peer-to-peer mobile payment, social networks can be used to authenticate the payee to the payer. Note the *https* service only authenticates that the webpage does belong to a certain social network. And the rating of the web-page indicates the level of authenticity of all the information (the context) displayed. The payer can then evaluate the context and make a decision of whether or not to trust the digest displayed on the payee's web-page.

The use of social networks in remote mobile payment has an obvious benefit. It is not economy and practical to have every Internet user to require a public key certificate, but those who runs a small business online can easily display their social network accounts on their personal web-pages, their customers can therefore be able to obtain security via social networks even without using PKI.

Note in mobile payment scenario, $R \longleftrightarrow_E S$ can be changed to $R \longrightarrow_E S$. As we have discussed in Section 1, in a payment scenario, the payer's identity is less important, and current technology provides the payee convenient methods to have the assurance that he or she has been paid by the payer.

An additional benefit is that the payer can download the payment details automatically from the payee once the secure connection has been established.

5.2 On-Body Sensor Registration

The authentication between the patient and the hospital should be symmetric: the patient needs to make sure that his or her medical data are delivered to his or her hospital; the hospital needs to know the data collected are from the correct patient. As in practice the hospital always require the patient to be registered first before receiving any treatment, we can use telephony or postal service to form the empirical channel from the hospital to the patient, the opposite empirical channel can be made by using the hospital's *https* web-site. The bootstrapping of the connection between sensor and mobile phone can be made by using the "resurrecting duckling" method introduced in [10].

Social networks can be used when the sensor is registered to a person rather than a doctor in a hospital.

6 Future Research: Group Authentication by Context

In this section we discuss a possible approach to authenticate a group by context. The "binary trust" discussed in Section 3.3 is suitable in the implementation of pair-wise authentication by context, for example, the mobile payment scenario and the on-body sensor registration scenario. But in practice the condition may change in a group (size > 2) scenario because members of a group may not readily to "trust" each other. In addition, there would be conflicts, for example, in a group (size is N) with members M_1 to M_N, M_i's "binary trust" value is true to M_j, but this value may be false to M_k. When the value of N increases, the bootstrapping of security for the group may fail frequently.

Note such conflicts can be easily solved when the members of a group are physically close to each other, for example the scenario of on-site authentication. However, the complexity of solving those conflicts will increase in remote authentication scenarios, especially when the group size is big.

It is reasonable to use more sophisticated rating systems in scenarios of group authentication by context, for example, a rating system with values from 1 to 10. And then the group session will be given a value α. We call it threshold value. Therefore the condition will be changed to $\min(\text{rating}) \geq \alpha$. This method has two benefits:

1. It can increase the efficiency of bootstrapping a group by reducing the amount of conflicts as well as mistakes, for example, a scale of 1 to 10 can be rounded up to 0 or 1, if the threshold value of a session is 8, which is rounded up to 1 if we use "binary trust", then we may mistakenly allow members with value of 6 or 7 to join in this session.
2. It provides more context for the user to complete the evaluation process. Because in practice each value in the rating system may have a specific corresponding meaning or description. This is useful because in a remote group session, each member will receive a list of members of his or her group from the initiator, in order to symmetrically authenticate each other, one member M will be required to evaluate all the other members' context information, the ratings and their corresponding descriptions can be served as short but concise context information for M to conduct more accurate and faster evaluation.

However, it also brings a new challenge to future research on security: quantifying the level of risks of a specific task according to the ratings of trust on social networks. Researches on solving this challenge would have a significant impact on the future implementations of HISPs.

7 Conclusion

When the authentication by identity is not available or inconvenient, authentication by context can be exploited by using a HISP, which formalises the human evaluation of context. The advantage as well as the limitation of a HISP is the use of the empirical channel. Current researches on HISPs focuses on on-site authentication, where empirical channels are the easiest to find or create. Remote authentication frequently suffers from the lack of mutual trust as well as authentic context information. However, with the growing pervasiveness of social networks in our daily life, a new form of trust-based communication system is emerging. By allowing ratings of trust over social networks, we can effectively transform social networks or social network related communication into empirical channels. This allows the wider use of HISPs.

References

1. A. Rice. A Continued Commitment to Security, `http://blog.facebook.com/blog.php?post=486790652130`
2. Adamic, L.A.: The Small World Web. In: Abiteboul, S., Vercoustre, A.-M. (eds.) ECDL 1999. LNCS, vol. 1696, pp. 443–852. Springer, Heidelberg (1999)
3. Albert, R., Jeong, H., Barabasi, A.: Diameter of the world-wide web. Nature 401, 130–131 (1999)
4. Christianson, B., Harbison, W.: Why isn't trust transitive? In: Lomas, M. (ed.) Security Protocols 1996. LNCS, vol. 1189, pp. 171–176. Springer, Heidelberg (1997)
5. Dey, A.K.: Understanding and using context. Personal Ubiquitous Comput. 5, 4–7 (2001)
6. Dolev, D., Yao, A.: On the security of public key protocols. IEEE Transactions on Information Theory 29(2), 198–208 (1983)
7. Golbeck, J., Hendler, J.: Accuracy of metrics for inferring trust and reputation in semantic web-based social networks. In: Motta, E., Shadbolt, N.R., Stutt, A., Gibbins, N. (eds.) EKAW 2004. LNCS (LNAI), vol. 3257, pp. 116–131. Springer, Heidelberg (2004)
8. Kindberg, T., Zhang, K., Shankar, N.: Context authentication using constrained channels. In: Proceedings of Fourth IEEE Workshop on Mobile Computing Systems and Applications, 2002, pp. 14–21 (2002)
9. Nguyen, L.H., Roscoe, A.W.: Efficient group authentication protocol based on human interaction. In: Proceedings of the Workshop on Foundation of Computer Security and Automated Reasoning Protocol Security Analysis (FCS-ARSPA), pp. 9–33 (2006)
10. Stajano, F., Anderson, R.: The Resurrecting Duckling: Security Issues for Ad-Hoc Wireless Networks. In: Malcolm, J.A., Christianson, B., Crispo, B., Roe, M. (eds.) Security Protocols 1999. LNCS, vol. 1796, pp. 172–182. Springer, Heidelberg (2000)
11. Vaudenay, S.: Secure communications over insecure channels based on short authenticated strings. In: Shoup, V. (ed.) CRYPTO 2005. LNCS, vol. 3621, pp. 309–326. Springer, Heidelberg (2005)
12. Wong, F.-L., Stajano, F.: Multi-Channel Protocols. In: Christianson, B., Crispo, B., Malcolm, J.A., Roe, M. (eds.) Security Protocols 2005. LNCS, vol. 4631, pp. 112–127. Springer, Heidelberg (2007)

When Context Is Better Than Identity
(Transcript of Discussion)

Bangdao Chen

University of Oxford, Oxford, UK

My talk today is when context is better than identity. Imagine we are making a cash payment to a small shop, we do not care who is standing in that shop, or we do not know the name of the small shop, it is the location and the environment, or the condition that we have already received the goods makes us believe that the risks of making this payment is very low. When you have made payment to this small shop, it gives you assurance that you have paid the correct instance of that shop. So we know that when authenticating the small shop it is frequently the best to run a test of the context. And when authenticating the customer or the payer, for example, when you are using your credit card, the current payment infrastructure allows this to be done very easily, and in this case, the shop acts as a proxy for the banks.

Think, when you are passing private information stored on your own device, for example a mobile phone, to a checkpoint, such information can be your private identity, or an e-ticket. It is the location and environment or the condition that this is the only one standing in front of you tells you that you are actually dealing with the correct checkpoint, or somebody else you trust tells you that this is the correct checkpoint. It doesn't matter who is standing in front of the checkpoint, and usually there is no personnel at all.

So in the future context can be used in authentication more often than identity, because more payments will be made electronically, which means they will become more ad hoc than ever. Devices like mobile phones will be integrated with all kinds of electronic identities, for example, bank cards, ID cards or other tokens. So more often in the future we will use our own device to pass information to others. We also need to take into consideration the human factor, because humans can sometimes become lazy, and sometimes identities can become too complicated or too long for humans to use.

So what is context? There are many definitions, but most of them are too general. If we try to use context in authentication we may conclude the problems into the following three challenges. The first one is, it is difficult to define what is proper context, or what is context at all. The second one is, quite a few contexts cannot be automatically assessed by machines, for example, human faces, or human trust. The third one is, some contexts can easily be false, for example, you may use your own mouse to click to choose where you're supposed to be; one can easily find photos, or even steal photos from others, especially from famous people. We're actually looking at context that can be used in bootstrapping security, but context varies in different scenarios, it is very difficult to design

B. Christianson et al. (Eds.): Security Protocols 2011, LNCS 7114, pp. 126–131, 2011.

a universal secure system for all applications. So instead of designing different, sometimes sophisticated and expensive systems, we may choose rely on human evaluation, in which we assume that humans can make their own judgements based on their own risks. We can generalise the authentication into two types, on-site authentication and remote authentication. Clearly remote authentication, which involves human interaction, is the most difficult one to design.

In the on-site authentication where humans can see, hear and touch, the situation is easier, but with remote authentication we must find a proxy, which can refer trust over distance. In practice it is very difficult to find such a proxy, for example, Alice may not know Bob's telephone number, or Bob cannot recognise Alice's voice on a phone call. We observe the problem is to find each other in distance. If we look at social network, which is rich in context, it is easy to search, for example, you can search by telephone number, you can search by name, search by company name, search by events, so it is easy to find one another. In this way we can simplify the above three challenges into the following question, whether or not the user choose to trust the data received from the empirical authentication channel, a channel that is resistant to man-in-the-middle attack, and in most cases it involves with human interaction.

Jonathan Anderson: So if the benefit of relying on humans is that they're not vulnerable to man-in-the-middle attack, I mean, if you're talking about a social network in the computer sense, you're in fact talking about a digital representation of what might be a person at the other end, which is very vulnerable.

Reply: This is in fact the question I am going to address. So social networking, it is becoming more and more popular. Facebook alone today has over 500 million active users, and each user has an average of 130 friends, each of them spends at least forty minutes a day in chatting with others via this. If to use a social network like Facebook as an empirical channel we must first answer this question, how do I know that what I'm seeing on the web-page comes from the person, or other entity, that I think. This simple question can be broken down into two sub questions: (a) how do I know the web-page I am seeing is authentic within the social network; (b) how do I know it belongs to the person I think it does. The first question can be answered by using https service. For example Facebook has just covered all it's online services by using https on the 26th January this year. The second question, if we consider social network as a trust-based communication system, the second question can be answered in two ways. The first one is implicit, that is, we trust this person, and we know his social network web-page, and I'm pretty sure of the authenticity of the context displayed on his web-page. The second is explicit, which can be made by relying on so-called crowd knowledge, which can be drawn from online images, photos, messages, profiles, online interactions. This can be done automatically or manually, which sometimes is in the form of rating by trust.

Rating by trust is actually a common practice in research on social networks. So when using ratings it is mostly useful when two persons do not know each other. Based on the 6-degree of separation theory laid down by sociologist

Stanley Milgram, we can find a connection between any two of us by using a certain algorithm, and when we look at the second question, the answer is actually binary, true or false. So there is no credibility involved, which is different from the ratings on eBay. So the empirical channel here we're looking at all assume binary trust, because we do not take into consideration the process of why to make payment, or why to proceed with action. But in general the web-based social network provides us a convenient way to exploit human trust as well as rich context.

Such a process can be formalised by using a so-called human interactive security protocol, a HISP, which is familiar to many of us here, for example, those invented by Frank and Ross, and those invented by the Nokia Group. A HISP exploits empirical authentication channels, current research and current practices on HISPs focus on on-site authentication where empirical channels are the easiest to find, or to create. We can however extend the use of HISP by using social networks as I have discussed before. In the future if we look at the problem of bootstrapping security for a group, we find the complexity of doing this is much higher than pairwise authentication by context. Imagine you are required to share your location with your colleagues, you will receive a list of accounts from the initiator, if the group is very large, so the list will be very long. It is very difficult and very inconvenient for you to authenticate all of them one by one. The initiator may be trustworthy, but he may not be capable to guarantee that he has checked each one. So by allowing a more sophisticated ratings, for example, a scale from 1 to 10, we can facilitate this human evaluation process because each rating may have a corresponding meaning or description, which can be served as a short but concise indicator of authenticity of the person that has been displayed. And it can also reduce conflicts. For example, A may trust B, but B may not be trusted by C. But there are also challenges, for example, how to quantify the risks of a specific task according to the ratings of trust on social networks, and this is an ongoing experiment that I'm currently working on. And that's all. Thank you. Any questions?

Dieter Gollmann: Comment, you make the remark in human-to-human interaction it's easy to establish trust, but I will have to do the contrary. There are people who are very good at tricking you. If they're nice, they are friendly, we trust them, and then they cheat you. There is this confidence fraud, people make an excellent living out of it, if they have the right looks, if they have the right manners, so I think this kind of chain of arguments based on trust in humans is bad for security.

Reply: It's not about trusting humans. I have indicated that the authentication here does not involve credibility. It's about how you can complete a certain transaction, you believe what you are seeing, you believe what you have heard, you may not choose to trust somebody else, you may choose to, this is based on the risks you have perceived from specific tasks, it doesn't necessarily mean you have to trust others, at least you trust yourself, right. For example, I am discussing how to complete a task rather than why we do such a task.

Dieter Gollmann: I'm not quite following the argument, sorry.

Reply: For example, secure interaction does not necessarily mean you are interacting with others, you may be the only human in some cases, so you believe what you are seeing.

Dieter Gollmann: Yes, but what kind of transactions are you talking about? In the beginning it was paying in a shop. And you had this slide where you had a border control and you had this bullet point of human trust, I do not trust the people at border controls, they are the enemy, I want to have as little to do with these guys as possible, and I have been travelling to Eastern Europe when it was still part of the Soviet empire, these people you would not trust, and they would not trust you.

Reply: We are discussing the scenario of payment in a small shop, our concern is that when you need to make a payment, how to bootstrap security. Even if you do not trust this shop, you have to make the payment because you have to purchase some goods. And it's not about the trust in humans, it is the trust you perceive from the information you have sensed by yourself in a specific situation.

Dieter Gollmann: Again, if I stick with this border control example, I know I'm in this situation, there is no argument of trust, and there at the gate, we want to see your passport, can you open your suitcase, can open the boot of your car, and can we look under your mattresses, can we look under whatever, we have these mirrors to look under your car.

Reply: Well if you use traditional security, you use a password, or other tokens. They are also vulnerable to some kind of scam. If attackers can earn your trust, there is hardly anything to stop that kind of scam.

Bruce Christianson: How does your use of trust relate to the two channel protocols that you're looking at?

Reply: Right, for example, if I make a phone call to you and I can recognise your voice, you can just read the number, which is generated by digesting the whole range of messages transmitted before. So if I do not recognise your voice or phone number, I may choose to search your social network webpage, right, and you can just display all your context information, so I know this is the information that originates from you. The point is, you can always find a channel to communicate with your counterparts in a way you can trust.

Jonathan Anderson: Well maybe, I mean, I've created fake people on Facebook who look an awful lot like the real person, and I've had their friends come up to me and say, oh I didn't know you had a Facebook account, let's be friends.

Reply: You can do that, yes.

Jonathan Anderson: And once there are financial incentives involved I think there will be more attacks like this.

Reply: Actually the level of trust can be measured by using some kind of algorithms, for example, authenticity can be measured by measuring the intensity of interactions.

Alf Zugenmaier: I think all these measures are very good after, like you want to measure things in the past, but once you have this metric public then you can start gaming it, so yes, by just looking at the intensity of interactions you can measure authenticity somehow in the past, but once it is clear that you are going to look at the intensity of interactions then you just put up a incentive there that will increase interactions.

Reply: I mean, this could be a more sophisticated algorithm, which takes into consideration of several factors, rather than just based on intensity.

Alf Zugenmaier: And then it's not gameable?

Virgil Gligor: Yes, there are sociologists that have published four or five parameters which they call, which characterise strength of ties, so you could use that in a social network graph which is just arbitrary friends, some arbitrary friends, and then you can quantise using the sociological methods which cannot be gamed all that easily, the strengths of tie, and then there's a context that he is talking about, not just on interaction, but on the whole set of strengths of tie parameters.

Alf Zugenmaier: But were these metrics designed not to be gamed?

Virgil Gligor: Yes, designed not to be gamed, and they did a lot of experiments at the time, I can mention a few tomorrow.

Reply: If you look at the research on social networks about ratings by trust, then there are many similar models that have been established by defining what is the most useful factor to define the level of trust. Any more questions?

Alf Zugenmaier: Do you differentiate between what the trust is supposed to be used for?

Reply: Yes, in pairwise authentication the trust is simply binary, it means whether you believe this context is true or not, but in a group scenario, for example, in order to reduce conflicts, you may rely on a more sophisticated rating system to define the level of trust, in order to justify the level of risks, for example, you may receive a task to share your location with others for one hour, then the threshold value for this session is much lower than sharing your location with others for one year. You can just make reference to the ratings.

Dieter Gollmann: It may be, one slight comment, does it use language, speech for a few times. I heard some stories a few years ago in the UK when people very good at voice impersonating impersonated various politicians, rang up people to get very good quotes, and they are really good with this, so this doesn't work as simply as you have described it.

Reply: Well if someone can earn your trust, he can just steal other's identity. There is no way to protect you when you actually trust someone you're supposed not to.

Bruce Christianson: But the attack is slightly different here because, if you trust someone and they don't do what you are relying on them to do then clearly there's a threat there that you have no countermeasure for, because if you had a countermeasure you wouldn't need to trust them.

Reply: Yes.

Bruce Christianson: But the impersonation attack is a different one where someone that you think is a person you can trust, and therefore you trust them, actually isn't the person you thought.

Reply: Yes, indeed. For example when you are using NFC mobile payments, you touch the touch pad, and you're supposed to verify the information displayed on your own screen, on your own device. I just find it's very interesting when I ask people whether they do this every time, and check the payment account to check the payment amount, they didn't. So there are vulnerabilities when you rely on humans to verify identities.

Bruce Christianson: But if you treat this stuff that they're supposed to verify as part of the context and you require the transfer of some digest or something like that, where the human has to participate or the transaction won't proceed, you know, the real threat is not from dishonest participants, it's from lazy ones, and most people will be honest seeming.

Reply: Yes.

Selective Location Blinding Using Hash Chains

Gabriele Lenzini[1], Sjouke Mauw[1,2], and Jun Pang[2]

[1] Interdisciplinary Centre for Security, Reliability and Trust, University of Luxembourg, Luxembourg
[2] Computer Science and Communications, University of Luxembourg, Luxembourg

Abstract. Location-based applications require a user's movements and positions to provide customized services. However, location is a sensitive piece of information that should not be revealed unless strictly necessary. In this paper we propose a procedure that allows a user to control the precision in which his location information is exposed to a service provider, while allowing his location to be certified by a location verifier. Our procedure makes use of a hash chain to certify the location information in such a way that the hashes of the chain correspond to an increasing level of precision.

1 Introduction

The main challenge faced in security protocol design concerns the need to satisfy a number of conflicting security requirements. In the domain of location-based services, this conflict shows in the tension between location assurance and location privacy. On the one hand, service providers must know their clients' location with some level of assurance while, on the other hand, clients do not want to expose more location details than strictly needed for the requested service.

A second factor complicating the design of a security protocol is that its functional requirements and the assumptions concerning the system strongly depend on the intended usage scenario of the protocol. This factor clearly shows in location-based service scenarios, each of them leading to essentially different solutions. In the following, we briefly exemplify three of such scenarios.

A common usage scenario is that of *e-tolling*, in which the location of a car is periodically sensed and used to determine the amount of toll due. In this particular scenario, which gave rise to solutions like VPriv [11] and PrETP [1] assumptions dictate that location data must be stored at the car for offline usage. However, for online usage data must be stored at the server, on the condition that they are used by this service only. Location integrity requires either tamper resistant hardware (a solution which preserves drivers' privacy) or on-road checking spots for a-posteriori assurance (which weakens privacy). Location privacy suggests that cars can hide in the crowd of other vehicles, but service providers need to have enough information to bill correctly.

Another scenario is the use of positioning information to inform the client of the availability of services near his current location, such as the nearest Chinese restaurant or the closest gas station for which the user has a fidelity card. In this

B. Christianson et al. (Eds.): Security Protocols 2011, LNCS 7114, pp. 132–141, 2011.

scenario location-spoofing by the client does not harm the service, allowing protocol designers to mainly focus on the associated privacy concerns.

Yet another scenario is that a client makes use of a number of different services in a certain area or region. Examples of such services are physical access control, a loyalty program of a filling station, location-dependent congestion or parking charges, etc. Such services have in common that the client's location must be assured in order to prevent *theft of service*, but they differ in the required precision of the client's location data. Thus, the disclosure of the location data has to adhere to the *need-to-know* principle.

The latter usage scenario so far has not received as much attention as several other scenarios, while this particular setting allows for novel approaches. In this paper we will design a simple solution for this particular usage scenario. The main characteristic of the proposed protocol is that the client's location only has to be assured once, while the client can later decide for each particular service used with which precision his location will be revealed. This is achieved by using *hash chains.* We will design our solution under the assumption of a *location verifier.* This is a trusted entity that can assess and certify a user's claimed location, based on a set of raw location data coming from, e.g., a GPS satellite.

This paper is structured as follows. In Section 2 we describe the general architecture that we assume for location-based service provision and location assurance. In Section 3 we develop the basic notations used in our design and we provide our location-blinding protocol, together with an informal validation. In Section 4 we discuss some related work and in Section 5 we summarize our findings and draw some conclusions.

2 General Architecture

We address the problem of balancing location reliability and privacy in the particular infrastructure which relies on the Global Positioning System (GPS) to calculate locations. This choice is motivated as follows. Recently, Harpes et al. propose to fix the absence of assurance in GPS location by introducing a location verifier, which is accountable to verify and sign the user's location [7]. If this solution was implemented, it would be possible to provide assurance that a given device was at a given place at a given time. We will provide a global description of this architecture and the underlying assumptions.

We describe our architecture for location-based service provision in terms of roles involved and of communication links among them (see Figure 1). A *User Device* (e.g., a GPS-enabled phone) processes the signals coming from the GPS satellites to calculate its own geographical position. Usually, the calculated position is communicated directly to the *Service Provider*, who uses it to adapt the service on the basis of the user's location. The communication between the user device and the service provider flows over channels for wireless connectivity such as those used in Wi-Fi or in the 3G wireless technologies.

As explained in Section 1, our architecture also includes a *Location Verifier.* Its task is to certify the integrity of the location information that the user is

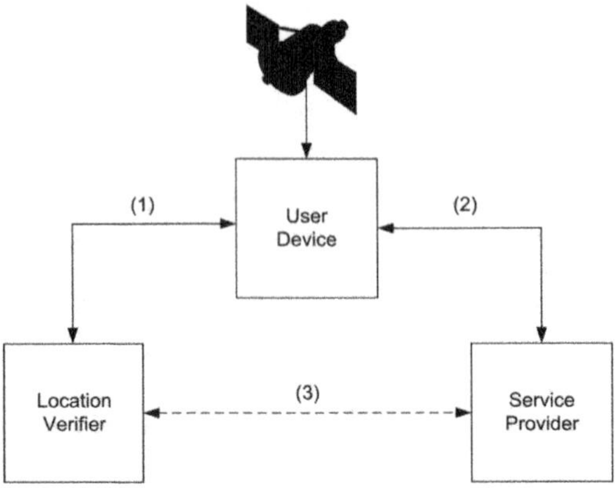

Fig. 1. The architecture for location-based services with location assurance

going to send to the service provider (see also [7]). In fact, the user device sends its location claim to the location verifier first. In Figure 1 this link is labeled (1). If the claim is verified to be correct, the location verifier sends back a *location certificate* to the user who, in turn, presents it to the service provider. This link is labeled (2). If the service provider has questions about the proof, he might contact the location verifier directly. This link is labeled (3).

There are many reasons to have a location verifier responsible for a high level of location assurance. Many location-based applications, for instance speed-limit enforcement, high valued assets tracking, and forensic reconstruction, actually can function properly only with reliable location data. However, the user device can fail in providing a correct location. First, user devices can be targets of meaconing or spoofing attacks [14]. In fact, satellite information is neither encrypted nor authenticated, thus an adversary can generate counterfeit satellite signals and mislead the user's device over its own location. A device can miscalculate a location, e.g., because the device is compromised by a malware accidentally downloaded while updating the device's software or firmware from the Internet. Finally, a user can intentionally manipulate the algorithm that generates the device's position to deceive the location-based service provider, for instance, to avoid to be billed while driving on toll roads. The presence of a location verifier prevents certain attacks against the integrity of locations that originate from the user device. For example, the location verifier can apply state of the art navigation message assurance mechanisms, or it can assign and revoke localization assurance certificates [7].

Admittedly, the availability of a location verifier is a rather strong assumption. Clearly, the system does not provide the user's location, but the location of his device. A relay attack, in which the user provides location data of a remote device, will indeed be hard to counter and distance bounding techniques will only partially be able to mitigate this type of attacks. Manipulation of the user device can be prevented by assuming that the device is tamper resistant. If we even assume that the antenna and its connection to the device are tamper resistant, direct manipulation of the incoming raw data will even be ruled out. This will require that the attacker has to resort to more complicated and expensive means of attacking the system. A further observation is that location assurance is not a yes-no question. Based on the raw data provided, the location verifier will only be able to assign a trust or assurance level to the location. Despite these possible concerns on how to realize a proper location verification service, we will simply assume the availability of such an entity.

In the following we will further assume that the communication channels between the User Device and the Location Verifier and between the User Device and the Service Provider ensure an authenticated and confidential exchange of messages. This assumption will allow us to concentrate on the information to be exchanged between the parties, without having to give a precise protocol for securing this communication. We consider authentication and confidentiality as services that are provided at another layer in the communication stack.

3 Selective Location Blinding

In this section we explore a solution that helps users to have control on the precision of disclosed location information while still allowing certified location assurance.

3.1 Locations and Hash Chains

The central concept of our study is the notion of a *location*. We use the word *location* as a generic term for describing a user's position-related parameters, such as latitude, longitude, elevation, velocity, acceleration, orientation, temporal information, etc. An example of a location is $x = (lat, long, t)$, where parameter lat is the (normalized) latitude, $long$ is the longitude and t is the time.

Without loss of generality, we assume that a location is represented by n location parameters and that each parameter is a natural number. Location x is therefore defined as a list of natural numbers,

$$x = (x_1, \ldots, x_n) \in \mathbb{N}^n.$$

We assume that each x_i is denoted in base $B > 1$ and that, possibly after padding with zeroes, it consists of d digits. For $1 \leq i \leq n$, we have

$$x_i = x_i^{d-1} x_i^{d-2} \ldots x_i^0,$$

where x_i^{d-1} is the most significant digit of x_i and x_i^0 is the least significant digit.

The accuracy of a parameter x_i can be controlled by hiding its rightmost digits. The granularity of this hiding is determined by the base B in which the numbers are expressed. By $x|_p$ (for $d-1 \leq p \leq 0$) we denote location x of which the p least significant digits of each of the parameters are blinded. Phrased differently, only the $d-p$ most significant digits are exposed. Thus, $x|_d$ contains no information on location x, $x|_{d-1}$ exposes one digit, and $x|_0$ equals x.

We will use a hash chain to selectively hide the least significant bits of a location parameter. Let h be a cryptographic hash function that satisfies *preimage resistance*, *second preimage resistance* and *collision resistance*. We assume that h is publicly known.

For every location parameter x_i $(1 \leq i \leq n)$, we construct a hash chain $K_{x_i} = K^d_{x_i} K^{d-1}_{x_i} K^{d-2}_{x_i} \ldots K^0_{x_i}$, where $K^0_{x_i}$ is a randomly chosen seed and $K^{j+1}_{x_i} = h(x^j_i, K^j_{x_i})$ (for $d-1 \geq j \geq 0$). Thus, the next hash in a chain contains the next more significant digit of the location parameter. Creating the hash chain requires the following calculations: $K^0_{x_i}$, $K^1_{x_i} = h(x^0_i, K^0_{x_i})$, $K^2_{x_i} = h(x^1_i, h(x^0_i, K^0_{x_i}))$, etc. We combine the hash chains for the different location parameters $(x_1, \ldots, x_n)$ by defining $K^j_x = (K^j_{x_1}, \ldots, K^j_{x_n})$ and $K_x = (K_{x_1}, \ldots, K_{x_n})$.

3.2 A Selective Location Blinding Protocol

Next, we show how to use these hash chains to selectively blind certified location data. In our protocol, we will only focus on which information is exchanged and we assume that authentication and confidentiality of the information exchange is dealt with at other levels of the communication stack. Figure 2 shows the entities involved and their interaction.

In our protocol, a *User Device* (e.g., a GPS-enabled phone) processes the signals coming from the GPS satellites to calculate its own geographical position. The calculated position will be verified and certified by the *Location Verifier* and communicated to the *Service Provider*, who offers the service, adapted to the User Device's location.

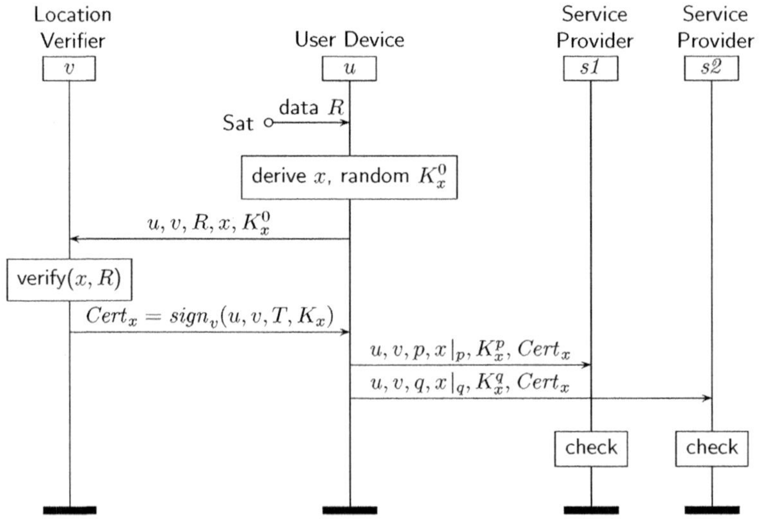

Fig. 2. The location blinding protocol

In full detail, our protocol consists of the following steps. First, based on raw data R (e.g., satellite signals), the User Device u calculates its location x and generates the list of random seeds K_x^0 for the hash chain. This information is sent by u to the Location Verifier v. Based on its own context and observations v verifies whether location x corresponds to raw data R. We will not specify this context and observations because they are specific to the positioning system used. We simply assume that v has sufficient information to assess u's calculated location. If the location is correct, v calculates the key chain and offers u a signed certificate $Cert_x = sign_v(u, v, T, K_x)$, where T is a time stamp. Such a certificate is also called a *location proof* [12]. At this point, u can use this certificate in subsequent communications to Service Providers. For each such communication, u determines a precision p (for $d-1 \leq p \leq 0$) and sends the hash corresponding to this precision, K_x^p, together with the partially blinded location $x|_p$ and the location certificate $Cert_x$.

Using this information, the Service Provider reconstructs that part of the hash chain that follows after K_x^p and compares the final hash value, say K_x', with the one from the certificate, K_x. In this way the Service Provider receives and verifies the $d-p$ most significant bits of the User Device's location parameters, while the least significant bits remain unknown to him.

An important feature of this protocol is that the User Device (i.e., the user who owns the device) can decide upon the precision p *after* the certification of his location. This will prevent the Location Verifier from having to certify the User Device's location for every possible precision p in advance. The same certificate can be used for different service providers, while adapting the precision to the needs of each of the particular services.

In the above protocol all location parameters are blinded with the same precision. The protocol can be easily adapted to provide a different precision for each location parameter. The only difference is that in the message from the User Device to the Service Provider all location parameters have to be treated separately.

The user device and the service provider should be able to agree upon how much privacy will be disclosed according to the *need-to-know* principle. Here, the user device and the service provider can run a service level agreement (SLA) protocol which supports the two parties in determining the level of privacy satisfying both the user's privacy policy and the service's requirement on location details. In certain cases, the level of privacy can be decided by bilateral agreement between a client and a server at the time of the client's enrollment to the service.

3.3 Validation

In this section, we give a basic reasoning why our protocol can guarantee the secrecy of the least significant p bits of the location parameters and the authenticity of the claimed location. In the previous section we made the assumption that the communication channels between the user device and the location verifier (link (1) in Figure 1) and between the user device and the service provider (link (2) in Figure 1) ensure the authenticated and private exchange of messages. This makes sure that any outside attacker cannot learn any information about, or modify the raw data R, the location x, the randomly generated seeds K_x^0, the hashes K_x and the certificate $Cert_x$, as exchanged between these protocol entities.

From the perspective of an insider, under the assumption that the location verifier is fully trusted, we see two threats: (*i*) a user spoofing his location and (*ii*) a compromised (or malicious) service provider learning more about the user's location than he is allowed to. The first threat is prevented by the certificate. Because the location verifier verified the user's location and because the hash function is second preimage resistant and collision resistant, the service provider can detect a location spoofing attack by checking the hash chain with the provided input. The second threat is prevented because the user only sends the most significant digits of his location to the service provider. Further, because the hash function is preimage resistant, the service provider cannot derive additional location information from the hashed values.

It is possible that from a series of observations a service provider (by conspiring with other service providers) can derive more accurate data on the whereabouts of a user than strictly allowed by the set precision, for example, using a Kalman filter [8]. Another possibility is that conspiring service providers can collaboratively calculate a precision which is better than the best precision for each of them as they can calculate the intersection of the location data that each of them received. To mitigate this type of attacks, we can combine our protocol with techniques providing anonymous usage of services (see Section 4). Since users cannot be identified, the conspiring service providers have no means to link location certificates to a particular user. There is one exception when a service requires a sequence of location data from the *same* user. In this particular case, anonymization cannot help as the service needs to ensure that several location certificates come from the same user.

4 Related Work

A major concern for large-scale deployment of location-based services is the potential abuse of users' locations, a recognized sensitive information. Papers on achieving location privacy can be classified into two classes: one uses location cloaking and the other studies user anonymity.

Location cloaking [6,2,3] is a popular approach for providing location privacy – a user's location is cloaked (by a third party or the user's device) before it is given to a service provider. For instance, Gruteser and Grunwald [6] develop an algorithm to adjust the resolution of location information based on the entities who may be using services in a given area. Cheng et al. [2] study a system model, which can be used to find the balance between privacy and the quality of location-based services. In their model, users can specify their location, service request and privacy requirements to the cloaking agent, which in turn produces the cloaked location and an "imprecise" service request. In this way, the service provider only knows the region where the user is, but does not know where exactly. In order to achieve location privacy based on the notion of k-anonymity, Zhong and Hengartner [16] develop a protocol based on homomorphic encryption which can cloak a user's location in a way that there are at least $k-1$ other people within the cloaked area. The system Casper* [3] uses a location anonymizer to blur a user's exact location information into a cloaked area to satisfy user specified privacy requirements. Our solution differs from these papers in several aspects. First, we allow the users to have control on their location privacy using hash chains – the user can provide an appropriate decryption key depending on which level location information is required by the service provider. Second, the above solutions require a trusted third party (cloaking agents or location-anonymizers) to protect the user's location privacy. Instead, we use a trusted third party, a location verifier, only to certify a user's location. Location cloaking is performed and controlled by the users.

Anonymous usage (of a service) is another important feature in LBSs. It is closely related to location privacy, in the sense that in LBSs it is desirable to make sure that the precision of location information cannot be used to identify a user. For this purpose, the algorithm developed by Gruteser and Grunwald [6] can be used to achieve a certain degree of anonymity for users by decreasing the accuracy of the revealed location information. Li et al. [10] propose a method to prevent an adversary to track the location of users, by allowing users to change their pseudonyms. Through a game theoretical analysis, Freudiger et al. [4] suggest some improvements on this protocol by Li et al. [10]. Our proposed solution has its focus on location privacy, it can be extended to satisfy more properties like user anonymity.

Papers on verifying the correctness of location proofs provided by a user are also related. Sastry et al. [13] present a simple protocol to securely check a user's location to be at some location within a region. By increasing the number of verifiers in the protocol, it can verify the user's location more precisely. Køien and Oleshchuk [9] develop a protocol which can be used to check whether the location reported by a user is inside of a polygon. Graham and Gray [5] propose a protocol for verifying location claims using proofs gathered from the neighboring devices/users. In our solution, we assume the existence of a location verifier, which is in charge of certifying location information. This can be achieved, for example, using techniques proposed in [7].

5 Conclusion

We proposed a procedure for the selective blinding of location information. The underlying idea is to hide the least significant digits of location data. This is a rather simple idea, but the problem becomes more complex in the context of a location verifier, when we require that the certificate does not depend on the precision which will be set later by the user. Our solution based on hash chains neatly enables the independence of a certificate from the required precision.

Because the procedure is based on hiding digits, the granularity of precision is determined by the number base used to represent the location data. In our current solution, the location verifier's certificate depends on this base, which implies that the granularity has to be decided upon before verification. An interesting question is whether we can use homomorphic encryption to allow the user to change the base of his certified location without requesting a new certificate.

In this paper we mainly focused on location data represented by natural numbers. Other flexible and versatile means to represent location information can also be supported. A wide range of solutions for representing location in Internet protocols are proposed in RFC 5491 [15]. Furthermore, our results can be extended to other types of contextual data that support a notion of precision, such as a person's age.

In our procedure, security properties of location certificates, such as secrecy and integrity, are easily achieved as we employ a trusted location verifier. Combining our protocol with other techniques (e.g., see Section 4) to provide users with properties like anonymity and untraceability is part of our future work.

As part of a project with industry, we plan to experimentally implement the architecture from Section 2. Our procedure will be validated by a prototype application using a mobile network with existing GPS or the upcoming Galileo receiver. The main challenge will be how to combine the different techniques concerning location verification, location privacy and user anonymity.

References

1. Balasch, J., Rial, A., Troncoso, C., Geuens, C.: PrETP: Privacy-preserving electronic toll pricing. In: Proc. USENIX Security Symposium, pp. 63–78. USENIX (2010)
2. Cheng, R., Zhang, Y., Hwang, J., Prabhakar, S.: Preserving User Location Privacy in Mobile Data Management Infrastructures. In: Danezis, G., Golle, P. (eds.) PET 2006. LNCS, vol. 4258, pp. 393–412. Springer, Heidelberg (2006)
3. Chow, C.-Y., Mokbel, M.F., Aref, W.G.: Casper*: Query processing for location services without compromising privacy. ACM Transactions on Database Systems 34(4), 1–48 (2009)
4. Freudiger, J., Manshaei, M.H., Hubaux, J.P., Parkes, D.C.: On non-cooperative location privacy: a game-theoretic analysis. In: Proc. 16th ACM Conference on Computer and Communications Security, pp. 324–337. ACM Press (2009)
5. Graham, M., Gray, D.: Protecting Privacy and Securing the Gathering of Location Proofs - The Secure Location Verification Proof Gathering Protocol. In: Schmidt, A.U., Lian, S. (eds.) MobiSec 2009. LNICST, vol. 17, pp. 160–171. Springer, Heidelberg (2009)
6. Gruteser, M., Grunwald, D.: Anonymous usage of location-based services through spatial and temporal cloaking. In: Proc. 1st Conference on Mobile Systems, Applications, and Services. USENIX (2003)
7. Harpes, C., Jager, B., Gent, B.: Secure localisation with location assurance provider. In: Proc. European Navigation Conference - Global Navigation Satellite Systems (2009)
8. Kalman, R.E.: A new approach to linear filtering and prediction problems. Journal of Basic Engineering 82(1), 35–45 (1960)

9. Køien, G.M., Oleshchuk, V.A.: Location Privacy for Cellular Systems; Analysis and Solution. In: Danezis, G., Martin, D. (eds.) PET 2005. LNCS, vol. 3856, pp. 40–58. Springer, Heidelberg (2006)
10. Li, M., Sampigethaya, K., Huang, L., Poovendran, R.: Swing & swap: user-centric approaches towards maximizing location privacy. In: Proc. 5th ACM Workshop on Privacy in the Electronic Society, pp. 19–28. ACM Press (2006)
11. Popa, R.A., Balakrishnan, H., Blumberg, A.J.: VPriv: Protecting privacy in location-based vehicular services. In: Proc. USENIX Security Symposium, pp. 335–350. USENIX (2009)
12. Saroiu, S., Wolman, A.: Enabling new mobile applications with location proofs. In: Proc. 10th Workshop on Mobile Computing Systems and Applications. ACM Press (2009)
13. Sastry, N., Shankar, U., Wagner, D.: Secure verification of location claims. In: Proc. ACM Workshop on Wireless Security, pp. 1–10. ACM Press (2003)
14. Warner, J.S., Johnston, R.G.: A simple demonstration that the global positioning system (GPS) is vulnerable to spoofing. Journal of Security Administration 25, 19–28 (2002)
15. Winterbottom, J., Thomson, M., Tschofenig, H.: GEOPRIV Presence Information Data Format Location Object (PIDF-LO) Usage Clarification, Considerations, and Recommendations. Tech. Rep. RFC 5491, IETF Network Working Group (March 2009)
16. Zhong, G., Hengartner, U.: Toward a distributed k-anonymity protocol for location privacy. In: Proc. 7th ACM Workshop on Privacy in the Electronic Society, pp. 33–38. ACM Press (2008)

Selective Location Blinding Using Hash Chains

(Transcript of Discussion)

Sjouke Mauw

University of Luxembourg, Luxembourg

The work that I am reporting on is work that we recently started with a Luxembourgish company, itrust. Together with this company we are working on the design of a security architecture and security protocols to enable location-based services.

The general architecture of the system consists of a satellite and a local user device, such as a mobile phone. This user device helps you to use location-based services offered by a service provider. Because the service provider needs to be sure about your location, we have also introduced a location verifier. You receive the data from the satellite, calculate your location and forward the data and the calculated location to the location verifier. In some way, the location verifier then validates your location and returns a certificate. Then you can use this certificate to convince the service provider that you are really at the location where you claim to be.

In developing this kind of protocols, you always have the tension between opposing requirements and here we have the tension between the requirements of privacy and location assurance. Privacy means that you don't want to give away more information about your location than strictly needed, and assurance means that the service provider is indeed sure that you are where you are.

I'm not at all an expert in the field of satellite communication, so I will only briefly explain the relevant technical issues. GPS is the one you all probably know, but Russia is developing its own system, the European Union are developing their own system, as well as China.

Let's consider the attacker model. It's easy to jam such a system. You can buy a low-cost jammer which can jam the main communication band over several kilometres, but such jamming can easily be detected. Spoofing is also an option. A literature study shows that software-based spoofers are available for several thousands of Euros. We are currently investigating how to detect such spoofed signals. One can look, for instance, at the strength of the signal, the bias of the clocks, or the Doppler shift. Of course, there's not one single method to detect spoofing and we are looking at the use of different logics to combine the various methods.

Mike Burmester: Since we're allowed interruptions, why don't these satellite companies sign the messages?

B. Christianson et al. (Eds.): Security Protocols 2011, LNCS 7114, pp. 142–149, 2011.

Reply: That was my initial reaction as well: let's modify the GPS protocol. They said, no way. These companies will never do that.

Mike Burmester: But they could do it not all the time, they could do it, for instance, every 10 or 20 seconds.

Joseph Bonneau: If the signal from the satellite is signed, then you can still spoof. You just need to relay it from any valid point to the location verifier.

Reply: Yes, of course, you can. There are several possible attacks like that. Some of these attacks can be defended against by extending the protocol with proper authentication, but that was a no-go area. So we had to solve it at the receiver's side.

Frank Stajano: If there are going to be four more different systems by 2020, is none of them going to authenticate the signal from satellites?

Reply: I haven't looked into that. I assume they will use the GNSS standard, but I'm not sure what the developments are.

If an attacker would use a spoofing device to spoof the signals of all visible satellites, he would not be able to simulate the relative speeds of the satellites. This could easily be detected by looking at the Doppler shifts of the signals. For this you only need to observe one of the communication bands. If you look at both communication bands you can compare the power of the signals, frequency based modulation, etc. This will also give you an idea if something went wrong. You can also build a database with satellite positions and calculate from which direction the signal comes. This can be compared to the actual data from the user device. Finally, you can compare signals from different sources to find irregularities. So there's quite a range of measures that you can think of, but they haven't been researched in full detail.

But that's not what I'm going to talk about now. I was just trying to motivate why we need this special service that has knowledge and algorithms, allowing it to decide whether a given set of data, in its context, can be considered as a genuine location or not.

So far for the location assurance part. From now on I will consider that as a black box that is still to be developed and we will focus on privacy-preserving protocols. We started from two kinds of techniques, first the privacy concept of hiding in the crowd, where you make yourself similar to all other people around you. Your privacy problem is then solved because you cannot be distinguished. An alternative technique is that you will not give your precise location data, but only an approximation of your position, meaning that you can only be localised within a certain area.

While looking at the problem we found out that there are many different usage scenarios, and that they all have their own extra requirements. It appears that for every particular group of applications you will have to develop a new class of protocols. Of course you recognise this from other application areas, but here it shows very clearly. For example, for e-tolling where you pay what you drive. The scenario is that you have frequent interaction with some machine that collects your location data over a certain time period, and in the end you hand it over to some company, and they will assure that the data is correct and complete, etc. This gives a different type of protocols than if you are at a certain location and want to use various local services, such as borrowing a book or parking your car at preferential rates, etc. Here you collect your data, have it assured, and use the same data several times for all local services.

Frank Stajano: I'm sorry, I didn't quite get the point of the local services. If I am using a local service, then the fact that I am interacting with the service provider locally should tell them that I am there. Why do I need anything from satellites?

Reply: If you want to park your car somewhere at a preferential rate, you only have to assure that you are in the area where the preferential rate applies. You don't need to precisely state where in that area you are. The same applies to making cheap phone calls if you are at a certain place and to customer loyalty programs that are location aware. You can get, for instance, bonus points if you are near a certain building.

Frank Stajano: Right, so I was assuming that the location thing would be based on some interaction in that location, such as buying something from that shop, or paying the parking meter in that place.

Reply: Exactly, if you have interaction with people, or directly with real systems, then there's no point in doing this, but there are services being developed for which you only have to certify your location electronically.

The first two protocols that we developed are for two of these scenarios. One is for electronic tolling and the other is for the local services scenario. Today I will only talk about local services, but I will first briefly sketch the intricacies of the other scenario, just to give you an idea of how diverse solutions can be.

Suppose you're driving a car and you would like to preserve your privacy, while still being able to prove your location to, for instance, the insurance company. A possible solution is to hide yourself in a group, and every time that you provide location data you use a group signature to sign your location. The signed location is sent to the service provider and based on the location data you calculate the fee that you will have to pay. The service provider then adds the payments of all group members and if this doesn't sum up to the expected group total, one of the users must have cheated. In this case, the group signature can be opened and the user who paid too little money can be identified. In this class of solutions a user hides himself in a group by using some kind of cryptographic mechanism, for instance group signatures, and loses his privacy only if he cheated.

Frank Stajano: Is it the case that if I don't pay, then everybody else who was in the group who has paid has their location privacy annulated?

Reply: In fact that is not the case. There is the assumption that there is a trusted authority, say the government, that handles these cases. The location service provider then hands over all data to the authority who can calculate who is the culprit, and then only gives back to this location provider the information about who is in fact cheating. The authority has the power to break the group signatures.

Frank Stajano: Then the group signatures don't give us much protection, because we could do everything just by telling it all to the location authority.

Reply: Yes, but the location authority will never know all details. It will only learn the details for a particular group if the location provider has a complaint. So, normally the location authority will never see anything; only if there's conflict.

Frank Stajano: It's a kind of separation of duties.

Reply: Yes.

I want to come to a much easier solution for the local services problem. It's almost trivial with hindsight. You use a hash chain to encode your location data. First let's clarify who the stakeholders are and then where the threats come from. A client determines its own location and wants to use several services at that location, but he wants to apply the need-to-know principle. The service provider should not know more than he really needs to offer his service. Furthermore, a client has an incentive to cheat since he has to pay for several services. He wants to claim to be somewhere else sometimes to get, for instance, cheaper phone calls. Then we have the trusted location verifier, who takes data from the client, and certifies this location data. Next, we have the service provider who wants to offer services. He really needs to be sure about the client's location; he offers location based services which maybe cheaper at some places. He doesn't always need to have millimetre precision, sometimes it's a mile precision, or even state precision, that you need for your service, but he's also curious about the user's precise location data. If he can collect that in a database, he can do a direct mail, and sell the information. He has an incentive to know learn more than he is allowed to know.

We use some simple abstractions. A location is simply a list of natural numbers after normalization and scaling. For example, you have the parameters latitude, longitude, and time, and whatever context information that can be expressed as natural numbers. Then we can control the precision by simply nulling out the least significant digits of your numbers. So uncertainty level 0 means you will have the full data, and uncertainty level 8 will mean that you have no data at all. You determine for each of the services what precision level they require, and that's the precision level that you want to send. Of course this precision depends on the base that you have chosen.

Jonathan Anderson: And of course reducing the precision doesn't necessarily mean that you've actually given a lot of information. If, for instance, you have an uncertainty level 7 but my value keeps switching back between 8 and 9 every 30 seconds, then you can still have a fairly precise estimate of where I am.

Reply: Yes, then you will go one up level in precision.

Frank Stajano: I think the other point is that you may be in the middle of the Sahara where there's only you anyway, so it doesn't really matter. (Hiding in the crowd of one.)

Reply: That's why I started showing you these two pictures. Hiding yourself in a crowd is a different approach from hiding the precision of your location, and you cannot attack one of the solutions by assuming the other approach, of course.

Joseph Bonneau: If you're getting these reduced precision things at a constant time, you can see that you were at 9000 for 10 seconds, and then you were at 10000. Can you linearise and assume a path if you're travelling at constant speed?

Reply: Yes, if you have a sequence of location data then there are several methods to extrapolate your location, such as Kalman filters. They allow one to predict where you're going. Here we assume that you don't give a sequence of data. You have one position and stay there for a while, or walk around in a small area.

Bruce Christianson: If I run a car park with a fractal shape, then I can just say, that I need to know whether you're in the car park or not. So you have to give me latitude and longitude to a very high precision, because the boundary is fractal.

Reply: That's true, this approach only works with square areas, but I think this can be refined.

Next, we look at how to create the hash chains. You create the sequence of keys as follows. You have a sequence of digits of your number, with the least significant digit at the right. K_0 is a random initial nonce. You insert it in the hash together with the least significant digit. Hashing now gives K_1, etc. Then you take K_n, which is the final element of your hash sequence. You give it to the location assurance provider together with all data that might be relevant for him, and then he certifies K_n if he is convinced that you constructed it in the right way.

Now you have a kind of certificate. If you want to use a service from a service provider, you want to only give him the initial segment of your location data, leaving out the least significant digits up to point p. Then you give him the key K_p plus the certified value K_n, plus these bits. In this way the service provider can reconstruct your hash chain by starting to count from K_p, which is given. Finally, he verifies if the calculated K_n corresponds to the certified K_n.

We look at a typical scenario of the protocol. Here we have the location verifier and here the user device. We assume two service providers at this location. Say, you want to address one service provider with precision p, and the other service provider with precision q. Then we take the satellite data, which is the raw data R, from which we calculate our location, and we derive the random key K_0. We send all relevant data to the location verifier and he verifies whether the location that you claim to be in corresponds to the raw data. He can use his database, and all other contextual information that can help him to verify the location. If this is correct he will reconstruct the key chain, and then he will certify your K_n as belonging to you, and you can use this certificate later in your application.

Omar Choudary: I think verifying based on the raw data R is not sufficient because you can lie on both R and your location.

Reply: Yes, but normally it is very hard to spoof R. This is quite a large amount of data that you can't really interpret yourself.

Omar Choudary: You can just send the data from another location. Maybe you can send data from two days ago when I was in another city, or something like that.

Reply: But then you can find out that it is spoofed because the time stamp in the raw data is different from the current time.

Omar Choudary: OK, maybe if it was just different location, not a different time necessarily.

Joseph Bonneau: So it seems like you can put a device on your roof at home and then relay it to wherever you are in the world, and then transmit the R like it was received at your home, and it will look like you're always there.

Omar Choudary: So I guess the question is, what is the purpose of the verifier.

Reply: The purpose of the verifier is to check whether the technical information received from the satellites and all the contextual information that can observed is consistent with the location that you claim to be at.

Alf Zugenmaier: But that will probably mean that you need to do some distance bounding.

Reply: Yes, you will need some kind of distance bounding.

Omar Choudary: Or the service provider can just accept the location and give him a bad service.

Alf Zugenmaier: It's like a location commitment, you can do whatever you want to, but then you're committed to having that location at that time.

Omar Choudary: You are getting a service based on a different location. That might be OK.

Jonathan Anderson: I think it's not entirely clear that you could do distance bounding. You can do distance bounding to a thing that is close to you. But you can't do any kind of distance bounding that would prove that the user device is in fact using the GPS coordinates from its current location, and not GPS coordinates that it is receiving from, for instance, my house. I don't think there's any way you can tie those two things together. You can't do anything that relies on computing your actual location from a bunch of data that has come down from a satellite on an embedded processor that might be really slow.

You can't make good time guarantees, so I don't think you could distance bound this.

Frank Stajano: The only thing I can see as a use for distance bounding is that if the user device does a distance bounding protocol with the location verifier, then it is not able to claim data from the roof of its house, if the roof of its house is outside the diameter.

Jonathan Anderson: That's true, but then we're back to the scenario where the satellite doesn't do anything. All you need is a transponder that says, I'm within so many feet.

Frank Stajano: No, because then the difference is that when you use the satellite it tells you where you are, as opposed to just within what rate.

Alf Zugenmaier: It is very unlikey that you could start bouncing around at local speed greater than light. The location verifier can try to find out what is the trajectory that you are on. So the verifier could in fact be some kind of big brother that finds out whether you can be where you're claiming to be.

Bruce Christianson: But if I'm always claiming to be in my house watching television, I'm not going to move at all.

Joseph Bonneau: If you're paying for a car or something based on the usage, then it's very useful to say, I was in one location.

Jonathan Anderson: But that's a scenario where then you just have to assume that Ford or BMW, or whoever, is going to have a little TPM somewhere in the car that keeps track of your actual location. And so you're back to the transponder case where the thing that you trust is in fact the hardware. Then you trust that the user probably couldn't get the hardware open and modified without leaving tamper evidence.

Joseph Bonneau: The tamper resistant hardware then has a private key, and it signs that it received R and X. You can send this to the location verifier, but even if you have untrusted software, you can't sign a different location.

Alf Zugenmaier: But that's not going to help because you can just feed simulated GPS signals in there. You can buy boxes that would simulate your GPS signal for any point of time.

Joseph Bonneau: The TPM has to somehow have spoofing detection.

Alf Zugenmaier: If you want to have it as a verifier you would have to rely on some tracking infrastructure. Positioning: the device finds out it's own location. Tracking: someone is trying to find out the location of the device.

Reply: But it was not the intention to do tracking. You can only spoof this device from the outside, not by connecting wires. Then the device will have ways to measure all this data itself, and that's the data that will be sent to the location verifier. So you can only spoof it by making some fake satellites, and hopefully you can detect that scenario.

Omar Choudary: We have someone working in the lab on spoofing satellite data. Because you only see four or five satellites, it's not hard to spoof them.

Reply: There's so much information that you can use to detect spoofing. It is very hard to simulate, for instance, the Doppler effect in practice.

Alf Zugenmaier: You're not generating the signal from the outside. You're buying a box and a cable that runs into the antenna connector. There is no reason that you can't do it in software. You're shifting frequencies a bit by heating some insulator or cooling it down. It's reasonably easy, and you can buy, for testing the GPS receivers, hardware that will simulate your position, the time, and any speed that you want to set it at. It will just calculate what is the wave form, that would be received at your antenna, and that's it.

Omar Choudary: Maybe you can use GSM data. You can control it much more than the GPS. I think that it's easier to detect a relay attack in GSM.

Alf Zugenmaier: We are now slowly moving away from this nice idea of not having to change any protocol, and we're discussing now to install distance bounding for GSM operators.

Frank Stajano: Why would the verifier take on the liability of producing the signed certificate. What's the benefit for it, and what's the penalty in case it gets it wrong? Is it going to refund the service providers if it signs something that turns out not to be right?

Reply: That's an economic issue that I didn't consider. It's like virus software. You pay for it, and you get only about 50% of all viruses detected. At the moment people simply accept this. The location verifier can extend the certificate with the amount of belief that he has in the correctness of the location.

Joseph Bonneau: Your solution progressively loses one digit every time. It seems to me you could just have an arbitrary sequence of locations that are more precise.

Reply: Yes, every progressive sequence of location areas would work.

Risks of Blind Controllers and Deaf Views in Model View Controller Patterns for Multitag User Interfaces

Alf Zugenmaier

Munich University of Applied Science, Munich, Germany
{firstname.lastname}@hm.edu

Abstract. Electronic tags such as 2D bar codes and NFC are used to connect physical and virtual worlds. Beyond pure information augmentation of physical objects, this gives rise to new user interfaces, so called multitag interfaces. A salient feature of these interfaces is that the user sees a physical object, a poster, but interacts with its electronic augmentation. We present two attacks that exploit this feature along with first thoughts of how these attacks may be countered. We analyze the possibility to introduce secure bindings into these novel user interfaces.

1 Introduction

Tagging of objects with 2D bar codes or NFCs allows personal electronic devices to easily identify them. This connection of physical and virtual world makes it possible to interact with these physical objects. The simplest type of electronic interaction with such objects is to retrieve additional information about the object. [WFGH99]. In these interactions, the user has a personal device being able to read the content of the tags and connect to a server as indicated in the content of the tag.

O'Neill et al. [OTGW07] studied the use of tags to implement small applications such as music downloads. The personal electronic device, which was a mobile phone with an NFC reader in their study, had to be positioned directly on top of the NFCs embedded in the posters in order to read the tags. Depending on which NFC tag the phone was reading, the phone initiated different actions. A label describing the actions was printed on the poster at the location of the tag. Thus, areas of the poster where a tag was embedded could be used like buttons in a graphical user interface to trigger an action of the phone.

The next step is to print a complete user interface on a poster. This can be used to perform more complex transactions involving multiple tags. Such kind of user interfaces, called *multitag interfaces*, were studied by Broll et al. [BSR+07, BRP+09]. While their original proposal had substantial user interaction involving additional user input on the mobile phone, in a later paper [HRHW10] they show that, from user interface perspective, performing all user input by holding the phone over the active areas on the poster is preferable.

B. Christianson et al. (Eds.): Security Protocols 2011, LNCS 7114, pp. 150–155, 2011.

The applications used for demonstrating these multitag interfaces were a tourist information service [HRHW10], as well as ticketing applications for train tickets and for movie theater tickets [BSR+07]. for each of these applications, NFC tags were embedded in a printed poster.

From a security perspective it is interesting to see that in the experiments there were no concerns reported about the perceived security of the applications. To be fair, it is also not reported whether the questionnaires used to evaluate the user interface included security.

2 Multitag Interfaces

Multitag interfaces as described by Hardy et al. [HRHW10] support three types of interaction widgets: static widgets, in which all information is contained on the tag, and the interaction is purely local, i.e. displaying information on the phone. Phone-only widgets present user interfaces on the phone. Server widgets allow state changes on an application server. In the described ticketing applications, payment takes place in a server widget. Therefore we will look at server widgets in greater detail.

Server widgets follow a model view controller design pattern [Try79]. The MVC design pattern has become *the* standard user interface pattern. While there are many different variants to implementing the MVC pattern, Krasner and Pope describe the most widely accepted variant [KP88]: The model reflects the current state of the system. Views display this state of the system, while the controller deals with user interaction. Views are often associated with a controller, such that when a user input takes place correlated to a view, the controller knows which part of the model to update.

For the ticketing applications, the process to purchase a ticket was as follows: First, the user starts an application by reading the tag associated with task. Then, the phone is used to read the tags corresponding to the required input. The order in which tags are read is not relevant. The phone gives haptic feedback to the user that an NFC tag has been read successfully by vibrating shortly.

3 Cut and Paste Attack

An attacker could separate the labels printed on the poster, which is what that the user sees and attributes a semantic to, from the tags, and rearrange them. This could be done by cutting out the tags and pasting them into the poster at a different location. Or an attacker could print a poster with a different layout and paste it on top of the original poster with its tags. In the movie ticketing application, the user may think he is interacting with the tag that selects movie X because this is what he sees (View U), while the phone interacts with the tag that selects movie Y (View T).

The basic reason why this cut and paste attack is possible is that the control of the MVC pattern doesn't have an association to the view that the user sees. The control can be considered blind. The user also has no indication what is happening really: as the poster is static, the view is not updated, it is not listening to the update broadcasts of the model. In that respect the view can be considered deaf.

Feedback to the user could be used to defend against this attack: The view could be updated to reflect the current choice of the user. However, when using static views as would be the case with a printed poster to implement a multitag user interface, the view can't be updated with the changes a control makes to the model. Dynamic views could be presented by using a projector to project the image of the poster or by using phone-only widgets. Hardy et al. [HRHW10] also studied the usability of dynamic displays and found that static displays are favorable. While the preference of static displays was statistically significant, the difference was not so much that it seems impossible that security concerns could tip the balance in favor of dynamic displays.

4 Man in the Middle Attack

A man in the middle attack is is similar to the cut and paste attack in that the attacker replaces the poster to present a view that is unrelated to the embedded tags. However, in this attack the application that is printed on the poster (the view) is unrelated to the model that the controller interacts with. As an example, on the poster of the train ticketing application, tags representing the cinema application can be embedded. In that case, the user would imagine updating a different model (model U) than the model the controller is interacting with (model T). Again, this is made possible by the controller being blind. In this case, user feedback could be deceptive, as the man in the middle could also control the feedback channel.

Note that the man in the middle attack is especially dangerous when a phone-only widget is used for entering a pin. Because the user doesn't know which application he is interacting with, the user may make false assumptions about the security of the application.

In order to avoid man in the middle attacks, it would necessary to bind usage of tags to the view that is being presented. However, the problem remains how to determine which application the user wants to perform. For as long as there are only few applications, it may be possible to let the user decide using an interface on his mobile. Once the application space gets more crowded, application authentication will suffer from the same problems as web site authentication.

5 Possible General Solutions

In this section some first ideas on how to defend against the attacks described above are presented. Unfortunately, none of the ideas so far are great.

One general solution would be physical binding of tag and poster. If posters could be made tamper evident, cut and paste attacks would be avoided. However, tamper evidence for posters in public spaces may not be practical. In applications

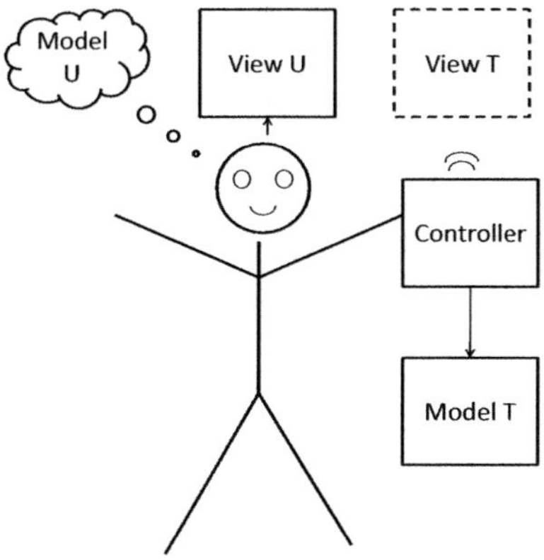

Fig. 1. The problem: controller and user may be perceiving different views and interacting with different models

in which there is only authorized access to the posters, simple physical security could be an option.

The most promising type of binding would be to ensure that the controller actually sees what the user sees, i.e. introduce optical recognition of what the user tries to achieve. Steps to achieve that would be first to determine which poster the user is interacting with, then load the appropriate information which can then be used to determine which control is activated depending on the optical input of the camera. However, in order to avoid man in the middle attacks it would have to be possible to reliably automate determination which application the poster belongs to.

Mutual authentication of application server (the model) and mobile device (the controller) would solve the problem of man in the middle attacks if authentication were easy for the user to understand, i.e. the user doesn't get confused as to which authenticated application the controller is talking to. A way to get to there could be a walled garden approach. When mutual authentication is in place, the mobile device can function as trusted input and output device.

As a more general approach to solving the security problems, it could be possible to adjusting the architecture of the application to minimize risk. In the case of the movie ticketing application, risk for the application user to lose money could be minimized by postponing payment until the service is consumed, i.e. the application provides only a reservation to the movie. However, this would expose the cinema owner to an attack in which large number of seats are reserved but not paid for.

Further attacks could also involve implementation level details of the multitag interaction framework or the specific application using such an interface. This would be similar to the RFID virus described by Rieback et al. [RCT06]. However, the issues arising from these attacks could be addressed in similar way as for web based applications, i.e. input checking even for tag inputs.

5.1 Possibility of an Impossibility Result

Considering the failure to present an obvious solution, it may be that the problem is unsolvable in general. Under the assuption that there is no way of binding how the user interprets what he sees to the action that the device will execute, there will always be a possibility of confused deputies. Thus it may be necessary to change the mode of interaction. Instead of the device interacting with machine readable tags, the device needs to use optical recognition of the content of the poster coupled with a heuristic of how the user interprets what is seen. The device would need to try to simulate the users thought processes, a task that is highly unlikely to succeed.

6 Conclusion

While multitag interfaces allow usable pervasive service interaction, they also create new security problems. There may be applications in which the risk is smaller than the benefit provided by the convenience.

Two attacks were described:

- The first attack described here is similar to clickjacking [HG08]. The principal countermeasures against clickjacking is making sure that user input is only directed at the controls that are visible. This is easier to realize because the environment clickjacking attacks can take place in are usually under the control of the user who can install browser or operating system updates and not under control of the attacker.
- The second attack described here is similar to what happens in phishing: the user is lured to a server that is not the one the user expects. The usual countermeasure against phishing is to train the user to not follow links found in emails in order to perform sensitive tasks. However, the idea of electronic tags is to make it easy for a user to follow links that are provided by the environment.

Both of these attacks could be considered instances of the confused deputy problem [Har88].

The lack of a convincing general solution indicates that there is still work to be done to make these multitag user interfaces applicable in situations where security is important.

References

[BRP+09] Broll, G., Rukzio, E., Paolucci, M., Wagner, M., Schmidt, A., Hussmann, H.: Perci: Pervasive service interaction with the internet of things. IEEE Internet Computing 13(6), 74–81 (2009)

[BSR+07] Broll, G., Siorpaes, S., Rukzio, E., Paolucci, M., Hamard, J., Wagner, M., Schmidt, A.: Supporting mobile service usage through physical mobile interaction. In: Fifth Annual IEEE International Conference on Pervasive Computing and Communications, PerCom 2007, pp. 262–271 (2007)

[Har88] Hardy, N.: The confused deputy (or why capabilities might have been invented). SIGOPS Oper. Syst. Rev. 22, 36–38 (1988)

[HG08] Hansen, R., Grossman, J.: Clickjacking. SecTheory (December 2008), `http://www.sectheory.com/clickjacking.htm`

[HRHW10] Hardy, R., Rukzio, E., Holleis, P., Wagner, M.: Mobile interaction with static and dynamic nfc-based displays. In: Proceedings of the 12th International Conference on Human Computer Interaction with Mobile Devices and Services, MobileHCI 2010, pp. 123–132. ACM, New York (2010)

[KP88] Krasner, G.E., Pope, S.T.: A cookbook for using the model-view controller user interface paradigm in smalltalk-80. J. Object Oriented Program. 1, 26–49 (1988)

[OTGW07] O'Neill, E., Thompson, P., Garzonis, S., Warr, A.: Reach Out and Touch: Using NFC and 2D Barcodes for Service Discovery and Interaction with Mobile Devices. In: LaMarca, A., Langheinrich, M., Truong, K.N. (eds.) Pervasive 2007. LNCS, vol. 4480, pp. 19–36. Springer, Heidelberg (2007)

[RCT06] Rieback, M.R., Crispo, B., Tanenbaum, A.S.: Is your cat infected with a computer virus? In: Fourth Annual IEEE International Conference on Pervasive Computing and Communications, PerCom 2006, pages 10, p. 179 (2006)

[Try79] Reenskaug, T.: Models - Views - Controllers (1979), `http://heim.ifi.uio.no/~trygver/1979/mvc-2/1979-12-MVC.pdf`

[WFGH99] Want, R., Fishkin, K.P., Gujar, A., Harrison, B.L.: Bridging physical and virtual worlds with electronic tags. In: Proceedings of the SIGCHI Conference on Human Factors in Computing Systems: The CHI is the Limit, CHI 1999, pp. 370–377. ACM, New York (1999)

Risk of Blind Controller Patterns for Multitag User Interfaces

(Transcript of Discussion)

Alf Zugenmaier

Munich University of Applied Sciences, Munich, Germany

I think I made mistakes with this presentation: one is that I actually think it might have something to do with the theme, and secondly, I don't really have a protocol to solve my problem. When I wrote this up I thought, ah I've got a problem here, and this is just an indicative submission, and by the time the workshop is there I'd have a nice protocol that can be destroyed in a discussion, and then creatively reconstructed. I didn't even get that far, and I'm very sorry, so it's more of a problem statement than an actual protocol solution.

Mike Burmester: Can you prove there is no protocol solution?

Reply: So far I have an indication of one person thinking hard occasionally did not come up with a solution. That is not a proof. It's not even a proof that I can't find a solution. It can just be an indication that I may have to work harder.

So what I want to talk about is multitag interfaces. That is an idea a colleague of mine at a previous company had. Just when multi-touch interfaces came out he said: "ah yes, we can also use multitag interfaces!" I'll say what they are in a second. I'll show some attacks that I came up with. And that, surprisingly, these can be phrased in a way of Alice Doesn't Live Here Anymore. I have some ideas for security solutions, but I don't think any of them are great. And then some conclusions.

I think we've seen this idea of tags. There is in ubiquitous computing this idea of having physical machine interactions with everyday object. What you often do is you tag them, either with a QR code that you would read with a camera on your mobile device - and they are used quite extensively, especially in Japan, where pretty much every billboard you see has a QR code, and you can use your mobile phone's camera to read it and find where it's pointing at. I've even seen some very nice artistic QR codes where this in the centre, even though this looks like the Japanese island Honshu, this actually is a QR code that will direct you to the US Red Cross website.

Frank Stajano: US?

Reply: Yes, they have for many different countries this kind of QR code, this is from the Red Cross, and they have this design pointing to various different websites. I've seen one for Hong Kong one for the US, that one is the US.

B. Christianson et al. (Eds.): Security Protocols 2011, LNCS 7114, pp. 156–169, 2011.

Mike Burmester: So actually you have this, you take a picture of it?

Reply: You take a picture of it, and then you try to detect those four dots, and then you find out what is the information that is encoded in the QR code.

Mike Burmester: So these are RFIDs so they will send back

Reply: No, this is a QR code.

Mike Burmester: Oh I'm sorry.

Reply: No that's a barcode. But RFIDs look like this, they're cheap. You can buy them in bulk, stick them wherever you want to. As example, in Japan they are used for "route-annai" so to would find out what route you should be taking. You can either use this QR code here, or you take your mobile, in Japan lots of mobiles are nowadays equipped with RFID tag readers, you point there and they go: "beep", and it would give you the route that you want to take. Again, it's redirecting your browser, so the information that you have here, is most of the time it's an http link, but you can also have just plaintext information. I think that one up here says Security Protocols Workshop, which is not a link. What you also often do is you just stick serial numbers on the code. This is for an industrial application.

Joseph Bonneau: Do you know off the top of your head how many bits you can fit on a standard QR code?

Reply: It all depends. As far as I understand, the more information you want to fit the smaller the pixels get.

Frank Stajano: This size is not fixed, you can have more pixels and have a bigger codes.

Reply: Yes, it's variable, so the more you try to put on there you the higher resolution you will have to have to be able to read it.

And so this is what my colleague came up with, this idea of multi-tagging a place where you have multiple active areas on the same poster. These tags contain links and information, so what you would to buy a movie ticket you'd say, OK, I want to go to this movie theatre, and this number of people, at that time, and now order the ticket. It is a quite simple idea, but the usability, and they tried this in the lab, is just phenomenal. People pretty much instantly understand that when given this thing, now you can buy the ticket by just holding it next to here, just like pressing the buttons. People just take seconds to pick up this idea, and they play around. They [my colleagues] built this as a platform, so it's like a widget toolkit that you have for windowing applications. They have widgets that, let's say, follow links, or you can display information directly. So you have a text widget, or a user input widget. User input means you could in theory use that for PIN entry, something you wouldn't like to do in public, just go and enter your PIN. And that's when I started worrying about the security of it, because when you start entering PINs it goes beyond pure entertainment and fun, it comes to something where, let's say you are putting something that is worth protecting with a PIN.

It's quite cool, you get haptic feedback so it vibrates a little when the tag is actually being read, so it's like pushing a button, you know when the interaction has happened. you don't even have to look at the display of your mobile anymore. Which again, when you think about the security implications, it's also a bit of a threat that, you can just do this without looking at your sort of secure back channel. You just use it because it's easy to do.

Bangdao Chen: Is it possible to tamper the attacks?

Reply: Exactly, that's where I'm getting at. So you see this, and it's really cool, you want to play with it. But as a security person you start thinking: how can I break this? What is the fun that can be had? And they [my colleagues] did loads of usability studies. Almost any question you can ask about the general usability of this, they have done studies on. And one of the things was that the usability of the static poster is better than if you have a mixed interface where, let's say, for setting the time when you want to go and see the movie you have to go and do a selection on the phone. So it is really preferable to have a poster like this. They also tried non-static posters so that, like in this projection situation, they project a poster, and you can change obviously then what is being displayed on the projection. They found that actually a static poster from a usability perspective works best. The users look at it, they understand what it is, and then they do things, while when it changes it gets too complicated for many users, suddenly things change and other things pop up.

As I said, they built this as a widget toolkit. It's using this standard model view controller approach where you put the model on where the application is running. That is some kind of backend server. You have display widgets, and controller widgets also on the mobile phone, and you have a physical interface where you can interact with a tag that is embedded in the physical interface.

Now we are coming to your idea of tampering, which is, the first idea was that you take a poster that says, buy now, on this active area, the NFC tag says, well this is a link that would be equivalent to the buy now button. Some attacker could come up and say, actually I have this nice icon that I would like to cut out, and glue on top of this. Now the icon says, information, but the action that you're going to present is going to be the buy now, so you probably are going to buy something even though you just wanted information.

Bangdao Chen: So what is the new threat here, if you have the ordinary barcode and go to the supermarket and you buy a product with a barcode, you scan the barcode, then someone can paste in your barcode on the package to the value of a different price. So what is the new threat if you introduce RFID?

Reply: One of the threats is that when you do this barcode scanning you are doing the scanning in a reasonably controlled environment by a reasonably trained or maybe not reasonably trained person, so the person who's doing the scanning can actually check what is happening. If you find, the supermarket finds out that there is too much fraud happening they will try to figure out how to stop it, that is by training their cashiers better. These interfaces are meant for the general public, and training the general public is much harder than training a few cashiers.

Mike Burmester: If you go to some supermarkets where there are no cashiers, in the States there are places where cashiers are disappearing, you're going too fast with barcodes

Reply: If there are no cashiers there's no reason for you to do that with barcodes, you just take something that's quite cheap, you scan it a couple of times, and you just put your expensive item between the cartons of milk and everything else just into your bag.

Mike Burmester: They weigh the thing that goes into the bag

Reply: Well if you do weight detection then this also may not work unless you figure out the exact weight of the item with barcodes that you have, that you've just put on.

Jonathan Anderson: The attack at the automated Sainsburys is that you have an expensive bottle of wine and a cheap bottle of wine, and they both weight exactly the same thing because they're the same amount of glass and the same amount of wine. However, that's mitigated because you can't buy wine at an automated thing without somebody coming and looking at it anyway.

Mike Burmester: But you can do it with other goods as well by detaching the code.

Jonathan Anderson: So is it fair to say that the real problem here is that that when you scan an NFC tag there is an implication of user intent, which doesn't have to be confirmed by the user, doing something here?

Frank Stajano: So in this case it looks like, if I understand correctly, the cut and paste is a cut and paste of the image on top of an existing tag, and this can't be any more harmful than what was already on the poster. So at worst it's just annoying you by making you buy something from that cinema, you can't, I mean, the attacker can't profit, unless they replace the tag with one that says, buy something from me, because all they can do is make you buy something from the cinema that is the cinema's profit.

Reply: Well whether it's possible to profit relies on the exact business model.

Omar Choudary: So why don't they replace the poster then?

Reply: They can replace the complete poster, but in this attack you actually are limited to only the actions that are on there, I mean, you could have something like sponsored links on there, or some kind of revenue sharing systems where you get something, higher percentage if more people use this than the other links.

Jonathan Anderson: Or maybe a cashier who's highly incentivised for people not to like the automated system, because then you'll be out of a job.

Sandy Clark: I also have the image of pranking like Banksy, designing all of this posters and icons and things that people will then think they're getting one thing, and they'll get a completely different image or an email or something that

Reply: Yes, something that, I have to admit I did it myself, not high tech, but we used to have in the university coffee vending machines, and you could have extra whitener, and extra sugar, and they also had a soup button, so the soup button we replaced by a label with extra caffeine, and at university that was a very popular option until people figured out that this was not actually a real flavour.

Mike Burmester: What happens here is actually there's something missing, because you can buy something you don't want to buy, that tag can say the simple fact saying you bought something, now your cell phone will recognise that that is not an action you wanted, you wanted information. I want to actually make it an interactive process, so that you are aware, you become aware that you're buying something, and that your phone will immediately tell you this is not an action somehow you expected.

James Malcolm: Yes, but most of the time you do want to

Sandy Clark: But you need something like a low power electric shock, you need some real disincentive to purchase, don't buy this hat.

Frank Stajano: But the attack could still work by making you buy something different from what you want, if you click on buy link, and it's actually buying something else.

Mike Burmester: But then if it then says, buy, and gives you the information of what you've bought, because that's supermarkets will

Bruce Christianson: But I think Alf's argument is that using the back channel in that way significantly reduces the usability of the technique.

Reply: Yes, the users were really happy not to have to look at this image, by not looking at the mobile phone display because that's a different media, so that's just, the usability was their big issue.

Sandy Clark: The other thing you could do is really quietly raise the price, charge the customer more than they think they're being charged, they won't pay attention anyway.

Reply: So we'll probably just increase the power of the electric shock.

Jonathan Anderson: Almost all of these matters would be improved if you were talking about things that are undoable. So whether it's, you know, I tapped the movie poster and printed the wrong ticket, then I could go to the cashier and say, hey what's going on, I tapped this movie and it gave me that one, she says, funny, you're the third person, you know, this morning. Then that's not so bad, or if you can undo a payment and say

Mike Burmester: Which is what happens in supermarkets, this is what happens in supermarkets when there are such mistakes.

Jonathan Anderson: Yes, you get home, and then you realise, hey, they charged me for two bottles of milk and I only bought one, and then you go back and they say, ah, fine we'll

Mike Burmester: So somebody takes responsibility, they just give you a free bottle, in the States you get a free bottle of wine.

Joseph Bonneau: Maybe another example though would be you see some poster that says, you know, cheap auto insurance, and then you scan the thing, and then the tag has been replaced so you go to a website of their competitor, or somebody else is doing a knock-off, and even if you realise it and go to what you're looking for, some percentage of people will just go to the thing and basically hijack their advertising.

Reply: Yes, so there's also this denial-of-service aspect with it, you replace the information button and say, buy now, and you want to buy something, you just get information, this is not worth it, and go and do it somewhere else.

Jonathan Anderson: Or you paste over something that says, don't touch, warning, mobile phone viruses, or something.

Reply: Test the newest mobile phone viruses.

Feng Hao: But this is quite a fundamental, difficult problem because it could be an attack or could be a feature, for example, if something is printed wrong on the poster instead of changing the whole poster you just attach a different tag, or you won't have the service.

Reply: Brilliant for the localisation of the poster, you know, you just want to change the name or language.

Mike Burmester: Yes, so if the user doesn't check the display how can the user actually tell the difference

Reply: Well that's exactly the problem.

Mike Burmester: What if you have a hash of the whole picture (laughter), you can check that no tampering has occurred.

Reply: Brilliant. But just look at the next thing, it's a standard man-in-the-middle attack. There we have alice.co.uk, and what the bad guy does, he zaps Alice, and puts in bob.com, puts the NFC tag here. Well we have to do some clever attachment there so it's not that obvious, then you combine with a cut and paste type attack, and then when you interact with the poster you end up at the bad guy's server. Then you can relay this. And this is especially nice when you have this PIN entry, because that's ideal for phishing, it is very, very difficult to determine that really you are not talking to the server that you want to be talking to. This is like following a random link in an email you've received only because the physical thing, people tend to have more trust in it. Phishing letters, like proper paper letters, signed by hand, have most likely a higher success rate, than one email that comes in telling you of another great business opportunity by just clicking on this link and entering all your bank details.

Omar Choudary: There may be one option to solve above, but I am sorry if I interrupted

Reply: Well I had some ideas, but I, none of them seemed to be really

Omar Choudary: I was thinking about the possibility that maybe the server, so you are saying that you are relaying information from the back of the server. The server could send you back like, I don't know, a certificate or something, saying, OK, if you retouch this, that means that the value for indicator should have this value, or this unique identifier, and then the phone can detect that it was actually touching a different identifier.

Reply: Well what's happening here in this phishing kind of setup, maybe this address is only very slightly changed.

Omar Choudary: No, I mean the unique identifier of the tag is a physical identifier.

Reply: But this my tag, the bad guy's tag.

Omar Choudary: Yes, so you can really identify the tag.

Reply: This is the bad guy answering, so the bad guy is saying, this is the tag that you should have been touching.

Omar Choudary: No, but you should, I need to communicate to the server, right, to get my product or whatever, to the good server, you are also communicating with the good server.

Reply: You're also communicating with the good server, but

Omar Choudary: So the good server, there maybe something encrypted that the bad guy can not modify, and that tells me the actual data that should be there

Reply: That would work in a walled garden approach, where there are only a very limited number of good servers. Where you know, you've vetted all your servers, and none of the servers that are vetted and have a certificate actually can be bad.

Omar Choudary: OK, why are we relaying the information to the good server then?

Reply: Because you actually want to see whether there is something, you know, you want to get a sort of similar user experience.

Bruce Christianson: You might be phishing to get a password or

Reply: Yes, or the

Omar Choudary: When you are trying to get the password or something, might give you some, I don't know, if the goal is to go out somewhere to the good server, then the good server can give me some hint, of which is the tag you should be touching

Reply: But how would you

Bruce Christianson: But how are you ever going to get that information.

Jonathan Anderson: That only works if you have like a client cert in your phone.

Mike Burmester: Sounds like all the PKI authentication bootstrapping in the client

Reply: But would a client cert work?

Jonathan Anderson: Well if in order to login to the server, you know, they send you

reply: But then that kills the phishing idea but not the kind of sitting in the middle and doing

Jonathan Anderson: Well once you can do reliable crypto between two end-points, then you can see the person in the middle, but that, you know, I'm not actually proposing a solution that involves everybody knowing about client certificates in everybody's phones.

Mike Burmester: So this is an active man-in-the-middle, so the relay, the man-in-the-middle changes?

Reply: Yes, can change things, but the proper server can't do anything.

Mike Burmester: If it alters the information and you cannot find a way of bypassing it? Relay attacks are difficult, where you don't change anything, but you change things, can't you actually, is this a Diffie-Hellman, they are authentic, you've got strong crypto.

Reply: But what do you use to bootstrap that strong crypto, it's the standard certificates that you get online from various

Mike Burmester: Well maybe the certificate, you have a server, one backend server, which is

Reply: Per poster, per application. So think of this, the poster, as the webpage that you see. It's not that there is one single server. It is not the walled garden approach, in that case it would work. If you have a walled garden you say, OK, there's only a hundred servers there, and I know all these people that put up the servers, they're good guys. Then you can say, OK, this went to one of the good servers. But if you assume the open model where anyone on the internet can put up a server that makes use of this certificate.

Mike Burmester: Well you can then restrict it to, I mean, at the beginning I asked you, do you have a proof that it is impossible, now you have a proof that it is impossible.

Reply: Well I kind of

Mike Burmester: No, if you actually allow the server, the backend server, at which all the trust is compromised, because that's effectively what you're saying, then you can prove that it can never be done.

Reply: Well it's exactly like

Mike Burmester: You have a negative result now. You can prove, if you allow now the possibility that your server is compromised, which effectively is the case, then you can prove that you can never do it. So either you have a trusted entity which, for which there is some kind of trust you can link to, or you don't. If you have the first one then there is a possibility that you can work out some kind of proof, it may not be practical, but nonetheless, but if that backend server, if the trust is completely lost, then no way do you unlose it (?), you need some kind of trust link, if that trust link is broken for good then you're finished.

Reply: But I was hoping that I can find a way of linking the poster, as I said, with a hash, to the server, so that you have

Mike Burmester: To a trusted server, not to a compromised server.

Reply: To whichever server, so you want to make sure that the poster that you're seeing, and the server that you're communicating with, are a pair, that they match.

Mike Burmester: And if they're both compromised?

Reply: If they are both corrupt then you're hoping that you will, well

Mike Burmester: You're finished, you're part of the, you're in adversarial territory, you're the only honest guy, everybody else, all the other trust links are broken.

Bruce Christianson: But you can't protect people against making bad choices, that's not an objective, the question is, are they making the choice they thought they were making. And most of the ways of verifying that involve changing some small number of bits changing hands over a second high integrity channel, which is like the back channel that you don't want to use for usability.

Reply: Yes. Well we have this, the classic confused deputy problem. You are seeing a certain view, which is the poster, and you have an idea of what is the model behind it, but what you are using is a controller that may be seeing a different view because the tags maybe changed, or the poster may be different, and you may even be interacting with a completely different model. And if you remember this confused deputy problem that you have with overlay for user interfaces that were not visible, so you were clicking on the button that was behind the overlay, when in fact the click was directed to a different application, this is also very much the same problem. But here we just have a physical user interface so there is not a tightly controlled access to, let's say, the operating system of the poster, because the operating system of the poster is just the ink and the paper, and it's much easier to, maybe easier to tamper with than a complex operating system where you have to find exploits that are not patched yet and all these things.

Jonathan Anderson: But maybe that's OK because you have, for some of the scenarios that you're talking about in bulk buying things like movie tickets, if the machine then prints out the wrong movie ticket you'll notice pretty quickly, and if it happens to three people in a row someone will come and change the poster, and say, oh this poster is defective. Or similarly, if you are looking for a route to a place on the subway and, oh, this is routing me to somewhere that is not the place I wanted to go, those things won't last very long.

Reply: Yes, they are not on a global scale, because it's a physical interface. You actually have to be there and do things, you can't just have global impact, unless you have phishing attack.

Frank Stajano: I think the thing that you were mentioning about the hashing and using a visual code and others, you can have a multichannel protocol where you have the radio on one hand, and the hash acquired by camera on the other hand, and so on, but the only purpose of a multichannel protocol is that you use some other channel which has an extra property, and the extra property that we want here is that the user actually checks what's seen. So if you had a channel where the user actually reads the text and verifies that that's just where they want to go, then maybe a multichannel protocol would solve that. But if what the user does is, OK, I'll go for the green button and click, whatever is on there, whatever, it doesn't matter what extra things are there if the point is that the user doesn't want to check them.

Reply: So I had this idea of trying to bind the tag and posters. The first idea was to tamper proof, you put holograms everywhere, and it makes it very expensive to actually mount any of these attacks. And that's an increase in cost, and who's verifying these tamper proof posters? It's people that are probably not trained in finding out all the weaknesses. It's a bit like trying to ask the user to verify that there's no skimming device on your ATM. How do they know that this is not an anti-skimming device, or what should the ATM look like if every month they change their interface. Of course if you have physical access control to the poster then the problem may even just go away, so you can imagine these kind of posters, for example, in control rooms of ...

Bruce Christianson: Nuclear power plants.

Reply: I was trying to avoid that example. And then you could use this as an interactive thing, because you assume that people going there, they might just as well on purpose do other things rather than trying to move around the images or doing any of these attacks. So as a user interface in that situation it may actually work well, and I've seen a similar approaches where the cashier has to say, it's this product, and it's this colour, and do multiple interactions with different barcodes just to get to a price. We could try what you said with a hash. So my idea was to have optical recognition of the user readable text tags, so that if as a user you read something, then the phone that you're holding next to it will use optical recognition, so it's not using multichannel but it's using the same channel, so you're binding those two channels together by making them the same. And of course, question is, how reliable is it? (1), how reliable is the text recognition, and (2) how reliable are you in reading the text tags themselves. And of course the usability might go down when you actually put proper multi-line links on an area where normally there would just be an i for information.

Mike Burmester: So one of the proposals to physically prevent forging currency comes to mind, so one of the proposals for the $100 bill to prevent forgery would be to have random little sort of metal sort of strings or threads, and then sort of digitally signed, scan them, and then digitally sign the, whatever the code gets, and that would be a way of sort of

Matt Blaze: But there are seals that work on the same technology as that.

Mike Burmester: And do you know who first proposed it, I thought it was Rivest but it was earlier, I forget his name, he worked for

Matt Blaze: Yes, Garcia.

Mike Burmester: Garcia. So we could actually do something like that I think to authenticate it in some way.

Reply: The whole poster you mean authenticate?

Mike Burmester: Yes, everything.

Reply: The problem there is then again that you have this semantic mismatch potentially. You have it signed but you still have to then verify that in fact what has been signed is what you want to interact with, or you could

Mike Burmester: So it's not the $100 bill case, it is

Reply: No, it's $100 bill, that's all you want to know, you don't have millions of different ones.

Bruce Christianson: It would be alright if all, if you knew all the poster publishers and their public keys, and that could be a problem.

Frank Stajano: Even in that case you could have, actually you could have something where the guy just doesn't read what's on the poster.

Mike Burmester: Whereas if he doesn't read

Mike Burmester: It's a genuine poster, but

Reply: Well it depends on if you could enforce that the posters are, well so far separate that if he doesn't read you can reasonably argue that it's his fault, rather than there were just two letters swapped around which

Frank Stajano: For example, if I am a company that is well-known for having a public key and so on and making posters, and then as a customer I just click on the green one to get the bottle of Coca Cola, and then they decide, OK, let's just charge 30 cents more for Coca Cola, and I still paid that, and I never noticed it.

Reply: Yes, that's your problem really.

Frank Stajano: But the user is going to still click regardless, they won't rescan the poster, once they've acquired the poster in their cognitive model, they will not re-parse it every time they

Reply: But if you're going to the supermarket when you buy the Coke, and they increase the price, you know, you have pretty much committed to it, unless at checkout time you

Omar Choudary: I think, coming back to Frank's statement earlier, this is a bit of an artificial problem I would say, because it's something we are trying to make ourselves, it's easily solved by the fact that, you know, you just, as a user just check whatever it is, click on the link, and then it's just another phishing problem, and the fact the you're spending 30p and not 60p, and if doesn't check that, he's a lazy user, he pays whatever he wants

Jonathan Anderson: So you're saying if we reduce it to phishing the world will be a better place. And we solved that so well. (laughter)

Bruce Christianson: We're saying there's a fine line between a security attack and very clever marketing.

Jonathan Anderson: Right, that's true.

Frank Stajano: So when we did the study on scammed victims, we said, after looking at fraudsters what can we look into next, and let's look at salesmen, because after all they're exactly the same as fraudsters, except that some of what they are doing is legal.

Reply: So we had these authentication discussions and I'm not convinced that authentication would solve things very well, because can the user understand what is being authenticated.

Mike Burmester: But if you didn't have authentication it would be even worse. It won't solve, you're right, because it's multi-dimensional, you are only by addressing one dimension you don't solve the problem, you need another dimension.

Reply: Yes, pretty much what you would have to authenticate is the user interface rather than the server.

Mike Burmester: No not rather, it's an "and", user interface and the server.

Reply: The server is reasonably easy to authenticate, we can do that like in the current internet

Mike Burmester: But you would have to do that because otherwise

Reply: But the user interface is the new dimension that you're running into.

Mike Burmester: You need both

Reply: Yes, and it would be nice in a walled garden approach, where you know everyone is good. I think we had some discussions, so I'm going to quickly wrap up now, so that coffee doesn't get too cold outside. If we use this in applications where the risk is very low, for example, just information provisioning, as you said, the idea of, you just use it on a map, and if instead of showing King's College Chapel it shows the caf across the road, what is the real damage of that, the risk is actually quite low. So you could have it for information provisioning, or just reservations where you say, redo this ticketing application for the cinema, until you actually go through the turn-style to get into the cinema no payment has been made. So, you know, what would be the damage if you bought the wrong ticket, or you didn't get a ticket. It's a denial-of-service thing.

Matt Blaze: But I think there's a risk here in designing a protocol in which we're making that many assumptions about the security properties of the application. Right, this is, well, there's no harm if this attack happens, because of the application we happen to be envisioning, and then somebody comes up with an application of it in which that would be quite harmful.

Reply: Exactly, it would probably slowly push the boundaries of, where instead of being good because it's the i on this map application, nothing bad is happening, so we might want to use it for buying soft drinks, OK, soft drinks is fine. Eventually you end up with a banking application.

Joseph Bonneau: So I think you should modify your statement to say, not that attacks won't be harmful, but they won't be scalable, because it's hard to imagine a case where you can copy and paste a different tag onto millions of posters simultaneously without a huge amount of manpower, which you can do on the web in some cases.

Reply: So definitely we have, if we have something with an interactive commitment, it has to be local, immediately we should see a physical effect. If all these things happen then you can't scale, that's equivalent to ATM fraud. I mean, that also has to be local, the immediate effect and there's a physical effect of it if. Because now you can skim cards and transfer everything somewhere else, you can get the physical effect removed, and the locality or immediateness of it also goes away, that makes ATM fraud bad. Where before if you put up an ATM, it would just eat your card, and you immediately knew something was going wrong. So there, if you have all interactions on these interfaces that follow this approach, get the ticket, it says the wrong thing, and there you immediately know something is wrong. So you can fix it, and they're not going to do you harm.

Jonathan Anderson: So you said at the beginning that the studies that you guys have done found that the usability properties were poor if you required users to look at the screen after doing something. But as long as something happens, and if you're looking for information about how to get from A to B then you are going to look at the screen, as long as something happens every time you use the NFC thing, then the user, one way or another, can evaluate whether that's the thing they expected, did the parking meter time go up.

Reply: Right, or did I actually manage to get into the cinema now.

Jonathan Anderson: And so it is in fact a multichannel protocol.

Reply: Yes, well this is if you limit yourself to interactions with these kind of properties that let us see what's going to happen, so like there's transferring money from one account to another, that's going to be much more difficult to

Jonathan Anderson: It's probably a bad idea to build a banking app that will transfer money into another country just by scanning the QR code, scan here to transfer me £10,000.

Joseph Bonneau: The worst application though which you mentioned is the, scan this and we will donate £5 to relief for Japan, which is also one of the worst cases for phishing on line I guess because people have no way of telling if they got phished or not.

Reply: I mean, that was just directed to the website where then enter stuff, it wouldn't automatically donate. But I think in terms of, well if you think of the marketing impact, it would be actually brilliant, put up this poster saying, if you scan here you're going to donate £5, would be, in terms of the marketing effect, and reduce the activation you need from your customer, just scan that and it's done, you don't have to enter your credit card details or all this stuff, would be brilliant for that side. But from the security perspective I would rather not have it work that way.

Joseph Bonneau: So they've already figured that out with the, after I guess Haiti, the text message to donate became extremely popular, and also there were a large number of fake premium numbers that were put out there that people texted, and they saw money deducted from their account, and that's the only verification you have.

Jonathan Anderson: And you definitely donated $10 to something.

Reply: OK, I think, here are the conclusions, I think we came to the same conclusions pretty much in this discussion. Thank you very much.

How to Sync with Alice

Feng Hao[1] and Peter Y.A. Ryan[2,⋆]

[1] School of Computing Science
Newcastle University, Newcastle, UK
feng.hao@ncl.ac.uk
[2] Faculty of Science
University of Luxembourg, Luxembourg
peter.ryan@uni.lu

Abstract. This paper explains the sync problem and compares solutions in Firefox 4 and Chrome 10. The sync problem studies how to securely synchronize data across different computers. Google has added a built-in sync function in Chrome 10, which uses a user-defined password to encrypt bookmarks, history, cached passwords etc. However, due to the low-entropy of passwords, the encryption is inherently weak – anyone with access to the ciphertext can easily uncover the key (and hence disclose the plaintext). Mozilla used to have a very similar sync solution in Firefox 3.5, but since Firefox 4 it has made a complete change of how sync works in the browser. The new solution is based on a security protocol called J-PAKE, which is a balanced Password Authenticated Key Exchange (PAKE) protocol. To our best knowledge, this is the first large-scale deployment of the PAKE technology. Since PAKE does not require a PKI, it has compelling advantages than PKI-based schemes such as SSL/TLS in many applications. However, in the past decade, deploying PAKE has been greatly hampered by the patent and other issues. With the rise of patent-free solutions such as J-PAKE and also that the EKE patent will soon expire in October, 2011, we believe the PAKE technology will be more widely adopted in the near future.

1 Introduction

The past two decades have seen the gradual evolution of a computer. A computer used to be a luxury, but now it is a necessity; it used to be bulky and fixed at one location, but with the rise of smartphones and tablets, it is becoming smaller and more mobile; it used to store data locally, but now data storage is moving to the cloud (which can be accessed anywhere from the Internet).

One trend from this evolution is that an individual now tends to own several computing devices. At home, he may use a good-performance desktop PC for entertainment; on the road, he may use a smart phone to read news and check emails; at meetings, he may use a laptop or a tablet to deliver a presentation. The possession of multiple computers naturally raises a practical problem: how to keep data in sync across different platforms?

⋆ Sponsored in part by the FNR Luxembourg.

B. Christianson et al. (Eds.): Security Protocols 2011, LNCS 7114, pp. 170–178, 2011.

Dropbox offers a popular solution. According to the report, it has a population of 25 million users worldwide [3]. To set up a sync account, the user needs to provide a username/password. Once installed, the software will centrally store the user's files on the company's servers, automatically tracks the changes, and synchronizes the changes across the user's computers. The sync process happens in the background and is transparent to users.

However, there is a serious lack of privacy protection in the Dropbox solution. As Dropbox states its security policy on its website [3], "Dropbox employees are prohibited from viewing the content of files you store in your Dropbox account, and are only permitted to view file metadata (e.g., file names and locations)." Meanwhile, the company also acknowledges: there are a small number of employees who must be able to access the files whenever necessary. Although this is stated by the company policy as "rare exception, not the rule", the security is hardly reassuring. (If an insider attacker leaks users' personal files to the government, the users will probably never know.)

Browser vendors face exactly the same problem. Every browser keeps a user profile, which includes history, bookmarks, cached passwords and so on. The user profile used to be stored locally, but it has become increasingly necessary to store it remotely (in a "cloud "), and synchronize the profile across the user's computers. This can significantly improve the usability and productivity. For example, if a user buys a brand new laptop, after sync he will be able to instantly re-use the same bookmarks, history etc that were previously accumulated on another laptop. This is quite convenient.

As browser vendors recognize, security is a key issue. The user profile contains security-sensitive information – for example, it may contain passwords for on-line banking or other accounts. If the data is stored on the vendor's "cloud" and the vendor can read data, users must completely trust the vendor (just as in Dropbox) not to misuse it. But, the problem goes deeper than the mere trust. If the vendor has ready access to all the user's on-line account passwords in the cloud, what are the legal implications if the user accounts are compromised? How can the vendor establishes the public confidence that it did not leak any user's passwords nor misuse them?

The right solution seems to have an end-to-end encryption between the two sync computers. All data between the computers is encrypted. The user is the sole holder of his own encryption key; no one else is able to read data – not even the cloud provider. Both Mozilla Firefox and Google Chrome aim to provide such a solution. In the following sections, we explain their solutions in detail. The same sync design in the browser is instrumental and can be generally applied to many other applications (e.g., to address the security loophole in Dropbox).

2 Background

In this section, we briefly explain the Password Authenticated Key Exchange (PAKE) technology in general and the J-PAKE protocol in particular. They are relevant to solving the sync problem.

2.1 Password Authenticated Key Exchange

Password Authenticated Key Exchange (PAKE) is a foundational building block for a wide range of security applications. This technique allows establishing secure communication between two parties solely based on a shared password without requiring a Public Key Infrastructure (PKI). A PAKE protocol shall fulfill the following security requirements:

1. **Off-line dictionary attack resistance** – It does not leak any information that allows a passive/active attacker to perform off-line exhaustive search of the password.
2. **Forward secrecy** – It produces session keys that remain secure even when the password is later disclosed.
3. **Known-session security** – It prevents a disclosed session from affecting the security of other established session keys.
4. **On-line dictionary attack resistance** – It limits an active attacker to test only one password per protocol execution.

A secure PAKE protocol has several compelling advantages over PKI-based schemes such as SSL/TLS. First, it does not require a PKI, which is particularly expensive to set up and to maintain. Second, it allows zero-knowledge verification of a password: in other words, the user can prove to the other party the knowledge of a shared password without revealing it. Since the password is never disclosed to the other party (unlike in HTTPS), a PAKE protocol is naturally resistant to phishing attacks.

The first PAKE protocol was called the Encrypted Key Exchange (EKE), designed by Bellovin and Merrit in 1992 [5]. Subsequently in 1996, Jablon proposed another solution called Simple Password Exponential Key Exchange (SPEKE) [7]. Many other PAKE protocols were proposed. In 2000, IEEE P1363.2 formed a working group to study all available PAKE protocols and to select secure ones for standardization. However, in 2008, the project ran out of the maximum eight years; no concrete conclusion seemed to be made.

Two hurdles emerged during the standardization process. First, patent was a big issue. Many PAKE protocols were patented. In particular, EKE was patented by Lucent Technologies [6], SPEKE by Phoenix Technologies [8], and SRP by Stanford University [4]. Second, these protocols were found vulnerable. EKE was reported to leak partial information about the password, hence failing to satisfy the first requirement [9]. SPEKE was found to allow an active attacker to test multiple passwords in one protocol execution, therefore it does not fulfill the fourth requirement [11]. Similarly, the SRP does not satisfy the fourth requirement, as explained in [12]. None of these protocols have security proofs.

2.2 J-PAKE

It became clear in 2008 that the PAKE problem was still unsolved. In the same year, Hao and Ryan proposed a new PAKE protocol, called Password Authenticated Key Exchange by Juggling (J-PAKE) [1,2]. The protocol follows a completely different approach from past schemes. It works as follows. Let G denote a subgroup of Z_p^* with prime order q, and g be a generator in G. Let s be a shared password between Alice and Bob, and $s \neq 0$ for any non-empty password. The value of s is assumed to be within $[1, q-1]$. Alice selects two secrets at random: $x_1 \in_R [0, q-1]$ and $x_2 \in_R [1, q-1]$. Similarly, Bob selects $x_3 \in_R [0, q-1]$ and $x_4 \in_R [1, q-1]$.

Round 1. *Alice sends out g^{x_1}, g^{x_2} and knowledge proofs for x_1 and x_2. Similarly, Bob sends out g^{x_3}, g^{x_4} and knowledge proofs for x_3 and x_4.*

The above communication can be completed in one round as neither party depends on the other. When this round finishes, Alice and Bob verify the received knowledge proofs, and also check $g^{x_2}, g^{x_4} \neq 1$.

Round 2. *Alice sends out $\mathcal{A} = g^{(x_1+x_3+x_4)\cdot x_2 \cdot s}$ and a knowledge proof for $x_2 \cdot s$. Similarly, Bob sends out $\mathcal{B} = g^{(x_1+x_2+x_3)\cdot x_4 \cdot s}$ and a knowledge proof for $x_4 \cdot s$.*

When this round finishes, Alice computes $K = (\mathcal{B}/g^{x_2 \cdot x_4 \cdot s})^{x_2} = g^{(x_1+x_3)\cdot x_2 \cdot x_4 \cdot s}$, and Bob computes $K = (\mathcal{A}/g^{x_2 \cdot x_4 \cdot s})^{x_4} = g^{(x_1+x_3)\cdot x_2 \cdot x_4 \cdot s}$. With the same keying material K, a session key can be derived $\kappa = H(K)$, where H is a hash function. Alice and Bob will subsequently perform explicit key confirmation as described in [1]. In the protocol, the knowledge proof can be realized by using, for example, Schnorr signature. Overall, the J-PAKE protocol has been proved to fulfill all the four security requirements. In addition, the protocol is unpatented. The J-PAKE protocol and security proofs have been available on the IEEE P1363.2 website[1] for public review for over three years; no attacks have been found.

3 Sync Solutions in Browsers

In this section, we will explain how major browser vendors try to tackle the sync problem. In particular, Firefox 4 presents an interesting case study as it is the first browser to adopt the PAKE technology in the sync design.

3.1 Overview

Sync has become an important feature for a modern browser. With the exception of IE 9, new releases of browsers generally have built-in support for sync (see Table 1). In the following sections, we will focus on comparing sync in Firefox 4 and Chrome 10, as their solutions are representative.

3.2 Chrome Sync

Chrome 10 provides a straightforward sync design, based on using a password as the encryption key. Setting up sync in Chrome 10 is almost zero effort – as long as you have an Gmail account. The user can then configure what to sync. By default, that is everything: apps, auto-fill, bookmarks, extensions, preferences, themes and passwords (Figure 1). The browser offers two options to encrypt the sync data: re-using the Gmail password (default) or choosing a new password (Figure 2).

[1] http://grouper.ieee.org/groups/1363/Research/contributions/hao-ryan-2008.pdf

Table 1. Overview of Sync solutions in browsers

Browser	Release date	Built-in	Sync-key	Price
Firefox 4	Mar, 2011	Yes	128-bit	Free
Chrome 10	Mar, 2011	Yes	Password	Free
IE 9	Mar, 2011	No	–	–
Opera 11	Dec, 2010	Yes	None	Free
Safari 5	Jun, 2010	Yes	None	$99 per year

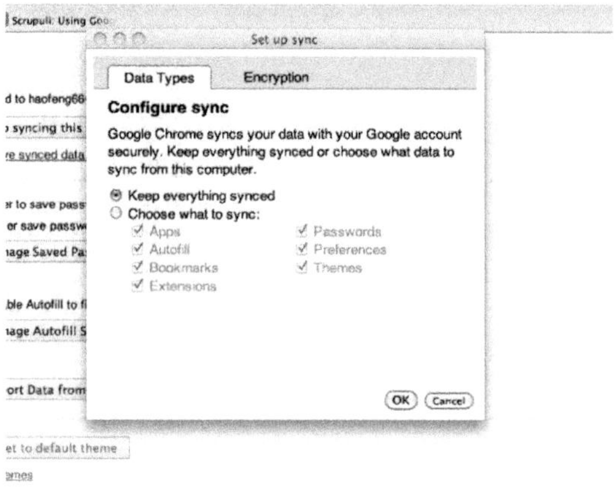

Fig. 1. Confgure sync in Chrome 10

However, Google's solution provides virtually no guarantee of privacy. In both options, the encryption key is directly derived from a password. Due to the human's inability to remember cryptographically strong secrets, a password normally only has 20-30 bits entropy. Thus, although Google encrypts the sync data in its cloud, the encryption key is inherently weak. Anyone who has access to the ciphertext can readily break the key by exhaustive search and fully uncover the sync data.

3.3 Firefox Sync

The previous version of Firefox (3.5) used to have a similar sync solution. To set up sync, the user needed to remember two passwords: one for the sync account, and the other for encrypting data. The encryption works basically the same as in Chrome 10 – using a user-defined password as the encryption key. One subtle difference is that in Chrome 10, the default option is to re-use the Gmail password as the key, while in Firefox 3.5, the default is to let the user define a new password.

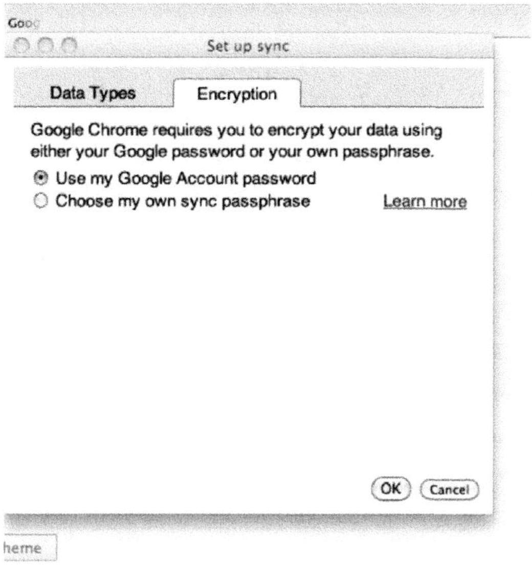

Fig. 2. Encryption options in Chrome 10 sync

Because the encryption was inherently weak, Firefox 3.5 had the same problem as in Chrome 10. Similar to Google, Mozilla was at a privileged position: it was able to read all the user's data despite that the data was encrypted (by a password). In recognition of this problem, the company has been trying to find a solution.

From Firefox 4 beta 8 (released in Dec, 2010), Mozilla made a complete change in the sync mechanism. The new solution adopts the Password Authenticated Key Exchange technology – in particular, it chose J-PAKE. Figure 3 shows an overall diagram about how sync works in Firefox 4. First, the browser generates a random 128-bit key, called the sync-key. This sync-key is never sent to Mozilla. It is used to encrypt the browser bookmarks, history, cached passwords etc. Only the encrypted data is stored at the Mozilla "cloud". Alternative servers can be used, and one can even set up his own server.

To set up sync in Firefox 4 is relatively straightforward. First, one needs to configure what data to sync (see Figure 4). Second, the J-PAKE algorithm is used to securely transfer the sync-key between different Firefox clients. (Otherwise, the user will need to manually type in the sync-key, which can prove tedious especially on a mobile phone.) Using the J-PAKE protocol, the user reads a 12-character secret code from the new device (as shown in Figure 5) and enters it to the host device. Since the secret code is exclusively shared by the two devices, a secure end-to-end channel can be created and through this channel, the sync-key is transferred to the new device.

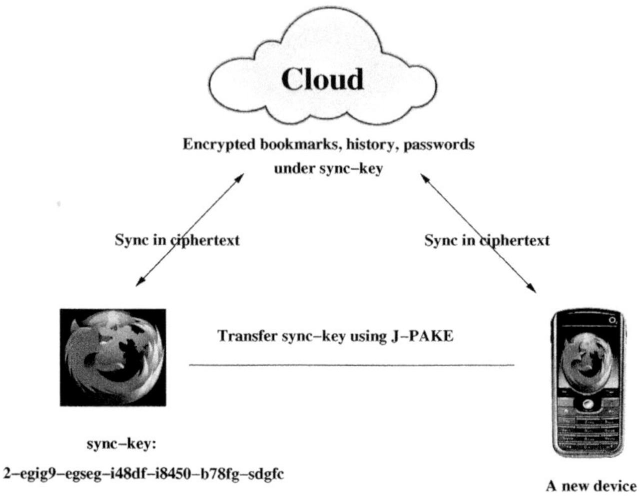

Fig. 3. Sync mechanism in Firefox 4 (beta 8 and later)

4 Discussion

4.1 Comparison between Firefox and Chrome

Between the two sync mechanisms, which is more appealing to users? Obviously, the Firefox sync is more secure than the Chrome's. On the other hand, many average users find the Chrome sync attractive as it is so simple and easy. It is yet unclear to what extent do users care about their privacy or whether they care enough to make a switch. In the Mozilla solution, users are in control of their data. The data is encrypted by a cryptographically strong key and only the user has access to the key. The use of J-PAKE facilitates the transfer of the sync key between devices without compromising security. However, the crypto process is not easy to understand by the common people. To many users, the sync setup in Firefox 4 happens almost like a magic. Will the Mozilla's efforts in honoring the user privacy pay out in the long term? Perhaps, only time can tell.

4.2 Outlook of PAKE

To our best knowledge, the use of J-PAKE in Firefox 4 is the first large-scale deployment of the PAKE technology. The adoption of PAKE had been greatly hampered in the past due to patent and technical issues. The obstacles are disappearing. With the rise of J-PAKE as a patent-free solution and also that the EKE patent will soon expire in October 2011 (see [6]), it looks likely that the PAKE technology will be more widely adopted in the future.

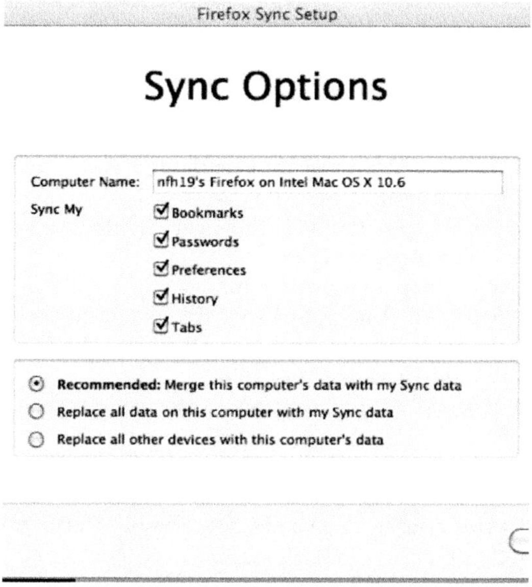

Fig. 4. Sync options in Firefox 4

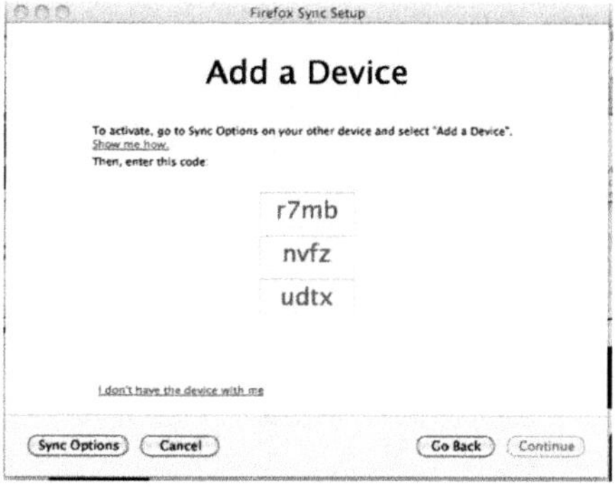

Fig. 5. Add a new sync device in Firefox 4

5 Conclusion

The Password Authenticated Key Exchange (PAKE) protocol is a useful cryptographic technique. In this paper, we explained how PAKE could be applied to tackle the sync problem. In particular, we described how sync works in Firefox 4, which is the first browser to adopt the PAKE technology. After over twenty years of intensive research in PAKE, the field finally starts to see its use in a large-scale practical deployment.

References

1. Hao, F., Ryan, P.: J-PAKE: Authenticated Key Exchange Without PKI. In: Gavrilova, M.L., Tan, C.J.K., Moreno, E.D. (eds.) Transactions on Computational Science XI, Part II. LNCS, vol. 6480, pp. 192–206. Springer, Heidelberg (2010)
2. Hao, F., Ryan, P.Y.A.: Password Authenticated Key Exchange by Juggling. In: Christianson, B., Malcolm, J.A., Matyas, V., Roe, M. (eds.) Security Protocols 2008. LNCS, vol. 6615, pp. 159–171. Springer, Heidelberg (2011)
3. Dropbox, `http://www.dropbox.com`
4. Official SRP, `http://srp.stanford.edu/`
5. Bellovin, S., Merritt, M.: Encrypted Key Exchange: password-based protocols secure against dictionary attacks. In: Proceedings of the IEEE Symposium on Research in Security and Privacy (May 1992)
6. Bellovin, S., Merritt, M.: Cryptographic protocol for secure communications, U.S. Patent 5,241,599
7. Jablon, D.: Strong password-only authenticated key exchange. ACM Computer Communications Review 26(5), 5–26 (1996)
8. Jablon, D.: Cryptographic methods for remote authentication, U.S. Patent 6,226,383 (March 1997)
9. Jaspan, B.: Dual-workfactor Encrypted Key Exchange: efficiently preventing password chaining and dictionary attacks. In: Proceedings of the Sixth Annual USENIX Security Conference, pp. 43–50 (July 1996)
10. IEEE P1363.2 Working Group, P1363.2: Standard Specifications for Password-Based Public-Key Cryptographic Techniques, draft available at `http://grouper.ieee.org/groups/1363/`
11. Zhang, M.: Analysis of the SPEKE password-authenticated key exchange protocol. IEEE Communications Letters 8(1), 63–65 (2004)
12. Hao, F.: On small subgroup non-confinement attacks. In: Proceedings of the 10th IEEE International Conference on Computer and Information Technology, CIT 2010, pp. 1022–1025 (2010)

How to Sync with Alice
(Transcript of Discussion)

Feng Hao

Newcastle University, Newcastle, UK

This talk is about How to Sync with Alice. It is joint work with Peter Ryan. Life used to be simple; you have only one desktop computer. Then you have laptop, which is more convenient, and is becoming inexpensive. In the past five years you've seen the rise of smartphones, and tablets. So the computer has been evolving. It used to be bulky, and fixed at a permanent location, but now it is mobile and can be anywhere. A person commonly owns more than one computer.

Back to the theme of this workshop, Alice Doesn't Live Here Anymore. First, who is Alice? Alice could be a PC, a smartphone, or a tablet, or anything with a chip. Her location is not important, because she can be anywhere. Identity is not important whether it is PC, laptop, or mobile phone. The device is only a platform for you to access Internet. With the cloud computing you no longer store data on the laptop; you store data in the cloud.

For these computing devices, laptop, Android, iPhone, iPad, Kindle, they all have a browser. The browser is a window for the user to interact with the Internet. One important feature of browsers is syncing the personal profile. Here, we're not talking about syncing the bookmarks; we are talking about syncing the whole personal profile. People may have different opinions about privacy of bookmarks. Some view the bookmarks as not very security sensitive. But we are talking about the personal profile which includes the cached passwords. So, data in the profile is clearly security sensitive. Since the browser saves data in the cloud, the question is: is this safe?

For that we need to first look at the trust in the cloud. Since you store data in the cloud, you have to trust the availability of data. But other than that we don't really trust cloud for confidentiality, and we don't trust it for integrity. Therefore, we need security protocols to address those issues.

Different browsers have different solutions. We have the latest versions of browsers released this year. For example, Firefox 4 was released in March this year. It has a built-in sync function, and the function is based on a protocol that Peter Ryan and I proposed in this workshop three years ago. I am going to explain that in more detail a bit later. Chrome 10 was also released in March this year, and we have IE9 released in the same month. It is a full-fledged war between all the major browser vendors. Opera also has added its own built-in sync, and the mechanism is quite similar to the one of Chrome. As for Safari, it has built-in sync, but it is not free. It costs you $99 a year. There are some rumours saying that it is going to be free but it has not happened yet. So at the

B. Christianson et al. (Eds.): Security Protocols 2011, LNCS 7114, pp. 179–188, 2011.

moment, Firefox and Chrome are the two major browsers that have full support for sync, so I will focus on comparing these two browsers.

Let's look at Chrome first. How to set up sync? First, you choose what to sync. By default that is everything, including apps, auto-fill, bookmarks, extensions, passwords. One thing I'd like to highlight is that previously there were no passwords, and previously there was no encryption in Chrome. To sync your data, you just need to have a gmail account, and as long as you login to your gmail everything is automatically synced. But, you don't have any encryption. In Chrome 10 Google realised that it is quite a useful feature to synchronise your passwords, so they added "passwords". Suddenly, security becomes crucial. You must add encryption to protect the data.

For encryption, we have a standard algorithm. However, the difficult part is how to manage the encryption key. In Chrome there are two ways to derive the key. The first one, the default choice, is to use a gmail password. You devise a key from it.

Matt Blaze: In the application you're talking about, Chrome is a browser, not the operating system?

Reply: It's the browser.

The first option is to reuse the gmail password. The second option is that you choose a different password. Let's look at each option. If you use the option one, which is default, Google knows your gmail password, so it knows your key. In the second option, the user chooses a new password. But remember that a human is incapable to choose a strong password. The best the human can do is choose probably a 10 character password, but for proper encryption you really need about 40 characters. So the encryption key is inherently weak. Anyone who gets ciphertext can brute-force the key.

And let's look at Firefox. Firefox used to have a sync solution, which is the same as Chrome 10. Firefox realised the sync problem about three or four years ago so they started working on this. The initial solution was an add-on to Firefox 3.5 released about two years ago, and it was very similar to Chrome 10. Basically it uses a password, and generates an encryption key based on the password. There are two passwords, one is for a sync account, and the other one is for encrypting sync data. This is essentially the same as what currently Chrome 10 has been doing. The only difference is that in Chrome, the default is using the gmail password, but in Firefox the default is to choose a new password. Most users will choose the same password anyway.

Frank Stajano: So in the Chrome the gmail password is used for gmail even if you don't do this sync. In the other one, in the Firefox, what's the use of the account password?

Reply: That is to set up a sync account with Mozilla. For Chrome, many users already have a gmail password, but if they don't, they will need to set up a gmail account. With Mozilla you also need an account, which is common for all the browsers.

Chrome's default is to use a gmail password, and in the old Firefox the default is to choose a new password. But Firefox realised it is a problem: it requires the users to completely trust Mozilla. In principle, because the encryption key is weak, so you have to trust that Mozilla doesn't read your data, doesn't modify your data, and that is the kind of an assumption which makes Mozilla developers feel uncomfortable. They don't want to be in such a privileged position.

Mozilla did investigate that problem, and then made a dramatic change in sync since Firefox 4 beta 8, which was released in December last year. Actually Mozilla had worked on this problem for over a year, and in December they made a switch to the new mechanism. And their solution is based on a technique called Password Authenticated Key Exchange, and in particular, Mozilla chose J-PAKE, which was first proposed at this workshop. One nice thing about Mozilla is that they made the discussion about the whole process open. So if anyone wants to know why they choose J-PAKE, it is all on their website. And they have regular meetings so for anyone who wants to know what's going on, they can phone into the meetings. The whole process is quite transparent.

The Password Authenticated Key Exchange by Juggling – I'm not going through the technical details of this protocol, but basically what this protocol does is two things. We have Alice and Bob. We don't have PKI, and we don't have any trusted third party. What's in common is that Alice and Bob have a password, a low entropy secret. The protocol does two things: the first is zero knowledge proof of the password, so if you are talking to a phishing website, and you prove that you know the password, but if the other party is a phishing website, you don't lose the password. And the second thing it does is authenticated key exchange. If the other party has the same password, then you will be able to establish a strong crypto key. So essentially you establish a high entropy session key based on a low entropy secret. It sounds a bit mind-boggling, and something impossible, but it is possible. The reason is that the two parties have the password, and you need to make a commitment that proves what password you have, so if you make the wrong commitment, the protocol will fail, and you get the mere information that the passwords are different. That's all. You don't learn the other party's password.

Let's see how this technique can fit into Firefox. So we have a desktop here. If you set up a sync account, it will generate a sync key, which is a 128-bit key, and all the data, including the bookmarks, history, passwords, is all encrypted by that key. The cipher-text is stored in the cloud. The sync key is cached at client so is never sent to Mozilla. You can set up your own cloud, basically a server, if you don't trust Mozilla cloud. But it doesn't make any difference because all the data is encrypted, and the encryption key is controlled by the client. So this is all known knowledge. The challenging part as it turns out is how do you actually transfer this encryption key to a new device. One trivial way is that you take a mobile phone and you enter the key into your mobile. But this was considered unacceptable to the users, because the mobile phone has a small screen, and it is tedious to enter like a 128-bit character string, and from the usability point of view is unacceptable. So they decided to use J-PAKE to transfer the key. Some people may ask why not use a Bluetooth so the transmission is local. But not every device has Bluetooth, however, all devices have Internet access, so you can always connect to another device through the Internet, through the cloud, and you need an end-to-end encryption channel. You only trust the two ends, and you don't trust anything in-between.

How does it work in Firefox? First you choose what to sync, and it's basically the same as in Chrome. Next you choose to add a new device. Suppose you already have a desktop, and you just bought a new laptop. Now you want to sync it with the existing desktop so that you will have the same bookmarks and history. What you need to do is two steps. First, from the new device there is a function called generate a code. You click that function on your laptop, it will generate a 12-character code. You will take that code, go to your existing desktop, and enter the code to your browser. It's a 12-character code, so it's not that bad to enter to the browser. Now, the sync has finished. It feels like magic, and the process is transparent to the user. As we can see, Password Authenticated Key Exchange is a really useful technique.

And I'm going to briefly review this research area. Basically there are two types of PAKE, one type is balanced, another one is augmented. The balanced like EKE, SPEKE, J-PAKE, and augmented like SRP.

Omar Choudary: So it seems to me that what you're trying to say is that, OK, it's hard to type into the phone, but let's type now into PC in order to get that done.

Reply: Yes.

Omar Choudary: But what about in the case where in five years time the other computer is actually my phone. Now I'm, I still need to type into the phone?

Reply: That's correct. You can only do the best you can. If you have two phones, and you have to enter the code to one phone.

Omar Choudary: And so then I can just enter the key hash.

Jonathan Anderson: I don't think you mean hash the sync key?

Bruce Christianson: In five years time the phone will project a holographic keyboard.

Reply: But the point is that the user is not going to enter the crypto key to the mobile phone keyboard.

Bruce Christianson: Why couldn't you acquire a visual code from one phone to the other? All phones have a camera.

Reply: You could, but I think it's not a general solution because you rely a lot on facilities on the phone, and in this case we want to minimise assumptions. The only assumption we have is that the phone can connect to the internet. That's all.

Omar Choudary: Well the simple approach that you're using is that the initial PC is always a computer, but even today, OK, not in five years time, maybe your initial computer is actually the phone, so there is still a problem by entering a long string of characters.

Reply: In that case you have two mobile phones that you want to sync together. Of course you need to enter one, but the point of using the PAKE technology is that you don't have to enter 128-bit code, you just enter a short code.

Omar Choudary: But 128-bit is like 16 characters, which is not that long.

Alf Zugenmaier: But you can't enter those 16 sixteen characters, especially not on a mobile phone keyboard, because you run out of characters that you want to distinguish.

Joseph Bonneau: There's about 20 characters that you do a 64-bit.

Omar Choudary: It's 16 characters, is exactly what Google is using, and it's numbers and letters.

Bruce Christianson: Yes, but letters are a pain on a mobile phone.

Sjouke Mauw: The software can do it automatically.

Omar Choudary: But that is based on the fact that I have a desktop. That's my problem.

Alf Zugenmaier: And the other thing is, if you say 16 characters then you have to enter 12 plus press some other symbol.

Omar Choudary: Yes, so that's losing four, that's the other thing you're doing basically.

Alf Zugenmaier: On the telephone you're asking for digits.

Reply: So you can see there's actually more than digits, there are letters here too.

Omar Choudary: Yes, because everything is alphanumeric.

Reply: Yes, they don't want to go like capital letters, small letters, because that will be a pain for the user.

Joseph Bonneau: You can do bit 64 slightly better than, you know, 16 characters is a little short.

Reply: OK, so we have two types of PAKE, balanced and augmented. The only difference lies when the server is compromised. In general the PAKE is a practically very useful technique, and it has a wide range of applications. One particularly attractive aspect is that it takes usability into account because you accept that a user can only use short passwords. But you can bootstrap that to a strong key, and also you don't require a PKI.

A natural question is, why PAKE hasn't been more widely used. Let's briefly review the development. In 1992, the first PAKE solution was proposed by Steven

Bellovin and Michael Merritt, and in 1996 there was another solution called SPEKE proposed by Jablon, and also SRP proposed by Tom Wu in 1998, and many solutions proposed around 2000. Probably there were a few hundred papers on the subject. So people were optimistic in 2000. They thought, the problem is solved. We have so many papers, and how difficult could that be just to select one paper which is good and let's standardise it. That's what IEEE did in 2000. They got a working group, and reviewed all the techniques, and then they tried to standardise one. The initial project was four years. In 2004 they couldn't reach any conclusions, so they extended their project by one year, and every year they extended the project, and finally in 2008 the project ran out of maximum eight years. Eight years is a limit for standardising technique project. If you couldn't standardise a technique within eight years then there's probably something wrong.

So what is wrong? Actually there are two problems. The first problem is the patent. Unfortunately, a lot of techniques are patented like EKE by Lucent, SPEKE by Phoenix, SRP patented by Stanford, and the companies are usually not happy to clarify the patent. They want to make it as fuzzy, as muddy as possible. It's in the best commercial interest. And the second problem is technical. All these techniques have various flaws, and they're subject to different kinds of attacks, and that is quite problematic for a standard. If you have a standard then it needs to be resistant to attacks.

Matt Blaze: So if I recall, the EKE patent is quite broad and it covers all EKEs practically? It should be running out soon.

Reply: Yes, it runs out next year, and we will see more deployment of PAKE once EKE has run out of patent. In 2008 we proposed a technique called J-PAKE which solves this problem, motivated by the belief that we think the problem was unsolved. We used a completely different approach from all past solutions. And the core part in our solution actually comes from a technique that I did during my PhD, and I presented that technique in 2006 in this workshop. So we adapted that technique, and it turns out that it's suitable to solve the PAKE problem. After that workshop we gave the paper to IEEE P1363.2, and they put it on the website. We also have a blog on the lightbluetouchpaper to invite everyone to attack it. We want to make the process transparent. If anyone finds a flaw then it should be immediately noticed. Three years now, no attacks have been found, and a journal paper has been published just end of last year.

About the security of this protocol, here is just a summary. I'm not going into too much details. We proved that the protocol fulfils four security requirements. The first one is offline dictionary attack resistance. The password is weak, but we've designed the protocol in such a way that if an attacker captures the data, it couldn't have exhaustive search. And second is forward secrecy. This is a quite interesting property. If means that when you have two devices doing the sync, there is a code, and you use a short code to do the key change. Tomorrow the code may be disclosed. In that case it doesn't have any effect on the session key established in the past. So forward secrecy is quite a useful property. And the third one is known key security. So using this technique you can have multiple sessions between two devices, and if some sessions may be compromised, it doesn't have the effect on other sessions. And finally is online dictionary attack resistance. By nature you can't prevent an attacker from taking a random guess of passwords. He can just take a random guess of the password and see whether it matches. So, the best you can do is to minimise that guess to exactly one password for one protocol execution. If the other side guesses the password for more than three times, then you just terminate. By comparison, there are counterexamples to show that EKE doesn't fulfil property one, and SPEKE, SRP6 don't fulfil four. They don't have security proofs, and there are some heuristic attacks which show that they don't satisfy certain requirements.

So far the feedback has been positive, but to be honest, there are some criticisms, which could suggest potential for future work. In general there are three criticisms. The first one is actually criticising J-PAKE for being a balanced scheme, not an augmented PAKE, I will explain that in the next slide. And the second one is that it uses non-interactive zero knowledge proof, so it uses random oracles, and then some people said, no it's not attractive because you use random oracles. And the third one is, it does not have formal model, and people were saying, no, you must have a formal model. I will address each of those criticisms in the next few slides.

First, server compromise resistance, what does that mean? I'm sorry I couldn't tell you because I don't know how to describe it. Basically this requirement says if the server is compromised, you want to prevent an attacker from authenticating to the server without doing the exhaustive search. It sounds confusing. Let's break this down. The attacker tries to authenticate to a compromised server. But why? You've already compromised the server, and now it tries to authenticate to the compromised server. And the second one is more interesting. So the assumption is that an attacker has compromised the server, and he got all the verification data, for example, a hash of the password, but for some reason he decides not to have an exhaustive search, so why? But people will say: that's an assumption. You assume that an attacker doesn't do the exhaustive search. But the fundamental assumption in the whole research theory is that the password is weak, and is subject to exhaustive search. So if you have the verification data of the password, and then you do an exhaustive search, you will have a quite high chance of breaking the password. So what is the point when you assume the attacker doesn't want to do that? It's not really a logic requirement, but it's quite amazing to see quite a number of papers with formal security proofs to prove that protocols fulfil this requirement. It's amazing to me because how can you prove it, when you couldn't formulate this property in the first place.

Frank Stajano: Can you explain what the first one means, attacker tries to authenticate to a compromised server?

Reply: So now an attacker compromises a server. He has stolen all the data on the server, and now this requirement says that an attacker couldn't authenticate back to this compromised server.

Bruce Christianson: The intention is that compromising the server shouldn't allow the Mallory to masquerade as the client to another server.

Frank Stajano: To another server or to the same server?

Reply: It's the same server.

Bruce Christianson: Well to the same server.

Frank Stajano: Is that the assumption that the guy is going to re-use the weak password somewhere else?

Reply: Yes.

Frank Stajano: So in that case the other one would not be compromised?

Reply: Yes, that's why, you would have techniques to hash passwords differently for different server.

Bruce Christianson: But they have in their mind the idea that revealing the cookie doesn't reveal the password, so just capturing the cookie doesn't allow you to masquerade, and the protocol requires you to know the password to pass authentication, but they can't formulate it.

Reply: The big problem is that if we assume an attacker is really powerful, and if he has a hash of a password, for example, we would assume he will do the exhaustive search, so you couldn't really limit what the attacker can do. And it's interesting that when Mozilla investigated this problem, and they compared J-PAKE with SRP, they found J-PAKE more suitable for the sync, because J-PAKE doesn't have this property, which is something quite interesting.

Matt Blaze: So let me propose a possibility. I'm not sure I believe it, for where this might be a realistic distinction to make. I mean, exhaustive search, even if it's feasible, can't be done in real time, possibly, so there may be scenarios under which you'd be able to, you'd want to prevent a server from doing a real, a model in which a real-time attack, preventing a real-time attack is sufficient.

Reply: Yes, but here you've got data, and you've got the data offline, so you make a lot of assumptions, like how fast an attacker can break it. The main problem here is that if you state this requirement and you need to prove it, but how can you prove it, when you couldn't formulate properly what exactly is this requirement, and that is a big problem. You can't just assume, OK, we have an attacker, and attacker doesn't do the exhaustive search. That's not a valid assumption. And the second one is random oracles, and this is a long standing debate within the community. The random oracle is basically a secure hash function, and the argument against it is usually that it's very difficult to design such a hash function which behaves like a random oracle. So if you design a protocol without using random oracle, that's good, and it makes sense. But then you ask, if you don't use random oracle, what are the alternatives, and you look at the alternatives, and they are often much worse off.

Bruce Christianson: Random oracles have been introduced to model certain actual protocols that we have like the Schnorr's signature, which is readable, so it's a kind of a self-inflicted wound isn't it.

Reply: Yes, I agree. It's quite an intuitive assumption. You have input, and you get some random output, but some people don't like this. And the formal model, especially in the last ten years, if you look at the crypto conferences, they have this compulsory requirement. Everything you design has to be formally proven, otherwise your paper goes nowhere.

Bruce Christianson: That's why we're never going to be a major crypto conference.

Reply: I'm not so sure that is really the right trend, but it seems to be the state in the current crypto research. So one simple question to ask, OK, if you make this compulsory for everyone to use some formal model, what model are you talking about. There are so many models, so which model should people follow. It turns out this is very difficult to answer, and as far as I know, no-one has really a good answer. After 20 years research there is still no consensus.

At least in the PAKE area we have a few models, for example, one very famous model is proposed by Bellare, Pointcheval, Rogaway in 2000 at the Eurocrypt, and the paper was widely cited. They proposed this idea of ideal cipher model, and they applied the model to prove that EKE is secure. That is quite amazing because earlier back in 1997 Jaspan analyzed EKE to show that the encryption is actually not secure. It leaks data, and the reason is quite intuitive. EKE uses a password as an encryption key to encrypt data, but the password is too short as an encryption key. If you use a password which only has 20-bit entropy to encrypt data then it will leak information, and somehow you have the theory to prove that it's actually secure. So we've got a contradiction here. And the explanation is that, what is that ideal cipher? It was not defined in the 2000 paper, and it was only clarified by some other researchers like two years later. It's a kind of the block cipher, but it has peculiar properties, and the encryption and decryption are not even symmetric, so it doesn't exist. And people would say, this doesn't matter: the proof is still right. We have the definition of this cipher, and go to find it. But then there will be some people say, no, you are not solving the problem, you're just pushing the problem down to the implementation, and the problem is unsolved.

There are other formal models, and the very popular one is called common reference string. For some reason I don't understand, people often use the term common reference string model and the term standard model interchangeably. The key motivation is to get rid of random oracle because people don't like it.

This is just to highlight some of the protocols, because they are widely established. What is a cache here? All these protocols assume a trusted third party to set up the protocol group parameters. So in J-PAKE it is the same setting as in DSA. You have a generator, which could be any arbitrary element in a group, and it is easy to verify. But in all those protocols you have two generators, and they have to be uncorrelated and they have to be random. The question is, how do you actually verify it? You can't really verify it. So in the model they assume a trusted third party could do this difficult part, for example, in this Jiang-Gong paper[1], it said to use a trusted third party or a threshold scheme to define the public parameters. What is this threshold scheme? The paper doesn't explain. And in another KOY paper[2] it says to use a trusted third party, or a source of randomness. So I ask what is the source of randomness? The paper doesn't explain. So this paper[3] by Gennaro and Lindell in 2003 is a bit more explicit on this. They assume there is a large organisation as a trusted third party to define the parameters, so this party will be trusted by everyone. But it we think about it, the fundamental purpose of the PAKE is that you have Alice and Bob, and they want to do the key exchange, they don't want to involve anyone else. They don't want to involve the PKI, because they don't trust the certificate authority. They don't trust anyone else, and now you introduce another trusted third party, and everyone has to trust it, not only Alice and Bob. That's all the people who use the protocol. So it kind of defeats the purpose.

That's the conclusion. So I reviewed the latest developments of sync amongst the browsers, and the trend seems that sync is going to be quite an important feature for the modern browser, and I compared with Chrome and the Firefox sync. The Chrome sync has better usability, whereas Firefox has better privacy protection. And with EKE patent expiring next year I believe PAKE will be more widely used. And also there are some open research problems of it. The formal analysis, I agree, is important, but for the moment the practical results have been far from satisfactory, so a lot more work needs to be done.

Bruce Christianson: So the conclusion is that security protocols are potentially quite a good methodology for doing research into formal methods.

[1] S.Q. Jiang, G. Gong, "Password based key exchange with mutual authentication," Selected Area in Cryptography, LNCS 3357, pp. 267-279, 2004.

[2] J. Katz, R. Ostrovsky, M. Yung, "Efficient password-authenticated key exchange using human-memorable passwords", Advances in Cryptology, LNCS 2045, pp. 475-494, 2001.

[3] R. Gennaro, Y. Lindell, "A framework for password-based authenticated key exchange," Eurucrypt'03, LNCS, No. 2656, pp. 524-543, 2003.

Attack Detection vs. Privacy – How to Find the Link or How to Hide It?

Jiří Kůr, Vashek Matyáš, Andriy Stetsko, and Petr Švenda

Masaryk University, Brno, Czech Republic
{xkur,matyas,xstetsko,svenda}@fi.muni.cz

Abstract. Wireless sensor networks often have to be protected not only against an active attacker who tries to disrupt a network operation, but also against a passive attacker who tries to get sensitive information about the location of a certain node or about the movement of a tracked object. To address such issues, we can use an intrusion detection system and a privacy mechanism simultaneously. However, both of these often come with contradictory aims. A privacy mechanism typically tries to hide a relation between various events while an intrusion detection system tries to link the events up. This paper explores some of the problems that might occur when these techniques are brought together and we also provide some ideas how these problems could be solved.

1 Introduction

A wireless sensor network (WSN) consists of resource-constrained and wireless devices called sensor nodes. WSNs are considered for and deployed in various scenarios such as emergency response or energy management, medical, wildlife or battlefield monitoring. When deployed in an area, they monitor some physical phenomenon (e.g., humidity, temperature, pressure, light) and send measurements to a base station. Since the communication range of a sensor node is limited to tens of meters and the area of deployment is often large, not all sensor nodes can directly communicate with a base station and hence use hop-by-hop communication.

In WSNs, the risk of an attack happening is higher than in conventional networks, since the area of deployment is rarely protected physically. If an attacker captures some nodes, she becomes an authenticated participant of the network and can launch a variety of attacks. For an example of attacks, see [KW03]. The active attacks can be detected by a network intrusion detection system (IDS). Both centralized and distributed approaches can be applied. We believe that the distributed one is more reasonable in WSNs since it is more robust and less energy consuming. In this approach, every sensor node can run an IDS monitoring its neighbours and trying to detect an attack by itself or in cooperation with close neighbouring sensor nodes. We do not assume that every sensor node runs an IDS, although this would be possible. Further in the paper, when we mention an IDS we mean one IDS (instance) running on a certain node. Nevertheless, a centralized IDS is also worth considering in the future.

B. Christianson et al. (Eds.): Security Protocols 2011, LNCS 7114, pp. 189–199, 2011.

However, an IDS is usually inadequate for defending the network against a passive attacker, who quietly monitors the network communication. This type of attacker may infer sensitive information in the presence of packet encryption using traffic analysis techniques. Sensitive information leaked by traffic patterns may include location of certain nodes and events, movements of monitored subjects, frequency of events, location of a base station, etc. Thus privacy mechanisms, e.g., obfuscating the traffic patterns, should also be included in the defence line of WSNs.

It seems natural to employ both IDSs and privacy mechanisms to protect a WSN yet they have contradictory aims as we shall see. The aim of an IDS is to detect an attack and preferably to identify/eliminate the source of the attack. Detection accuracy of an IDS often depends on its ability to link certain events, e.g., packet X was sent by node Y and received by node Z. When privacy mechanisms are enabled, the IDS ability to link certain events is likely to decrease – implying a decrease in its detection accuracy.

The aim of this paper is to find out whether it is possible to use both IDSs and privacy mechanisms in WSNs at the same time, and how they might influence the functionality of each other. We focus on this conflict only within WSNs since these networks differ from other environments w.r.t. some important aspects for both IDSs and privacy mechanisms – energy and communication constraints, processing power, etc.

The roadmap of this paper is as follows – in Section 2, we first present several problems that may appear when both IDS and privacy mechanisms are employed in the network. In Section 3, we discuss possible approaches to mitigate these problems. Section 4 sketches details of possible solutions to some of the problems, and the following section then concludes the paper.

2 Possible Problems

In this section, we present problems that might occur when both IDSs and privacy mechanisms are used simultaneously. These problems are divided into four categories based on the cause and nature of the problems. Subsection 2.1 discusses problems within the first three categories, concerning issues that privacy mechanisms may cause to IDSs. The last category, concerning problems that IDSs may cause to privacy mechanisms, is then discussed within Subsection 2.2. The problems are denoted with Roman numbers, with continuous numbering throughout the following subsections.

2.1 Problems that Privacy Mechanisms May Cause to IDSs

Multiple or hidden identities. Privacy mechanisms usually intentionally hide the identity of nodes, assign multiple pseudonyms to a single node or use dynamically changing pseudonyms [MX06]. Thus a single node may have different pseudonyms for communication with different neighbours and these pseudonyms may change in time. Packets sent by the node then contain identifiers that are understandable only to this node and the intended recipient. This may cause trouble to an IDS since it is not able to link overheard packets with a particular sender or recipient. The IDS will also not be able to decide whether the claimed pseudonym of a node is true or not. Let us consider the following problems:

I An IDS concludes that a particular node is malicious. However, it may not be able to mark the node as malicious since it has no suitable identifier of the node that could be unambiguously understood by other nodes. Thus it will have trouble providing other nodes with the information that the certain node is malicious. A usual way to cope with this problem is to use the physical location of the malicious node. However, the nodes may only have some information on the radio signal strength of the attacking node received packets, not its accurate location.

II An IDS may not be able to detect a Sybil attack [KW03] since it is legitimate for every node to have multiple identities. An IDS without additional information is not able to distinguish between a true identity and a malicious identity either fabricated or stolen.

III Detection accuracy of an IDS may decrease if it does not know the identities of its neighbours. For example, in order to detect a selective forwarding attack an IDS (running on the node A, see Figure 1 below) monitors packets in its communication range. If the IDS overhears a packet (from the node X), it may want to check whether the packet is properly forwarded by the recipient (the node Y). If the IDS assumes that the recipient is in its communication range, while it in fact is not, false positives might occur. On the contrary, if the IDS assumes the recipient is out of reach and it is not true, false negatives might occur.

IV An IDS may not be able to detect a selective forwarding (jamming) attack in case a forwarding (jamming) node has multiple identities and the IDS does not know that these identities belong to that node. Then the IDS cannot link two dropping (sending) events that look innocent when separated and

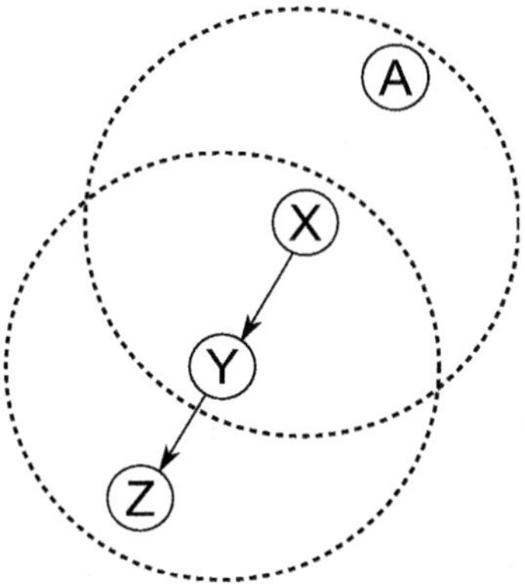

Fig. 1. The node A does not know whether the recipient (node Y) is in its communication range

would be recognized as an attack when linked together. Furthermore, the IDS has to maintain larger tables in the memory due to a higher number of identities monitored.

Randomized sending rate and route diversity. Attacks are usually detected by monitoring the sensor nodes behaviour [OM05, KDF07, LCC07, SFM10], e.g., packet sending rate, packet dropping rate, received packet signal strength. When privacy mechanisms modify network behaviour of sensor nodes in order to decorrelate traffic patterns, an IDS might have problems to differentiate legitimate and malicious behaviour.

V Privacy mechanisms may use dummy packets to suppress traffic patterns [OZT04]. A node introducing a dummy packet or dropping a dummy packet may be considered malicious by an IDS. On the contrary, if such behaviour is tolerated, a malicious node can introduce malicious or drop legitimate traffic without being detected.

VI Privacy mechanisms may route data through multiple different and randomly chosen routes [OZT04]. Thus, an IDS does not get a steady flow of packets to analyze.

VII An IDS monitors other nodes for packet dropping by checking if an incoming packet is resent in a reasonable time frame [SFM10]. Privacy mechanisms that will use some kind of anonymity mixing technique [HWK+05] will interfere with such detection, because a packet may be delayed for some time (therefore increasing the detection window that needs to be tolerated on IDS's side).

VIII Honest nodes may intentionally imitate the behaviour of a base station (BS) to hide the location of the true BS [BMM07]. These nodes may be then considered malicious by an IDS. On the contrary, if such behaviour is tolerated by IDSs, a malicious BS may remain undetected.

Encryption and changes of packet appearance. Privacy mechanisms usually employ packet encryption to hide the content of packets or to change the packet appearance hop-by-hop [SGR97, DHM04].

IX If encryption is used and an IDS does not posses appropriate keys, it cannot analyze packet content.

X If privacy mechanisms use some kind of hop-by-hop or onion encryption, an IDS without encryption keys is not able to decide whether the forwarded packet corresponds to the received one. Then a malicious neighbour would be able to modify packets in an undetected manner or to drop original packets and send dummy ones instead.

2.2 Problems That IDSs May Cause to Privacy Mechanisms

Not only privacy mechanisms cause trouble to an IDS, also the IDS can negatively influence privacy mechanisms.

XI Privacy mechanisms may decrease the relevant anonymity set by excluding potentially compromised or misbehaving nodes detected by an IDS. An attacker may influence the IDS decisions and therefore indirectly influence the privacy mechanism. Cooperation between an IDS and a privacy mechanism actually opens new attack vectors.

XII IDS traffic or decisions may leak sensitive information on node identities or relations between nodes. Privacy mechanisms thus also have to take care of the IDS traffic.

3 Towards a Successful Cooperation of IDSs and Privacy Mechanisms

We have presented several problems that may arise when privacy mechanisms and IDSs are employed together, though we believe that they can successfully coexist and even cooperate. We do not aim to discuss possible solutions in their entirety at this stage, we shall provide the necessary details of selected solutions in the Section 4. The following approaches may be adopted.

3.1 Both Privacy Mechanisms and IDSs Are Designed in a Non-interfering Way and Still Achieve Their Goals

The simplest way to avoid all of the aforementioned problems is to run protocols that do not cause these problems. However, the likely cost for this evasion will be a decrease in performance (security functionality) of either IDSs, privacy mechanisms or both. Another impact can be an increase in protocol complexity. For example, the IDS may use a node behaviour to identify this node (see Problem I) instead of the node identifier. Such behaviour may be represented by hashes of messages sent by the node recently. This information can be understood by all nodes in the communication range of the malicious one.

3.2 Privacy Mechanisms and IDS Cooperate

Privacy mechanisms "make a mess" in a network by hiding identities of nodes, introducing new traffic, etc. Privacy mechanisms might share some (secret) information with an IDS, in particular should this sharing help the IDS to "organize the mess" and successfully detect active attackers. A problem to solve is that a certain IDS node may accumulate a lot of secret information, becoming a sweet spot for an attacker.

1. **Pre-shared secret.** Privacy mechanisms employ a trapdoor function for pseudonym generation, content protection or dummy traffic identification. The trapdoor information is pre-shared between a privacy mechanism and an IDS, thus the IDS knows all the information necessary to run properly. No further cooperation is needed. However, the IDS knowing the trapdoor information is tempting for an attacker. The impact of an IDS compromise can be minimized by sharing only partial information or information that is valid only for a certain time.

2. **Delayed information disclosure.** Certain information is retrospectively revealed by privacy mechanisms, especially if this information helps the IDS to understand audit data recorded in the past. This approach assumes that an attacker needs the information immediately and delayed disclosure is not helpful for her. This approach can be used, for example, to retrospectively differentiate dummy and real traffic w.r.t. Problem V.
3. **Information is revealed on demand.** The information necessary to cancel the effect of privacy mechanisms' protective actions can be obtained by an IDS on demand, if the IDS executes an additional protocol and a privacy mechanism cooperates. The key characteristics are that IDSs cannot obtain the information without cooperation of privacy mechanisms and the obtained information is limited to cancelling effects of privacy mechanism protective actions only for a certain subject or time period (one message, one identity, etc.).
4. **Threshold scheme for information availability.** Information available to an IDS running on a particular node is intentionally limited to provide additional resilience against the node compromise. To obtain full information required, multiple nodes with an IDS/privacy mechanism must cooperate, potentially with the support of a suitable cryptographic threshold scheme.

3.3 Involvement of a Trusted Third Party

Another option to solve problems between privacy mechanisms and IDSs is to introduce a trusted third party, which will possess all necessary information to resolve the problems. E.g., Problem VIII could be solved by cooperation with a real BS. The BS could grant a ticket to a particular node to act as a BS. This node can later broadcast this ticket to its neighbours, so that the IDSs are sure that this node is either the real BS or a legitimate node imitating the BS.

3.4 IDSs and Privacy Mechanisms Leverage Properties of Each Other

Co-existence of IDSs and privacy mechanisms may benefit both when used properly. If an IDS has several identities, it can, for example, send a probing message (using one identity) that should be forwarded back to itself (represented by another identity). These probing messages increase the amount of traffic and may play the role of dummy traffic. This also makes the traffic analysis harder and helps the privacy mechanism. Another benefit is that an attacker cannot easily avoid an IDS by selecting one (static) path without IDSs if a privacy mechanism ensures that multiple routes or randomly chosen routes are used.

4 Sketching Some Solutions

The problems described in Section 2 can be solved to some extent by approaches suggested in Section 3. The details of a particular solution are usually dependent on many parameters of the protected network and requirements on IDSs and privacy mechanisms. Here, we will provide a more detailed outline of the techniques from Subsection 3.2 with their demonstration on a common privacy scheme and an IDS. The goal is *not* to provide a detailed new scheme for co-operation of IDSs and privacy mechanisms, but rather to provide an evidence that the techniques from Subsection 3.2 are not completely theoretical and can be used in the context of existing schemes.

4.1 How to Hide a Link

A privacy mechanism can operate in various modes that offer different levels of privacy protection. For example, the privacy mechanism can hide:

- both sender and recipient identities;
- either sender or recipient identity;
- neither of them.

We consider and describe a privacy mechanism operating in the mode when sender and recipient identities are hidden, which is the worst mode for the IDS. The chosen example mechanism is based on commonly accepted principles and assumes a network where each sensor node has a unique identifier that is known to all the neighbours. Instead of using the unique identifiers X and Y (see Figure 2), the node X generates a new pseudonym every time it sends a new packet to the node Y. Based on the pseudonym, only the recipient Y knows that the packet is addressed to it and that the packet comes from the node X. An instance of such privacy mechanism can be found in [MX06].

The pseudonym generation can be done in various ways. In order to present the ideas from Subsection 3.2, we consider two schemes both of which assume that any two communicating nodes share a pairwise key K_m:

- *Scheme 1* – The sender X directly uses the pairwise key K_m to create pseudonyms, for example, by encrypting a counter using the key. The counter increases every time a new packet is sent to the recipient Y.
- *Scheme 2* – The sender X does not use the pairwise key K_m directly to create pseudonyms. Instead, it uses the key to derive n session keys. Every session key is then used to create a limited number of pseudonyms. Note that this scheme applies common security principle of short-time-secret derivation that limits the master secret usage.

Both alternatives of the privacy mechanism cause the following problems to an IDS that runs on the node A (see Figure 2):

- It cannot deduce that all three packets were sent by the same node X and all of them were addressed to the same node Y. Thus Problems II, III and IV arise.
- It cannot decide what traffic must be logged and what traffic can be left out, which leads to the storage memory problem (see Problem IV).
- It cannot decide whether the packets were forwarded or not (see Problem IV). For example, if the node Y encrypts the content of the packets received from the node X and forwards them to the node Z using other pseudonyms (P_{21}, P_{22} and P_{23} as depicted on Figure 2).

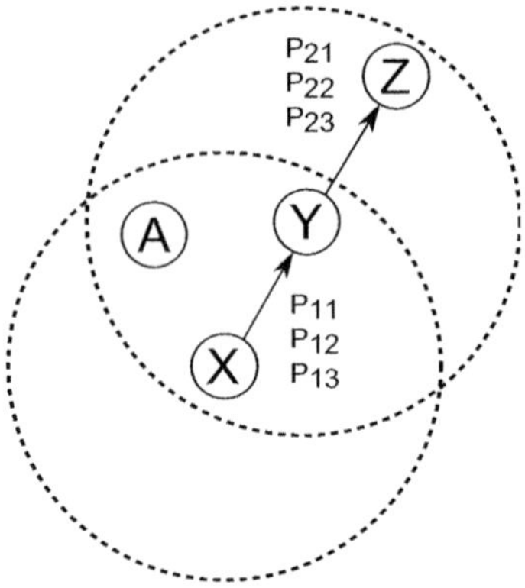

Fig. 2. The node X sends three packets to the node Y using three different pseudonyms P_{11}, P_{12} and P_{13}. The node Y forwards the received packets to the node Z using other pseudonyms P_{21}, P_{22} and P_{23}.

4.2 How to Find a Link

The problems previously described can be solved by adopting approaches sketched in Subsection 3.2. Note that in both the schemes the pseudonyms are generated using a trapdoor information, namely the pairwise key in the *Scheme 1* and the session key in the *Scheme 2*. Hence if the IDS has access to this trapdoor information, it can effectively uncloak the pseudonyms. This access can be granted by the following methods:

Pre-shared secret – full disclosure. Nodes X and Y pre-share the pairwise key K_m also with the IDS. This enables the IDS to uncloak the pseudonyms and analyze the traffic in realtime. This solution is straightforward, efficient and works for both the *Schemes*, yet it suffers from several drawbacks. The IDS becomes a sweet spot for an attacker as it is able to uncloak all the pseudonyms and even impersonate nodes in the neighborhood. The problem escalates if an IDS is running on every node.

Pre-shared secret – partial disclosure. The drawbacks of the full disclosure can be mitigated by pre-sharing only *partial information* that is valid only for a certain time period or a certain number of messages. When the *Scheme 2* is in use, the nodes X and Y pre-share with the IDS only a limited number of session keys and thus limit the information available to the IDS. A tradeoff rule applies: the more information is shared, the more accurate the detection and the worse the impact of a potential IDS compromise is.

Note that the *Scheme 2* can be particularly useful if every node runs an IDS. Each node may then possess different session keys. So every pseudonym can be uncloaked by some IDS, but there is no IDS that has access to all of them.

Delayed information disclosure. To partially avoid problems with pre-sharing, the trapdoor information may be disclosed to the IDS retrospectively.

In the case of *Scheme 2* the session keys would be shared with the IDS once they become obsolete. This is very useful in situations when the communication has to be protected only during a certain short time period. After this period the used session keys can be shared or even made public, because the protected information is obsolete. Yet the fact that a certain node is malicious may be important even with a short delay. Furthermore, the delayed session key disclosure does not enable anyone to forge the pseudonyms.

A drawback of the delayed disclosure is that the IDS has to maintain a log of past traffic and is not able to analyze it until the session key is revealed. Thus the detection of malicious activities (if present) is delayed and requires more storage memory.

The delayed disclosure of information is not limited only to the disclosure of the session keys. Each IDS may control only partial trapdoor information and these pieces can be put together only at a certain time or after a certain event. Thus an attacker that has compromised only a fraction of the IDSs does not gain access to the complete trapdoor information prior to its delayed disclosure.

Information is revealed on demand. The trapdoor information can be disclosed on demand. This method may combine pre-sharing with delayed information disclosure. The time of the disclosure and the type of the disclosed information is specified by the IDS which requests the information. Yet the decision whether to fulfil the request or not (e.g., based on the previous requests) is left to the owner of the information.

Assume the *Scheme 2* is in use. In order to analyze the traffic, the IDS needs to gain access to the session keys. So it requests the session keys from the nodes X and Y when necessary. Depending on the IDS, it may request past, current or even future session keys. However, in all the cases it should be able to make only a limited number of such requests. This limitation is vital as it prevents the IDS from accessing all the session keys in case the IDS is compromised. A drawback of the limitation is that a misbehaving node has a chance to cheat and remain undetected since the IDS cannot ask for and uncloak all the pseudonyms. Note that the limitation on requests sets the security tradeoff – the more requests are allowed, the more accurate the detection and the worse the impact of a potential IDS compromise is.

5 Conclusion and Further Work

We explored some of the problems that might occur when both intrusion detection systems and privacy mechanisms are employed in wireless sensor networks at the same time. Problems with an intrusion detection system might occur when a privacy mechanism changes packet appearance, hides identities of nodes or changes a network traffic pattern. On the other hand, an intrusion detection system may leak sensitive information or enfeeble a privacy mechanism. We provided some ideas on how these problems could be solved. We demonstrated that some of these ideas can be applied in the context of existing schemes. Yet some of them still await a deeper examination.

We encountered several open issues that are worth exploring in the future. We highlighted only the most promising ones – from our point of view. We plan to explore the threshold schemes for information availability in a greater detail. Furthermore, we would like to examine solutions involving a trusted third party. Yet such solutions need to be efficient and without any significant communication overhead – and this will be a tricky task. Another issue arises with the on-demand information disclosure. This approach requires an anonymous scheme for limiting the number of requests an IDS can make. Finally, we would like to investigate the issues of active probing/testing, where an IDS may actively probe suspicious nodes by sending them probing messages. Such probing need to be done in an efficient and preferably anonymous way.

Acknowledgement. We are grateful to our colleagues from the Laboratory of security and applied cryptography, namely Filip Jurnečka, Marek Kumpošt, Marián Novotný, Zdeněk Říha, Tobiáš Smolka and Roman Žilka for the discussions and suggestions that improved the paper.

This work was supported by the project GAP202/11/0422 of the Czech Science Foundation. Jiří Kůr and Andriy Stetsko were additionally supported by the project GD102/09/H042 "Mathematical and Engineering Approaches to Developing Reliable and Secure Concurrent and Distributed Computer Systems" of the Czech Science Foundation.

References

[BMM07] Biswas, S., Mukherjee, S., Mukhopadhyaya, K.: A countermeasure against traffic-analysis based base station detection in WSN. In: Web Proceedings of the International Conference on High Performance Computing, HiPC 2007 Posters, poster session (2007)

[DHM04] Deng, J., Han, R., Mishra, S.: Intrusion tolerance and anti-traffic analysis strategies for wireless sensor networks. In: DSN 2004: Proceedings of the 2004 International Conference on Dependable Systems and Networks, pp. 637–646. IEEE Computer Society, Washington, DC, USA (2004)

[HWK+05] Hong, X., Wang, P., Kong, J., Zheng, Q., Liu, J.: Effective probabilistic approach protecting sensor traffic. In: IEEE Military Communications Conference, MILCOM 2005, vol. 1, pp. 169–175 (October 2005)

[KDF07] Krontiris, I., Dimitriou, T., Freiling, F.C.: Towards intrusion detection in wireless sensor networks. In: Proceedings of the 13th European Wireless Conference (2007)

[KW03] Karlof, C., Wagner, D.: Secure routing in wireless sensor networks: attacks and countermeasures. In: Proceedings of the 1st IEEE International Workshop on Sensor Network Protocols and Applications, pp. 113–127 (2003)

[LCC07] Liu, F., Cheng, X., Chen, D.: Insider attacker detection in wireless sensor networks. In: Proceedings of the 26th IEEE International Conference on Computer Communications, pp. 1937–1945 (2007)

[MX06] Misra, S., Xue, G.: Efficient anonymity schemes for clustered wireless sensor networks. International Journal of Sensor Networks 1(1), 50–63 (2006)

[OM05] Onat, I., Miri, A.: An intrusion detection system for wireless sensor networks. In: Proceedings of the IEEE International Conference on Wireless and Mobile Computing, Networking and Communications, vol. 3, pp. 253–259 (2005)

[OZT04] Ozturk, C., Zhang, Y., Trappe, W.: Source-location privacy in energy-constrained sensor network routing. In: SASN 2004: Proceedings of the 2nd ACM Workshop on Security of Ad Hoc and Sensor Networks, pp. 88–93. ACM, New York (2004)

[SFM10] Stetsko, A., Folkman, L., Matyas, V.: Neighbor-based intrusion detection for wireless sensor networks. Technical Report FIMU-RS-2010-04, Faculty of Informatics, Masaryk University (May 2010)

[SGR97] Syverson, P.F., Goldschlag, D.M., Reed, M.G.: Anonymous connections and onion routing. In: Proceedings of IEEE Symposium on Security and Privacy, 1997, pp. 44–54 (May 1997)

Attack Detection vs Privacy – How to Find the Link or How to Hide It

(Transcript of Discussion)

Jiří Kůr and Andriy Stetsko

Masaryk University, Brno, Czech Republic

Alf Zugenmaier: What exactly does the IDS try to detect, what kind of intrusions?

Jiří Kůr: The IDS tries to detect the malicious nodes and the malicious activity of these nodes.

Mike Burmester: So anomalous behaviour?

Jiří Kůr: Yes, in principle. The particular examples may be packet dropping, packet injection, packet modification, jamming, and so on.

Alf Zugenmaier: Do you have a list of that coming up, because these are so various examples. How far do you want to push the IDS, what it is supposed to detect and what it is not supposed to detect?

Andriy Stetsko: We tried to look on this as a general problem, so we don't have the complete list of all attacks.

Alf Zugenmaier: There are lots of attacks that you may want to defend against, or where you say, actually these kinds of attacks is something that we don't care about in the settings that may require a different knowledge inside the IDS, or a different kind of monitoring capabilities of the IDS.

Jiří Kůr: We didn't try to take a particular IDS, and a particular privacy mechanism, and find a conflict. We tried to stay on a more general level: this is what IDS typically wants to detect, and this is what privacy mechanism typically does. But you are right; in particular instances the problems may not be present. However, in most cases, if we don't want to apply unfavourable security trade-off, the problems are likely to appear.

Jonathan Anderson: You're also talking about IDS as a distributed application running on all the nodes, right?

Andriy Stetsko: Yes.[1]

Jonathan Anderson: So to say that you're pre-sharing a key with the IDS is to say that you're pre-sharing a key with all of the nodes around?

[1] This issue is clarified in the paper. We do not assume that every node runs an IDS, although it would be possible.

B. Christianson et al. (Eds.): Security Protocols 2011, LNCS 7114, pp. 200–204, 2011.

Andriy Stetsko: No, in the case of a key pre-sharing, by the IDS we mean a single IDS instance running on a single node.

Jiří Kůr: We are pre-sharing a key with a single node only. The key which is shared between nodes X and Y is pre-shared only with their direct neighbour and we do not pre-share this particular key with nodes in a distant part of the network.

Jonathan Anderson: So the IDS is only monitoring exactly what's happening at its nearest neighbours, and which end of the communication it can see, or what's going on with its nearest neighbours.

Jiří Kůr: Yes. Of course you can have local IDS that makes local decisions based on the information available in its neighbourhood, or you can have a global one which puts all information from the whole network together and decides in a centralized way. But in our work we are focused more on the local IDS and direct neighbourhood of the IDS nodes.

Jonathan Anderson: Can you give examples you've demonstrated, or somebody's demonstrated that an IDS can actually do something useful in a wireless sensor network? Even when you give IDS an absolute global view of what's going on in the whole network, even on the best of days it's foggy, and easily fooled. So I'm somewhat sceptical that it would actually be a useful thing to put in a wireless sensor network where either you have a very local view, and you can only see what your neighbours are saying to each other, or you have this global view that's been computed from aggregated stuff where you assume that some of the nodes in the network are compromised, and so some of those could be the IDS nodes.

Andriy Stetsko: Just a simple example when a malicious node drops packets. It's a very simple attack, but it may cause a big damage to the operation of the network. If there is an IDS near the malicious node, it may detect the attack.

Jonathan Anderson: But, how would you detect it with any certainty? (a) I have to know that Frank has received a packet and then he's supposed to pass it on to somebody else, and (b) I have to see that he hasn't passed it on to the person he was supposed to pass it on to. And it seems like, especially when I can only see what Frank's transmitting, and not everything he's receiving, because we're not in the exact same place, it seems like that would be very difficult to do within its capability.

Vashek Matyáš: Well to be honest, we still have to run quite a few experimental simulations which show whether actually the benefits of the IDS will balance the cost associated with deployment.

Alf Zugenmaier: But even if you have that, what will you do? An IDS then suddenly becomes a weak point in your system. The way I understand it, this IDS has to sit everywhere, so it has to monitor everything, which is like implanting an attacker. Once you can take over an IDS you can take over the network. An IDS just gives you some information, which is probably not so exciting, or it is going to allow you to actually do something about the attacks that are ongoing. You have created a great tool for an attack or anyone who can take over an IDS.

Vashek Matyáš: One point is that what Andriy said was not actually precise. The IDS is not in every node, or we don't expect an IDS to be in every node. And second, you always get information with a certain level of uncertainty.

James Malcolm: Why don't we put the IDS in every node, because you've got local information. Each node has got the best position to know what's going on.

Vashek Matyáš: That is already one of the assumptions that we will use only local information. If we introduce things like the probing techniques that are not strictly set on local information only, you might get some benefits from that, but you will pay with communication and energy costs.

Jonathan Anderson: I always thought that the win that you get out of an IDS, even though it's really stochastic and really easy to fool, etc, was that it's a box that you can plug into a mirror port on your switch, and it has a global overview, so if it's easy to find stuff it will see it. But in a situation like this it seems like you don't have enough benefit, and so really you are just scattering kind of police everywhere in a crowd, and one policeman for every protestor or something, just to see if any of them are saying or doing anything dodgy.

Frank Stajano: The other thing is that when you plug it into the port you know it's something that isn't interfering with the network because it can't be interfered from the network, whereas if you scatter in the field you don't know if they're tampering with IDS nodes as well.

Alf Zugenmaier: What is the reason why you are assuming misbehaving nodes but not misbehaving IDS nodes?

Vashek Matyáš: We didn't say this.

Bruce Christianson: They assume IDS nodes can be subverted.

Alf Zugenmaier: So you need another IDS system for the IDS.

Bruce Christianson: Secret policeman.

Petr Švenda: The response taken as a result from the suspicious behaviour detected by IDS must be also limited in impact. For example, if you are the IDS then you can blame your neighbouring nodes for misbehaviour, but you must also do some time-limited suicide where you and the node you are blaming is out of work for some period of time. As a result, you as the IDS cannot convince all nodes in the network that something is wrong.

Bruce Christianson: You might be a provocateur.

Petr Švenda: And also we don't really need to have the IDS on every node. What is important is that the attacker is not aware which are the nodes with the IDS, and set of these nodes can possibly change in time. An attacker then can't count on the fact that given area is clear with no nodes running IDS, because he doesn't know where the nodes with IDS are. It's better than having the IDS on all nodes because then an attacker is aware that every node he will pick will be running IDS, and he can do something with such a node and accompanied keys. And with respect to Jonathan's original question, the global overview, I think that's the attacker on different level then we assume - here we are not able to detect a very sophisticated attacker doing something in one part of the network and then doing something else related in distant part, because the nodes with IDS positioned in different parts of the network are not communicating between each other. But you can still detect the part of the larger attack consisting from several actions like dropping of the packets. If you can detect this dropping and block offending node, it might cause that larger attack will not be successful.

Jonathan Anderson: But it seems that the kind of attacks you'd want in a wireless sensor networks are things like when you see the enemy tank rumbling through we just don't report. Or if the temperature has changed and this indicates something about the stress on the building, then you just don't indicate as much of the temperature change as you should. And that's something where, how do I tell that that's an attack; versus how do I just tell that temperature over there is not the same as right here?

Petr Švenda: But still if the attacker decides that he likes to suspend the message, which is signalling that the temperature is going up, then he will be dropping the message containing this information somewhere in the network and therefore can possibly be detected as message dropper.

Jonathan Anderson: Or he may be just subtly changing it, saying that the temperature raises is .1 instead of 1.

Petr Švenda: If an attacker can change the message in transit (even when message is encrypted and integrity protected as an attacker is assumed to know relevant cryptographic keys due to compromise of some nodes), then you can still detect message change, if you are using fake probing messages (we refer it as an active probing technique) where attacker cannot be sure whether he is modifying genuine message with real temperature or fake one and will get caught afterwards. Fake messages act as a kind of agent-provocateur and will test if you are honest and are passing the unmodified message(s) or you are malicious and modifying the message(s).

Jonathan Anderson: Right, then I guess the only way to check whether a node is honest is to have absolute redundancy, and to have two nodes right next to each other seeing the same thing, and one is doing something, and the other is computing what the other one should have done, and so you have the fault tolerant thing through redundancy. And that seems to be the only way of being able to detect that he received a packet. Say Bruce sent Sandy a packet, and Sandy should have given it to Frank, the only way for me to know that she did in fact send it to Frank and not to Frank prime, who doesn't really exist but for me seems to be just out of my radio range, is for me to have the same routing table as Sandy, and update it in the same way, and make all the same decisions.

Petr Švenda: That's true, but these nodes are just one hop away, therefore IDS running on separate nodes and communicating locally (one or two hops only) can still obtain information necessary to detect packet effectively dropped by transmission between Sandy and (non-existent) Frank prime.

Matt Blaze: Let me just refine that attack, now what Sandy does is sends message to Frank prime, and spoofs Frank's responses as well to make it appear that Frank is responding, and you have no way of, assuming you're the IDS, you have no way of distinguishing yourself being out of Frank's range, and Sandy's misbehaviour.

Petr Švenda: If you assume that nodes can plausibly have multiple unlinkable identities, and it's allowed by overall scheme to have these, then you can send fake probing messages effectively to yourself. An attacker will not be able to tell that this message is suspicious, because from his viewpoint, the message is sent from and addressed to a different node. Because the node running IDS possesses multiple identities itself then it needs no other node to cooperate in active probing technique, it will just wait for its own packet to come back (node is both Bruce and Frank in your example). Spoofing Frank's responses will not help the attacker. It's kind of a Sybil attack (multiple identities on single node) but in a reverse way, where it's used for defence.

Bruce Christianson: Civil defence.

Petr Švenda: Yes.

The Sense of Security and a Countermeasure for the False Sense

Yuko Murayama, Yasuhiro Fujihara, and Dai Nishioka

Graduate School of Software and Information Science, Iwate Prefectural University, 152-52, Sugo, Takizawa-mura, Iwate 020-0193 Japan
{murayama,fuji}@iwate-pu.ac.jp, D.Nishioka@comm.soft.iwate-pu.ac.jp

Abstract. In this paper, we report the two issues from our recent research on the human aspect of security. One is the sense of security and the other is a warning interface for security threats. We look into the emotional aspect of security technology and investigate the factors of users' feelings based on the user surveys and statistical analysis. We report the difference in those factors of the sense of security in the U.S.A. and Japan as well. We also introduce the multi-facet concept of trust which includes security, safety, privacy, reliability, availability and usability. According to the results of our surveys, no matter how secure systems and services are, the users may not get the sense of security at all. On the contrary, the users may well feel secure with insecure systems and services. It suggests that we would need another type of protocols and interfaces than merely secure protocols, to provide the users with secure feelings. We propose an interface causing discomfort — a warning interface for insecure situations. A user could be aware of security threats and risks by a slight disturbance. Such an interface has been researched to a great extent in the safety area for protection from human errors.

Keywords: the sense of security, security, trust, user survey, warning interface.

1 Introduction

Security technology has been evaluated in terms of theoretical and engineering feasibility and mostly from service providers' viewpoints. What has been missing is evaluation from users' viewpoints. The term, "security" includes objective viewpoints of security engineering as well as such subjective factors as sense of security.

In this paper, we report the two issues from our recent research on the human aspect of security. One is the sense of security and the other is a warning interface for security threats.

We look into the emotional aspect of security technology and investigate the factors of users' feelings based on the user surveys and statistical analysis. We report the difference in those factors of the sense of security in the U.S.A. and Japan as well.

B. Christianson et al. (Eds.): Security Protocols 2011, LNCS 7114, pp. 205–214, 2011.

We also introduce the multi-facet concept of trust which includes security, safety, privacy, reliability, availability and usability. According to the results of our surveys, the sense of security is related closely to the well-known trust factors. The factors such as the integrity, competence and benevolence of trustees affect the users' sense of security. On the other hand, we did not get a factor such as security technology in use. No matter how secure systems and services are, the users may not get the sense of security at all. On the contrary, the users may well feel secure with insecure systems and services. It suggests that we would need another type of protocols and interfaces than merely secure protocols, to provide the users with secure feelings. Moreover, we need those protocols and interfaces for insecure feelings against security threats and risks.

We propose an idea on an interface causing discomfort — a warning interface for the insecure situations. A user could be aware of security threats and risks by a slight disturbance. Such an interface has been researched to a great extent in the safety area for protection from human errors. The work is still under investigation for the moment. We present our current work and issues so that we could discuss our future work.

Throughout this paper, we use a Japanese word for the sense of security, Anshin. Anshin is a Japanese noun which is composed of two words: An and Shin. "An" is to ease, and "Shin" indicates mind. Anshin literally means to ease one's mind [1–3].

The next section presents related work. Section 3 reports our investigation into the sense of security based on previous work. Later sections describe result of the experimental survey and factor analysis of the results. The final section gives some conclusion and presents future work.

2 Related Work

In this section, we introduce related work in the area of trust as well as in human interface. We introduce work on Anshin in different disciplines as well. Trust has been studied in various disciplines such as sociology, psychology and economics. From a psychological viewpoint, Deutsch defined trust in an interpersonal context [4]. Gambetta defined trust as a particular level of one's subjective probability that another's action would be favorable to oneself [5]. Marsh proposed the first computational trust model with quantized trust values in the rage of -1 to +1 [6].

Traditional studies on trust were concerned primarily with cognitive trust, however, Lewis as sociologist defined one type of trust as follows:

> *Trusting behavior may be motivated primarily by strong positive affect for the object of trust (emotional trust) or by "good rational reasons" why the object of trust merits trust (cognitive trust), or more usually some combination of both* [7].

Popularly, cognitive trust is defined as a trustor's rational expectation that a trustee will have the necessary competence, benevolence, and integrity to be relied upon [9]. On the other hand, the emotional aspect of trust is defined as an emotional security, or feeling secure, or comfortable [8]. Xiao says that emotional trust is feeling, while cognitive trust is cognition [9]. Emotional trust is an interpersonal sensitivity and support [10] which is feeling secure about trustee. More recent work [11, 12] includes the emotional aspect of trust in their frameworks for trust in electronic environments as well.

¿From a sociological viewpoint, Yamagishi [13] gives distinct definitions of Anshin and trust. He says that Anshin is the belief that we have no social uncertainty, whereas trust is needed when we have high social uncertainty. Trust is expectations of others' intentions based on trustor's judgment of others' personalities and feelings.

Camp identified that trust included security, safety and reliability [14]. Later Hoffman et. al. presented such a structure as well with security, safety, reliability, privacy and availability [15]. Accordingly, we presume that emotional trust is composed of the senses of security, safety, reliability, privacy and availability. Indeed, in Japanese, Anshin presents the senses of security, safety, reliability, privacy and availability; therefore, Anshin is emotional trust[16]. ¿From the viewpoint of risk communication, Kikkawa introduces two Anshin states: one with knowledge and the other without knowledge [17]. Kikkawa suggests that it is necessary for users to study and obtain information in an active way to get more Anshin feeling. To create Anshin experts on technology need to provide information to users as well as reducing technological risks.

Yamazaki and Kikkawa suggested that there is a structure in Anshin through their study on Anshin in epidemic disease [18].

¿From a human interface viewpoint, Whitten and Tygar point out that user interfaces in security systems need special interfaces [19]. Stephens gives design elements, such as page layout, navigation, and graphics which affect the development of trust between buyers and sellers in e-commerce [20]. Pu also reports that how information was presented affected trust building in user interfaces [21]. According to Riegelsberger [22], affective reactions influence consumer decision-making.

3 User Survey on Anshin

Among the multiple concepts of trust introduced in the previous section, we started with security and looked at Anshin as the sense of security. We have conducted several surveys on the sense of security and exploratory factor analysis (EFA) as follows [2, 3, 16, 23]:

1 425 subjects; our university student resulted with 6 factors

1.1 307 subjects: computer science students resulted with 6 factors

1.2 118 subjects: non-computer science students resulted with 4 factors

2 88 subjects: non-computer science, university students in the U.S.A. resulted with 4 factors

3 756 subjects: local government officers resulted with 5 factors

In this section, we introduce the survey results briefly.

3.1 Questionnaire Survey

We have produced a series of survey questions based on the results of our previous survey [2]. The previous survey was conducted on two hundred and ten students of our university in July 2006. We asked students for their opinion about the sense of security when they have when they use a security system or service through the Internet. Our past survey has thirty five questions.

Our survey includes the following question: "Do you feel that the following thirty five items account for the sense of security when you use a service or system through the Internet?" Some of the items are listed in Table 2. We used the seven-point Likert scale system ranging from strongly disagree (1) to strongly agree (7), as many such survey have used this scale.

We used a paper questionnaire for the students in Japan, whereas we set up a web site for the survey in the U.S. as well as the one with the local government officers.

We analyzed the survey responses using exploratory factor analysis (EFA) using the maximum likelihood method under the normality assumption over the data [24]. We used Promax rotation since the factors are co-related.

3.2 Survey with the Students in Japan

We conducted a questionnaire survey on Anshin with four hundred and fifty two students in the faculties of software and information science, nursing, policy studies, social welfare of Iwate Prefectural University, Japan in 2006. After eliminating incomplete answers, there were four hundred and twenty five valid entries used for the analysis.

The analysis identified six factors, those with Eigenvalue at least 1.0 and others from inspection of the scree plot. We named the six factors: security technology; usability; experience; preference; understanding; and cognitive trust.

Security technology consists of seven questionnaire items which are concerned with the particular security technologies that the system or service uses. Most items indicate security measures such as protection of personal information.

Usability consists of five items which address the users' satisfaction with aspects of the user interface such as usability, attractive design and user-friendliness.

Experience consists of six items which are concerned with how much the users have used the system or service as well as with recommendations of the users' family and friends.

Preference consists of three items which are concerned with the users' preference for interface design. In other words, it shows the user's tastes.

Understanding consists of four items which address the users' knowledge about information technology. Particularly, it shows their perception and understanding of risk or threat based on their prior knowledge.

Cognitive trust consists of four items which are concerned with the users' confidence in service providers and systems.

3.3 Survey of CS Students

In the survey of the students, 307 out of 425 subjects were computer science students who had some knowledge on security. We conducted analysis of variance (ANOVA) between students in the various faculties on the factor scores, and found that there was significant difference only in the understanding factor [25]. The students whose major is Software and Information Science have Anshin based on their knowledge, whereas those with other majors rely more on Preference. This suggests that the two types of the students have different structures of Anshin.

With the students majoring in software and information science we found six factors with five of them being almost same as the ones presented in the previous subsection — i.e. Security Technology, Usability, Preference, Knowledge and Understanding, and Assurance. The new factor is subjects' belief in systems — that even if an incident occurred that they could get around it. The items identified as the Experience factor previously each fall into either the Usability or Assurance factor for this subgroup.

3.4 Survey of Non-CS Students

With the students majoring other than software and information science we found four factors [16]: User Interface Design, Cognitive Trust in the Competence of the Systems and Services Provided, Cognitive Trust in the Integrity and Competence of the Service Provider; and Experience.

The first factor is a combination of Usability and Preference from the previous survey, and we name as User Interface.

The second factor consisuts of seven items which could be regarded as Cognitive Trust in terms of competence of the systems and services provided, as well as users' Knowledge.

The third factor consists of a combination of Security Technology and Cognitive Trust from the previous survey; this factor represents the subjects' belief in service providers; we could regard it as Cognitive Trust in terms of integrity and competence of the service provider. The fourth factor consists of three items is concerned with Experience.

3.5 Survey of Non-computer Science, University Students in the U.S.A.

We surveyed non-CS students from Eastern Washington University (EWU) and Washington State University (WSU) in March 2008 [16]. Out of one hundred and forty subjects we selected eighty eight non-CS respondents.

For these students we identified four factors using the same techniques as before. Although the number of factors is the same as the one with the non-CS Japanese students, the factor structure is somewhat different. The first factor is cognitive trust in the competence of the systems and services provided. The second factor, usability, is almost identical to the first factor for the Japanese students.

The third factor is slightly different from the survey with the non-CS Japanese students consisting of six items that nevertheless still represent cognitive trust in the competence of the systems and services provider.

The fourth factor is completely different from that of the non-CS Japanese students. It consists of six items which are concerned with understanding, representing their knowledge of risks, technology and systems.

3.6 Survey of Local Government Officers

We modified the questionnaire so that some sentences became unambiguous and some redundant items as to have 28 question items finally [23]. After the survey, data for three question items had to be excluded due to ceiling effect. As the result from EFA, we had five factors. The first factor is Cognitive Trust in terms of integrity, competence and benevolence of the service provider. The second factor is Kindness in terms of usability and reactions from the service provider. The third factor is Understanding which is concerned with knowledge of security technology as well as risks. The fourth factor is Preference which is concerned with the design of user interface and information presentation. The fifth factor is Familiarity which is concerned with user experience and reputation from family members and close friends.

3.7 Discussion

According to the results of our surveys, the sense of security is related closely to the well-known trust factors, such as the integrity, competence and benevolence of trustees affect the users' sense of security. On the other hand, we did not get a factor such as security technology in use. No matter how secure systems and services are, the users may not get the sense of security at all. On the contrary, the users may well feel secure with insecure systems and services. We would need another type of protocols and interfaces than merely secure protocols, to provide the users with secure feelings.

4 An Interface Causing Discomfort

In this section, we introduce an interface causing discomfort. Human interface has been researched to a great extent in terms of usability [25]. On the other hand, researches have also been conducted on methods to avoid human errors in safety engineering. Some interfaces are deliberately designed such that it is difficult to operate the systems that employ them.

In the following subsections, we introduce the related work and then present the result of user survey on discomfort factors when one uses computer systems.

4.1 Related Work

Sankarapandian et al. [27] suggested an interface to make the user aware about the vulnerabilities posed by unpatched software. They implemented a desktop with annoying graffiti that showed the number and seriousness of vulnerabilities. Egelman et al. [28] conducted an experiment on the rate to avoid the damage caused by phishing; the experiment was based on a C-HIP (Communication-Human Information Processing) model [29] in which the interface warns users about vulnerabilities. They reported that the user responses to a warning differed depending on the type of interface used.

4.2 User Survey

We have conducted a user survey in order to measure the degree of discomfort caused by the individual discomfort elements. We prepared forty six questions for simulating discomfort on the basis of the results of our preliminary test. We asked subjects to rate each discomfort element. The rates included five ranks: from calm (zero points) to acute discomfort (four points). In total, one hundred forty six men and one hundred sixty four women of the second-, third-, and fourth-year students from four different departments participated the survey. The survey was conducted from November 14, 2007 for one week.

We collected three hundred ten data; forty nine from the faculty of Nursing, fifty two, from the faculty of Social Welfare, one hundred thirty four from the faculty of Software and Information Science, and seventy five from the faculty of Policy Studies. Most subjects had completed the course on liberal arts of computer use and used a computer daily.

We analyzed the three hundred ten data by exploratory factor analysis using the maximum likelihood method. We made the initial analysis with the maximum likelihood method and a promax rotation. We present seven factors that contribute to discomfort feeling. Factor 1, Time-consuming, consists of eleven high factor loading items related to looking for things that are difficult to find or to input information using a keyboard or a mouse. Factor 2, Information-seeking, consists of eight high factor loading items related to a situation in which a user is attempting to find information that is difficult to locate. Factor 3, Message, consists of seven high factor loading items related with messages that interrupt a user's activity. Factor 4, Unexpected-operation, consists of five high factor loading items related with a system malfunction that is unexpected or unintended by a user. Factor 5, Difficulty-in-seeing, consists of three high factor loading items related with the sense of sight given by a physical aspect. Factor 6, Time-delay, consists of three high factor loading items related with waiting time and system delay. Factor 7, Noise, consists of three high factor loading items related with the sense of hearing given by a particular sound.

We have been working on implementing those factors in the user interfaces for email user agent systems.

5 Conclusions

We looked into the users' feeling of security technology and introduced our work on user survey to find out factors contributing to it. We also introduce the multi-facet concept of trust which includes security, safety, privacy, reliability, availability and usability. According to the results of our surveys, no matter how secure systems and services are, the users may not get the sense of security at all. We proposed an idea on an interface causing discomfort — a warning interface for the insecure situations. A user could be aware of security threats and risks by a slight disturbance. Such an interface has been researched to a great extent in the safety area for protection from human errors. The work is still under investigation for the moment.

Acknowledgement. This research has been supported by Grant-in-Aid for Scientific Research (B) from the Ministry of Education, Culture, Sports, Science and Technology (MEXT). Special thanks to Carl Hauser and to Atsushi Inoue for our survey on Anshin in the United States. We thank Ginny Hauser for her assistance with the translation of our questionnaire into English.

References

1. Murayama, Y., Hikage, N., Hauser, C., Chakraborty, B., Segawa, N.: An Anshin Model for the Evaluation of the Sense of Security. In: Proc. of the 39th Hawaii International Conference on System Science (HICSS 2006), vol. 8, p. 205a (2006)
2. Hikage, N., Murayama, Y., Hauser, C.: Exploratory survey on an evaluation model for a sense of security. In: Proc. of the 22nd IFIP TC-11 International Information Security Conference (SEC 2007), pp. 121–132 (2007)
3. Fujihara, Y., Murayama, Y., Yamaguchi, K.: A user survey on the sense of security, Anshin. In: Proc. of the 23rd IFIP TC-11 International Information Security Conference (SEC 2008), pp. 699–703 (2008)
4. Deutsh, M.: The effect of motivational orientation upon trust and suspicion. Human Relation 13, 123–139 (1960)
5. Gambetta, D.: Can we trust trust? In: Chapter 13 Making and Breaking Cooperative Relations, electronic edition, Department of Sociology, pp. 213–237. Basil Blackwell, University of Oxford (1988), `http://www.sociology.ox.ac.uk/papers/gambetta213-237.pdf`,(Last access: February 9, 2007)
6. Marsh, S.P.: Formalising trust as computational concept, PhD Thesis, Department of Mathematics and Computer Science, University of Stirling (1994)
7. Lewis, J.D., Weigert, A.: Trust as a Social Reality. Social Forces 63(4), 967–985 (1985)
8. Xiao, S., Benbasat, I.: The formation of trust and distrust in recommendation agents in repeated interactions: a process-tracing analysis. In: Proc. of the 5th International Conference on Electronic Commerce (ICEC 2003), pp. 287–293 (2003)
9. Xiao, S., Benbasat, I.: Understanding Customer Trust in Agent-Mediated Electronic Commerce, Web-Mediated Electronic Commerce, and Traditional Commerce. Information Technology and Management 5(1-2), 181–207 (2004)
10. McAllister, D.J.: Affect- and cognition-based trust as foundations for interpersonal cooperation in organizations. Academy of Management Journal 38(1), 24–59 (1995)

11. Chopra, K., Wallace, W.A.: Trust in Electronic Environments. In: Proc. of the 36th Hawaii International Conference on System Science (HICSS 2003), p. 331.1 (2003)
12. Kuan, H.H., Bock, G.W.: The Collective Reality of Trust: An Investigation of Social Relations and Networks on Trust in Multi-Channel Retailers. In: Proc. of the 13th European Conference on Information Systems, ECIS 2005 (2005), `http://is2.lse.ac.uk/asp/aspecis/20050018.pdf` (last access: February 9, 2007)
13. Yamagishi, T.: The structure of trust: The evolutionary games of mind and society. Tokyo University Press (1998), english version `http://lynx.let.hokudai.ac.jp/members/yamagishi/english.htm` (last access: February 9, 2007)
14. Camp, L.J.: Design for Trust. In: Falcone, R., Barber, S.K., Korba, L., Singh, M.P. (eds.) AAMAS 2002. LNCS (LNAI), vol. 2631, pp. 15–29. Springer, Heidelberg (2003)
15. Hoffman, L.J., Lawson-Jenkins, K., Blum, J.: Trust beyond security: an expanded trust model. Communication of ACM 49(7), 94–101 (2006)
16. Murayama, Y., Hauser, C., Fujihara, Y., Nishioka, D., Inoue, A.: The Comparison Study between the US and Japan on the Sense of Security, Anshin with non-Computer-Science Students. In: Proceedings of the 44th Hawaii International Conference on System Sciences, HICSS 2011 (2011)
17. Kikkawa, T., Shirato, S., Fujii, S., Takemura, K.: The pursuit of informed reassurance ('An-Shin' in Society) and technological safety ('An-Zen'). Journal of SHAKAI-GIJUTSU 1, 1–8 (2003) (in Japanese)
18. Yamazaki, M., Kikkawa, T.: The Structure of Anxiety Associated with Avian Influenza and Pandemic Influenza. The 47th annual meeting of the Japanese Society of Social Psychology, 676–677 (2006) (in Japanese)
19. Whitten, A., Tygar, D.: Why Johnny Can't Encrypt: A Usability Evaluation of PGP 5.0. In: Proc. of the 9th USENIX Security Symposium, pp. 169–184 (1999)
20. Stephens, R.T.: A framework for the identification of electronic commerce design elements that enable trust within the small hotel industry. In: Proc. of ACMSE 2004, pp. 309–314 (2004)
21. Pu, P., Chen, L.: Trust building with explanation interfaces. In: Proc. of the 11th International Conference on Intelligent User Interfaces (IUI 2006), pp. 93–100 (2006)
22. Riegelsberger, J., Sasse, M.A., McCarthy, J.D.: Privacy and trust: Shiny happy people building trust?: photos on e-commerce websites and consumer trust. In: Proc. of the SIGCHI Conference on Human Factors in Computing Systems (CHI 2003), vol. 5(1), pp. 121–128 (2003)
23. Fujihara, Y., Yamaguchi, K., Murayama, Y.: A Survey on Anshin of the Users without Technical Knowledge on Information Security. IPSJ Journal 50(9), 2207–2217 (2009) (in Japanese)
24. Johnson, R.A., Wichern, D.W.: Applied Multivariate Statistical Analysis, 4th edn. Prentice Hall (1998)
25. Murayama, Y., Hikage, N., Fujihara, Y., Hauser, C.: The structure of the sense of security, Anshin. In: Proc. of 2nd International Workshop on Critical Information Infrastructures Security (CIRITS 2007), pp. 85–96 (2007)
26. Nielsen, J.: Usability Engineering. Academic Press (1993)

27. Sankarapandian, K., Little, T., Edwards, W.K.: TALC: Using Desktop Graffiti to Fight Software Vulnerability. In: Proceedings of the 26th Annual SIGCHI Conference on Human Factors in Computing Systems (CHI 2008), pp. 1055–1064 (2008)
28. Egelman, S., Cranor, L.F., Hong, J.: You've been warned: An empirical study of the effectiveness of web browser phishing warnings. In: Proceedings of the 26th Annual SIGCHI Conference on Human Factors in Computing Systems (CHI 2008), pp. 1065–1074 (2008)
29. Wogalter, M.S.: Communication-Human Information Processing (C-HIP) Model. In: Wogalter, M.S. (ed.) Handbook of Warnings, pp. 51–61. Lawrence Erlbaum Associates (2006)

The Sense of Security and a Countermeasure for the False Sense

(Transcript of Discussion)

James Malcolm

University of Hertfordshire, Hatfield, UK

This talk has two parts, I think: what makes users of computer systems feel secure *and* a countermeasure for when that sense of security is unjustified. I'm clearly not Yuko; Yuko Murayama was actually a colleague of mine many years ago, and of Mike shortly after that, but she's unable to travel to Europe to present this paper because of the earthquake in Japan. So I'm going to do my best to explain the work that she's done.

The traditional assumption is that users would like secure systems, and that they might feel secure if their systems were secure. And the key thing behind both parts of what Yuko and her colleagues have done is to question that connection between feeling secure and being secure. And so we have the more or less objective idea that you *are* secure, but there's also the sense of security. She wants to identify that sense of security, that feeling that everything is OK; some people would describe it as "trust". But we had long debates in previous workshops about what trust is. And perhaps with an eye to that, Yuko has taken the word "anshin", which literally means an easy mind, a feeling that everything is OK.

Bruce Christianson: It's almost the same in English: "se" means without, and "cure" means care, so secure means without care, or without anxiety, or possibly careless.

Reply: So what is the saying, Bruce?

Bruce Christianson: The way to be safe is never to be secure[1].

Reply: Never to be without care, always be on your guard.

[1] Many attribute this to Franklin, in his Poor Richard's Almanac, but he seems to have taken it from Francis Quarles (1592-1644) on temptation: "When the flesh presents thee with delights, then present thyself with dangers; where the world possesses thee with vain hopes, there possess thyself with true fear; when the devil brings thee oil, bring thou vinegar. The way to be safe is never to be secure."

B. Christianson et al. (Eds.): Security Protocols 2011, LNCS 7114, pp. 215–222, 2011.

Bruce Christianson: That's a quote from Shakespearean times[2] which indicates that the word has changed its meaning by 180 degrees during the course of the last 400 years.

Reply: So the first thing that these authors have done is to look at what are the factors that contribute to somebody feeling that they are secure.

This diagram emphasises the difference between whether something is technically secure or not, as opposed to whether the user might feel secure or not.

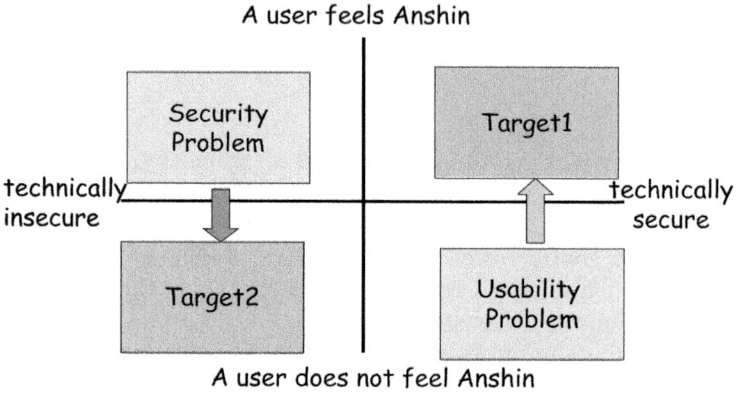

So on the right-hand side there are technically secure systems, on the left-hand side we have insecure systems, at the top we have systems where the user feels comfortable, happy, at ease with the system they are using, and in the bottom half we have systems where the user does not feel comfortable with the system. So on the top right-hand corner are those systems that are secure and where the user feels secure. There are other systems (bottom right) which are secure but the user does not feel secure, the user does not feel this "anshin", and those are clearly systems with a usability problem. They are actually secure, but they don't feel right, and so there are user interface issues.

Jonathan Anderson: So bottom left is the old thing about, in New Zealand where they said, you should mount a big spike on the front of the car driver, and ban seatbelts, because driving is so dangerous people don't feel dangerous enough[3].

---

[2] The closest in Shakespeare itself is Macbeth Act 3 Scene 4, where the queen of the witches says: "And you all know security is mortals' chiefest enemy" suggesting that the saying was familiar to the audience: does she mean carelessness or the desire to be safe?

[3] This seems to be a hardy perennial: several people seem to come up with the idea each year, including John Adams who used it in a report for the Adam Smith Institute in 1999, see `http://www.adamsmith.org/publications/regulation-and-industry/risky-business/`

Bruce Christianson: You should realise that you're about to do something that's very terrifying and dangerous, and you should be in an appropriate state of mind.

Reply: Exactly, you've jumped umpteen slides. So yes, if you have a system which feels secure but is not secure then you have a security problem, and if you can take your insecure system and make it secure (which is what we all talk about in this workshop), that's one solution to the problem. But another solution to the problem is to take the system which is insecure and make it *feel* insecure, make the user aware that he's got a problem. And that's at least part of a solution.

If the user feels comfortable, but is not in fact secure, and is about to fall for some scam, we would like the user to become aware that something is dangerous, something is wrong.

Bruce Christianson: Be aware that they have a need to buy one of the security products that we hold the patent for. [laughter]

Reply: So there's a lot of stuff in these slides about trust and security, and one of the problems we have is that trust has so many different meanings, and some of them are almost diametrically opposite to others. Basically the idea of anshin is the emotional, or the touchy-feely part of whether something is secure. I'm not quite sure if I completely agree with this, but there's a technical part and an emotional part to trust, and anshin is the idea of how do you feel about the system, how do you feel when you're using it. But sometimes when we talk about trust, we do not mean the systems that we *have* to rely upon, and if we don't trust them we can't do anything because if we do trust them it's possible for them to do us harm (I think that's the definition that we've agreed upon here over the years). But other people use the word trust to mean what kind of reasons do we have for trusting that the floor will not collapse under my weight, or whatever. So there may be good rational reasons that we have seen lots of floors before that have not collapsed, or we might have an emotional reason for feeling that things are alright. And many people, I think, don't have rational reasons for trusting systems, they have perhaps emotional reasons.

Sandy Clark: That's why we call that religion.

Bruce Christianson: The interaction between trust and faith is a very healthy one.

Reply: I think the definition we have in this community is closer to faith than some of these other things. You're relying on something that you can't see.

Bruce Christianson: It's what philosophers would call true unjustified belief.

Jonathan Anderson: It's not entirely unjustified, I mean, I have faith in the building inspector who approved this place being put up, but buildings don't usually fall down in the UK because there's a process by which they usually do their job. That faith is actually justified, not completely, but, you know.

Reply: OK, so if you have a feeling of trust, you're not actually aware that you need to do anything about trusting, although in fact you probably are trusting things. Whereas if you rely on measuring how reliable things are, then you may be in a problem, because you can't actually work out how much reliability to put on other things.

In order to get a better feel for the basis on which people actually feel secure about the computer systems they're using, they conducted a survey, quite a large survey. They did a preliminary survey with 122 students in their university, and having done that, they did a larger survey with 425 subjects in the university, and also further surveys with government officers and in the USA as well. The American one unfortunately was a little bit smaller.

The purpose of this survey was to try and identify what was the basis that people felt they could trust various computer systems. And they received 35 items, which could answer the question, do you feel that the following items account for your sense that you have security when you use your system through the internet, and people basically had to say, I strongly or mildly agree, or disagree, whether these factors contributed to their sense of comfort, well-being, or anshin, related to using these systems. So questions like, I trust the service provider and the company that own it, the service provider and its owner have the confidence of society, I am in confident in the competence of the provider, I'm not afraid because I am quite experienced, I have a sense of security because my friends or family use it, or whatever. The people who were surveyed were mostly university students, relatively young, perhaps not old enough to have become excessively cynical, and mostly computer science related students, but quite a number of non-computer science students too. For analysis, the questions could be divided into a number of factors: security related, or usability related, or subject experience, etc.

And one interesting result, there is an absolutely huge difference between computer science or information science students, and other students. The computer science students have a strong indication, the most significant part of their judgement of whether they're happy to use a system is based on their computer science knowledge, and to some extent preference, and trust in the knowledge that the organisation behind it is sound. Whereas for other students, cognitive trust, trust in the provider and personal preference are still quite strong, but knowledge is almost disappeared.

Bruce Christianson: Those are negative correlations, so it's the opposite of the computer science students: preference and cognitive transfer are actual disinhibitors.

Mike Roe: You expect that if both sets of people are being rational: the people who think they know how a system works are basing their judgement on knowing how a system works, and the people who think they don't know how it works are basing their judgement on other things.

Reply: Yes, but it certainly highlights that there's a very big difference between the computer science community and others, even if we look at our students and say, they don't know very much.

Sandy Clark: But they think they do.

Dieter Gollmann: They actually do; they know a lot compared to the rest of the population.

Reply: I think the difference is significant, it's not just statistically significant, but there is a very big difference between the man in the street, even if well educated and about to become a professional in some other area.

Frank Stajano: I could see some things which were correlated with the things in our scam victim study[4], such as "I have a sense of security as my friends or family use it", which would be the herd principle. So it would be interesting to know how many of these get scammed because of this false sense of confidence: in which cases is the confidence well-placed, in which cases it is wrongly placed.

Bruce Christianson: Or is it just that computer scientists don't have any friends.

Reply: So there's a fair number of other questions that could be asked.

Frank Stajano: Is it going to come later?

Reply: Apart from this summary that I've just shown you, there's no detailed report on these groups, apart from the clear difference between computing students and non-computing students. She also looked at some students in America, not so many, but there was clearly a difference in ranking between Japanese students and American students. It seemed that Japanese students were more influenced by the design of the user interface for some reason. Trust in the competence and integrity of the provider of the system was ranked third with Japanese students, but was ranked top with American students, the interface went down to second, and trust in the competence and benevolence of the system, as opposed to the provider of the system, has also moved down.

So there's some difference between the different communities, and the most noticeable one being that trust in the organisation is lower in Japan than it is in the United States.

Dieter Gollmann: I think what you said is wrong; it's much lower, it's ranked further down, because in a society where you assume by default that a provider's competence and integrity is a given, it does not discriminate.

Mike Burmester: I think what's quite interesting is that experience versus knowledge, and fundamentally I think ranking experience over knowledge is very sensible. Because you may believe you know how the system works, most of the times you don't really know how it works, you just have a mental model of what

[4] "Understanding scam victims: Seven principles for systems security" by Frank Stajano and Paul Wilson, Communications of the ACM 54(3):70-75.

you think that they would be doing if they would be doing it the way you would be doing it.

Alf Zugenmaier: Is something say where I interact with the service a couple of hundred times and not been defrauded, so, you know, just take a risk for a couple of hundred plus one times. So I think that is actually quite interesting.

Bruce Christianson: It begs the question of how you interacted with it 200 times without that assurance though.

Reply: And why it was so patient before it decided to scam you.

So I think the survey gathered a lot of data, but we haven't fully understood all the details because unfortunately the people that did the work cannot be here.

The other thing that follows on from Jonathan's point about the dangerous motorcar, is the suggestion that if we can make people more aware that they are using a system in a way that might potentially be dangerous, then we could move systems which remain insecure, but move them to a position where the user is aware that they are in an insecure situation. And I thought that this is entirely in keeping with the theme of the workshop, because as you know, as you walk through Oakland, you begin to feel insecure, you notice that some of the shops are boarded up, you notice that the street light has failed, there's somebody a bit dodgy on the other side of the street.... It's not, suddenly I know I'm insecure, you are kind of gradually aware of things not being quite right, and it strikes me that in making the user interface somehow uncomfortable, which is their suggestion, it doesn't have to make a true/false decision for you, it can be gradually getting more uncomfortable.

Matt Blaze: But with phishing, I guess the user interface is what the attacker most obviously controls, right, they're exploiting the fact that their user interface looks very trustworthy.

Reply: The phishing site looks exactly the same as the real one.

Matt Blaze: Yes, but there's nothing that the good guys can do to prevent the bad guy from making a more comforting user interface than the real system. My bank's website has pictures of criminals, you know, running around, shooting, pointing shotguns at you, and the phishing website has a picture of a policeman.

Bruce Christianson: Firefox has a little frame that the browser is in, and you can have that change to become quite threatening, and the background music become discordant.

Frank Stajano: In the good old days, some 15 years ago or so when Java was introduced it had an orange bar that said this is put up by Java, it's not the web site, so beware because anything in here could be fake, but it could not get out of that window so at least you knew. That has of course been lost now.

Bruce Christianson: But just being able to do it the other way round would be nice.

Reply: Some simple things would be easy, for example this is a website in Russia. We are allowed to go to websites in Russia, some of them are perfectly fine, but it's just a little bit suspicious, so you think maybe I should just be a bit more careful here. And something that just raises the emotional tension might be quite helpful because it is not possible to make a clear-cut distinction between safe and dangerous. For example, I think Alf you mentioned that you had a phone call from somebody, and you honestly didn't know if it was a scam or not.

Alf Zugenmaier: Actually people were coming to my door, and I was not able to get any confirmation that these people were in fact coming from the telephone company.

Reply: And my daughter had the same thing, we had this phone message, and it sounded like it was from her credit card company, but then it didn't sound like it; we were unable to come to a definite conclusion as to whether it was genuine. You could imagine that an expert system or something attached to your browser would not need to prove that you're about to do something fatal, they can just raise the tension, as it were.

Jonathan Anderson: They can just recommend things that will make you feel more comfortable, like if I am the one calling the number of the back of my card, then that increases my comfort level, even though, yes, it's possible that somebody's done nasty things to my phoneline, but I feel more comfortable, and justifiably so.

Sandy Clark: The browser, that extra frame, could also go out and correlate, if you're going to visit this site here are ones that we know to be good domains that you can trust, or something.

Alf Zugenmaier: Just the fact that a phishing email is most likely to come from a slightly different sounding, looking address. You clicked on a link therefore you are going to get this spooky background music while you type in the words yourself, you get more relaxing music.

Frank Stajano: In Thunderbird, for example, if you get an email which has a link, and the link is not the same as what's displayed, then it will put up a warning, it sounds like a scam, you really wouldn't want to do it.

Matt Blaze: So let's look at the evolution for 419, Nigerian scams. You notice that there are at least two classes, at least for the ones that I'm seeing, that get through my spam filters. There is the raw "please help me transfer this money out of the country" scam, and then there is the "we're investigating this fraud that is being attempted against you, please let us know and we'll get you your money back" form of scam. And it's interesting that by raising the kind of noise level of the underlying scam ones, you're actually making the ones that are ostensibly helping you recover your money look better by comparison.

Reply: Because it's getting you more context that fits with your model of what's going on[5].

Matt Blaze: But there we have the example where the adversary is maybe not deliberately, but effectively manipulating your whole context of what you're looking at in ways that go outside the individual message.

Frank Stajano: I guess manipulating the context gives them more credit than they deserve, but this is what they want, so when they see that this is what happens, they say, right, we can reframe this.

Reply: Like Haiti, and Japan, the earthquakes, or you know there's a royal wedding coming up really soon, and you need to make sure that you invest in the right company to deliver flowers, or whatever, anything topical they will grab hold of.

[5] See "The snooping dragon: social-malware surveillance of the Tibetan movement" by Shishir Nagaraja and Ross Anderson: UCAM-CL-TR-746.pdf.

Towards a Theory of Trust in Networks of Humans and Computers

Virgil Gligor and Jeannette M. Wing

Carnegie Mellon University,
Pittsburgh, Pennsylvania 15213, USA
gligor@cmu.edu, wing@cs.cmu.edu

Abstract. We argue that a general theory of trust in networks of humans and computers must be build on both a theory of *behavioral trust* and a theory of *computational trust*. This argument is motivated by increased participation of people in social networking, crowdsourcing, human computation, and socio-economic protocols, e.g., protocols modeled by trust and gift-exchange games [3,10,11], norms-establishing contracts [1], and scams [6,35,33]. User participation in these protocols relies primarily on trust, since on-line verification of protocol compliance is often impractical; e.g., verification can lead to undecidable problems, co-NP complete test procedures, and user inconvenience. Trust is captured by participant preferences (i.e., risk and betrayal aversion) and beliefs in the trustworthiness of other protocol participants [11,10]. Both preferences and beliefs can be enhanced whenever protocol noncompliance leads to punishment of untrustworthy participants [11,23]; i.e., it seems natural that betrayal aversion can be decreased and belief in trustworthiness increased by properly defined punishment [1]. We argue that a general theory of trust should focus on the establishment of new trust relations where none were possible before. This focus would help create new economic opportunities by increasing the pool of usable services, removing cooperation barriers among users, and at the very least, taking advantage of "network effects." Hence a new theory of trust would also help focus security research in areas that promote trust-enhancement infrastructures in human and computer networks. Finally, we argue that a general theory of trust should mirror, to the largest possible extent, human expectations and mental models of trust without relying on false methaphors and analogies with the physical world.

1 Introduction

Consider this fundamental question: How can I, a human, trust the information I receive through the Internet? This question's relevance has grown with the advent of socially intelligent computing, which includes social networking, crowd sourcing, and human computation. Socially intelligent computing recognizes the increasing opportunities for humans to work with each other relying on input from both humans and computers in order to solve problems and make decisions. When we read a Wikipedia page, how can we trust its contents? We need to

B. Christianson et al. (Eds.): Security Protocols 2011, LNCS 7114, pp. 223–242, 2011.

trust the person who wrote the page, the computer that hosts the page, the channel over which the message that contains the page contents are sent to the reader, and finally the computer that receives the message that contains the page contents.

We seek a general theory of trust for networks of humans and computers. Our main idea is that for a general theory we need to build on both a theory of *behavioral trust* to complement and reinforce a theory of *computational trust*. Behavioral trust defines trust relations among people and organizations; computational trust, among devices, computers, and networks. Towards building a general theory of trust through combining ideas from behavioral trust and computational trust, we moreover argue that there is *new economic value* to be gained, raising new opportunities for technological innovation.

The True State of Affairs. Toward a general theory of trust, let's review from computer science and the social and economic sciences, the state of the art, since it is not as rosy as we would like. Over the past three decades, research on trust in computer networks focused on specific properties, e.g., authentication and access-control trust, in traditional distributed systems and networks [4,22,13]), mobile ad-hoc networks [12,31,25,36,5,32,38,27,26,18], and applications [19,21]. Lack of a formal theory of trust has had visible consequences: definitions of trust are often ad-hoc, and trust relations among different network components and applications are hidden or unknown. Often trust definitions underlying the design of secure protocols are misunderstood by both network designers and users, and lead to unforeseen attacks [30]. Similarly, despite a vast body of work on trust in the social sciences [16,24], we do not have a formal theory of trust among groups of humans, social and business organizations. Instead, trust is defined by example in different areas of economics, sociology and psychology, and no generally accepted theory of trust exists to date. Hence, we neither have a formal theory of trust for computers nor one for humans; and we certainly do not have a formal theory of trust for networks of humans *and* computers to date. Yet it is quite clear that such a theory is needed in the light of complex interactions in networks of humans and computers in the Internet.

This paper's main contributions to the computer security community are: (1) asking our opening question of trust where humans are as much a part of the system as computers; (2) introducing behavioral trust as a seed toward answering the question; (3) arguing the new economic value introduced by a general theory of trust based on the combination of behavioral trust and computational trust.

2 Impact of a Theory of Trust

We anticipate that a new theory of trust will have significant impact on several important areas of network economics, security, and usability.

New Economic Value. A new theory of trust should explain the establishment of new trust relations where none existed before. The expansion in the kinds of and numbers of trust relations in human and computer networks clearly helps create new economic opportunities and value. New trust relations increase the pool of usable services, remove cooperation barriers among users, and at the very least, take advantage of "network effects." Cloud computing is the most obvious example of new kinds and numbers of trust relations: people trust companies, e.g., Google, Facebook, and Amazon, with all sorts of personal data, and moreover people trust these companies' computing infrastructure to store and manage their data. New trust relations also help increase competition among network service providers, which spurs innovation, productivity, expanded markets, and ultimately economic development.

New Focus for Security Research. Much of the past research on trust establishment focused on (formal) derivation of new trust relations from old ones; e.g., trusted third-party services, transitive trust relations, delegation. In contrast with prior research, we seek a theory of trust which explains how to create new trust relations that are *not* derived from old ones, and create new opportunities for cooperation among users and among services. For example, it should be possible to establish private, pair-wise trust relations between two untrusting parties that do not necessarily share a common trusted service, such as eBay, which enables reputation systems to work; or a common social network, which might enable recommendations systems to work. While helpful in many cases, trusted third parties create additional complexity and uncertainty, and sometimes become an attractive attack target (e.g., Google). Instead, we seek network infrastructures that enable *unmediated* trust relations, which take us beyond the realm of various (re)interpretations of the end-to-end argument at the application level [7]. In this paper, we argue that network infrastructures that support the establishment of *behavioral trust*, which lower risk and betrayal aversion between untrusting parties and increase beliefs in trustworthiness between these parties, will spur establishment of unmediated trust relations, and as a consequence create new economic value.

Usable Models of Trust. A new theory of trust should be useful for casual users, not just for network and application-service designers. To be useful, such a theory must be easily understandable by designers and users alike. And to be understandable, *a theory of trust has to mirror, to a large extent, human expectations and mental models of trust.* For example, users understand how to separate and protect physical and financial assets in everyday activity. Similarly, they would understand and expect computer systems networks to enable them to separate information assets, be they local system services or financial data held by bank servers. Furthermore, a new theory of trust must not create false metaphors and analogies with the physical world. The email trust model is an example of false expectations: the widespread user expectation that electronic mail would mirror the trust model of physical mail (e.g., authenticity, confidentiality, non-repudiation of receipt, delivery in bounded time) has misled many unsuspecting users into accepting spam, misleading ads, and malware. In contrast, the trust model of eBay follows a well-established, traditional human trust example:

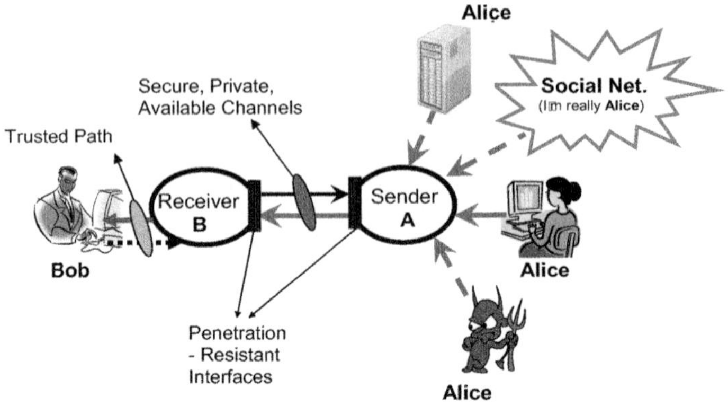

Fig. 1. Simple Communication Model: Entities and Channels

it establishes trust relations based on reputation, and to counter inevitable protoctol non-compliance and trust failures, it uses insurance-based recovery mechanisms.

We begin with a simple communication model (Section 3), primarily to state our assumptions. In addressing our opening motivating question, we focus on notions from computational trust (Section 4) that leads us naturally to introduce notions from behavioral trust (Section 5). We explore in Section 6 the implications of behavioral trust for the creation of novel computing and institutional infrastructures. We close in Section 7 with directions for future research.

3 A Simple Communication Model

We assume a network of parties who exchange information with each other over communication channels. When party A (Alice) sends information to party B (Bob), we call A the *sender* and B the *receiver*. Senders and receivers could be human users, network hosts, network applications, and even purveyors of malware (see Figure 1). To focus on trust in networks of humans and computers, we need a simple communication model that allows us to separate questions of sender/receiver *behavior* from more traditional questions of trust specific to communication-channel security, privacy and availability.

Communication-Model Assumptions. Figure 1 summarizes our main assumptions: communication channels are secure and private, and trusted paths can be used by users to communicate with their local computers. We also assume that all communication channels are available for sender-receiver communication whenever needed. Furthermore, we assume that the receiver's and sender's interfaces to communication channels are penetration resistant. Properties of penetration resistance are relatively well understood and have already been formally defined [15]. Recent research [17,28] illustrate how attack surfaces exposed by these, and other, interfaces can be measured and reduced.

4 Computational Trust Overview

Let's tease apart the opening motivating question "How can I trust the information I receive?" in a purely computational setting. This information is produced by another, possibly anonymous party, or multiple parties, and arrives via messages on communication channels. Thus, first we equate "information" to be literally "contents of messages" (or for brevity, "messages"). We then decompose this question into two separate sub-questions: "Is the communication channel via which I receive messages from a sender secure?" and "How can I trust the sender of the messages I receive?" This decomposition allows us to equate trust in the information I receive with the *act of trusting the sender*. Let's consider the first sub-question. Since we assume secure communication channels, we rule out undetectable corruption, insertion, and replay of the messages received by a third party. Similarly, receipt of secret information over a secure channel rules out non-negligible secret leakage to a third party and reduces any confidentiality concern to trusting the sender with keeping that secret.

In short, assuming the security of communication channels, the question of "How can I trust the information I receive?" (possibly via an anonymous channel) reduces to: "How can I trust the sender of the message I receive?" For example, if I click on a link to a website, can I trust the contents of the message received from that website? Of course, similar questions can be asked in the context of multiple message exchanges and multiple protocol participants. For much of the balance of this paper, we focus on possible answers to this question and assume that communication takes place over secure channels; i.e., we separate concerns of communication security from the act of trusting the sender by the receiver.

Value Underlying the Act of Trusting the Sender. In sender-receiver communication, both the sender and the receiver must derive some *value*, i.e., the benefit of communication must exceed the cost. If there is no value for either sender or receiver, the question of trusting the message sender does not arise, since communication does not take place. For the receiver, value materializes whenever the receiver depends on that information for further action, e.g., the receiver uses the information to invest resources. For example, reading the contents of a message may be very beneficial to the receiver, as the message may contain a program which solves a problem the receiver could not solve himself. However, executing that program on the receiver's system may also have an unexpectedly high cost, e.g., the program may contain "malware" that damages his system, or provides incorrect results, which may cause the receiver to take costly future actions. Hence, the receiver has to decide whether the value derived from reading a message received exceeds the cost of the potential damage caused by that message.

Similarly, a sender derives value in responding to a request from a receiver. The sender benefit materializes whenever there is a payment transfer from the receiver, or when a request represented by a click on a link to the sender's website is monetized. However, when processing the response, a sender uses its resources at some cost, which must be lower than its benefit.

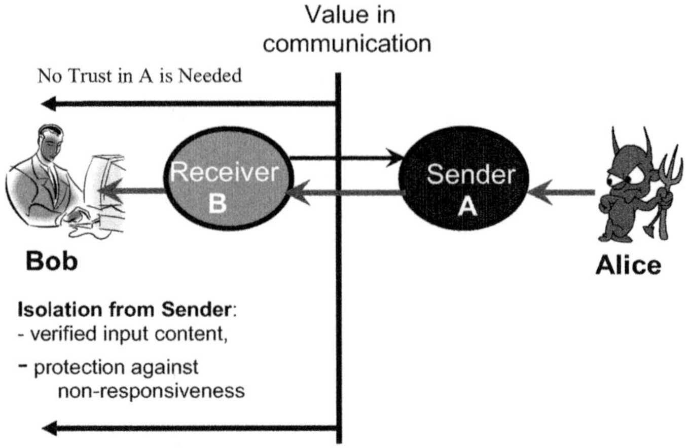

Fig. 2. Receiver's Isolation from Sender's Behavior

4.1 Isolation

Isolation from Sender's Behavior Implies No Trust is Needed. Let's return to our simple question of "How can I trust the sender of the message I receive?" Suppose that the receiver can verify the validity of the message at a reasonably low cost, certainly lower than the benefit derived from it. That is, the receiver can derive value from the message received by verifying all its properties that could affect his resource investment and future state. For example, suppose that the receiver can verify whether the message contains malware, incorrect solutions to a problem of interest, incorrect proofs, or other disinformation. If verification indicates that the received information is valid, then the receiver can act on it and be better off than before. Otherwise, the receiver can reject it, and avoid negative consequences. In short, verification of message properties isolates the receiver from a malicious or incompetent sender. That is, regardless of what message the sender sends the receiver, her input to the receiver cannot damage the receiver. Hence, there is no need to trust the sender. Isolation establishes a well-defined boundary or interface between the sender's and receiver's interests. Figure 2 illustrates the role of a receiver's isolation from the sender's behavior.

In practice, support for isolation can be implemented by means other than direct receiver verification. One way is to get a *second opinion* from a different independent sender, thereby protecting the receiver from the interests and/or competence of the first sender. For example, two independent *authorities* that provide acceptable answers on a subject matter may offer independent advice in response to a query. A positive comparison, which indicates that the two independent advice messages are similar, would cause the receiver to trust the (original) message more than before, and perhaps simply to accept the first sender's message as valid without further checking. However, a negative comparison would mean that the advice messages are contradictory, and thus the second opinion would offer no help in isolating the receiver from a malicious or incompetent authority. Furthermore, for a second opinion to be useful, it also has to be available whenever needed. Receiving messages from an authority on a particular subject of interest to the receiver can be expensive, and the cost of soliciting advice from multiple authorities may exceed the receiver's benefit. The notion of "second opinion" generalizes to "n opinions," but at a cost.

Another way to achieve isolation from a sender is by *outsourcing validation*, e.g., via a recommendation system whereby multiple parties independently evaluate (e.g., score) the validity of the message received from that sender. Unlike the case where the receiver gets a second opinion from an independent *authority*, a recommendation system allows inconsistent evaluation of a sender's message by independent parties. In effect, the receiver outsources the decision to trust the message (and thus implicitly trust the sender) to a crowd of recommenders. The receiver's decision whether to accept a message from a sender would be based on the dominant recommendation made by a crowd of independent evaluators. To be useful, however, recommender systems must make available a sufficient number of independent recommendations when needed by a receiver. Availability of a sufficiently large number of independent evaluations helps assure that various biases about the particular message content (and thus sender) are diminished. A more challenging situation is when there is lack of independence of the recommenders.

While receiver verification of a sender's input message represents a major part of receiver isolation from sender behavior, it is not the only isolation property that protects against a malicious or incompetent sender. Isolation from a sender's behavior also requires the receiver to protect against the event that the sender does not reply to the receiver's query in due time. In short, because a sender may not comply with communication protocol requirements (e.g., protocol norms, use agreements) *receiver's isolation from sender's behavior*, comprises: (1) the verification of a received message and (2) protection against deliberate sender non-responsiveness (independent of any network availability concerns, which we assume away by our communication model).

4.2 Trustworthiness and Correctness

Trustworthiness is Stronger than Correctness. Traditionally, the notion of trustworthiness in computer security has been identified with that of correctness. For example, this interpretation of trustworthy computer systems is embodied in all evaluation criteria, from the Orange Book (1985), to EU's ITSEC (1987), and to Common Criteria (1996). In fact, these evaluation criteria have tiered levels of correctness (assurance). However, the notion of trustworthiness is *strictly stronger* than the notion of correctness. In our example, the correctness of the sender's code is a necessary condition for sender's trustworthiness, but it is not a sufficient condition. Why? A sender (computational entity) that satisfies its specifications may still use input of uncertain validity from a human in preparing its response to the receiver. Or the sender may not start in a correct initial state (e.g., after a crash). Or it may not be configured correctly. As a result, we must think of a sender's trustworthiness as a combination of computational correctness properties *and* human trustworthy behavior. In other words, whenever we have a *human in the trust loop*, the notion of trustworthiness must incorporate both a computational primitive, namely correctness, and a behavior trust primitive, namely beliefs of human trustworthiness.

To establish a sender's trustworthiness a receiver needs to verify the validity of *trustworthiness evidence* both in a computational (e.g., by checking proofs of response validity or using proof-carrying code, to protect herself from incorrect, stale, inconsistent evidence) and a behavioral setting (e.g., beliefs established as a results of trust and gift-exchange games—see discussion below). Also, the delivery mechanism for obtaining evidence of sender's trustworthiness, whether on-line via secure and available channels or off-line, ultimately raises different, but separate, questions of trust, as already discussed above.

We note in passing that sender trustworthiness itself may require sender's isolation from receivers. For example, in traditional security settings, a sender responds to multiple receivers' requests via channels with fairly complex interfaces (e.g., large, complex sender code typically has a wide attack surface). Competing receivers may, in fact, penetrate the sender and invalidate all sender's evidence of trustworthiness. This explains the key underlying requirement that security kernels (and trustworthy computing bases, in general) need isolation to be trustworthy, and illustrates further the need for our penetration-resistance assumption of channel interfaces.

Separation of Sender's Trustworthiness from Receiver Isolation. Suppose that the receiver can obtain incontrovertible evidence that the sender's trustworthiness; i.e., both computationally and behaviorally. Then the receiver can accept all messages from the sender *without additional* verification. The sender is *trustworthy* by definition, and hence the receiver need *not* isolate himself from the sender.

4.3 The Act of Trusting the Sender

Now suppose that the receiver cannot isolate himself from a sender. For example, isolation is not possible in cases when the receiver cannot verify the output behavior of a program contained in a sender's message, since such verification may lead to an undecidable problem. Or, the verification cost may exceed the value of the response to the receiver; e.g., the receiver may have to verify the solution to a co-NP complete problem, which is very unlikely to be possible in polynomial time. Or, a second opinion regarding the validity of a message received and outsourced message-validity checking may be unavailable. Furthermore, suppose that the cost of obtaining and checking evidence of sender's trustworthiness may be too high.

In such cases, the receiver can extract the value of communicating with the sender only if the receiver agrees: to wait for the response to his query *without* any guarantee of a response, and to accept the sender's message received *without* verifying its validity. That is, the receiver benefits only if the receiver *trusts the sender*. There must be value to the receiver in waiting for the sender's message and accepting it without verification, even in the absence of evidence of sender trustworthiness or protection against invalid sender messages. The essence of trusting the sender is that the receiver places himself and his resources at the disposal of the sender *without* any protection against being cheated, misinformed, or otherwise led down a garden path. Why would the receiver do this? Because there is tangible value to be had.

Value Outcomes of the Act of Trust: The act of trusting transfers value from the receiver of information to the sender and back, at a cost.

Here now is the link between computational trust and behavioral trust. Consider henceforth the receiver to be the "trustor" or "investor" and the sender to be the "trustee." The trustor incurs a cost by clicking on a link to the trustee. This cost, for example, could be the cost of executing the action or opportunity cost (of not clicking on a different link). Yet the trustor willingly transfers value to (e.g., pays) the trustee. In addition, the market may amplify the trustor's transfer, as it may help the trustee monetize the trustor's click. The trustee can choose to transfer value back to the trustor, as it expands resources to respond correctly to the trustor's request, instead of cheating, i.e., instead of providing an arbitrary response, if not a malicious one, a partial response, or no response at all. However, if the trustor anticipates that the trustee will cheat, the trustor would avoid contacting the trustee (i.e., by not clicking on the link for a website), and no value would be exchanged. In summary, the *act of trusting* has the following three possible value outcomes:

1) if the trustor trusts the trustee *and* the trustee is *trustworthy*, then both the trustor and trustee are better off than before executing the protocol, i.e., cooperation pays off.
2) if the trustor trusts the trustee *and* the trustee is *untrustworthy*, the trustee is better off and the trustor is worse off than before, i.e., trustee has strong incentive to cheat in the absence of a mechanism that protects the trustor.
3) if the trustor suspects that the trustee will cheat and hence, does not initiate the protocol, no value is exchanged.

By building on computational techniques (e.g., cryptography, verification, fault-tolerance) that give us trust among computational entities (e.g., computers and networks) we are left with non-computational entities. Thus now when we talk about trustors/receivers and trustees/senders we are talking about humans: the person (sender) who wrote the code to be run remotely or who wrote the Wikipedia page and the person (received) who requested the message contents, e.g., by clicking on the webpage. This means we need to look at theories that explain trust relations among humans.

5 Behavioral Trust Overview

One-shot Trust Games. Recent research in behavioral economics defines a game that captures the notion of trust described above [3,11,10], which we present as

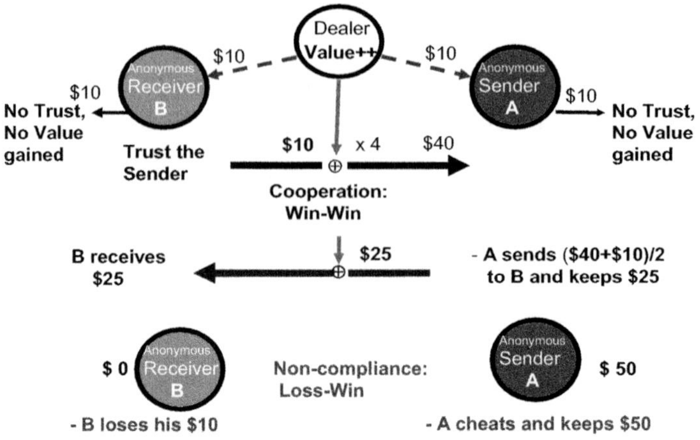

Fig. 3. Outcomes of an One-shot Trust Game

a motivation for the foundations of *behavioral trust*. In a typical one-shot trust game (illustrated in Figure 3), two players, the trustee A and trustor B, both of whom remain anonymous, are endowed with $10 each by a dealer. Player B must decide whether to hold on to his endowment or send it to A. If he sends it to A, the dealer quadruples the transferred value received by A. Player A is supposed to return half of her accumulated value (i.e., ($40 +$10)/2) to B. So both players end up with $25 each if they cooperate, and only with their initial $10 endowment, if they do not. If B transfers his endowment to A and A does not comply with the protocol (i.e., A cheats and transfers less than $25), B loses his endowment and receives less than the $25 expected, if anything. Depending upon her behavior, A is left with as much as $50, and certainly with more than the $25 guaranteed by cooperation, in worst-case cheating. That is, A retains her initial endowment of $10 plus $40 representing the quadrupling of the value transferred by B ($10) by the dealer. Hence, player A has an incentive to cheat.

The trust game mimics a sequential economic exchange in *the absence of any mechanism* that would enforce a contract between players A and B, and has the same flavor as the sender-receiver protocol outlined above in the absence of the receiver B's isolation and sender A's trustworthiness; i.e., it illustrates receiver B's *act of trusting* sender A. Experiments in neuro-economics [11] show that the vast majority of players in the role of B, namely 14 of 15 players, trust the players in the role of A contrary to rational economic theory, which would have each player pocket the $10 endowment and not play.

The trust game also illustrates the definition of cooperation and fairness *norms in sender-receiver protocols*. Specifically, player A is supposed to send half of her accumulated value to player B; i.e., ($40+$10)/2. If A decides not send $25 to player B, then B interprets this as a norms violation, or a protocol non-compliance act.

The same experiments [11] also show that protocol non-compliance evokes a sense of betrayal in player B and a desire to punish violator A, even if *punishment*

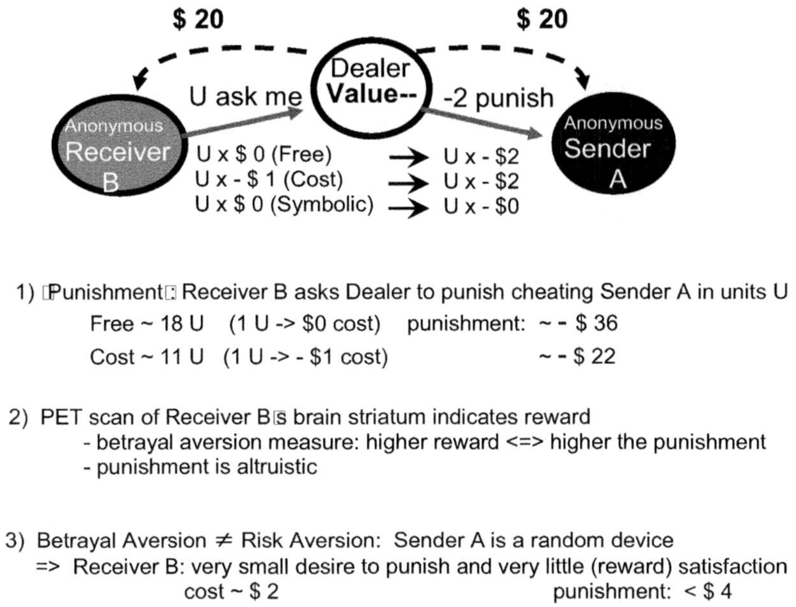
$ 20
$ 20
Dealer
Value--
U ask me
-2 punish
Anonymous
Receiver
B
Anonymous
Sender
A
U x $ 0 (Free)
U x - $ 1 (Cost)
U x $ 0 (Symbolic)
U x - $2
U x - $2
U x - $0
1) Punishment Receiver B asks Dealer to punish cheating Sender A in units U
Free ~ 18 U (1 U -> $0 cost) punishment: ~ - $ 36
Cost ~ 11 U (1 U -> - $1 cost) ~ - $ 22
2) PET scan of Receiver B's brain striatum indicates reward
- betrayal aversion measure: higher reward <=> higher the punishment
- punishment is altruistic
3) Betrayal Aversion ≠ Risk Aversion: Sender A is a random device
=> Receiver B: very small desire to punish and very little (reward) satisfaction
cost ~ $ 2 punishment: < $ 4

Fig. 4. Experiments Illustrating Betrayal and Risk Aversion

comes at a cost to B. In the continuation of the trust game, player B is informed of A's protocol violation, is given one minute to decide whether, and how much, to punish A, and his neural reaction is measured. Specifically, in a first experiment, where punishment costs, player B is given 20 punishment units, U, each costing B \$1 and A \$2; i.e., for every punishment unit U, B pays \$1 so that A loses \$2. In another experiment, punishment is free; i.e., it costs B nothing to reduce A's ill-gotten gain by \$2. In the third experiment punishment is symbolic; i.e., neither B nor A incur any cost. Finally, in the last experiment A's decision to cheat is made by a device, at random; i.e., the device replaces cheating player A. To measure player B's neural response to punishment, a PET scan of B's brain was taken during the one-minute interval B's decision was made. Figure 4 summarizes three outcomes of these experiments. First, player B is willing to *incur a cost to punish*, and the amount of punishment inflicted was higher when punishment was free. Second, player B derived satisfaction (i.e., felt rewarded) proportional to the amount of punishment inflicted on cheating player A; i.e., the stronger the satisfaction player B derived, the higher the cost he was willing to incur. This indicates the strength of B's *aversion to being betrayed* by A. It also illustrates the fact that B's *punishment is altruistic*, since he is willing to pay to punish even though he is not deriving any material gain. Third, when cheating player A was replaced by a random device that is protocol non-compliant, B's desire to punish is negligible. This indicates that B's *aversion to the risk of losing* money when faced with an ambiguous outcome was different (i.e., lower) from his aversion to being betrayed.

The analogy between our sender-receiver protocol and a one-shot trust game in economics can be valuable because behavioral economics has already discovered the fundamental primitives comprising the act of trusting. Some of these primitives have analogues in computer networks. Others complement these primitives as they refer to *the act of trusting* among humans and apply directly to human networks. In both cases, they address the need for network infrastructures that promote value creation by trustor and trustee cooperation (as suggested by Figure 5).

Behavioral-Trust Primitives. Behavioral trust is characterized by three *independent* primitives studied extensively in economics. As the trust game suggests, these are:

1) A trustor's *risk preferences.* This captures the trustor's (player B above) degree of risk aversion when faced with ambiguous outcomes; i.e., the trustee's (player A above) trustworthiness is uncertain. Much of the research on decision making under uncertainty relies on these *asocial* preferences [37,20].
2) A trustor's *social preferences.* This captures the trustor's degree of *betrayal, or non-reciprocation, aversion* when faced with a trustee who may cheat or perpetrate a scam [10,8,9]. Recent research also indicates that betrayal aversion—a social preference—is very different from and independent of asocial risk preferences. For example, in the one-shot trust game above, player B's neurological reaction is very different when the cheating player A is a human as opposed to a device, e.g., a computer. Recent research also suggests that trust is partially heritable [10].
3) A trustor's *belief in trustworthiness* of trustees. The trustor forms probability beliefs about a trustee's actions and uses these beliefs to guide the trusting act; e.g., it measures the difference between the expected utilities of trust and distrust, both of which are computed using probability beliefs. Recent research also indicates that *trustworthiness beliefs* are independent of a trustor's *risk and social preferences.* Trustworthiness beliefs can be enhanced by reputation building opportunities, including reputation protocols, with or without recommender features, etc. Gift-exchange games capture reputation building in behavioral economics [10].

Standard models of trust, both in the social sciences (i.e., economics, sociology and psychology) and computer science, rely on two of the three primitives above: risk preferences and formation of trustworthiness beliefs. Hundreds of articles have been published on these two primitives separately in the social sciences [16,24] and computer science. However, there is little practical experience applying these notions in networks of computers and humans; e.g., only eBay's model of trust attempts to diminish risk aversion by offering insurance to trustors and enhance trustors' beliefs in trustees' trustworthiness by reputation protocols. With the exception of recent research in behavioral trust, both theory and practice missed the notion of betrayal aversion and its application in networks of humans and computers.

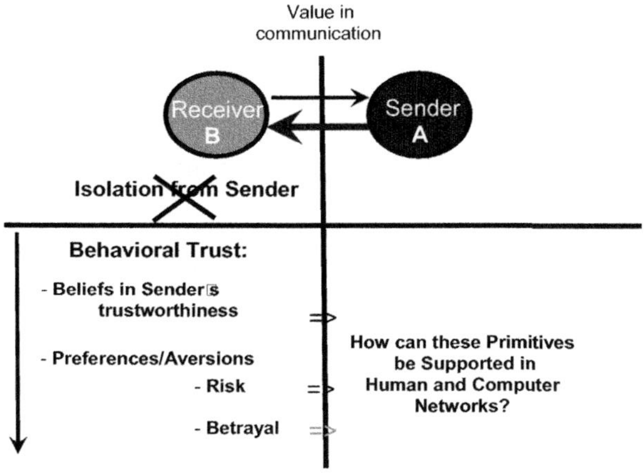

Fig. 5. Summary of Behavioral-Trust Primitives

6 Usefulness of Behavioral Trust in Networks of Humans and Computers

Is there Anything New in "Behavioral Trust?" Yes, betrayal aversion (as characterized by social preferences). Standard economic models of trust account only for trustors' risk aversion and the role of reputation-formation institutions. These models emphasize reputation and guided-belief-formation games, typically using Bayesian updating procedures. Similarly, in computing, there have been several reputation-building exchanges [19] and recommender systems with collaborative filtering [29,14]. The experiments in neuro-economics mentioned above show that betrayal aversion has a larger inhibiting role in the act of trusting than risk aversion. Intuitively, people are more willing to take risks when faced with a certain probability of bad luck than when faced with an identical probability of being cheated by others.

Behavioral trust shows that standard economic models miss the betrayal-aversion component of trust altogether, and hence they miss opportunities to deal with it in a constructive way, i.e., build system infrastructures that deter untrustworthy trustees from cheating. Intuition suggests that *deterrence* requires punishment, and punishment requires accountability [23]. (Accountability is also necessary in reputation-building exchanges, not just for deterrence.) However, intuition does not explain what punishment and accountability infrastructures are sufficient for deterrence; e.g., accountability does not prescribe any punishment and it is unclear what type of punishment deters cheating and encourages trustworthy behavior. Research is needed in this area.

Why Do We Expect Behavioral Trust to Create Value in Networks of Humans and Computers? Trustworthiness beliefs are positively correlated with economic prosperity (as measured by GDP), though no causal relationship has been established, yet [10]. More acts of trusting (e.g., based on lower risk- and betrayal-aversion and higher belief in trustworthiness), however, should lower the cost of economic transactions, promote trade, and hence create wealth [10]. Also, restrictive security mechanisms designed to protect parties involved in economic transactions should diminish the need for acts of trusting but increase transaction cost. By analogy, the spread of the Internet and the Web, which was largely built on (often unwarranted) acts of trusting, could be curbed by overly restrictive security mechanisms.

If causality between the act of trusting and wealth creation has not been proven, why should we really look at economic primitives to encourage acts of trusting in networks of computers and humans? Because we need *usable security* by humans. Current approaches have not been particularly successful and are not scaling up to meet the increases in both functional demands and numbers of participating entities. Most communication infrastructures built in computer systems and networks to date rely either on receiver-isolation mechanisms, namely on verification of input content, or on (often unwarranted) beliefs of sender's trustworthiness. While isolation mechanisms are often necessary, they can be: (1) cumbersome to use, (2) costly to obtain, set up and administer [23], and (3) often psychologically less than acceptable; e.g., enforcing them promotes mistrust and may be unappealing to use. In contrast, unwarranted acts of sender trust have proven to be very dangerous as they can lead to breaches of security, ranging from social scams, to identity theft, and to failures to protect the national interests. We propose this alternative: the *act of trusting* based on *evidence-driven* beliefs of trustworthiness and *robust infrastructures* for diminished risk- and betrayal-aversion. In short, behavioral trust appears to be a good place to start.

Are the Three Primitives of Behavioral Trust Sufficient? Or Are There Other Trust "Determinants" That Are Unaccounted For (e.g., Religion, Ethnicity, Geography, History)? Current economic theory emphasizes that *all* individual behaviors, such as the act trusting others, are captured by (1) preferences and (2) beliefs. To date, economic thought indicates that all other determinants are already captured by preferences and beliefs primitives. The three independent primitives discussed above, namely *risk preferences*, *social preferences*, and *beliefs in trustworthiness* are sufficient to characterize behavioral trust completely [10].

Behavioral Trust Answers the Question "How can I believe the input I receive from a trustee?" What About Trusting the Trustee with the Secrecy of the Trustor's Sensitive Output? Behavioral trust captures both cases. In the latter, the trust game can also be gauged in terms of trusting the trustee with maintaining the secrecy of output, e.g., digital rights management, information leakage via covert channels, traitor tracing, and personal data. Output trust is not explicitly addressed herein because we suspect it has similar behavioral characteristics of those for input trust, though the details need to be worked out.

How Can Social "Institutions" (aka Infrastructures) Enhance The Act Of Trusting? Economic theory shows that risk and social preferences are less malleable than beliefs in trustworthiness. Then does it make sense to try to affect them in an attempt to induce more trusting behaviors? First, since *betrayal*

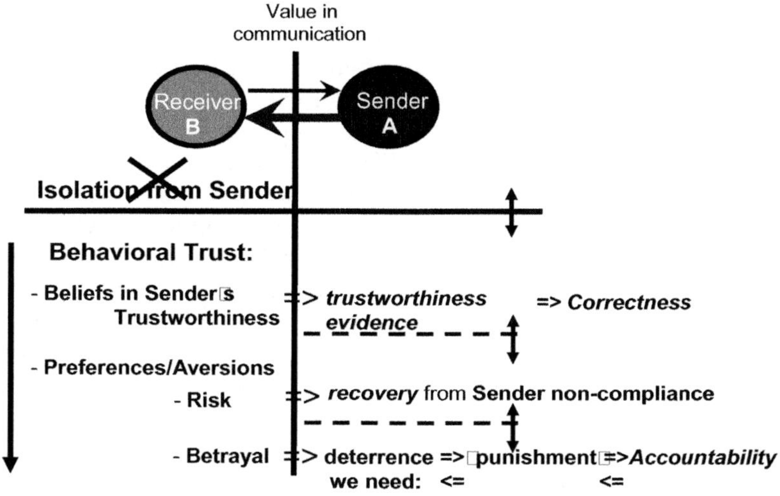

Fig. 6. Behavioral-Trust Primitives and their Infrastructure Requirements

aversion is an inhibitor for the act of trusting, any institution that promotes *deterrence* against cheating trustees can lower betrayal aversion and increase trust. Second, beliefs in trustworthiness of others, the most malleable of all three trust primitives, can be institutionally increased; viz., different gift-exchange games presented by Fehr et al [10] illustrate the formation of trustworthiness beliefs. In computer networks, the formation of trustworthiness beliefs can illustrated by reputation protocols, such as the ones used by eBay. Hence, creating network and social infrastructures that lower betrayal and risk aversions and increase beliefs in trustworthiness makes intuitive sense. This is summarized in Figure 6.

Like betrayal aversion, risk aversion can also be reduced institutionally to encourage acts of trusting. However, institutional reduction of risk aversion may create "moral hazard," and hence trustors may become imprudent, e.g., may take unwarranted risks in transactions where risk reductions are absent. Moral hazard can be countered by infrastructure mechanisms that reduce risk at some cost to trustors; for example, cost is incurred in invoking recovery mechanisms, in purchasing and exercising insurance, and with credit misuse. Ebay's insurance protocol illustrates this idea in practice.

All proposed infrastructures must be carefully designed and analyzed since adversaries (e.g., cheaters, scammers) may find ways to exploit weak mechanisms and perpetrate more fraud. As always, the design of robust infrastructures must account for the presence of (rigorously defined) adversaries. Note that the mix of infrastructure protocols that would respond to adversary attacks can vary. The vertical arrows of Figure 6 represent a graphical illustration of the idea that the boundaries between different behavioral trust primitives and isolation mechanisms are flexible, and can be moved as applications demand. For example, in some applications, one can rely on isolation alone, and then one need not develop protocols that enhance beliefs of trustworthiness, reduce risk and deter. In other applications where isolation is impractical, one might rely more on recovery and less on deterrence. Yet in others, accountability may lead to deterrence, in which case one would rely on recovery to a smaller extent.

Are Beliefs in Trustworthiness of Others Long Lasting? Are They Self Reinforcing and Can They Reach Stable Equilibrium? Available evidence in this area is mixed; e.g, see research work cited in [10]. For example, it is unclear whether trustworthiness beliefs are self-reinforcing, despite some empirical evidence that this may be the case. Furthermore, there is some evidence which indicates that, although beliefs in trustworthiness can increase, initial high levels of trustworthiness beliefs are not always sustainable. A consequence of this possibility would be to sustain acts of trusting by external factors; e.g., periodic administrative action.

Can We Explain Social Scams as Games Based on Unwarranted Acts of Trusting? Some scams illustrate how a trustee, often aided by social collaborators, can induce an unsuspecting trustor to engage in social protocols and games where eventually the trustor is cheated. The social scams described by Stajano and Wilson [35] and Ryan [33] include, but are not necessarily limited to, some trust-and gift-exchange games [10]. Christin et al. [6] illustrates how a trustee extracts value from a trustor in one-click requests by delivering only blackmail. The challenge seems to be in representing scams as sequences of games and then studying their composition.

If Behavioral Trust Is So Useful, Why Hasn't It Been Already Adopted By Security Economists? We see three reasons for this: (1) most security economists [2] have used the standard economic models mentioned above, which include only risk preferences and beliefs in trustworthiness of others, but have not incorporated betrayal aversion in their models, and hence missed the related notions of *institutionalized deterrence*; (2) recent work on social scams and what we can learn from them in security [35], though very interesting, has focused only on the relevance of risk preferences of unsuspecting victims, decision making under uncertainty [20,37], and bounded rationality [34]; (3) the value of institutionalized deterrence via norms-based punishment has been investigated only very recently [1] and is largely unknown in security economics to date. Provably effective norms definitions must be provided to deter. Unreasonable norms seem to fail; e.g., folk tales have it that during the Paris Commune (May–March, 1871), public hangings for those who pick-pocket did not deter pick-pocketing at public hangings.

7 Directions for Further Research

7.1 Foundations

In our introduction we argued for the need of a general theory of trust in networks of humans and computers. We pointed out the lack a theory of computational trust, though we believe elements of this theory need to build on concepts such as isolation, correctness, and trustworthiness as introduced in Section 4. So towards a general theory of trust, our first task is to identify primitives of computational trust akin to the three primitives of behavioral trust as introduced in Section 5.

A second task is to understand the precise relationship between concepts from computational trust and those from behavioral trust. Where are they the same? Where are they different? How do they combine and interact? For example, behavioral trust shares with computational trust the notion of belief in others trustworthiness, e.g., gift-exchange games in economics and reputation-building protocols in computer science. Both areas target robust game design, which cannot be manipulated by unscrupulous trustees. The notion of risk aversion and risk management are common to both but are treated differently in practice to account for specific domain differences; e.g., one domain addresses social sciences concerns whereas the other addresses concerns of computer network design.

7.2 Computer Systems, Network Architecture, Computer Security

Another premise of our work is that a general theory of trust will elucidate potential for new economic value. In networks of humans and computers, there are new trust relations that neither computational trust nor behavioral trust address. A general theory will make these trust relations explicit and these new trust relations can be monetized. What implications does this potential economic value have on the design and implementation of computer systems, e.g., cloud computing, and network architectures of the future?

A new theory should provide necessary and sufficient conditions for practical network infrastructures that can enhance the creation of trust relations where none were possible before. Focus on network infrastructures that support behavioral trust poses an interesting challenge for security research: What security mechanisms and policies spur creation of new economic opportunities? This question is motivated, in part, by a direct analogy between security mechanisms in computing networks and those in transportation systems. For example, air breaks in railcars (a safety invention of George Westinghouses in 1869) and automated railway signals and train stops (developed at Westinghouses Union Switch and Signal during 1882-1901) played major roles in substantial safe increases of train speeds, railroad commerce, and economic opportunities. Much of the past security research has been dedicated to mechanisms and policies that prevent loss. In contrast, we expect that a similar causality to that between increased railroad commerce in the 19th century and increased economic value, which has been firmly established by economics, will be proven to hold between network infrastructures that promote trust and thus economic development. What evidence do we have for this seemingly unusual expectation? The correlation between increased trust and economic development, while not proven to be an economic causality yet, is unambiguous: countries where survey-measured trust among people is high have a higher GDP than countries where trust is lower [10].

Further research is needed to show the practical usefulness of a new theory of trust. In particular, the new theory should address new protocol areas. For example, it should model properties of protocols where trustees are required to maintain the secrecy of data provided by the trustor; it should model social scams and deception; and it should incorporate users' mental models of trust relations.

7.3 Promoting Cooperation in Networks of Humans and Computers

A new theory of trust should address the stability properties of trust relations. We hypothesize that we can get better security, namely more usable security at lower cost, with less emphasis on traditional mechanisms (e.g., isolation, restrictive security policies) and more reliance on system primitives that enhance trust (e.g., deterrence against non-compliance in trust games to decrease betrayal aversion, recovery and resiliency mechanisms to decrease risk aversion, and reputation-enhancement protocols to increase beliefs in others trustworthiness). Furthermore, if trust is eventually shown to be self-reinforcing (e.g., high levels of trust beget high levels of trust), then system primitives that support cooperation/trust become very desirable. If not, acts of trusting could be sustained by external factors; e.g., periodic administrative action that bring networks to known levels of trust.

To test this hypothesis, we should analyze and build network primitives and institutions (e.g., network infrastructures, protocols) that promote cooperation between trustors and trustees. To do so, we can draw inspiration from behavioral economics regarding the malleability of the three separate primitives that characterize behavioral trust: risk aversion, betrayal aversion, and beliefs in trustworthiness.

Addressing all these research tasks and more would bring a tangible contribution to understanding trust in today's networks of humans and computers.

Acknowledgments. We thank Butler Lampson and Manuel Blum who independently raised our opening question. Lampson first raised this question in the context of accepting input in green from red [23]. Blum raised it specifically in the context of reading Web pages but more generally in the context of networks of humans and computers. Both inspired us to explore this new research direction. We thank Jun Zhao for helping with the preparation of this manuscript.

This research was supported in part by CyLab at Carnegie Mellon under grant DAAD19-02-1-0389 from the US Army Research Office. The first author was also partially supported by the MURI grant W 911 NF 0710287 from the Army Research Office, and by the National Science Foundation (NSF) under grants CNS083142 and CNS105224. The second author was also partially supported by by the National Science Foundation (NSF) under grant number CNS-1064688. The views and conclusions contained in this document are those of the authors and should not be interpreted as representing the official policies, either expressed or implied, of any sponsoring institution, the U.S. government or any other entity.

References

1. Akerlof, R.: Punishment, Compliance, and Anger in Equilibrium. Job Market Paper, November 18. MIT Sloan School (2010), `http://mit.academia.edu/RobertAkerlof/Papers/163148/Punishment_Compliance_and_Anger_in_Equilibrium_JOB_MARKET_PAPER_`

2. Anderson, R.J.: Security Engineering, 2nd edn. Wiley (2008)
3. Berg, J., Dickhaut, J., McCabe, K.: Trust, Reciprocity, and Social History. Games and Economic Behavior 100 (1995)
4. Birrell, A., Lampson, B., Needham, R., Schroeder, M.: Global Authentication without Global Trust. In: IEEE Symp. on Security and Privacy, Oakland, CA (1987)
5. Chen, C.-H., Chen, C.-W., Kuo, C., Lai, Y.-H., McCune, J.M., Studer, A., Perrig, A., Yang, B.-Y., Wu, T.-C.: GAnGS: Gather Authenticate 'n Group Securely. In: ACM Annual International Conference on Mobile Computing and Networking (MobiCom), San Francisco, CA, September 13 - 19 (2008)
6. Christin, N., Yanagihara, S.S., Kamataki, K.: Dissecting One click Frauds. In: ACM CCS, Chicago, Illinois (2010)
7. Clark, D.D., Blumenthal, M.S.: The End-to-End Argument and Application Design: the Role of Trust. Federal Communications Law Journal 63(2), 357–390 (2011)
8. Falk, A., Fischbacher, U.: A Theory of Reciprocity. Games and Economic Behavior 54, 293–315 (2006)
9. Fehr, E., Fischbacher, U., Kosfeld, M.: Neuroeconomic Foundations of Trust and Social Preferences. In: Forschungsinstitut zur Zukunft der Arbeit, IZA (Institute for the Study of Labor), Bonn, Germany (2005)
10. Fehr, E.: The Economics and Biology of Trust. Journal of the European Economics Association (2009)
11. de Quervain, D., Fishbacher, U., Treyer, V., Schellhammer, M., Schnyder, U., Buck, A., Fehr, E.: The Neural Basis for Altruistic Punishment. Science, August 27 (2004)
12. Eschenauer, L., Gligor, V.D., Baras, J.: On Trust Establishment in Mobile Ad-Hoc Networks. In: Christianson, B., Crispo, B., Malcolm, J.A., Roe, M. (eds.) Security Protocols 2002. LNCS, vol. 2845, pp. 47–66. Springer, Heidelberg (2004)
13. Gligor, V., Luan, S.-W., Pato, J.: Inter-Realm Authentication in Large Distributed Systems. In: IEEE Symp. on Security and Privacy, Oakland, CA (1992); The Journal of Computer Security (1993)
14. Gligor, V., Perrig, A., Zhao, J.: Brief Encounters with a Random Key Graph. In: International Workshop on Security Protocols, Cambridge, UK (April 2009) (to appear in LNCS, Springer Verlag)
15. Gupta, S., Gligor, V.: Towards a Theory of Penetration-Resistant Systems and its Applications. In: IEEE Computer Security Foundations Workshop, Franconia, NH (1991); The Journal of Computer Security. 1(2), 133–158 (1992)
16. Bachmann, R., Zaheer, A.: Handbook of Trust Research. Edward Elgar Publishing (2006)
17. Howard, M., Pincus, J., Wing, J.M.: Measuring Relative Attack Surfaces. In: Lee, D.T., Shieh, S.P., Tygar, J.D. (eds.) Computer Security in the 21st Century, pp. 109–137. Springer, Heidelberg (2005)
18. Hsiao, H.-C., Studer, A., Chen, C., Perrig, A., Bai, F., Bellur, B., Iyer, A.: Flooding-Resilient Broadcast Authentication for VANETs. In: ACM Annual International Conference on Mobile Computing and Networking (MobiCom), Las Vegas, Nevada (September 2011)
19. Josang, A., Goldbeck, J.: Challenges for Robust Trust and Reputation Systems. In: 5th International Workshop on Security and Trust Management (STM), Saint Malo, France (September 2009)
20. Kahneman, D., Tversky, A.: Prospect Theory: An Analysis of Decision under Risk. Econometrica 47(2), 263–291 (1979)
21. Kim, H.J., Owusu, E., Gligor, V., Perrig, A., Hong, J., Yamada, A.: Robust Online Trust Establishment through Visualization of Tie Strength, CMU CyLab Technical Report (February 2011)

22. Lampson, B., Abadi, M., Burrows, M., Wobber, T.: Authentication: Theory and Practice. ACM TOCS (1992)
23. Lampson, B.W.: Usable Security: How to Get It. In: Comm. ACM (November 2009)
24. Bachmann, R., Zaheer, A.: Landmark Papers on Trust (The International Library of Critical Writings on Business and Management), vol. I, II. Edward Elgar Publishing (2008)
25. Luk, M., Whillock, B., Perrig, A.: Seven Cardinal Properties of Sensor Network Broadcast Authentication. In: ACM Workshop on Security of Ad Hoc and Sensor Networks, SASN (October 2006)
26. Lin, Y.-H., Studer, A., Chen, Y.-H., Hsiao, H.-C., Kuo, L.-H., Lee, J., McCune, J.M., Wang, K.-H., Krohn, M., Lin, P.-L., Perrig, A., Sun, H.-M., Yang, B.-Y.: SPATE: Small-Group PKI-Less Authenticated Trust Establishment. IEEE Transactions on Mobile Computing 9(12) (December 2010)
27. Lin, Y.-H., Studer, A., Hsiao, H.-C., McCune, J.M., Wang, K.-H., Krohn, M., Lin, P.-L., Perrig, A., Sun, H.-M., Yang, B.-Y.: SPATE: Small-group PKI-less Authenticated Trust Establishment. In: International Conference on Mobile Systems, Applications and Services (MobiSys), June 22-25 (2009)
28. Manadhata, P.K., Wing, J.M.: An Attack Surface Metric. IEEE Transactions on Software Engineering (June 2010)
29. Marbach, P.: A Lower Bound on the umber of Rankings Required in Recommender Systems Using Collaborative Filtering. In: IEEE Conference on Information Sciences and Systems, pp. 292–297. Princeton University, NJ (2008)
30. Marlinspike, M.: SSL Attack demonstrated at Blackhat (2009), https://www.blackhat.com/presentations/bh-usa-09/MARLINSPIKE/BHUSA09-Marlinspike-DefeatSSL-SLIDES.pdf
31. McCune, J.M., Perrig, A., Reiter, M.K.: Seeing-Is-Believing: Using Camera Phones for Human-Verifiable Authentication. In: IEEE Symposium on Security and Privacy (2005)
32. Raya, M., Papadimitratos, P., Gligor, V., Hubaux, J.P.: On Data-Centric Trust Establishment in Ephemeral Ad Hoc Networks. In: INFOCOM (2008)
33. Ryan, T.: Getting in Bed with Robin Sage. In: Black Hat Conference (2010)
34. Simon, H.A.: Rational choice and the structure of the environment. Psychological Review 63, 129–138 (1956)
35. Stajano, F., Wilson, P.: Understanding Scam Victims: Seven Principles for Systems Security. Comm. ACM 54(3), 70–75 (2011)
36. Surie, A., Perrig, A., Satyanarayanan, M., Farber, D.: Rapid Trust Establishment for Pervasive Personal Computing. IEEE Pervasive Computing 6(4), 24–30 (2007)
37. Tversky, A., Kahneman, D.: Judgment under Uncertainty: Heuristics and Biases. Science 185(4157), 1124–1131 (1974)
38. Wendlandt, D., Andersen, D., Perrig, A.: Perspectives: Improving SSH-style Host Authentication with Multi-Path Probing. In: USENIX Annual Technical Conference (June 2008)

Towards a Theory of Trust in Networks of Humans and Computers
(Transcript of Discussion)

Virgil Gligor

ECE Department and CyLab,
Carnegie Mellon University,
Pittsburgh, Pennsylvania 15213, USA

When I first noticed this year's SPW theme I realized that not only Alice isn't living here anymore, but that we do not really know who Alice is, after all these years. Is she a fictitious character of Oscar Wilde's *Importance of being Earnest* (1895) who tries to avoid the obligations of Victorian-era social protocols? Or maybe the fickle character of the Duke of Mantua's aria in Verdi's *Rigoletto* (1851)? Or, perhaps the fictitious and equally fickle character of our past Security Protocols Workshops who changes her goals and behavior from year to year? Whichever the case may be, one thing is clear: Alice may not always be trustworthy—as she sometimes seems to be involved in shady activities—but she must always be accountable in our protocols. Hence, we must look into what makes Alice accountable in networks that do not provide accountability for protocol participants by default; e.g., in the Internet. In particular, I argue that we could locate Alice in a multi-dimensional accountability space similar in spirit to that used in *online behavioral advertising* (OBA). Since in security protocols we often deal with networks of computers *and* humans, it seems useful to look at OBA, which also captures the behaviour of humans and computers well enough to become a source of (possibly anonymous) identity.

To gain precision, OBA uses a multi-dimensional space, which includes *location parameters* in at least six dimensions. These are: (1) geographic location, where current systems gather, for example, GPS coordinates of various users, Wi-Fi location, IP addresses, and physical address derived from IP addresses; (2) demographic parameters, such as sex, age, profession, income, ethnicity, education level, marital status, household size and composition; (3) psychographic parameters, such as personality traits, values, attitudes/beliefs, interests, and lifestyles; (4) sociographic parameters, such as relationships (i.e., acquaintances, friends, family), needs, and preferences/aversions/interests/passions; (5) on-line purchase parameters, such as product types, price sensitivity, offline correlations (e.g., credit card use); (6) on-line history, such as search space used, sites visited, and actions taken.

OBA also uses a variety of *location metrics*, including: (1) physical proximity to objects and services, such as bounded distance to cell-towers and known

B. Christianson et al. (Eds.): Security Protocols 2011, LNCS 7114, pp. 243–257, 2011.

Wi-Fi access points; (2) social proximity, such as presence in a certain social neighborhood; and (3) policy proximity, such as bounded difference between similar system policies. Typical location metrics also include the strength of preferences and beliefs used in product marketing; and deviation from the "normal" trajectory of service interaction. Per Adrian Perrig's example, suppose that my phone captures the path between my apartment building and my CMU office: the phone will develop my daily trajectory. If I lose my phone and someone finds it and guesses the pattern which unlocks it, my phone could, through OBA analysis, recognize that the phone's trajectory is not mine, and demand extra authentication for further use. Failure of the extra authentication test may trigger an exception, which would inform me (e.g., my desktop, or my work phone) of this discrepancy.

Another use of location metrics in accountability spaces is to determine whether a metric yields similar values for some user *persistently*; e.g., whether some (anonymous) user behaves repeatedly in the same way. Persistently similar behavior typically provides a good definition of (anonymous) *identity*.

Perhaps you remember that yesterday there was a discussion about *context* being better than identity. In fact, what I suggest here is that the same measured context of a user's behavior can become a proxy for that user's identity whenever it is persistent. In other words, in a network that does not provide accountable identity for users by default, we can still have, in principle, accountability mechanisms which yield identity.

A second important need of accountability arises from a simple question of trust. Suppose that we have a sender and a receiver of a message. The sender and receiver decide to communicate with each other, whenever there is value created by communication for both. That is, they are both better off if they communicate; if either is not better off, there would not be any reason to communicate. The trust question that arises here is this: how can the receiver of the messages trust the content of the message? Whether the receiver realizes the benefit of communication rests directly on a practical answer to this question.[1]

The first action the receiver takes is to verify the content of the input message. Verification, when possible, would isolate the receiver from sender's misbehavior: it would not matter what values the sender includes in the message, because receiver verification of the message content would reject inappropriate messages. The receiver would *not* have to trust the sender. Of course, input verification could be done in a variety of ways, in stronger or weaker ways. The verification may be probabilistic. Or, it may be based on the receiver's ability to verify a proof of message validity sent by the sender. Or, the verification may be outsourced by

[1] Note that there is an assumption here that the sender and receiver communicate via secure channels and that a third party cannot change the message content in an undetectable manner. Building secure channels has been the subject of past Security Protocol Workshops and, of course, there are some classic trust assumptions required, which evolve with communication technology. The secure channel may be anonymous in the sense that the receiver may not know the true identity of the sender and vice-versa.

the receiver to an authority, or to a crowd. The point is that the receiver would be isolated from the sender; and, of course, that isolation could be stronger or weaker in practice.

In reality, however, a receiver cannot always verify his or her input message. For example, if the input message contains an arbitrary program, the receiver may need to verify the output behavior of that program, and this leads to an undecidable problem. Even if the input message can, in principle, be verified by the receiver, the verification may be inefficient; e.g., the receiver may need to verify the results of a co-NP complete problem solved efficiently by the sender. However, it is extremely unlikely that such a verification could only take a polynomial number of steps in the length of the input. Even if the input message could be verified efficiently, the verification may not always be practical; e.g., it may involve the use of fully homomorphic encryption if the sender's execution of a recipient-outsourced computation needs to be verified[2].

In addition, even if all of the above verification hurdles are passed, input message verification may not always scale in terms of the number and variety of senders. The answer is not always positive. For example, practical input verification is always possible in systems that support mandatory integrity policies, such as Biba's[3]. That is, the receiver compares its integrity label with that of the sender's message, and if the latter dominates the former, the input message is always accepted with no further questions asked. Clearly, mandatory integrity policies do not scale to more than a few enterprises; and nor do other systems supporting integrity policies, which would also make input verification by the receiver simple, such as the Clark-Wilson model[4].

The key question is this: what should the receiver do if s/he cannot determine whether the content of the message received can be trusted? This question arises naturally in both networks of computers *and* humans. If one searches the web for the word "trust", one finds a very large number of articles published in different fields such as economics, sociology and psychology. In fact, there is a two-volume collection of papers entitled "Landmark Papers on Trust", containing over 50 papers[5], and a "Handbook of Trust Research", containing over 20 papers in these fields[6]. If one counts the references of all these papers, one realizes that (1) the notion of *trust* has been extremely well researched for the past two

[2] Gennaro,R., C. Gentry, and B. Parno, "Non-Interactive Verifiable Computing: Outsourcing Computation to Untrusted Workers", Proc. of CRYPTO 2010, Springer Verlag, August 2010.

[3] K. Biba, "Integrity Considerations for Secure Computer Systems", Technical Report TR-76-372, Air Force Electronic Systems Division, Hanscom Air Force Base, MA (1977).

[4] Clark, D.D., and D. R. Wilson, "A Comparison of Commercial and Military Computer Security Policies", Proc. of the 1987 IEEE Symposium on Research in Security and Privacy, May 1987, Oakland, CA.

[5] R. Bachmann and A. Zaheer, *Landmark Papers on Trust,* (vol. I and II), An E. Elgar Reference Collection, Cheltanham, UK, 2008.

[6] R. Bachmann and A. Zaheer, *Handbook of Trust Research,*, Edwrd Elgar, Cheltenham, UK, 2006.

decades, and (2) we could not begin to comprehend all its ramifications is all these fields without the benefit of a general theory. Luckily, there is an area of behavioral economics, which studies "behavioral trust"[7], which I believe is directly applicable to our simple trust question above.

Behavior economics explains the notion of trust, like everything else, in terms of *beliefs* and *preferences*. We find some commonalities between behavioral trust and trust primitives in computer science (e.g., network security). Hence, we explore the use of trust primitives in behavioral economics to explain the roles of trustworthiness, recovery, and accountability in network security. Specifically, I argue that we can learn what security properties our networks of computers and humans need to support in order to enable a receiver's trust of a sender whose message cannot be validated by the receiver. Without input validation, the receiver becomes dependent on the sender's behavior.

Matt Blaze: What is their definition of trust, meaning behavioral trust?

Reply: Behavioral trust comprises three primitives, namely beliefs of others' trustworthiness, risk aversion, and betrayal aversion[8].

In the context of our example, if the receiver cannot validate the sender's input, it might try to establish a degree of *trustworthiness in the sender*. Here, we have the first overlap between behavioral trust in economics and computer science. In computer science, trustworthiness in the sender implies the sender's correctness with respect to its specification. However, trustworthiness is strictly stronger than correctness. The reason for this is that the correctness of a program's behavior may also depend on inputs produced by humans. In networks of humans and computers we typically establish the trustworthiness of others by reputation (viz., eBay)—recommendation protocols, and combinations thereof.

The receiver's acceptance of a sender's message without validation also depends on the *receiver's risk aversion*. To increase chances of acceptance and trust in the sender, we can counterbalance the receiver's risk by enabling the receiver to recover from the sender's non-compliance; e.g., from a sender deliberately including malicious code in the message to the receiver. The need to decrease the receiver's risk by providing *recovery mechanisms* yields the second area of overlap between behavioral trust and computer science.

Finally, the last primitive of behavioral trust is the *receiver's betrayal aversion*. This captures the receiver's sense of being betrayed or angered by a sender's non-compliance with protocol norms. This component of behavioral trust (which I'll define more formally in a minute) has a lot to do with human interaction and less with a particular programme unless, of course, that programme is run by a particular human. Again, to increase the chances of acceptance and trust in the sender, we can counterbalance the receiver's sense of betrayal by *deterrence mechanisms*; i.e., by mechanisms that enable the receiver to punish a

[7] Fehr, E., "The Economics and Biology of Trust", *Journal of the European Economics Association*, 2009.

[8] Fehr, *op. cit.*

non-compliant (or cheating) sender. And, as argued by Lampson[9], punishment requires accountability. Hence, the importance of accountability arises from its necessity for deterrence against protocol non-compliance; i.e., accountability is at the end of the chain of implications *deterrence* $\Longrightarrow$ *punishment*, and *punishment* $\Longrightarrow$ *accountability*.

The more interesting question arises in the other direction from these implications. That is, what type of accountability mechanisms are sufficient for enabling punishment and, of course, what kind of punishment deters in what application domains?

Recall that deterring the sender from protocol non-compliance is the important goal. The other behavioral trust primitives have been covered, to a substantial extent, by the standard models of security economics; viz., Ross Anderson's excellent book[10].

Matt Blaze: So at this point, if I had to predict, your next slide is going to show some iterating payoff matrix, because now you have what looks like the setup for a standard Prisoner's Dilemma game, where either side has retaliation capabilities and both sides are envisioning harming the other.

Reply: You are basically right, but that is not what I'd like to focus on. The point that I'd like to make, which is missing on this slide, is that behavioral trust together with isolation is all one needs to think about for sender-receiver protocols, such as the one discussed here. In particular, behavioral-trust research[11] emphasizes that (1) the three trust primitives mentioned before are separate and distinct components, and (2) no other primitives are needed to represent trust. Hence, the three primitives are fundamental.

Alf Zugenmaier: Where would you put insurance, then?

Reply: Insurance against sender's misbehavior in our example would diminish receiver's risk aversion, since insurance is basically a form of recovery. Recovery may include other mechanisms in addition to insurance, such as transaction undo and transaction compensation.

Sandy Clark: Well, I was just thinking of the eBay analogy. There are certain eBay sellers who have a higher rating. If you purchase from them, eBay will give you an insurance so that if you don't get the purchased goods, you get your money back.

Reply: In fact, eBay's reputation protocols help establish beliefs sellers' trustworthiness, and the insurance is an instance of recovery intended to diminish risk aversion, as Sandy just suggested. However, eBay doesn't deal with this last primitive, namely with betrayal aversion towards non-compliant sellers.

---

[9] Lampson, B.W., "Usable Security: How to Get It", *Comm. ACM*, Nov. 2009.

[10] R. Anderson, *Security Engineering,* (second edition) Wiley 2008.

[11] Fehr, *op. cit.*

Let us return to Matt's guess. The game we have is a sequential one-shot trust game[12 13], which captures each player's behavior. Here the receiver is player 1 and sender player 2. Suppose that we have a dealer who endows each of the two players, which remain anonymous to each other, with $10. Moreover, the dealer, who also represents the value inherent in the communication protocol, establishes the following rules: if player 1 gives his $10 endowment to player 2, then the dealer quadruples that amount, and player 2 will ends up with $50; namely, his original $10 plus the $40 just received. The dealer also stipulates that player 2 is supposed to return to player 1 half of this bounty, namely $25. As a result, both players would be better off than in the initial state where each only had $10. However, if player 2 cheats (i.e., player 2 is protocol non-compliant) and does not return half of his money, he ends up with $50 and player 1 with $0. Hence, player 2 has an incentive to cheat. So the key question is: why would player 1 engage in such a protocol? Any rational player 1, as standard economics theory tells us, would quit after receiving the $10 endowment, and go home. Instead, most players 1 actually play the game. Why? Because there is value created for player 1, if he accepts to play *and* player 2 cooperates; i.e., $25 - $10. In other words, if player 1 accepts the input, which triggers his explicit act of trusting player 2, he is going to end up with more money than possible otherwise, whenever there is cooperation. So he has an incentive to play. However, if player 2 does not cooperate, player 1 loses his $10 endowment.

Frank Stajano: There may also be a cognitive bias in the fact that the $10 was obtained free from the dealer, whereas if player 1 was asked to send exactly the same amount, say $10 of his own money, he might not do it, because he would feel that it is his own risk.

Reply: True, absolutely.

Sandy Clark: But where's the communication, because what I see is that player 1 is taking a gamble, not communicating with player 2 at all.

Reply: Let me explain this game in terms of sender and receiver communication whereby the receiver accepts a message from the sender without verification. View the dealers' message to player 1 as a protocol invitation issued on behalf of player 2. Clearly, player 1, the receiver, is really taking a gamble in this case, since s/he cannot verify the effect of accepting the dealer's message that triggers his sending the $10 endowment to player 2. That is, player 1 cannot verify player 2's compliance with the protocol requirement, that it returns half of his bounty to player 1. In other words, player 1 cannot isolate himself from player's 2 cheating. On the other hand, player 1 would lose the value created by player's 2 protocol compliance, by not communicating with (i.e., by not sending his endowment to) player 2. Also, note that this game shows that cooperation

[12] Berg, J., J. Dickhaut, and K. McCabe, "Trust, Reciprocity, and Social History", in *Games and Economic Behavior*, no. 100, 1995.

[13] de Quervain, U. Fishbacher, V. Treyer, M. Schellhammer, U. Schnyder, A. Buck and E. Fehr, "The Neural Basis for Altruistic Punishment", *Science,* Aug. 27, 2004.

creates a value proposition for both sides, and hence the two sides would want to communicate. Otherwise, they wouldn't have any reason to communicate.

Now the remaining question is: what would player 1 do when s/he is cheated by player 2 (i.e., the non-compliance case)? Experiments reported in Science in August 2004[14] illustrate player's 1 reaction to being cheated in the trust game, specifically the "altruistic punishment" he is willing to inflict on a cheating payer 2. An experiment is conducted whereby the dealer comes back and tells player 1: "You can have up to 20 punishment units and you can tell me how many units you want me to inflict on the cheating player 2. In the first experiment, each punishment unit would cost you (player 1) $1, and for each unit, I'm going to take $2 from player 2." In a separate experiment, the dealer tells player 1 that "punishment comes for free; i.e., each unit of punishment costs $0." In the third experiment, the dealer tell player 1 that the "punishment is symbolic: it will not cost you anything, and nothing will be taken away from player 2."

The results of the three experiments show that (1) player(s) 1 asked, on the average, for about 11 units at a cost of $11 to punish player 2 by removing $22 from him, and (2) player(s) 1 ask, on the average, for about 18 units of punishment when punishment was free, which makes player 2 lose about $36. More importantly, during the "punishment" experiments, the PET scans of player' 1 brains indicate that player(s) 1 felt rewarded by inflicting punishment.

Bruce Christianson: Why do they punish more, because it's free?

Sandy Clark: It will cost them less.

Reply: Basically, the experiments also showed that player(s) 1 had a very strong aversion to being scammed, and that betrayal aversion is a biological and not psychological, trait. Further experiments showed that when the anonymous player 2 was replaced by a random device (e.g., a computer) that determines players 2 decision to cheat of not to cheat, players 1 showed only a very small desire to punish.

Frank Stajano: This is the kind of punishment we were talking about at lunch, a kind of survival of the species: the bugs that make themselves poisonous, it's not for their own benefit[15], but it's because they have evolved so that other bugs of the same species survive.

Reply: This is exactly right. This is *altruistic* punishment. Why? Because punishment costs you, and yet you are not punishing for your own gain: you may be losing money in the punishment proposition. Also, it is completely irrelevant whether you are motivated by the desire to punish in order to confer benefits onto specific parties.

Alex Shafarenko: It is still psychological rather than biological.

Reply: No, not by the way (neuro)economics defines psychological and biological games.

---

[14] de Quervain *et al, op. cit.*

[15] By the time the predator gets poisoned they have been digested.

Alex Shafarenko: But isn't it to do with the brain function?

Reply: Yes, but that does not necessarily mean that this is a psychological trait. In fact, the authors of these experiments[16] make it clear that these are biological games.

Alex Shafarenko: It's something to do with social conditioning of humans, and has something to do with the deeper instincts that we all have, right?

Reply: Yes.

Mike Burmester: So it is psychology of the soul.

Reply: This is opposite from what you might expect. One might feel really bad about wanting to punish and pretend otherwise, when in fact the desire to punish is biologically ingrained.

Dieter Gollmann: I would really like to know from which population these samples were taken, whether they came from a vindictive society, which has been vindictive over righteous; as my dear Icelandic friend has said, people of a different genotype type have been removed from the gene pool because they cannot survive in this society.

Reply: There may be some self-selection at work here. What surveys of trust have shown is that countries in which the population trusts more have a higher GDP. While this is a correlation and *not* a proven causality, it also seems that these countries have strict punishment for non-compliance to established norms, and consequently there is less cheating. Hence, cheaters "do not survive" in these countries.

Alf Zugenmaier: One question about the game: is it the same player 2 that had defrauded player 1 earlier? And the anonymous 1, do you know if it's the same player 1?

Reply: Yes. These experiments are designed as a continuation of the one-shot trust games described earlier.

Sandy Clark: According to that, player 2 wins if they cheat anyway, because they're going to home with $14.

Reply: Well, yes, if player 2 cheats and goes home with $50, s/he loses a maximum of $36 after s/he's punished according to the results of these experiments.
[Everyone talking!]

Matt Blaze: So the free punishment number is a kind of the measure of how much justice player 1 wants, right, and the cost number is how much they're willing to compromise, right?

Reply: Right.

---

[16] de Quervain *et al.*, *op. cit.*; Fehr, *op. cit.*

Ross Anderson: Is there a correlation, do you know offhand, with the amount of time that the society has been under the rule of law? Because in terms of frontier societies people were very punctilious and vengeance took the place of law.

Reply: I can't say that I have any information on the point that you're making, but I believe it's reasonable. The argument regarding the correlation between trust and GDP, really focuses more on recent surveys of trust included in recent German and US economic surveys.

Bruce Christianson: Sandy is making an interesting point though, because player 2 goes home with more money than they'd have had if they hadn't played (n.b., $14 vs. $10), but less money than they'd have had if they'd played honestly (n.b., $14 vs. $25).

Reply: Yes. Adequate punishment may, in fact, encourage compliance.

Matt Blaze: Well, player 2 should go home after cheating, and cheating should be, if this game is iterated, player 2's last move.

Reply: Yes. Player 2's last move can be determined by discounting the benefits of future cooperation with Player 1.[17]

Another interesting observation is that betrayal aversion and risk aversion are different notions. The way one can tell they are different is to substitute a device for player 2 that makes a random decision as to whether it returns money to player 1. As noted before, in this case there is little/no desire to punish. In fact the cost of punishment is under $2, and the punishment is under $4. In essence this says is that people prefer bad luck to being cheated/betrayed by a person.

Sandy Clark: Well, I think that we're just habituated to expecting our machines don't work well, and when we get cheated by machines, we do not react.

Reply: We don't kick them often enough.

Alf Zugenmaier: Well, people also play the lottery, which is similar to accepting cheating.

Bruce Christianson: One of my friends, who was an advisor to the chief statistician in New Zealand got into terrible trouble describing the national lottery in New Zealand, on nationwide television live, as a tax on stupidity.

Reply: Note that these two primitive preferences, namely risk aversion and betrayal aversion, are different, based on these experiments. In fact, behavioral economists also explain why beliefs in trustworthiness are different from preferences, namely from both risk and betrayal aversions. So these three primitives are separate and distinct.

Now let's see to what happens when we attempt to counterbalance or diminish risk and betrayal aversions. In essence, we need accountability for player 2,

---

[17] Dasgupta, P., "A Matter of Trust: Social Capital and Economic Development," in Lessons from East Asia and the Global Financial Crisis, (J. Y. Lin and B. Pleskovic, eds.) World Bank Publications , pp. 119 - 156.

or the sender in the original protocol, because we believe intuitively (and we may not be always right here), that accountability diminishes betrayal aversion. Lampson's argument[18] is that deterrence requires punishment, and punishment requires accountability. But his argument doesn't say that accountability actually deters, or even that accountability triggers punishment. So the other challenge is to find accountability measures that really trigger deterrence. Thus, we're not interested in the implications "deterrence $\Longrightarrow$ punishment $\Longrightarrow$ accountability". Instead, we're interested in implications that go the other way. That is the challenge for accountability and punishment.

The next question is: why recovery? Here the answer is actually a little bit simpler. We do want recovery because we want to diminish people's risk aversion. In other words, we want to make sure that the recipient of the sender's message is not dissuaded from communicating with the sender by his risk aversion. So we tell the receiver of a message that's not verifiable: "look, it's not too dangerous to accept this input without verification, (for instance if you accept this self-signed certificate), because you're able to recover; for example, we can undo the transaction; or, we can actually insure you against the sender cheating."

A related question that we have to ask is: do we create moral hazard by encouraging risky or hazardous behavior on the receiver's part; i.e., by encouraging the receiver to always input without any verification? This question resonates in the US and UK, where the respective governments bailed out financial institutions that took too much risk. This suggests that there is a hazard that they would do it again. So yes, recovery is good, but we have to be careful how we exercise it; e.g., at what cost to the insured.

To determine whether accountability enables punishment, and whether punishment leads to deterrence, let us look at accountability spaces again, in particular to their properties and design. One property that we want is *fairness*; e.g., we don't want to punish senders of messages to us that are not guilty of any misdeed. Also, we want accountability to be *certain*. In other words, we want to avoid false negatives. We don't want senders to get away with causing problems without assigning blame to them. I'll discuss three accountability spaces.

One example of a possible accountability space, which preserves anonymity, is provided by *proof of work*, and *proof of payments* requirements for service access. I can ask the sender of spam to pay \$1 to my favorite charity before they send me a message, and I want proof that this was done before I accept that message. Or I can require proof of work: I want to make sure that anyone that sends me a message will have to solve a computational puzzle whose result I can verify easily[19].

This type of accountability is *certain*: anyone, good or bad, who sends me a message has to provide and easily checkable proof of work or payment. However, this form of accountability is *unfair* because it punishes both legitimate (good) senders and (bad) spammers alike. It punishes and deters at a very high cost

[18] Lampson, B.W., "Usable Security: How to Get It", *Comm. ACM*, Nov. 2009.

[19] Aura, T., P. Nikander, and J. Leiwo, "DOS-Resistant Authentication with Client Puzzles", Securty Protocols Workshop, 2000, LNCS 2133, Springer Verlag, 2001.

and is unlikely to be used by any service. It's not the kind of accountability we want to design. Yes, it will deter spam, but it will deter too much.

Another accountability space is one that takes advantage of a neighborhood of strong ties in social networks. So I'll tell you more about it in a minute.

Frank Stajano: In the first case, it has been proposed that you could take the $1 from everybody who sends you mail, but if you actually wanted to read that mail, you send it back. In this case, that would match your definition of fairness. That it would be fair.

Reply: Well, it will not really, because I can send back $1 back to some legitimate senders but not others.

Frank Stajano: So I receive messages, and I pay back the ones that I was actually happy to get. If I don't press the button that says I rate it as *spam*, then I'm going to automatically give them back the $1.

Reply: Yes, that would make it more fair.

Alf Zugenmaier: And, if you're not giving it back, he can punish you.

Matt Blaze: Or all those messages that say, "Matt, you're late with your reviews", will cost them $1.

Reply: So that would be an improvement, of course, but it forces me to do some work, so it's not a totally cost-free solution.

Frank Stajano: You get paid for that work, you get paid $1 for each spam message, so it's OK.

Reply: Yes, I agree that this (n.b., increasing the penalty to pay for work performed) would be a good solution to making accountability fair.

Frank Stajano: I think I first heard this from Andreas Pfitzmann, namely the idea of giving back payment to the guys from whom I actually wanted to receive a message.

Bruce Christianson: There's a mechanism for a doorbell in 1905 in America to deter traveling salesmen. You have to put a nickel in the door for ringing, but you can give the nickel back to the caller that you're letting into your house.

Reply: Yes, this sounds like a good idea.

My goal is to give you some examples of fairness and certainty (or completeness) properties of accountability. These properties were recently discussed by Ralf Küsters and his colleagues at the University of Trier[20], in the context of cryptographic protocol analysis, though the notion of accountability in cryptographic protocols was first introduced by Raja Kailar in 1995[21]. Between 1995

[20] Küsters, R., T. Truderung, A. Vogt,"Accountability: Definition and Relationship to Verifiability", Proc. of ACM CCS, Chicago, Illinois, Nov. 2010.

[21] Kailar, R.,"Reasoning about accountability in protocols for electronic commerce", Proc. IEEE Security and Privacy, Oakland, April 1995 (also in *IEEE Transactions on Soft. Engineering,* 1996).

and 2010 there has been a lot of research on accountability in network protocols, much of it cited by Küsters *et al.* My focus is *not* on accountability mechanisms in general, but only on those that enable punishment and lead to deterrence.

In my second example, the accountability space is a neighborhood of *strong ties* in a social network where an individual can be located by his/her strong ties to other principals. Determining the strength of ties between individuals has been the subject of many sociologic studies[22]. For instance, the strength of ties can be fairly accurately measured by interaction frequency, evidence of recent communication, communication reciprocity, and the existence of at least one mutual friend. Hyun Jin (Tiffany) Kim and her colleagues at Carnegie Mellon University showed that we could measure the strength of tie in a practical way that is robust to impersonation, Sybil, and pollution attacks[23]. She used strength of tie measurements to capture, among other things, a basic notion of trust in social networks. Here, we have an example of accountability that could use her strength of ties measurements.

Suppose that I do not know anything about Matt when I receive a self-signed certificate from him. However, if Matt produces evidence of his strong ties with Frank, which comes with Frank's signature on it, then I accept Matt's certificate since I already trust Frank and his public key certificate. Here the accountability is *fair*, but the punishment that follows if Matt cheats in a protocol with me is *uncertain* and may not deter. At the very least, Matt should lose Frank's friendship, after I complain.

Frank Stajano: He would lose yours, or would *I* lose yours for having vouched for a fraudster?

Reply: ... or Frank would lose my friendship, yes. We haven't really figured out the actual value of friendships and strong ties, but behavioral economics has a model we can use; i.e., the social collateral model.[24] If, in fact, the value of strong ties is high, then loss of a strong tie may turn out to be a form of punishment that deters.

My last example of an accountability space is that of a sender's audit trail. Suppose that I am the receiver who accepts a message without verification and I can audit the message-sending action taken by a sender. Audit has been generally considered to be a *fair* and *certain* accountability mechanism, because whenever misbehavior is discovered in an audit trail, and the audit trail is protected, one can actually punish only the miscreants (i.e., the cheating sender).

Matt Blaze: But that assumes one can't escape the audit.

---

[22] Gilbert, E., and K. Karahalios, "Predicting Tie Strength With Social Media", Proc. of ACM CHI 2009, April 4–9, 2009, Boston, Mass., USA.

[23] Kim, H. J., E. Owusu, V. Gligor, A. Perrig, J. Hong, and A. Yamada "Robust Online Trust Establishment through Visualization of Tie Strength", Carnegie Mellon Univerity, CyLab Techncal Report, Feb. 2011.

[24] Karlan, D, M. Mobius, T. Rosenblat, and A. Szeidl, "Trust and Social Collateral," The Quarterly Journal of Economics, MIT Press, vol. 124(3), pages 1307-1361, August, 2009.

Reply: Right, so the audit has to be non-circumventable. And this requires that the audit mechanisms (e.g., audit event setting, audit trail) have to be protected, but in order to be protected they have to be located and managed within the same administrative domain, or in a domain which follows similar deterrence policies, as the punisher. This limits the scope of the receiver's punishment against a cheating sender.

Anyway, the fundamental point that I'm trying to make here is very simple.

Frank Stajano: I think example three shows that there is certainty of detection, but because there is no certainty of retribution, it doesn't link to deterrence.

Reply: That's true, but the point here is that when you have non-circumventable audit, accountability coupled with "adequate punishment" will deter. The question is, and this is a fundamental question for which research is still needed, what kind of punishment would cause deterrence? It turns out that there is a very good piece of work done by Robert Akerlof very recently[25]. in which he shows that in protocols, like the ones that I describe here, punishment can force deterrence, or protocol compliance, provided that the protocols have *norms* built in them. In other words, you have to have contracts that define norms, in order to be able to punish misdeeds to an extent that is sufficient for deterrence. A good research question would be to clarify the role of norms in computer security from the point of view of punishment and deterrence. That would be the desired linkage between accountability and deterrence.

Sandy Clark: Well, we were actually talking about this at dinner last night. The act of perfect punishment for identity theft would be that you would have to take on the rest of the stolen identity. You've got to do their laundry, you've got to walk their dog, you've got to take the kids to school.

Reply: There you go... society would define those norms.

Matt Blaze: If you can tie this cheating to their identity, you don't get anything special from computer security: you just revert to the legal system. If someone is stealing money from you, stealing money is not done by a computer, even if they use a computer to do it. The computer just makes it harder to catch them. If you can tie their behavior to their person, then you've already solved the problem—to the extent that it's soluble.

Reply: That's what I also thought myself. But let me give you a counterexample.

Matt Blaze: There's a *but* coming, by the way, and the *but* is that we don't always want to be able to tie things to the human identity, right? There are disadvantages to doing that: it may be cumbersome, there may be privacy implications, and so on.

---

[25] Akerlof, R., "Punishment, Compliance, and Anger in Equilibrium (Job Market Paper), MIT Sloan School, November 18, 2010.
`http://mit.academia.edu/RobertAkerlof/Papers/163148/Punishment_Compliance_and_Anger_in_Equilibrium_JOB_ MARKET_PAPER_`

Reply: Also, punishment procedures may force one to take actions that one may be unwilling to take. Punishment may be costly to the punisher, and yet the punisher may be legally required to pursue it. However, the counterexample I was going to give you was in a slightly different direction. In the mid to late 80s, audit trail data were not always accepted as evidence in US Courts, even if they were generated by relatively highly rated operating systems (e.g., B2-level Unix systems). The typical reason given for that was that the punisher couldn't prove, with any degree of certainty, that the audit trails were not, in fact, manipulated by a third party or by the accuser. That has changed with time.

I think we can draw several conclusions, at this point. A first conclusion is that we need to rethink security protocols not just in terms of networks of computers, but also in terms of *networks of computers and humans*. For example, the sender in my simple sender-receiver protocol may, in fact, have been under the full control of a human; e.g., it may take input from a human. As a consequence, security protocols could benefit from the notion of *behavioral trust*, because it describes fundamental primitives of human behavior, which we can expect to observe when humans interact with computers. Furthermore, behavioral trust primitives appear to be *complete* in the sense that they explain all aspects of trust for different protocol classes; e.g., one-shot trust games. This suggests that, if we find common ground between these primitives and computer security constructs, we can get some extra assurance of *fundamental relevance* of our security constructs. For example, we could create network infrastructures that support fair and complete accountability, punishment based on norms, and deterrence in a way that encourages communication and trust, and hence *create economic value*. That is actually a good place to start in building secure systems and networks.

Let me go back, for just one second, to our original figure and focus on how different protocols may mix the primitives discussed in different applications. In some applications, one can rely on isolation, and then one need not develop protocols that enhance beliefs of trustworthiness, reduce risk and deter. In other applications where isolation is impractical, one might rely more on recovery and less on deterrence. Yet in others, accountability may lead to deterrence, in which case one would rely on recovery to a smaller extent. The point is that all these primitives can be used in networks of humans and computers to different degrees. Basically, the use of these primitives in human and computer networks appears to be a reasonable starting point.

Another research area, which I think is absolutely fundamental, is the study of multi-run, multi-player protocols, and games, and their composition. This would enable us to decompose social scams and model them as trust games, and possibly gift exchange games. The latter are a different type of games that capture belief of trustworthiness in the reputation building space, which I did not address. I hope this would enable us to take advantage of the conclusions that Frank reached in his research[26]. We also need to look at several problems

[26] Stajano, F., and P. Wilson, "Understanding Scam Victims: Seven Principles for Systems Security", *Comm. ACM,* vol. 54, no. 3, March 2011.

of social-network protocols, for example, at how to accept invitations. The invitation protocols that we have right now in Facebook are insecure; e.g., there is little control over what Facebook discloses to a "friend". Maybe we could control these "friend" invitations, which are basically like the unverified message a recipient receives from an untrusted sender.

This concludes my presentation. Any other comments?

Ross Anderson: There was a story yesterday that illustrates how norms for punishment are askew online. A young lady, a student at Greenwich, who had been the money mule in a fraud where an Oxford professor lost £18,000, was sentenced to, if memory serves, 160 hours of community service. I thought this was a bit on the low side, so I looked up the sentencing guidelines, and it turns out that indeed you get smaller sentences for online fraud. Had she done a face-to-face confidence fraud against the victim, the starting point would have been three years in jail.

Reply: Right. There is an ongoing dispute in the legal domain about what kind of norms should be used for sentencing. This topic reminds me of a folk-tale about punishment administered during the Paris Commune (March – May, 1871), which suggests that sentencing norms may not necessarily deter. The story has it that pickpockets were sentenced to public hanging, and that, despite this, there was pickpocketing at the public hangings. While it is unclear whether this story is factual, it does illustrate the point that punishment based on absurd norms will not necessarily deter.

Matt Blaze: Perhaps pickpockets are suicidal.

Reply: That might be true...

Jonathan Anderson: I think different norms for an online scam versus a face-to-face con might actually be justified in that there is more risk when a crime is happening face-to-face in that it could get worse, and you never know.

Reply: You mean a face-to-face con could escalate.

Jonathan Anderson: Yes, it could escalate into physical violence. If the con isn't working, fine, I'm just going to bonk you over the head and take your wallet. In contrast, there's not much risk of violent crime coming out of somebody accepting an online banking transfer request.

Matt Blaze: On the other hand, Frank's research notwithstanding, I have the general sense that physical in-person con games of the kind Frank studies, are largely *not* a huge concern in our daily lives. Mostly we can get by without being conned too often; we have pretty good instincts. Online they're completely reckless. If you're not very careful, you will be conned online, whereas if you're not very careful in person you probably still won't be. So online scams appear to have become a social marketing tool.

Gearing Up: How to Eat Your Cryptocake and Still Have It

Alex Shafarenko and Bruce Christianson

University of Hertfordshire, Hatfield, UK

Abstract. Often Alice and Bob share a fixed quantity of master key and subsequently need to agree a larger amount of session key material. At present, they are inclined to be cautious about generating too much session key material from a single master key. We argue that this caution arises from their familiarity with keys consisting of a few dozen bytes, and may be misplaced when keys consist of many billions of bytes. In particular, if the proof that the master key was securely distributed depends on a bounded-memory assumption for Moriarty, then the same assumption also imposes constraints upon the cryptanalysis which Moriarty can apply to the generated session material. Block ciphers with (effectively) Terabit blocks allow a much higher ratio of session to master key than can be countenanced with current key lengths, and we construct one such cypher.

Session key material is handed off from the key agreement protocol to application software, and so we shall assume that all session keys, once generated, are immediately shared with Moriarty. We also assume that Moriarty has sufficient computing power to break a one thousand bit key almost instantly[1], but that he cannot do this with non-negligible probability for a thousand billion bit key. Finally, we assume that Moriarty's storage is limited to a few Yottabits[2].

Suppose that we have two master keys, a red key r of the order of five hundred bits, and a longer blue key b of the order of several Terabits. We use the red key to generate a very long pseudorandom bitstring (for example, two independent AES encryptions under counter mode which are then XORed together), which we interpret as a coded one-way transformation of the blue key. The transformed blue key becomes the session key:

$$r = r_1|r_2; \quad q^{(i)} = E_{r_1}[i] \oplus E_{r_2}[i]$$

$$q = q^{(1)}|q^{(2)} \ldots |q^{(N)}; \quad s = F_q[b]$$

We ensure that the transformation F_q is *collision-full*[3] by requiring that s is only half the length of b. For example, we might split $b = b_1|b_2$ and $q = q_1|q_2$ into

[1] Either by brute force, or by solving the equations.

[2] Actually, we can allow Moriarty more capacity, but the current estimated storage capacity of the world is considerably less than this. See Martin Hilbert et al, Science Direct, Feb 2011.

[3] Even with DES in OFB mode, the pairwise XOR of successive encryptions forms a keystream that is harder to break than triple-DES with two keys.

B. Christianson et al. (Eds.): Security Protocols 2011, LNCS 7114, pp. 258–259, 2011.

equal halves, define

$$F_{q_i}[b_i] = b_i \cdot (2q_i + 1) \bmod 2^n$$

where $2n$ is the length of b, and set

$$F_q[b] = F_{q_1}[b_1] \oplus F_{q_2}[b_2].$$

This gives us less session key material than the amount of master key that we started off with. But now what is to stop us re-using the blue key with a different red key r', giving rise to a different transformation q' of b? Moriarty knows that s and s' arise from the same underlying bits, but he cannot directly attack the keyspace of b. Nor can he mount a meet-in-the-middle type attack to recover b, because he cannot distinguish the different candidate values of b except by storing them, and Moriarty's storage capacity is limited - the binary logarithm of the ratio between his available storage and the length of a single candidate for b is less than forty bits.

The fact that r and r' are relatively short is of no help to him without some knowledge of b: even if he somehow knew r and r' (in spite of the fact that they are never revealed or reused) he still cannot invert F_q and store a significant proportion of the pre-image even for a single session key. This is because, for fixed s and q, the set $F_q^{-1}[s]$ has the same entropy as s originally did: exactly half that of b. Consequently Moriarty cannot learn even a single bit of b no matter how many session keys he has.

Suppose that Alice and Bob share 64 Terabits of master key, perhaps by using a Vintage Bit protocol[4]. They divide this equally into red and blue key material. Each red key consists of two 256 bit AES keys. These red keys are used successively to transform the blue key. The 32 Tb of blue key b is always the same. This allows Alice and Bob to generate a Yottabit of shared session key, all that they will ever need.

[4] Bruce Christianson and Alex Shafarenko, "Vintage Bit Cryptography", Proc. Security Protocols 2006, LNCS 5087, pp 261–265, Springer 2009.

Gearing Up: How to Eat Your Cryptocake and Still Have It
(Transcript of Discussion)

Alex Shafarenko

University of Hertfordshire, Hatfield, UK

This talk has to do with big, or rather huge numbers of bits, and how it affects security. I'm going to start with the observation that shared keys are not always small. Very long keys can be shared using the so-called beacon method, which is well-known in various shapes and forms. The principle is always the same, you have a high rate source of random data, by random I mean as random as you can get. This is the single vulnerability point, the source of data, if you compromise it you compromise the whole system, but you can secure that physically, just don't let Moriarty come anywhere near it, that's all you need. The high rate data source creates and broadcasts an enormous amount of data, exabytes. Then there are customers of the system, Alice and Bob, maybe George as well, and Charlie. The method is not sensitive to how many customers there are.

They share a weak secret, that is necessary for any key distribution system because otherwise you don't know who you're talking to, who's a member or who's not a member of the group, some kind of resilience is always necessary, but this is a weak secret, and it only needs to be a secret for a short while. And then based on that shared secret they select with a very slow rate, a subsequence of the bits that travel along that broadcast channel, and that becomes a strong secret, after a while. What's the basis of calling this a strong secret? Well simply because any eavesdropper, Moriarty, if he doesn't know the weak secret he has to record the whole high rate sequence, and if that high rate sequence runs into hundreds of exabytes, more than all the storage facilities of this planet, then you can safely state that there's no copy of that information anywhere, because the physical act of copying isn't possible. However, Alice and Bob have no such predicament because they just take small proportions of the bits.

Right, so that's all well-known, except the presentation of this method is usually in terms of a radio telescope looking at a some pulsar, but just to be clear I want to say that no radio frequency installation would create a sufficiently high rate source for it to overwhelm the capacity of this planet's storage system entirely, because according to the estimates the information of the world is about 300 exabytes, including everything, even non-digitised printing. And of course if you think in terms of the value of a radio channel of any kind, microwave or otherwise, there's no way, you will have to wait hundreds of years in order to implement the beacon. However, if you use fibre-optic instead, this is quite viable.

What's important about the beacon method, the reason it's relevant to my talk, is the fact that it has math-proof and tech-proof properties. It does not

B. Christianson et al. (Eds.): Security Protocols 2011, LNCS 7114, pp. 260–270, 2011.

rely on the one-way properties of any kind of functions, or any kind of mathematical properties at all, and it does not rely on any technology assumptions about the future, unlike quantum cryptography, and quantum computing. So if tomorrow they invent a high capacity hard drive, that would not allow them to reconstruct the shared key, unlike what happens with the Diffie-Hellman protocol when quantum computers become available. So any considerations of security are limited to what is available now, that makes it future-proof.

Matt Blaze: What you estimate your adversary to have now?

Reply: Yes, you should overestimate the adversary, if you are secure in your overestimation, then you are safe.

OK, now something that people are aware of a bit less, the fact that the beacon method has two parameters. One parameter is the strength w of the weak secret, and the other parameter is the size S of the strong secret, and what matters is that $2^w S$ is big enough, more than your 300 exabytes. So you can have a smaller strong secret, and a stronger weak secret, or you could have a weaker weak secret, and a stronger shared secret. Now, where's the optimal ratio? Well the rule of thumb is that if a commodity device has capacity X then you can rest assured that nobody has capacity a billion times bigger. To put in a billion of these devices next to each other, and wiring them up for resistance, is probably impossible, which means that the weak secret could be really weak, 32-bits: even a password is sufficient for completely impenetrable, unbreakable, physical security. However a strong secret has to be very strong, about a terabyte. So a combination of a terabyte selected at random from the beacon over say two months, and the beacon is running at 100 terabytes per second. Mind you, 20 terabytes per second has been demonstrated already over a 7000 kilometre optical line, so this isn't a fantasy, and with this method I think we should have about 100 terabytes per second, which is quite doable in optics. That would require me to have distributed a password, and then after a couple of months wait time, I have a terabyte that I share with Alice.

Alf Zugenmaier: What is the expected cost of distributing this random data?

Reply: The cost of the fibre, optical fibre?

Alf Zugenmaier: Yes, 7000 kilometres, at least one going across the ocean, and you have to hook it up to every household that wants to participate in this cryptography.

Reply: If you want a secret of this strength, yes. Well they actually run quantum optical lines around town at a cost. But this is not primarily aimed at end-users, end-users do not need such tremendous security, this is for banks, government offices, intelligence community, military, organisations.

Bruce Christianson: But one loop suffices, everyone can share. The different users don't have to trust one another.

Reply: Yes, this is based on a public optical network.

Matt Blaze: But this means you have to physically secure the optical network.

Reply: Absolutely not.

Matt Blaze: Because the adversary could replace the random source of bits with one based on a 32-bit linear feedback trip register.

Reply: This is where I started, I said that the security of the beacon is paramount.

Matt Blaze: But not just the beacon, the distribution system has got to be secure.

Reply: No, only the beacon itself. There is a protocol whereby the beacon authenticates the broadcast sequence to the end-user's server. Remember, until I finish my acquisition period, I'm not using anything, I'm still safe, and then I verify that I have acquired the correct sequence, and then I use it.

Matt Blaze: OK.

Feng Hao: So do you need a secure public channel to verify the bits?

Reply: No, not quite, integrity verified and authenticated.

Mike Burmester: Will you tell us more about the beacon authentication protocol you mentioned?

Reply: This is not really my talk today, I've already delivered that talk at this workshop a couple of years ago[1], I am delivering the next step.

Virgil Gligor: Remind us anyway.

Reply: OK, there is a Merkle-based protocol between the beacon and any end-users whereby they can verify statistically that this is the correct source, so Moriarty has an insurmountable challenge to replace the source by something else that randomly passes this statistical verification. There's also a challenge in making sure that at this huge transition rate, tens of terabytes per second, the errors of transmission do not screw this up, and any corrective measures do not expose security too much. This has all been done and patented, by us, so my talk is about the next step.

OK, so Alice and Bob now have a terabyte shared, does it mean that in fact they don't need to share anything anymore? And that's the point of this talk, if you share as much as a terabyte you do in fact share more than the terabyte. I'd like to stay within my original assumption that the only source of security is the

[1] See Vintage Bit Cryptography LNCS 5087, pp 261–275.

fact that Moriarty cannot acquire 300 exabytes of storage, nothing else should be assumed. Moriarty can do computation very fast, maybe he can hijack the whole computation power of this planet, but can't hijack more than the whole storage facility of the planet.

I propose to partition my crypto cake into two layers, the red one and the blue one, and the red one I slice thinly, about a kilobit each slice, and the blue one I keep in one lump, so this red is half of the shared terabyte and this blue is the rest. Now I take one slice of that red cake and use it as a seed for some kind of transformation procedure, which will generate bits from the blue layer, pseudo randomly.

As a result of these procedures I get a similar order of magnitude of new bits, green bits. These green bits are in fact the blue bits transformed according to a procedure selected based on one of these red slices. Next I use the green result as my key material until I use it up, and then I discard the first red seed, and move on to the second red seed. And if my seeds are about a kilobit each, then I'm hoping to get about 1000 exabytes of secure shared material out of this, and use it as a one-time pad between Alice and Bob forever. The need to share keys will cease at this point.

Virgil Gligor: How do you make sure there are no collisions on the left side, because if I have two slices that collide, they produce the same sequence.

Reply: Well they can't produce exactly the same sequence because they are different.

Virgil Gligor: But you took a random chunk of values, and you segmented them into small segments, so there is a chance that two small segments are alike.

Bruce Christianson: How small are the segments?

Reply: A kilobit, the chance is 2 to the minus 1024. But this isn't an index yet, this will be used to create an index into that array of transformations.

Virgil Gligor: So you want to make sure there are no collisions, because otherwise an index in the same array part will do the same thing.

Reply: Well yes, they will randomly hit the same places.

Bruce Christianson: But not in the same sequence.

Virgil Gligor: Sure, yes.

Omar Choudary: So can you explain a bit more how each 1 kilobit produces 100 terabytes?

Reply: Yes, this 1 kilobit produces an index, which is the size of 4 terabytes, and that index is just integer numbers, and then I use that index to transform the blue key.

OK, this is a specific example. I use 1 kilobit here as a seed, I split it four ways, each goes to an AES-256 enciphering in the counter mode, they produce 156 terabytes each that are dependent on the seed in this manner, and then I XOR them together and use them as an index.

Alf Zugenmaier: Does that mean that you depend on the fact that AES is not going to produce a repetitive key string after let's say a quarter terabyte, I've no idea what the cycle for AES will be.

Bruce Christianson: It's being used in counter mode, and it's reversible, so it won't repeat.

Ross Anderson: It's a 128-byte block, OK.

Reply: And after you've done the XOR, it's no longer a permutation, so it doesn't matter. So you have a new index, which you use once, and discard along with the seed that produced it, and then you move on to the next. So you're only using the blue bits once with every new seed. But you re-use them in a manner that never exposes the blue bits themselves, only the image under the indexed transformation. So if we assume that Moriarty intercepts all the green bits for each seed, then Moriarty has to solve the meet-in-the-middle problem. There's a seed, R1 here, and seed R2 here, he's got the images under those seeds, so he needs to crack it, and get to the blue bits from the green bits. Actually that is not even theoretically possible when you have just two realisations of the green array, it becomes possible after three.

The observation that I'm making here is that I can limit this by space rather than time. If the functional dependency of the green key on the blue is bi-complete, and my blue key is large enough, then Moriarty can't crack my coding scheme other than by recording at least the same amount of information as he would have done if he had the capacity for the beacon itself.

Basically the point of this talk is that given the beacon limitation on space, we can come up with a gearing-up mechanism, which gives you nine orders of magnitude more key within the same set of assumptions.

Jonathan Anderson: You're also assuming things about AES now.

Reply: Ah, no, all I'm assuming is that the transformation procedure on the blue key is not reversible, because it's many-to-one.

Bruce Christianson: The usual sort of information theoretical analysis says you can't end up with more bits of entropy than you started with, everything you learn has to reduce the amount of bits of entropy that you have. But information theory assumes not only that computation is free, but also that storage capacity is free, and that you can use an unbounded amount of storage in doing the computation.

The argument here is that one of your storage parameters is already close to the feasible limit. So even assuming that Moriarty just has a box that instantly solves the AES problem, so that putting the plaintext and ciphertext into the box gives him the AES key instantly, he doesn't have enough space to store enough candidate blue keys to actually do the attack that would reveal the true value.

Reply: The green key does not have to be the same size as the blue key, it's only half the size. This makes the internal strength of it absolutely enormous. How many ways are there to select half a terabyte out of a terabyte? It's absolutely unbelievably strong, and there's just no way you can store any significant proportion of that. So if you are producing half a terabyte every time you acquire this procedure, Moriarty will have to conquor the visible galaxy and more in order just to store enough data to start attacking.

Alf Zugenmaier: Can we use this for solving the sync problem, instead of this IP online that is paid, we're just going to use this instead.

Reply: If you already have a beacon that produces 100 exabytes, you can use a random bit. Then there's a lot you can do, but if you don't have that beacon this procedure doesn't help at all.

Alf Zugenmaier: The technicalities of getting 100 terabytes per second out of a beacon at fixed precision is not trivial, you have to do optical switching, and try to put into smaller channels.

Reply: No, you don't, what you do is create about 1000 distinct 100 gigabytes per second spectral channels in the buffer, you use physical randomness that creates zeroes and ones in each of the channels, you have 1000 laser diodes for controlled lasers that create that. Now the only problem that you have is synchronisation, so you need to cut them into blocks, these problems are well understood in the optical domain, already there is a 20 terabyte per second client for data transmission with a reasonable error rate, and our Vintage Bit protocols tolerate error rates up to the 10 to the minus 2, as opposed to 10 to minus 9 for normal optical transmission.

Matt Blaze: I guess some discomfort that I have is because we have a good idea about models of computational efficiency, of complexity theory, and so on, and to some extent we have models that relate to storage, although not perfectly. We have things like Moore's law, which is eventually going to run out for computation. What we don't really understand is, what is the relationship between advances in communication and advances in storage, that is, does the technological advance required to produce the gazilla bit and distribute it, imply in some unfortunate-for-this-protocol way, advances in storage that will allow someone to catch up.

Reply: That I can safely assume is a completely unrelated physics, storage facilities operate on a very different principle.

Matt Blaze: Well current storage technology does, but when ...

Reply: When this happens the beacon method will be dead, or dead for a while, but what's important is that everything that has happened before that would still be valid, and all the sequences that have accrued till that point would still be just as valid. This thing does not depend on anything in the future, it only depends on the state of affairs at the moment.

Matt Blaze: Well no, it does depend on something in the future, because I'm assuming there's an adversary who is maybe one generation of technology ahead of what's known, and there are going to be some technological jumps that make the advances in beacon generation and distribution technology improve, that that adversary is anticipating and maybe applying to storage.

Bruce Christianson: In your cellar you have various terabytes that you laid down in various years, and as you discover what technology Moriarty actually had then you say, OK, well the 1996 message is now looking a bit suspect, but the 1987 really is ready to use now.

What this approach we are introducing today proposes is a way that you can carry on using these vintage bits, instead of having to just XOR them once and then throw them away.

Matt Blaze: But there's an interval, during which I may make a catastrophic observation that bandwidth implies storage in some incredibly efficient way, and during the interval between my discovery of that in my national laboratory, and the commercial world's discovery of that, my national laboratory wins.

Reply: I don't see how this helps Moriarty. To break this he has to break my original assumption that this planet has only about two to three hundred, maybe a thousand exabytes of storage, of all forms. That assumption must be not just false, but grossly false. And not only that, but also somebody is using the fact that I'm deluded on this, and using it surreptitiously so that we don't know. If somebody has engineered a 100 exabytes facility that takes no power that we can notice, no space that we can spot, and is connected to my private channel ...

Matt Blaze: No, it's in Fort Mead, right, I know exactly where it is, and I know the power it's using.

Bruce Christianson: And the question is, how do we know that Moriarty can't do for this technique exactly what he's already doing for triple-AES? He cracked that already 20 years ago before the standard was announced.

Matt Blaze: Well, I mean, we do actually worry about that, we worry about that, you know, because we don't have an actual theory to tell us that AES is good. So this is not likely but paranoidly plausible.

Reply: For that I have another observation. This is a key distribution system, it distributes keys that are going to be used elsewhere, in symmetric encipher. If Moriarty has cracked all that, he doesn't need these keys.

Matt Blaze: Well he could be using it for a one-time event.

Bruce Christianson: Although I think that the beacon method means that this gearing-up is actually a convenient protocol, as well as one with interesting theoretical properties, but alternatively I could just load up a furniture removal van with CDs that I've burned randomly, and drive it to Australia, and distribute the key that way. Because I'm only going to have to do it once, and then it's laid down.

Matt Blaze: Right, as long as you secure that van.

Bruce Christianson: As long as the van is tamper-evident.

Reply: But this approach has the advantage of no human factor.

Alf Zugenmaier: How do you share the weak key secret?

Reply: The weak key secret only needs to survive for two months, and then you publish it in a newspaper.

Alf Zugenmaier: Yes, and you store your terabyte somewhere? Because someone has to clean that room.

Reply: There is a terminal that is connected to the public fibre network, this terminal is physically encased in something, you can't get inside, as soon as you get inside it explodes.

Alf Zugenmaier: The problem with this system in my view is that if we had a terabyte of shared secret we can do this wonderful thing, and it will last forever, but to select a terabyte we have to have someone walk over and hand over these weak key bits.

Reply: Only 32-bits.

Alf Zugenmaier: These 32-bits. Why don't you just hand over a DVD, and encase it in a way that is tamperproof?

Reply: This is the criticism that you can put to any key distribution system at all, anything at all, quantum distribution, public key cryptography, anything at all that distributes keys has the same problem, because at the end of the day the key should be with the correct principal, and the only way to authenticate the principal is to have a weak secret.

Jonathan Anderson: Well the DVD method actually has an additional problem, which is that I don't know how many people you gave the same DVD to.

In the beacon thing we're harvesting it, but then how many people did you give the same 32-bits to?

Reply: The terminal itself has its own secret key that it shares with the other terminal, and then you make a combination of all that. We assume Moriarty breaks every human connection here, so that's all you can do. You do need a weak secret at the end of the day, because otherwise you can't authenticate your key distribution group. Unless you have something implanted in humans that you could check by a computer, you have to rely on them behaving in a certain way. This minimises these assumptions, and it doesn't go beyond anything other than the beacon.

Alf Zugenmaier: The beacon is a very expensive thing, and it doesn't even have a sexy quantum word in it, which I think will make it harder to sell as something highly secure.

Reply: It's in every way superior to the quantum thing.

Alf Zugenmaier: Except for the marketing aspect.

Reply: No, actually it's superior in the marketing aspect because the quantum thing is weird, and you can't really feel whether it's secure or not just because scientists tell you, oh it's quantum.

Bruce Christianson: There have also been a couple of quantum hacks announced recently[2].

Reply: There was an announcement in nature[3] a few months ago, it was discovered that there's an accompanying phenomenon which is not quantum but classical but it allows Moriarty to remote-control the detector. So Moriarty does not need to break quantum which is unbreakable, just exploits the accompanying phenomenon, which is easily controlled, and gets access to the key that way. And the punters are scared now, because this wonderful quantum technology actually doesn't exist in a vacuum, it exists accompanied with various other technologies that cannot be verified secure when used with the quantum technology.

Alf Zugenmaier: Yes, and you may have similar issues with your beacon, that you can start feeding it certain, let's say, triggers which reduce the randomness of your beacon.

Bruce Christianson: But if Moriarty can control the coin that you're going to toss to make your PIN, what hope is there? The difficulty with these criticisms is not that they are wrong, but that they are too good. They apply to every key generation and distribution scheme ever invented.

---

[2] Lydersen et al, Hacking commercial quantum cryptography systems by tailored bright illumination, Nature Photonics 4, 686689 (2010)

[3] http://www.nature.com/news/2010/100829/full/news.2010.436.html Hackers blind quantum cryptographers

Alex Shafarenko: Absolutely, the question is, what are you criticising: the key distribution idea as such, or this particular method? Because whatever you say now applies to absolutely every method of distributing keys.

Alf Zugenmaier: Well here you have a large key that you're storing for a long period of time. Why not distribute it on a USB stick or on a DVD?

Reply: You can't control access to the USB stick and DVD, you will have to require physical security of every physical carrier that you use in that scheme, and there will be plenty of them, not just one, because you'll have multiple users.

Matt Blaze: But I have to trust the ferrier of the authentication key for the beacon once?

Bruce Christianson: Yes.

Reply: Once. Alice and Bob establish this connection once, and they never require trust from that terminal again.

Jonathan Anderson: There is a nice property, that you can lay down your 1980 vintage set of bits and 30 years later we probably would have heard if NSA had something to do that, so then alright, I'll start using the bits. But the problem is, I've got to keep those bits safe in a vault for 30 years, and that's also a difficult problem.

Reply: The main advantage of the beacon method is that nothing moves in this scheme.

Jonathan Anderson: But the bits have to be stored somewhere.

Reply: Yes, stored but never used in raw form. Only derivatives of it are used, and the information itself is stored physically in one place always, so you can secure it.

Jonathan Anderson: The computer that I store it on is not going to keep running for 30 years.

Reply: But the flash drive in it will, why not?

Bruce Christianson: You mean the mercury delay line.

Reply: Whatever. There are excellent error correction facilities that are around. This thing is even allowed to deteriorate significantly, so the fact that the disk is no longer readable because I have bad blocks on it, has absolutely no significance for this scheme.

You know that Voyager 1 and Voyager 2, are still out there 10 billion kilometres away from us, and they were launched in 1973.

Jonathan Anderson: No, I'm not talking about reliability. Nobody's out there actively attacking Voyager 2, as far as we know there aren't aliens trying to extract stuff from it. I'm saying that there's going to be various vintages down in my cellar, and sometimes I'm going to have a carpenter in to fix the shelf that broke in my cellar.

Reply: This can be attacked, but what I'm saying is, it cannot be attacked unnoticeably. If you attack it, fine, you destroy it, or it can destroy itself, it can be programmed to destroy itself, or explode physically.

Bruce Christianson: Actually it suffices to make the storage device tamper evident, because then I just say, oh bother the cork's been out, I won't use it.

Jonathan Anderson: As opposed to, this search device has been switched with another one.

Bruce Christianson: Yes, that's right, this is not the bottle that I bought.

Session Chair: OK, now that we are getting to bottles I think that we leave the rest of the discussion for tonight at the dinner.

Make Noise and Whisper: A Solution to Relay Attacks

Omar Choudary and Frank Stajano

University of Cambridge Computer Laboratory,
15 JJ Thomson Avenue, Cambridge, CB3 0FD, United Kingdom
first_name.last_name@cl.cam.ac.uk

Abstract. In this paper we propose a new method to detect relay attacks. The relay attacks are possible in many communication systems, and are easy to put in practice since the attackers don't require any knowledge about the underlying protocols or the cryptographic keys.

So far the most practical solutions against relay attacks rely on distance-bounding protocols. These protocols can provide an estimated maximum distance between two communicating devices.

We provide a different solution that can detect a relay attack regardless of the distance between the devices. Our solution relies on introducing intentional errors in the communication, providing a kind of hop-count metric.

In order to illustrate our idea we describe two idealized example implementations and we assess their theoretical performance with simulation experiments. There are several limitations in these two examples but we hope that the ideas presented in this paper will contribute towards practical implementations against relay attacks.

1 Introduction

Many systems are vulnerable to a relay attack, where an adversary can forward data, even encrypted, between two communicating parties in order to obtain some benefits (e.g. money or access to a building). Several solutions have been proposed to solve this problem, of which we mention distance bounding and multichannel protocols. These methods require precise time measurement or extra communication channels, respectively.

We offer a new approach to detect relay attacks that does not rely on distance bounding and which is distinct from multichannel protocols (though vaguely related). Our approach relies on creating a kind of hop-count metric based on introducing noise in the channel.

We suggest two possible physical implementations of the approach and discuss their advantages and limitations.

2 The Relay Attack Problem

A relay attack can be imagined as the extension (or even conception) of the communication channel between Alice and Bob without their knowledge.

B. Christianson et al. (Eds.): Security Protocols 2011, LNCS 7114, pp. 271–283, 2011.

The goal of the attacker is to relay the information between Alice and Bob in order to get some illegitimate benefit, even if the communication channel is encrypted.

These attacks can be carried out against most of the existing communication systems, where two parties (Alice and Bob) cannot control the entire communication channel between them. One of the first descriptions of the relay attack was made by Conway [1], referring to a little girl who played chess simultaneously against two Chess Grandmasters. She had to relay the moves from one of the Grandmasters to the other, so that in the end she either won against one of them or drew against both.

As a practical example, think about the situation where Alice is an ATM and Bob is a bank debit card. An attacker can try to mount the following attack to get money from Bob's account. Firstly the attacker creates a fake ATM, which we name MalvAlice (MA). Then he uses a fake card, named MalBob (MB), connected to MalvAlice. Now all the attacker has to do is to convince the possessor of the debit card to insert Bob into MalvAlice. At this point the attacker inserts MalBob into the real ATM, Alice, and relays the communication between Bob and Alice. Both Alice and Bob believe they are communicating directly since they are receiving the correct information; this works even if the data is encrypted, since the only goal of the attacker is to transfer the data between the two parties. At the end the real ATM happily gives the money to MalBob and MalvAlice simply outputs an error message to Bob. A graphical representation is shown in figure 1.

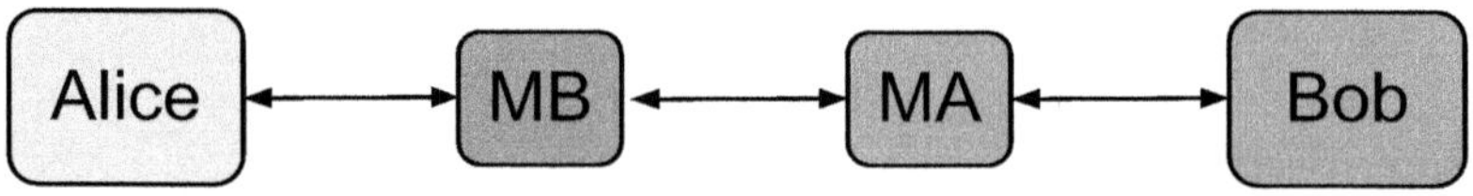

Fig. 1. An example of a relay attack, where a pair of devices forward the communication between Alice and Bob

Some solutions have been proposed to solve this problem, among which we mention distance-bounding protocols [3] and multichannel protocols [6]. The details and differences of these methods compared to our solution are discussed later in the paper, but for now we mention that in this paper we describe a new method to detect relay attacks.

In the following section we describe our idea for detecting a relay attack in a novel way.

3 Our Solution: Hop-Count Metric by Introducing Noise

The core of our idea is to exploit the noise on the channel between Alice and Bob: if the honest participants know how much noise there is on the channel, and if the middlemen cannot avoid introducing extra noise, then the honest participants can detect whether the middlemen are present or not. You can think of our solution as a kind of metric. The more noise received by Bob means the more steps between Alice and Bob.

This is the main intuition, but of course it wouldn't work straight away because the middlemen could use better equipment and better encodings in order to minimize the noise they introduce. So we develop a protocol in which the participants are *required* to introduce some established amount of noise—and it is possible to detect if they don't.

Now of course this wouldn't work either, because the middlemen could reproduce exactly the noise introduced by the honest participants and instead use a perfect noiseless channel between themselves for the relay. So we structure our system so as to make it impossible for the attackers to observe the inputs of the honest participants.

The situation is as follows. Honest participants Alice and Bob already share a secret. Alice has a communication channel with an entity that claims to be Bob. She wants to know whether that entity is really Bob or a middleperson MalBob who pretends to be Bob and relays the answers of the real Bob (in turn tricked by MalBob's accomplice MalvAlice).

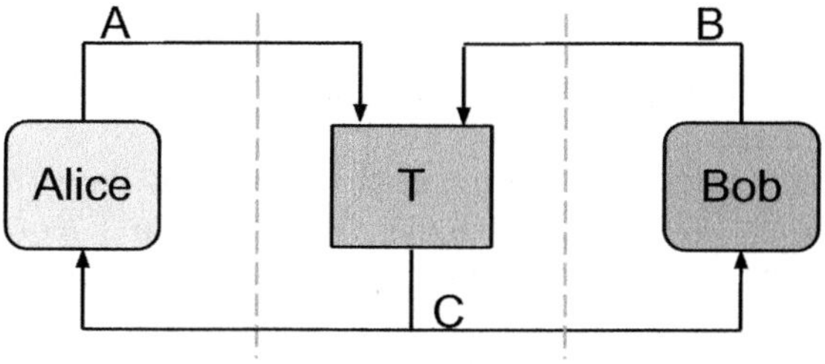

Fig. 2. Diagram of the communication from Alice to Bob when no relay attack is taking place

The verification works as follows. Alice generates a random bit sequence and transmits it to Bob. Bob is required to add a certain proportion of noise to the channel during Alice's transmission, meaning that he will not receive the exact sequence that Alice transmitted. Alice monitors the channel so she can tell whether Bob is adding the required amount of noise: if he isn't, then he is cheating and she can detect it. Bob is then required to send back to Alice the sequence he received (errors included) and to protect the integrity of the sequence with the secret he shares with Alice. Alice then checks how many errors there are in what Bob said he received. If there are more errors than expected, this indicates the presence of middlemen.

A representation of the communication channel is shown in figure 2. The T box is a trusted entity (perhaps the channel itself) that ensures all participants follow the rules described above. An illustration of a relay attack within this framework is shown in figure 3.

One important observation is that if Alice is able to detect all the errors introduced by Bob then MalvAlice can do the same and therefore replicate Bob's errors exactly to Alice. Therefore the protocol must be designed such that some

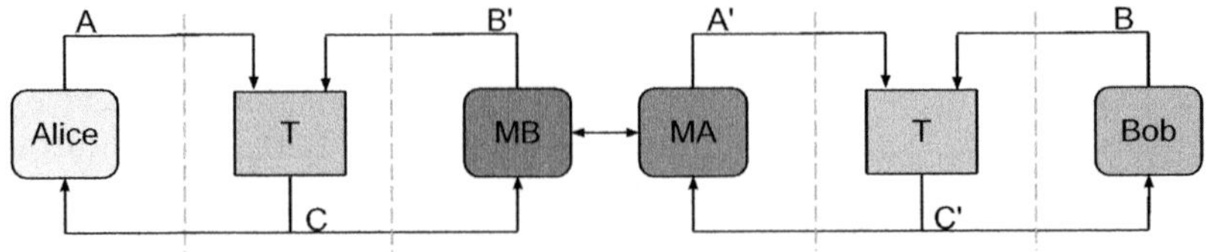

Fig. 3. Diagram of the communication from Alice to Bob when a relay attack is taking place

of the errors introduced by Bob are not detected by Alice (e.g. by colliding with her own inputs). This ensures that Alice can detect some of the errors introduced by Bob (where Bob will not be able to find Alice's input), while she will not be able to replicate them all (where Alice cannot find Bob's input).

Another key observation is that Bob must not insert errors on all of the bits from Alice, since this will cause him to receive a sequence independent of Alice's input and therefore would make the detection of a relay attack impossible.

Based on all these requirements we can extract the main features of our desired protocol:

1. Alice and Bob share a common secret which they use for confidentiality and integrity of the data sent between them.
2. Bob must introduce errors; some of them must be detectable by Alice while the others must be indistinguishable to Alice from her own input.
3. For the cases where Bob introduces errors he must be incapable to determine Alice's input.
4. A relay attack should be detectable in all the cases.

With this in mind, we ask ourselves: can such a protocol be implemented in practice? If so, what kind of communication channel can we use?

In the next section we provide two example implementations. These examples, despite limitations that make them unsuitable for deployment just yet, illustrate how to use our methods. Perhaps in the future we can find a more practical realisation.

4 Implementation

In this section we provide two ideal examples of implementation where the T box is the channel itself, with the intention that it therefore can't be bypassed. This channel is a bidirectional bus line that can be driven by both ends as the communication link between Alice and Bob. Such channels are used in many applications, including the banking Chip and PIN system for the communication between a smartcard and a terminal (ISO 7816).

4.1 Method 1

Our first example of implementation (figure 4) uses the following protocol.

Alice sends N bits, one by one, by driving the line to 0 (by closing the switch and connecting the line to ground) or 1 (by opening the switch and letting the line be pulled up to the supply voltage by the resistor) for each bit. The T box connecting Alice and Bob performs a logical AND function. On each bit, Bob must send either 1 (listen to Alice's bit) or 0 (reset the output without reading Alice's bit). Bob is required to send a 0 (reset without reading, i.e. introduce an error) with probability $p = 0.5$ (i.e. in approximately half the slots). If MalBob is in the middle and decides not to reset Alice's input (so that he can forward her exact N bits through MalvAlice to Bob) or to reset every bit (so that Bob will return a string of all 0's), then Alice will notice that her correspondent is not following the rules. Therefore MalvAlice cannot replicate Alice's sequence because MalBob cannot observe it (the Alice bits where MalBob drove the line to 0 are hidden).

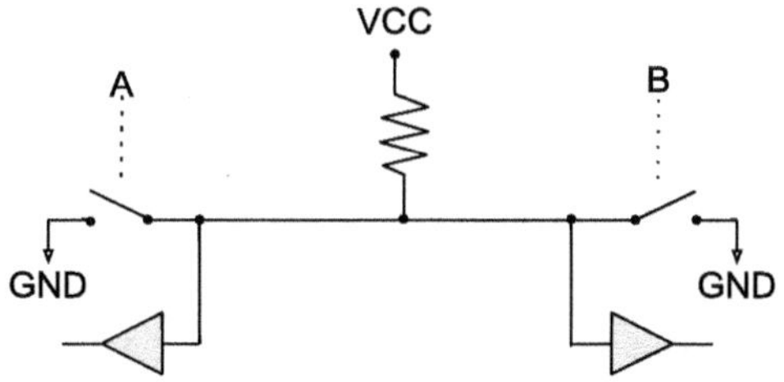

Fig. 4. Diagram of the T box implementation for the first method. Each switch can only be open or closed. A and B can send a 0 by connecting the line to ground or a 1 by leaving it floating. If either participant forces a 0, the result on the line will be 0 regardless of the other's input; otherwise the line will be pulled up to 1 by the resistor.

Remember, from the design requirements, that Alice should detect some of the cases when Bob introduces errors. In this method Alice can detect when Bob inserts an error (i.e. Bob sends 0) for the cases she sent 1 (since the output is different than her input); however Alice cannot distinguish between Bob sending 0 or 1 for the cases where she sends 0, since her input is masking his.

Table 1. Possible outcomes for method 1 from Alice's perspective in the case of a relay attack (see figure 3). When Alice and MalBob send 1 but Bob sends 0 (row 7), Alice detects a relay attack. When Alice observes an error (rows 5 and 6) she increases the observed error counter.

row	**Alice**	**MB**	**C**	**MA**	**Bob**	**C'**	**Outcome**
1	0	0	0	0	0	0	OK
2	0	0	0	0	1	0	OK
3	0	1	0	0	0	0	OK
4	0	1	0	0	1	0	OK
5	1	0	0	0	0	0	Increase error counter
6	1	0	0	0	1	0	Increase error counter
7	1	1	1	1	0	0	ATTACK DETECTED
8	1	1	1	1	1	1	OK

At the end of the protocol Bob sends to Alice, over the integrity-protected channel, all N bits he received, without Alice interfering. Alice compares this with what she observed on the line. If the pair of attackers MalvAlice and MalBob are involved then for every sequence where Alice and MalBob observe a 1 on the C line that joins them (they both send a 1, rows 7 or 8 in table 1) there is a 0.5 probability that Bob will get a different bit on the C' line between him and MalvAlice (this happens when he sends a 0 although MalvAlice has forwarded the 1 from Malbob). Alice will notice the difference, detect the men in the middle and refuse to proceed with the transaction. Please refer to table 1 for an illustration of the possible detection scenarios (excluding the implausible cases where the attackers introduce more errors than needed, thus making themselves more easily detectable). The attackers cannot avoid the probability of detection. If MalBob inserts too many errors, Alice notices because the counter increased in rows 5 and 6 reaches a higher value than expected; if he inserts too few errors, or even just the prescribed amount of errors, some of the time (one quarter of the cases in which he sends a 1 and thus inserts no errors: rows 3, 4, 7, 8) he'll fall into the situation of row 7 and will be detected immediately. In section 4.3 we describe in detail the probability of detection.

As we said, we implement the T box as a bidirectional data line between Alice and Bob, where each participant can either send a 0 by connecting the line to ground, or a 1 by leaving it disconnected and allowing the pull-up resistor to pull it up to VCC (see figure 4). Therefore, if any of the two parties forces a 0 the resulting bit on the line (independent of the other) is a 0. This line achieves our goals, assuming "ideal" 0 and 1 logic voltages and under the restriction that both participants can only read and write once per bit time (but see section 4.4).

4.2 Method 2

In this method we also implement the T box by means of a bidirectional channel (see figure 5), but this time Alice and Bob can select between connecting the line to GND (to send a 0), to VCC (to send a 1), or leaving it in a high-impedance mode (state Z, i.e. listen). If either of them decides to listen, then the output of the line is equal to the input of the other party. If both of them listen, the line is pulled up to 1 by the resistor. In the case where Alice sends 0 and Bob sends 1 or vice versa we get a short-circuit; since Alice and Bob will never send complementary values if they follow the rules, we take a short circuit as a sure indication of a relay attack.

The protocol works as follows. First Alice and Bob agree on a sequence of N bits based on their shared secret. Then for N consecutive bit-time slots they choose randomly (i.e. with probability 0.5) either to listen or to send the corresponding bit from the agreed sequence. For the slots where Alice decides to listen (approx. $\frac{N}{2}$), Bob can either listen as well (thus in $\frac{N}{4}$ of the slots) or send the bit from their known sequence (in $\frac{N}{4}$ of the slots). In the other $\frac{N}{2}$ slots, where Alice sends the corresponding bit from their known sequence, the result on the line is exactly this bit regardless of Bob's input (according to the rules of this protocol, he can only send the same bit or listen—otherwise he would

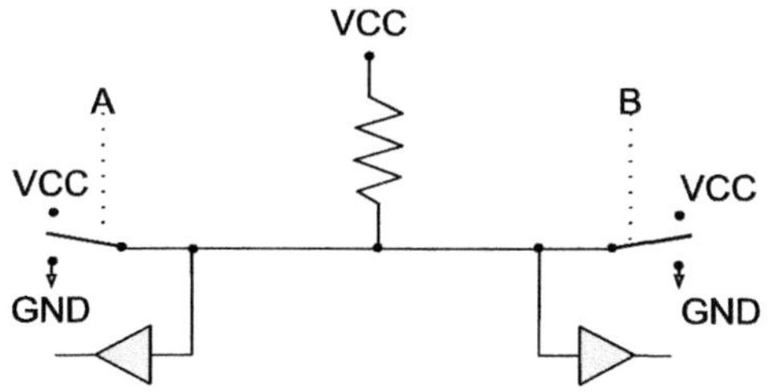

Fig. 5. Diagram of the T box implementation for the second method. Each switch can be connected to VCC, GDN or left disconnected. A and B can send 0 (connect to ground), 1 (connect to power supply) or leave the line floating (Z) to listen. If both parties select the same non-Z value, the line is driven to that value. If both parties select Z, the line is pulled to 1 by the resistor. If one party selects Z, the result on the line is determined by the input of the other participant. Complementary inputs (0, 1) or (1, 0) create a short-circuit.

create a short-circuit). As a result, Alice and Bob both leave their output in the high-impedance state (Z) for only $\frac{N}{4}$ of the slots (where they both decided to listen). They will suspect a relay attack if their counterpart appears to be listening more frequently than this (see the next section for more details on how to compute this score).

There is one more problem to solve. In the bidirectional channel we described, a listening Alice cannot really tell whether the other party is listening—he could be sending a 1 and it would look the same. We overcome this problem by considering the case where the bit of the agreed sequence is 0; in this case the correspondent is not supposed to send a 1 and so, if there is a 1 on the line, he must be listening, and Alice can count how frequently this happens. And if MalBob won't follow the rules, Alice detects him even more readily. We show how.

MalBob can either listen or send. If he sends, he must guess the bit of the sequence, because he doesn't know it. With probability 1/2 he will guess it incorrectly. If Alice was also sending in that bit slot, she will observe a short circuit. Honest players never cause a short circuit so Alice will know for sure that it was caused by a relay attack. So, in the case where Alice and MalBob both send, and MalBob guesses incorrectly, the relay attack is detected immediately during that same bit slot, without even having to run the protocol until the end.

On the other hand, if MalBob always listens (Z) in order to avoid short circuits, he will be detected probabilistically by the fact that Alice sees her correspondent listen more frequently than he ought to. But how can Alice reliably detect whether her correspondent is listening?

Alice considers the case in which the bit of the secret common sequence is 0 and she listens. If the correspondent is Bob, half the time he should be listening too (observed value: 1) and half the time he should be sending the correct bit (observed value: 0). If the correspondent is a MalBob who always listens, the observed value will be always 1, and Alice will know that something is wrong because she never sees any of the expected 0s. Interestingly, if MalBob attempts to guess some of the time, when the secret bit is 0 he'll be perfectly OK either way: if he guesses correctly and sends a 0, it will look to Alice as if Bob sent the right bit; while if he guesses incorrectly and sends a 1, it will look to Alice as if Bob listened. However, as we said above, on the whole the strategy of guessing is not sustainable for MalBob because, when the secret bit is 1 and Alice is listening, he will be detected immediately as soon as he guesses incorrectly: there, the observed outcome with MalBob will be 0, which the genuine Bob would never generate. Since MalBob doesn't know the secret bit, he can't tell the two cases apart and thus can't tell whether, in any given slot, he can safely get away with guessing or not.

If MalvAlice and MalBob want to relay the information between Alice and Bob they must trade-off between *guessing* the secret sequence agreed by Alice and Bob or *listening*. In the first case the attackers can be detected immediately as soon as they create a short-circuit or introduce a wrong bit. In the second case, in the long run Alice and Bob can notice that their counterpart is listening more than expected.

Table 2. All possible outcomes from Alice's perspective in method 2. There are a total of 12 possible combinations, out of which MalBob is detected immediately in 3 (rows 2, 4, 10). There is no case in which Alice can tell for sure that the other party is listening, but in rows 8 and 9 she knows that, if he didn't listen, then he cheated.

row	**Secret**	**Alice**	**Bob or MalBob**	**Line**	**A's conclusion**
1	0	0	0	0	OK (B sent 0 or listened)
2	0	0	1	S	ATTACK DETECTED (short-circuit)
3	0	0	Z	0	OK (B sent 0 or listened)
4	1	1	0	S	ATTACK DETECTED (short circuit)
5	1	1	1	1	OK (B sent 1 or listened)
6	1	1	Z	1	OK (B sent 1 or listened)
7	0	Z	0	0	OK (B sent 0)
8	0	Z	1	1	Increment counter (B listened or cheated)
9	0	Z	Z	1	Increment counter (B listened or cheated)
10	1	Z	0	0	ATTACK DETECTED (wrong secret bit)
11	1	Z	1	1	OK (B sent 1 or listened)
12	1	Z	Z	1	OK (B sent 1 or listened)

With reference to all the possible cases as listed in table 2, to detect whether her correspondent is listening too frequently, Alice assumes Bob knows the secret sequence (safe in the knowledge that, if it's instead MalBob, who doesn't, he will be discovered in rows 2, 4 or 10 at his first incorrect guess) and checks the case in which the secret is 0 and she is listening (third group, rows 7, 8 and 9). She expect to hear a 1 (indicating that Bob is listening, row 9) approximately half the time, and a 0 (indicating that Bob is sending, row 7) the other half. The more the frequency deviates from this, the more she should be suspicious.

Note that row 8 can only be generated by MalBob (by guessing the secret bit incorrectly), never by Bob. Alice can't tell the difference between rows 8 and 9, so this is the only case in which MalBob can guess incorrectly and not be discovered. But Alice doesn't care: if MalBob guesses rather than listening, in 3/4 of the cases in which he guesses incorrectly (thus in 3/8 of the cases in which he guesses) he will be immediately discovered.

Note further that, in the normal protocol, only Alice is the verifier: she performs all the checks and then lets Bob know, over their cryptographically protected channel, whether she detected a relay attack or not. A variant of the protocol, potentially yielding higher detection accuracy and fewer false negatives, would require that Bob perform the dual checks from his side to detect the presence of MalvAlice; then, at the end, Alice and Bob would exchange their local detection scores (see next section) over their cryptographically protected channel and then compute a common global score as the maximum of the two local scores.

4.3 Evaluation

Operationally, the differences between the first and second methods are only minor. In the first method we require Bob to send back to Alice the entire sequence of N bits that he observed, while in the second method the secret sequence is pre-agreed and the observed sequence does not have to be sent back to the correspondent. In either case, at the end of the protocol, Alice must send Bob the boolean verdict (was a relay attack detected?) over their cryptographically protected channel. A physical difference between the two methods is that in the second method the participants are required to detect and handle short-circuits without electrical damage, which might require extra hardware.

Having said that, are there any differences in performance?

Both methods proposed use a probabilistic approach to detect a relay attack. Therefore we have created a Python simulation[1] to test and compare the effectiveness of the two methods. Each method computes a detection probability score ($f \in [0,1]$) and, based on a set threshold ($r \in [0,1]$), decides whether to signal or not a relay attack detection. The detection probability scores are computed as follows. In the first method, Alice checks if the sequence she observed on the line is the same as the one received from Bob. If they differ she signals a relay attack (with certainty) by setting the detection score to 1. Else, she computes the score based on how many times Bob inserts errors:

$$score_1 = \left|1 - 2 \cdot \frac{seen\_errors}{sent\_ones}\right| \tag{1}$$

where *seen_errors* represents the number of times Alice detects an error (she sends 1 but observes 0, rows 5 and 6 in table 1) and *sent_ones* represents the number of 1's she sent. This score, between 0 and 1, is lowest when

[1] `http://www.cl.cam.ac.uk/~osc22/projects/tbox_norelay/pyscripts/tchannel.py`

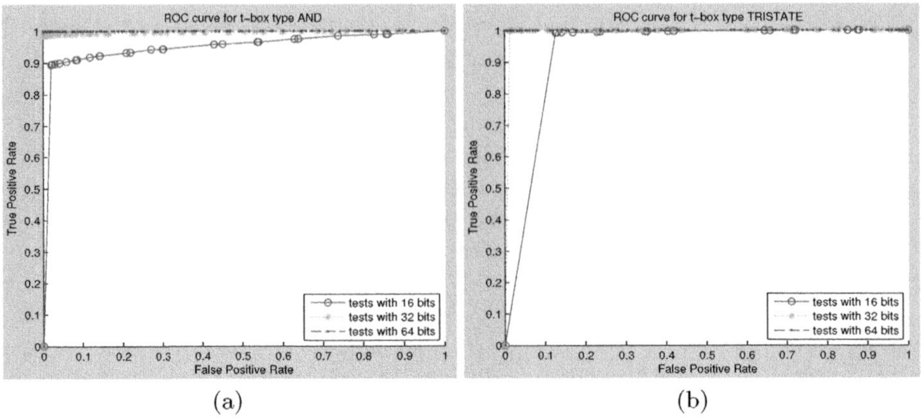

Fig. 6. The ROC curves for method 1 (plot (a)) and method 2 (plot (b)). These plots are based on tests with $n = 10000$ protocol runs and different message lengths ($l \in \{16, 32, 64\}$).

$$seen\_errors = \frac{sent\_ones}{2},$$

which is the expected number of errors that Bob should insert, and highest when Alice never sees any errors ($seen\_errors = 0$) or sees errors at each possible occasion ($seen\_errors = sent\_ones$).

In the second method, Alice checks for a short circuit (rows 2 and 4 of table 2) or a wrong secret bit (row 10) and if one is found she sets the detection score to 1. Else the score is obtained based on how often her correspondent listens:

$$score_{2A} = \left| 1 - 2 \cdot \frac{b\_listened\_or\_cheated}{a\_listened\_while\_0} \right| \tag{2}$$

where $b\_listened\_or\_cheated$ is the number of times that Alice saw a 1 on the line while the secret bit was 0 and she was listening (rows 8 and 9) and $a\_listened\_while\_0$ is the number of times that Alice listened while the secret bit was 0 (rows 7, 8 and 9).

This score, between 0 and 1, is lowest when

$$b\_listened\_or\_cheated = \frac{a\_listened\_while\_0}{2},$$

i.e. when Bob appears to listen in exactly half the cases examined, and highest when he seems never to listen ($b\_listened\_or\_cheated = 0$) or always to listen ($b\_listened\_or\_cheated = a\_listened\_while\_0$).

In the normal version of method 2, in which only Alice checks for the presence of a relay attack, this $score_{2A}$ is the final score: Alice compares it against the chosen threshold to yield a boolean verdict that she then also communicates to Bob. In the optional variant in which Bob too is a verifier, then Bob performs the symmetrical calculation and obtains $score_{2B}$. Alice and Bob exchange these scores and compute the overall

$$score_2 = \max(score_{2A}, score_{2B}). \quad (3)$$

Using this simulation framework we tested both methods for $n = 10000$ runs of the protocol, on both relay and legitimate scenarios and for different message lengths ($l \in \{16, 32, 64\}$). Based on this data and the algorithm described by Fawcett [9] we have plotted the Receiver Operating Characteristic curves shown in figure 6. From the two plots we can observe that method 2 is slightly better than method 1. With a sufficiently long message, relay attacks are very unlikely to remain undetected. In the $n = 10000$ relay scenario tests of our simulation, all attacks were detected when we used messages of length 64 bits (method 1) and 32 bits (method 2).

4.4 Limitations

The two examples above are meant to convey the flavour of our idea but, as presented, they are only ideal descriptions, not yet robust against real-world attackers.

First of all, we assumed time to be ideally quantized: we required that each of the participants connected to the bidirectional line (i.e. the T box) can only read and write once per bit slot. In the first method, once MalBob has decided to select a given input, we assumed he cannot change this input. In the second method, once MalBob has decided to listen, we assumed he cannot change his mind and send a value in that bit slot after hearing what Alice's value was. In practice, nothing stops MalBob from doing just that. Perhaps our examples could work if the two honest participants (Alice and Bob) had faster equipment than the attackers. But this creates a linear race between the hardware capabilities of the attackers and the honest participants. A great improvement would be to find an implementation that requires MalBob and MalvAlice to have communication equipment exponentially more powerful than Alice and Bob's.

We also assumed voltage to be ideally quantized, with values being either 0 or 1: but in practice we expect that enterprising attackers will be able to spot a difference in the analog voltage of the line between different combinations of the input. In method 1, for example, if MalBob is sending a 0 and thus the outcome is necessarily 0, he might still be capable of detecting a slight difference between Alice driving her end of the line with a 0 or a 1. There is also the question of who supplies VCC—the attacker might exploit that as a side channel.

Another limitation of our solution is that is vulnerable to the *long cable* problem. This problem refers to a particular case of the relay attack, where the attacker connects Alice and Bob via a longer cable than they would expect, without creating two separate communication channels (see Clulow et al. [8] for more details). In this scenario there is no extra noise created by MalBob so our method could not detect the attack.

5 Related Work

Relay attacks were first discussed by Conway [1], exemplifying a little girl that plays chess simultaneously against two Chess Grandmasters. By forwarding the moves from one of the Grandmasters to the other she is able to win against on of them or draw against both. A similar scenario, oriented towards payment protocols, was described as the *mafia fraud* by Desmedt et al. [2], who first proposed a countermeasure based on measuring the round trip time.

One of the first concrete solutions was proposed by Brands and Chaum, as *Distance-Bounding Protocols* [3]. Hancke and Kuhn proposed a distance-bounded protocol for RFID communications [4], which was later adapted by Drimer and Murdoch for the ISO 7816 (smartcards) scenario [7]. These solutions can provide an estimate of the distance between two communicating parties, based on the fact that a signal cannot travel faster than light. These protocols can provide a resolution of approximately 1.5 m using a dedicated hardware running at 200 MHz, although they only require powerful hardware in one side (e.g. the smartcard reader) while posing little computational constraints on the other participant (e.g. the smartcard).

Our solution, even though it does not yet have a secure implementation and so a direct comparison is unfair, doesn't have any distance limitations: a relay attack can be detected even if the attackers are arbitrarily close to the honest players.

Another type of defense against relay attacks was proposed by Stajano et al. [6] using multichannel protocols. The proposed protocols require that the two communicating parties use a digital channel for cryptographically secure data communication and a physical channel (e.g. a banknote that can be destroyed) that cannot be relayed. But the scheme does not yet have a practically usable implementation.

The *mafia fraud* kind of relay attacks, such as the demonstration on the Chip and PIN system by Drimer and Murdoch [7], could be blocked using an electronic attorney device [10]. The first author has created such device [5], which contains a trusted user interface and can detect if a fake reader is showing a false amount. However this solution cannot protect against similar attacks where the bandits are providing the expected request (e.g. withdraw money from ATM), which the more general solution proposed in this paper would instead detect.

6 Conclusions and Further Work

In this paper we have described a new idea to detect relay attacks. Such attacks are possible against most systems, since the attackers do not require any knowledge about the underlying protocol or cryptographic keys.

Our approach is based on introducing intentional errors (noise) between two communicating parties that share a common secret for confidentiality and integrity of the channel (whisper). We have designed our solution such that any pair of attackers trying to execute a relay attack must introduce extra errors in the communication and this should be detected by the honest participants.

In order to illustrate our idea we have described two examples of implementation and we have evaluated their detection performance using a simulation framework. However these implementations are idealized under several respects and, as presented, would not withstand a real-world analog attacker. We believe however that our idea offers a new strategy for detecting relay attacks and we hope that a more practical implementation may be found in the future.

Acknowledgements. We thank Markus Kuhn, Mike Bond and John Daugman for helpful discussions and contributions to this work.

Omar Choudary is a recipient of the Google Europe Fellowship in Mobile Security, and this research is supported in part by this Google Fellowship. The opinions expressed in this paper do not necessarily represent the views of Google.

References

1. Conway, J.: On numbers and games, p. 75. Academic Press (1976)
2. Desmedt, Y., Goutier, C., Bengio, S.: Special Uses and Abuses of the Fiat-Shamir Passport Protocol. In: Pomerance, C. (ed.) CRYPTO 1987. LNCS, vol. 293, pp. 21–39. Springer, Heidelberg (1988)
3. Brands, S., Chaum, D.: Distance-Bounding Protocols. In: Helleseth, T. (ed.) EUROCRYPT 1993. LNCS, vol. 765, pp. 344–359. Springer, Heidelberg (1994)
4. Hancke, G., Kuhn, M.: An RFID Distance Bounding Protocol. In: Proc. IEEE Securecomm 2005 (2005)
5. The Smart Card Detective: a hand-held EMV interceptor, Omar Choudary, MPhil thesis at University of Cambridge, Computer Lab, `http://www.cl.cam.ac.uk/~osc22/scd/`
6. Stajano, F., Wong, F.-L., Christianson, B.: Multichannel Protocols to Prevent Relay Attacks. In: Sion, R. (ed.) FC 2010. LNCS, vol. 6052, pp. 4–19. Springer, Heidelberg (2010)
7. Drimer, S., Murdoch, S.: Keep your enemies close: distance bounding against smartcard relay attacks. In: 16th USENIX Security Symposium (August 2007)
8. Clulow, J., Hancke, G.P., Kuhn, M.G., Moore, T.: So Near and Yet So Far: Distance-Bounding Attacks in Wireless Networks. In: Buttyán, L., Gligor, V.D., Westhoff, D. (eds.) ESAS 2006. LNCS, vol. 4357, pp. 83–97. Springer, Heidelberg (2006)
9. Fawcett, T.: ROC Graphs: Notes and Practical Considerations for Researchers. Kluwer Academic Publishers, Netherlands (2004)
10. Anderson, R., Bond, M.: The Man-in-the-Middle Defence. In: Cambridge Security Protocols Workshop (2006)

Make Noise and Whisper: A Solution to Relay Attacks (Transcript of Discussion)

Omar Choudary

University of Cambridge, Cambridge, UK

In the uninterrupted part of my presentation I explained the core of our solution and presented one example for method 1. The solution is described in detail in the paper. In the next paragraphs the discussion continues at the point where I present one example of transaction between Alice and Bob (see the image below).

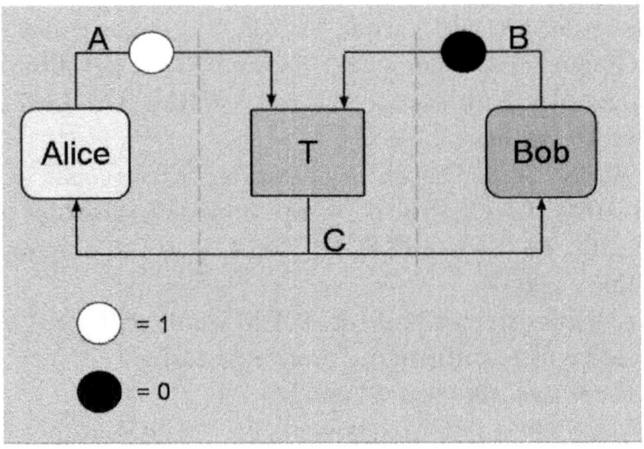

Fig. 1. The slide from which discussion starts. Example of a bit transmission between Alice and Bob for method 1.

OK, what happened in a different case? So in this case Bob will insert an error. Alice again sends the same bit, the white ball, which is a one, and Bob will insert an error this time. What would you expect to happen? Well, after the computation what you can see is that on the channel we get the black ball. What means that? From Alice's perspective that means that she can detect that Bob has inserted an error because the output was different than the input. From Bob's perspective, it's not very clear what happened, because he inserted a black ball which means that he was inserting an error. Therefore he has no idea if Alice was inserting a white ball or a black ball, so this was the same if Alice was inserting a black ball as well.

Feng Hao: So is T forming some kind of boolean OR function?

Reply: You could think so, actually an AND function.

Jonathan Anderson: T could stand for transistor.

B. Christianson et al. (Eds.): Security Protocols 2011, LNCS 7114, pp. 284–295, 2011.

Reply: It could stand for whatever you want, actually I will show you an example of implementation later.

Jonathan Anderson: It is just a gate.

Reply: T is a box I would say, which performs this operation: if Bob inserts an error at the end you get an error and I will show two examples of how to implement this T box.

Bruce Christianson: But if Alice and Bob put the same thing in there, that's what comes out? If they both put white in, white comes out?

Reply: Yes that's right, if they put the same thing that's what comes out.

Bruce Christianson: But you haven't specified what happens on other cases.

Reply: In this case it was different input. Alice sent a white ball, representing a one, and Bob has inserted an error, i.e. a black ball.

Jonathan Anderson: T is a gate and Bob can say: send Alice's result through or make it be zero.

Bruce Christianson: But it's crucial that Bob doesn't get any information if he inserts an error.

Reply: Exactly, so if Bob inserts an error the output is always an error; it's always a black ball, regardless of Alice's input.

Bruce Christianson: Oh, black means error does it?

Reply: Exactly.

Bruce Christianson: Black means error, white means correct.

Reply: Exactly, although from Alice's perspective you can think as one or zero.

Bruce Christianson: So for the moment we assume that T can tell white from black?

Reply: Exactly, that's correct.

Dongting Yu: In a given step, does the black ball that Alice sends represent the same thing as the black ball that Bob has sent in a previous step?

Reply: It could be, or it could different; it depends on your interpretation, as you wish. In this implementation is the same.

Dongting Yu: And also does Bob know that it's actually sending an error?

Reply: Bob knows that he's sending an error, yes. So if Bob decided to send an error is important that at the end he will see the same thing regardless of

Alice. In an implementation of the T box you must assure that whatever Bob sees is independent of Alice's input. So in this case Bob should see the black ball, regardless of Alice's input. So even if Alice sends a white ball, they should still get the black ball.

Dongting Yu: So how does Bob know that it's not sending the same thing that Alice is sending?

Reply: He doesn't, and that's the advantage.

Dongting Yu: So Bob knows he's inserting an error but he doesn't know what Alice is sending.

Reply: Exactly, that's what I want. I want to avoid Bob being able to relay Alice's input.

Bruce Christianson: And is this symmetrical, so if Alice puts an error in does the same thing happen?

Reply: Well we're assuming that only Bob is inserting the errors in our protocol, so only one side is inserting errors. So Alice is sending the bits, and Bob is inserting errors from time to time. And what is important is that Bob must insert errors on some of the bits, not on all. Alice should monitor this, and detect some errors. If Alice doesn't detect any errors that means the other party is not following the protocol, so we just reject the whole transaction.

Bruce Christianson: So when you say an error, Alice and Bob should be putting the same things in, is that right?

Reply: They should be sending values during the same slot, not necessarily the same values.

Bruce Christianson: Yes, but are they putting the same input values in using their shared key, or are they just making up the values?

Reply: No, in this solution Alice is sending some bits to Bob, without necessarily using a shared key, you will see, so the shared key is just at the end when Alice asks to Bob: Bob please send me all the bits that you've heard, and let's see if this is what I expect from you.

Bruce Christianson: OK, so sometimes Bob jams Alice?

Reply: Exactly, you can think as if Bob is jamming the input.

So in this third case Alice is actually sending a black ball, and Bob again is inserting an error. However, in this case, after the processing, the output is exactly the same as in the previous case. That means that Bob cannot make the difference between Alice inserting a 1 or a 0, and this is what we want, so this is the important property of the channel. And it is also important that Alice in this case cannot tell if Bob has been inserting an error or not. Why is that? Because even if Bob was not inserting an error, the output would have been exactly the same, because he was letting Alice's input going through. So this is the second important part of our protocol: Alice may not detect all errors because if she was able to detect all the errors that means that Bob in the first case (i.e. MalBob) is able to replicate the errors exactly on the same path and then recreate the same errors from one party to the other. But in this way we are stopping this problem from happening.

Matt Blaze: So can you remind me, what are the assumed security properties of the lines on this picture? So the line marked B is invisible to Alice?

Reply: That's correct.

Matt Blaze: And the line marked A is invisible to Bob?

Reply: That's correct.

Matt Blaze: And the line marked C is visible to the world?

Reply: Yes, you could think so.

Matt Blaze: Right, but nobody can see the A line or the B line?

Reply: Exactly, only Alice or Bob respectively could have access to that.

OK, before showing you how we actually detect the relay attack, let me give you an example of how we implemented the T box. So one example would be to use a directional line. This is used in smartcard communication, for example, using the ISO 7816 standard, and the idea here is that Alice is controlling the buffer on the left and Bob is controlling the buffer on the right. And they have two options: either they put the line to ground or they leave it up, floating, so that it will be raised to VCC by the pull-up resistor if, only if the other party is not pulling the line to ground. And this is basically satisfying the functional properties of what we define for. So if Alice is sending a 0, which means she's pulling the line to ground, it doesn't really matter if Bob is inserting an error, where the error is caused by pulling the line to ground again, because the result on the line will be 0 (ground). And Bob can either leave Alice's input by just leaving the line floating, which means that if Alice was sending a 0, you will see 0, if it was floating both of them will see the line at the VCC level because it was floating. But if Bob is inserting an error, which means that he is putting the line to ground, so he's connecting it here, that would be the result on the line, regardless of Alice input. And this is working exactly as we defined it earlier, so this is one example of implementation. I have another one if you want I will describe it at the end of the talk, but I think this is a simpler practical implementation to understand.

Matt Blaze: And this is an assumption that neither Alice nor Bob has access to any other components of this system, like the precise voltage of the power supply, and the current things that run from it?

Reply: Yes, you could say so. And also the big assumption that they cannot look at the output before sending their input.

Matt Blaze: But presumably there are, I mean, in any real implementation it's going to be very hard to avoid side channels from things like the power supply.

Reply: I agree. So this is the limitation of our practical solution example. We shown these examples to illustrate the concept.

Matt Blaze: So I mean, I did this work a few years back, isotropic cryptography which basically had this very nice and useful theoretical result that said that a channel in which direction is indistinguishable can be used for information theoretically proven secure communication. The problem is these directionless channels appear not to actually exist in nature, right, because of the presence of side channels. And this was actually a diagram that we drew and then threw out of an example of a directionless channel, because we couldn't actually figure out how to solve all these problems.

Reply: Yes, it would be great if we could find a practical implementation.

Matt Blaze: If it's purely digital this is very easy, but the problem is that nothing in nature is actually digital.

Reply: I agree. That was the main limitation of our current implementation.

[Here I was Talking a Few Minutes about How the Relay Attack Is Detected.]

What happens now is that MalBob sends the sequence to the accomplice, MalvAlice, and tries to forward this to Bob in order to try to fool the protocol, and somehow complete the relay attack. So she starts sending this sequence to Bob. However, the trick here, and what happens, is that Bob is using a different error sequence, instead of using errors in bits 2 and 3. Unfortunately for the Moriarty associates, he's using an error bit in the first bit. This means that for the first bit that MalvAlice is forwarding, which was a 1, unfortunately Bob will insert an error and thus they will both get a 0. So at the end of the protocol run, Bob gets four zeroes, and this is different from what Alice expects, which was the sequence *1, 0, 0, 0*. And then Bob sends this back to Alice over the channel that was using the secret keys, so they have confidentiality and integrity, where Moriarty adversaries are not able to interfere, and they detect the attack.

So this is basically how the framework works, as we've been mentioning already, there are two main limitations: one is that a physical channel is hard to create with this property, where you can create pure digital signals without the attacker intervening, and basically sniffing in the channel. So this is some work I would like to continue, although it seems very hard and was possibly proposed earlier.

Matt Blaze: Well it's not the same idea, it's a related idea.

Reply: So it's not exactly the same?

Matt Blaze: It's not exactly the same, but it depends on the idea of the directionless channel.

Reply: So it might be something to look more into. It has a nice property that it doesn't depend on the distance between participants. However, if you want it in a pure physical implementation then it does depend on time, yes, in order to be able to say that in this particular bit time there can be only one input. And we can even argue, for example, that if the two participants have a hardware, let's say that can communicate at a rate of 200 megabits per second or so, then the attacker, in order to break the protocol, must be able to communicate at over 200 megabits per second. However, the problem here is that it's a linear race between the participants, so as soon as the attacker is able to communicate at a double rate, he can break the protocol. So it would be great if we can find a solution where the attackers are forced to communicate at a speed that's exponentially greater than the honest participants.

And the second fundamental vulnerability of our solution is that it does not provide any kind of protection against a long cable attack, where you simply use a single cable between Alice and Bob.

Bruce Christianson: When you say a long cable attack, which cables are long?

Reply: As a long cable attack I mean that in the relay scenario instead of having computers connected – basically two instances of our protocol between Alice and Bob – what you do is just connect the card to Bob using the cable. This means that there are no two separate instances of the protocol between Alice and MalBob, and then between MalvAlice and Bob. There is a single instance, which you could say is hold at one end by MalBob and at the other end by MalvAlice.

Bruce Christianson: But the very long cable is attached to Alice?

Reply: Yes, to Alice directly.

Bruce Christianson: So if Alice has to plug into T, presumably she can check that she's plugging into T with a short cable.

Reply: She could, yes, but the problem is that is hard to check that you are plugging into T, because I said this is part of the communication channel, so you cannot physically see where you plug into.

Bruce Christianson: But what if I need to know whether I'm plugging into the real communication channel or somewhere else?

Reply: Imagine the case where you are inserting the card into the terminal. You have no idea if inside the terminal there is actually a chip that is communicating and that is creating the T box, or is just a cable, basically an extension of my channel.

Bruce Christianson: But if I can't tell whether I'm plugging into T or into not T, then I can't tell whether I'm running your protocol or not.

Reply: Well that's true, yes.

Bruce Christianson: But this is no good if I'm not plugged into the real diode. If the communication mechanism isn't really the box T, then the guarantee is not provided. Alice has to know whether or not she's plugging into a real authentic T, and so does Bob. And so the argument is, well if we trust T and we can tell whether we're plugging into the real one or not, then you can put the serial numbers on, and you can tell whether you're plugged into the same one or not, and then the problem goes away anyway.

Mike Burmester: So perhaps we can use a zero-knowledge proof. The bank can send a sort of authenticator, which includes the description of the T box. So the authenticator includes also the shop ID. When first Alice wants to buy something, she waits for the authenticator, and the authenticator says yes, there is an authorisation for a diamond to be purchased. Since Alice wanted to buy a loaf of bread she will not accept this authenticator.

Reply: We are trying to design a more general solution.

Mike Burmester: Agree, this was a related point.

Bruce Christianson: But if I can be sure of the digital key of the door that I'm standing in front of, there isn't a problem in the first place. There's only a problem to solve in the case where I am not absolutely sure which cash machine I'm talking to.

Mike Burmester: No, you are sure of this cash machine, but the danger is out there, so you go and buy at a legitimate shop a loaf of bread, you give your credit card, and then it's diverted to another Mafioso, who goes to buy a diamond from another shop. And that is then, he gets his diamond, and the whole zero knowledge is relayed to the bank, and it comes back, and the transaction is authorised, for the diamond, but the authorisation never reaches the bakery, the first shop. That is an authorisation for a ten dollar transaction, not for a one thousand dollar transaction; so you included that, but then you would have to break away from the zero knowledge proof, and you would have another.

Frank Stajano: That works at the application level. We were trying to do the fixed scenario.

Mike Burmester: I fully agree, I just said this is a different, so the motivating example has been addressed out of the box, but it's still a crucial example in relay attacks.

Frank Stajano: It exploits the fact that the fraud based on the relay attack will exchange different artefacts, of which one is worth a lot more, and you can tell which one it is, and at the application level you can tell the two cases. Whereas this one is a situation where you're saying, well I am Alice and I am in front of some entity that looks like a Bob. I want to know if the one that's in front of me is the same one that I am sharing the secret key with or if it's someone who doesn't know the key but who's relaying the information to the real Bob located somewhere else. That's the problem you are solving here.

Bruce Christianson: So I'm standing in front of a door and I'm saying, it's me Alice, don't shoot, but it's not the right door, and Moriarty is standing in front of the real.

Reply: Exactly. Also let me clarify the T box requirement. The idea is that the T box is created automatically, so it's part of the channel itself. Therefore when you insert a smartcard, if you want the smartcard to work, you need to follow the rules of the T box. The only thing the attackers can do is avoid creating two T boxes, not connecting or not to the T box. The attackers could try to to this by using the long cable, which means that Alice will be connected to Bob using a single cable, and then our solution will not work because Bob won't receive an increased number of errors. But such attack is hard because it requires the attackers to forward the analogue levels between the two parties.

Bruce Christianson: What you've done I think is a really neat mechanism, I'm fascinated by it. But you've got the problem of knowing that you're connected to the real T box, rather than the problem of knowing that you're talking to the real Bob.

Frank Stajano: No, you just need to ensure that you're connected into a T box.

Bruce Christianson: Now the argument that you're making, a good argument, is: now I don't care which T box it is, I just need to know I'm connected to a real T box and not a fake one, and I don't mind which is.

Frank Stajano: I mean, the possibly slightly dodgy assumption is that if you have a smartcard but in order for it to to talk to other things its physical interface only works with a channel that behaves like this T box.

Bruce Christianson: But then of course Moriarty is allowed to try and emulate that. But the sort of counter argument is to say, well why not put serial numbers on the T boxes, and then Alice and Bob can tell whether they're plugged into the correct T box or not. And actually the T boxes don't have to have any wiring inside them at all.

Frank Stajano: The T box doesn't exist, the T box is just the properties of the channel behaving like an AND gate, there is no AND gate, there's just a line that you drive up and down, there is no box to plug into.

Bruce Christianson: Well Alice has to plug into something.

Reply: What is important is that here what we're able to create, as Mike Bond was saying, a kind of metric. Basically, we know how many hosts are between Alice and Bob, which we haven't been able to do before.

Bruce Christianson: That's the really neat bit of it.

Reply: So that's the real thing basically, we're able to create a metric.

Bruce Christianson: But I'm not sure that it actually solves the problem that you think it's solving.

Alf Zugenmaier: What are the synchronisation properties that you require from your T box?

Reply: We should only been able to send and receive one bit per bit slot.

Frank Stajano: But the synchronisation property that you need is that you are not allowed by the rules of this game to let Alice do something, and then look at what she's doing, and then half way through decide what your bit is going to be.

Bruce Christianson: The rule is that the T box is either up or down, and when it's up you can put things in it, and when it's down it will push things out.

Matt Blaze: And instantaneous synchronisation.

Frank Stajano: So basically the value of the idea is in the 1 and 0 level, and the killer for what we've shown is what Matt has said: that if you try and implement it, and the attacker can control the power supply and so it will give away the game whether you are actually doing a 1 or 0. So we don't claim to have a physical implementation that would withstand a determined attacker. Yes, we have an idea, we have a sort of this is something that tells you how you might do it.

Bruce Christianson: But the T box could be a completely mechanical thing, that Alice and Bob just look at, it doesn't have to be electrical, or, you know, the T box can be any artefact that Alice and Bob can interact with, and they can know that they're talking to the same T box, and hence that they're standing next to each other. That's the idea isn't it? And you could implement the T box as a slot machine or any implementation you like.

Reply: Well my first thought is that we should try to make the T box as part of the channel so you don't have to bring extra devices.

Frank Stajano: The point is to not to have the T box as a separate device.

Feng Hao: So the T box is a kind of built mechanism inside the terminal?

Reply: No, for us the T box is actually the channel, so we made the properties of the channel such that the channel created this T box.

Jonathan Anderson: Does it work in the same way if instead of error condition being zero, Bob is just jamming or is not jamming, in such a way that Alice can tell: well nobody who's anybody anywhere near me would be able to detect what I'm currently transmitting.

Reply: I'm not sure what you mean.

Jonathan Anderson: So instead of having the output of the T boxes 1 or 0, if it were 1, 0 or error. So if that's the case, then that doesn't change your solution?

Reply: No, if you have a case of error that means that Alice can always see in that part, and that's what we don't want. We want Alice to be able to observe an error just on some of the cases, not all.

Bruce Christianson: You want something a little bit like the description of Ethernet for children: that any side can jam, and that's the same as holding your own.

Reply: Well the interesting thing is that when Bob is jamming, I want Alice to see that only on some of the cases. In some of the cases where Bob is jamming I want Alice not to see this; because if Alice could see every time Bob is jamming, it means that MalvAlice could see every time Bob is jamming, and then just do the same jamming with Alice, and then she'd be able to relay perfectly because the errors on MalBob's side and the errors on Bob's side would get exactly the same results. So it's important that Alice cannot see all the jamming.

Frank Stajano: You may think that Alice is good, and in fact she is, but there is a symmetrical Alice who's bad, so if you give powers of doing lots of things to the good Alice, then you're giving them to the bad Alice as well.

Reply: So we are limiting both participants here.

Bruce Christianson: It's just this abstraction that T is part of the communication channel, I'm not sure that that step is doing you any favours. If we can both be sure we're both plugged into the same channel we can solve this problem easily.

Feng Hao: The chip on the card must be part of the T box?

Reply: No. The idea is that if you don't comply with the T box rules then you will not be able to communicate. So MalBob and MalvAlice must create the T box somehow, by communicating using that particular protocol. If you are not using that protocol, the T box will not exist, and therefore there will be no communication at all. So that's why I say that T is the channel itself.

Feng Hao: Yes, if you are connecting into a malicious T box then the card should be able to tell. So the chip itself should be part of the T box.

Reply: You could say that the card is part of the T box, yes. The T box is an invisible thing that gets created as soon as both parties start communicating using the known protocol that Alice and Bob know. As soon as they communicate the T gets created basically. It's part of the channel.

Bruce Christianson: Alice and Bob have to have a way of verifying that they're communicating via a T channel.

Reply: And this kind of implementation fulfills that, within the limitation that there are some possible analogue level attacks. However, as someone was pointing out to me, it might be practical for some cases, let's say for 20% of the cases to do this, if you assume that the attacker has no interest in buying expensive equipment. So to limit some of the existing relay attacks, we could always try to implement it somehow, because this is just using the standard communication channel. But of course it has many limitations, and I'm not arguing it's a very good solution. But if we are able to design a solution where the attacker must use equipment with communication capabilities exponentially greater than the honest participants, then it might become very practical.

Frank Stajano: When we were drawing these diagrams, the kind of issues that we were sort of leaving under the carpet were in fact these VCCs in the centre of the diagram. Actually someone has to provide power. Does it come from one side, does it come from the other side? When we have a 1 and a 0, or a 0 and a 1, or a 0 and a 0, they all give 0, but is it going to be a slightly different 0? Those kind of things are fairly idealised, and if you go to practical implementation it's going to be very hard.

Frank Stajano: Another thing that Markus said, when we were worrying about the 1 and a 0, and a 0 and a 0 giving a different level, is this: if I'm going to attack this, and I control the power supply, then I'm just going to wiggle it slightly and make a wave that I can recognise later.

Jonathan Anderson: Well the other thing is that, if you wanted a really slow scheme, you could implement 0s and 1s in cryptographic terms where something is or is not a quadratic residue, in which case you would then have confidence that in fact a 0 is a 0, a 1 is a 1, and they combine in the way you expect. But then of course you're talking about doing modular exponentiation every time you want to transmit a 0 or a 1.

Reply: I think that would be fine as well.

Jonathan Anderson: But well then again, you have to have a T box.

Bruce Christianson: But that's the nice thing about the idea of a T box: both sides can look at it with the lid open and check that it's a T box.

Frank Stajano: Well actually, at this level, at the level that this talk has been given here for time reasons, there's no advantage in calling it the T box instead of just calling it an AND gate, except that we have another thing in the paper as well where it's not an AND gate because it's a tri-state thing, so it's slightly abstracted here, and all we are doing so far, and all we have played with, is just an AND gate.

Matt Blaze: Right, so the problem is that there's no such thing as an AND gate in a physical channel.

Frank Stajano: It's the same thing when we did romantic cryptography thing, where you basically want an AND gate between Alice and Bob who may or may not in love, and they only want to say it if the other guy is also going to say it, but nobody actually does it before the other one; it's the same thing.

Bruce Christianson: So the protocol involving cards that are either hearts or spades.

Scrambling for Lightweight Censorship Resistance

Joseph Bonneau and Rubin Xu

University of Cambridge, Cambridge, UK

Abstract. In this paper we propose scrambling as a lightweight method of censorship resistance, in place of the traditional use of encryption. We consider a censor which can only block banned content by scanning it while in transit (for example using deep-packet inspection), instead of attacking the communication endpoints (for example using address filtering or taking servers offline). Our goal is to greatly increase the workload of the censor by scrambling all data during communication, while maintaining reasonable workloads for the endpoints of the communication network. In particular, our goal is to make it impossible for the censor to effectively accelerate the de-scrambling procedure over what may be achieved by commodity PCs or mobile phones at the endpoints, a goal which we term *high-inertia* scrambling. We also aim to achieve this using the standard JavaScript runtime environment of modern browsers, requiring no distribution or installation of censorship-resistance software.

1 Introduction

Traditional approaches to censorship resistance include steganography and cryptography (including anonymity networks which usually bypass censorship by encrypting all data). Each has the fundamental problem of requiring some metadata to be communicated in the clear prior to communication of potentially censored content, namely the steganographic or cryptographic software which is not normally built in to web browsers.

Several proposals exist for censorship resistance through steganography, or careful hiding of banned content amongst innocuous content [8,5,4]. All of these proposals require special software for communicating parties. Steganography's drawbacks also include poor efficiency and a lack of robustness against a censor who may alter communications.

Other proposals involve the use of cryptography for censorship resistance, making it computationally infeasible for a censor to distinguish between banned and innocuous content. Proposals include storage and publication systems which "entangle" different types of content, making it impossible to delete banned content only [14], or overlay networks which protect all traffic cryptographically [3]. A general-purpose anonymity-network like Tor [7] can also be used for censorship resistance, as all traffic is encrypted.

While cryptographic solutions offer strong resistance to censorship, the protocols are complex and again require special client software and secure distribution of a set of trusted public keys to end-users. For example, censors in Iran

B. Christianson et al. (Eds.): Security Protocols 2011, LNCS 7114, pp. 296–302, 2011.

have recently attempted to block Tor by blocking the bit sequence of its public Diffie-Hellman parameters. The global Certificate Authority system underpinning TLS/SSL encryption, which is built-in to all web browsers, has recently been called into question for anti-censorship purposes due to the large number of government-controlled CAs and the recently-leaked existence of commercially available equipment to perform real-time middleperson attacks on TLS sessions given access to a CA's private key [12].

We focus on resisting *passive censors*, who will merely try to halt the transmission of banned content, and *active censors*, who may try to investigate and intimidate the end-points of communication. Cryptography frustrates passive censorship by making it computationally infeasible for censors to tell the difference between banned information and legal information. However, encryption is not strictly necessary for resisting passive censorship if secrecy of the banned content is not important. Cryptography may also be insufficient because, as we have outlined, it still requires distribution of trusted keys and decryption can often be accelerated by a censor (which is of considerable importance for censorship to scale to deep packet inspection of significant levels of Internet traffic).

Against a passive adversary who has potentially compromised the root of trust for cryptographic communication, we propose censorship without encryption but with simpler *scrambling*. We only require that endpoints have a trustworthy computation environment (for example, a modern web browser) which can compute a publicly available de-scrambling algorithm, which in practice can be transmitted as in-page JavaScript which de-scrambles data received through AJAX requests. This is similar to the function of many existing dynamic web pages.

Faced with a large volume of such scrambled messages (whether encrypted or due to simpler scrambling), a censor will be unable to block its desired set of data without either de-scrambling all data or over-censoring. Thus, a scrambling function which is sufficiently difficult to de-scramble can frustrate a central censor while not preventing endpoints from communicating. We are particularly interested in scrambling which cannot be practically accelerated, which we term high-inertia scrambling. That is, the censor must do as much work as all communication endpoints are willing to do and cannot "cheat" by investing in custom hardware. Another way of framing the problem is that we want de-scrambling to be optimised to run in the web browsers of commodity PCs, and have no significantly faster implementation on another platform.

In common with steganographic and cryptographic censorship-resistance schemes, scrambling can only be effective if some non-banned content is scrambled as well, preventing the censor from simply blocking any content which looks scrambled. However, scrambling possesses two potential advantages for web content. First, a large amount of content is already effectively scrambled in the form of obfuscated Javascript which unpacks page content dynamically in client browsers. Second, due to the ability of all current web browsers to descramble content, a large site such as Google or Wikipedia could scramble all served content without seriously inconveniencing any of its users. This would make blocking such a large site effectively all-or-nothing for the censor.

2 Scrambling

For our purposes, a scrambling function S is any function[1] which takes an input x and produces an output y from which no information about x can be recovered more efficiently than running the de-scrambling function S^{-1}. Encryption can be thought of as a special type of scrambling for which S^{-1} is intractable to compute without the secret key k. We are instead interested, however, in scrambling functions for which S^{-1} is either obvious[2] or is transmitted as a header along with the scrambled data y, enabling data to be transmitted in scrambled form without any key management.

2.1 Required Properties of a Scrambling Function

- **One-way.** An adversary given $y = S(x)$ should not be able to compute any information about x in a more efficient way than completely running $S^{-1}(y)$.
- **Randomised.** Computing $y_1 = S(x, r_1)$ and $y_2 = S(x, r_2)$ with different random seeds $r_1 \neq r_2$ must produce different outputs $y_1 \neq y_2$. Given y_1 and y_2, an adversary should be unable to determine if they represent the same input by any more efficient method than computing S^{-1}. If one-wayness is satisfied this implies an **indistinguishability** property, namely that an adversary given y_1, y_2 cannot determine if $S^{-1}(y_1) = S^{-1}(y_2)$ without computing both de-scramblings.
- **Universal and compact de-scrambling.** S^{-1} must be computable from a compact description on a widely available computing platform. This ensures that code for S^{-1} can be transmitted along with y to enable the scheme to be used by clients with no special set-up. In practice, JavaScript is an obvious choice due to its ubiquitousness and common use to de-pack websites.
- **Difficult to accelerate.** It should not be possible for an adversary seeking to compute S^{-1} on n inputs $y_1 \ldots y_n$ to do so using less than $\Theta(n)$ times more resources than an ordinary user computing S^{-1} once on commodity hardware. This should include resources of electricity, power, memory, and computation time. Fortunately, bulk hardware acceleration for JavaScript is not an active area of research.
- **Variable strength.** It should be possible to parameterise S such that the resulting S^{-1} can require any desired amount of resources to compute. Given with the difficulty of acceleration, this enables users to devote any available idle resources to computing S^{-1} and force the censor to perform as much work as possible.
- **Asymmetric cost.** Computing S should be significantly cheaper than computing S^{-1}. This is necessary to prevent bottlenecks if many users are accessing content from one server and to effectively push out all work the censor is being forced to do to the network edges.

[1] Technically speaking, S is likely not to be a true mathematical function but a randomised multivalued function which can map the same input to many possibly outputs.

[2] A classic scrambling function is ROT-13, a Caesar cipher with a fixed alphabetic shift of 13 which is used to hide "spoilers" in online forums.

- **Adjustable resource usage.** To avoid the problems of proof-of-work systems, for which adversaries can realistically expend more computation time than legitimate users [9], it may be desirable to make computing S^{-1} utilise other resources. In particular, memory latency-bound functions [6] are considerably more difficult for an adversary to compute relative to most end-user machines.
- **Human-interactive de-scrambling.** A particularly useful example of the above idea is to require human computational abilities in addition to standard machine computation to compute S^{-1}. This can be achieved by incorporating CAPTCHA-solving into S^{-1}. This is not a complete solution, as CAPTCHA-farming and other attacks exist, but puts additional burden on the censor.

3 Outline of a Practical Implementation

We imagine a practical implementation will be built using the AJAX architecture used in many modern dynamic web pages. A site with some potentially censored material will include JavaScript which will fetch the banned material M in multiple blocks, compute $S^{-1}(M)$ and display the results.

A key design tool is to use a package transform [11], which makes it impossible to compute any information about M until all blocks are available. While we are not aware of any implementations of package transform in pure JavaScript[3], one can be constructed relatively by computing the BEAR-encryption [2] of M using an all-zero key. This can be implemented using standard symmetric primitives like AES and SHA, for which widely-used JavaScript libraries are now available [13].

As a first pass, the server simply computes:

$$G_1, G_2, \ldots G_n = \mathrm{BEAR}_0(M_1, M_2, \ldots M_n)$$

And sends the G blocks to the client using individual AJAX requests. The client can undo the package transform once all of the G blocks are fetched.

This proposal already serves are a simple scrambling system as the cleartext blocks of M are not transmitted, but any client can still de-scramble M. By artificially delaying the transmission of the blocks, this system can force a censor to maintain a significant amount of state, as all blocks from all active transfers must be cached to enable de-scrambling. However, it is still not asymmetric or variable in cost, and admits significant acceleration by hardware implementation of the cryptographic primitives.

To add these properties, we use a technique similar to that proposed by Anderson to enable multi-party decryption [1]. Any transform applied to any of the G blocks must be undone prior to inverting the package transform and recovering the original message. This enables each block to be scrambled in a different way, allowing us to compose an arbitrary number of scrambling techniques.

[3] Practical desktop libraries do exist for all-or-nothing encryption based using package transforms [10].

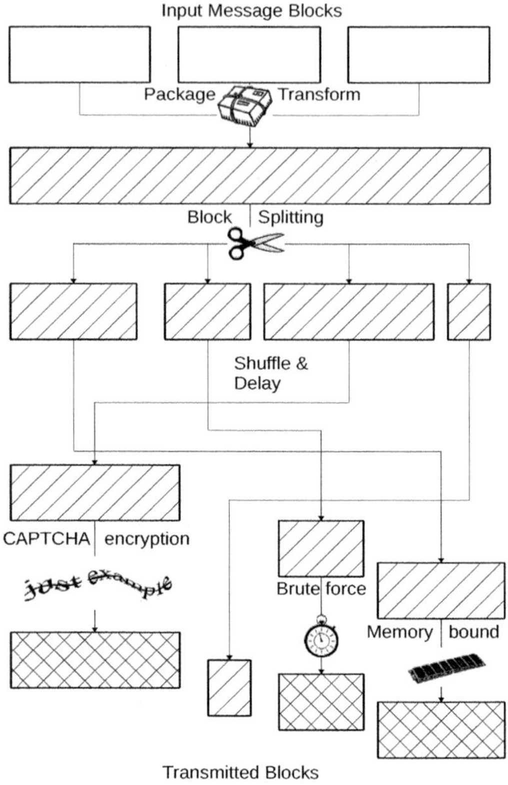

Fig. 1. Multi-stage scrambling of an input message. The package transform ensures that all steps must be undone to recover the original message.

A solid implementation would first perform a computationally-intensive scrambling for one or more blocks. This can be easily done in an asymmetric way by encrypting the block with a random 128-bit AES key, discarding 20 of the bits and transmitting the rest, forcing the de-scrambling routine to search over the rest. Another block could be transmitted encrypted by an AES key which is derived from the result of a CAPTCHA (likely with additional key-strengthening to frustrate brute-force of the input space). A third block could be transmitted encrypted by a key computed by a memory-bound function. Finally, some blocks could be transmitted with a de-scrambling function making heavy use of quirks in JavaScript as well as its built-in floating point, date, and string processing libraries, forcing a censor to implement all of these in any accelerated environment. A diagram of this implementation is shown in Figure 1.

3.1 Future Desirable Properties

We believe our simple proposal can be improved upon in many interesting and exotic ways. We propose two here as areas for future exploration:

- **Busy beaver traps.** Assuming the censor will attempt to compute S^{-1} for a large amount of content seen, it may be useful to introduce some functions S^{-1} into the system which in fact contain infinite loops and will never terminate. It can be assumed that end-users will simply give up on these and re-communicate the desired content, or perhaps will have agreed out-of-band on some messages to ignore. If some important content is scrambled with intentionally very high de-scrambling cost, then it may be difficult for the censor to detect which content will result in infinite loops. The existence of busy beaver functions in complexity theory which do an enormous amount of work before terminating despite their short descriptions indicates the difficulty for a censor detecting these traps.
- **Re-scrambling.** It may be very useful if scrambled content y can be re-scrambled by a re-scrambling function S', such that if $y = S(x)$ and $y' = S'(y)$, we have both $x = S^{-1}(y)$ and $x = S^{-1}(y')$. Ideally, computing $S^{-1}(y)$ or $S^{-1}(y')$ will be of similar difficulty and an adversary cannot determine that y and y' are scramblings of the same input without computing S^{-1}. Such re-scrambling would fit nicely with the existing theory of mix networks and re-mailers. If re-scrambling is considerably cheaper than initial scrambling, then it may also be a technique for asymmetric strength scrambling, as a server could scramble x once and then repeatedly re-scramble each time it must be transmitted.

Acknowledgements. We thank Steven Murdoch for providing inspiration for this project, as well as Ross Anderson and Richard Clayton for helpful comments.

References

1. Anderson, R.: The Dancing Bear: A New Way of Composing Ciphers. In: Christianson, B., Crispo, B., Malcolm, J.A., Roe, M. (eds.) Security Protocols 2004. LNCS, vol. 3957, pp. 231–238. Springer, Heidelberg (2006), doi:10.1007/11861386_26
2. Anderson, R., Biham, E.: Two practical and provably secure block ciphers: BEAR and LION. In: Gollmann, D. (ed.) FSE 1996. LNCS, vol. 1039, pp. 113–120. Springer, Heidelberg (1996), doi:10.1007/3-540-60865-6_48
3. Backes, M., Hamerlik, M., Linari, A., Maffei, M., Tryfonopoulos, C., Weikum, G.: Anonymity and Censorship Resistance in Unstructured Overlay Networks. In: Meersman, R., Dillon, T., Herrero, P. (eds.) OTM 2009. LNCS, vol. 5870, pp. 147–164. Springer, Heidelberg (2009)
4. Baliga, A., Kilian, J., Iftode, L.: A web based covert file system. In: Proceedings of the 11th USENIX Workshop on Hot Topics in Operating Systems, pp. 12:1–12:6. USENIX Association, Berkeley (2007)
5. Burnett, S., Feamster, N., Vempala, S.: Chipping away at censorship firewalls with user-generated content. In: Proceedings of the 19th USENIX Conference on Security, USENIX Security 2010, p. 29. USENIX Association, Berkeley (2010)
6. Crowcroft, J., Deegan, T., Kreibrich, C., Mortier, R., Susan, N.W.: Lazy Susan: dumb waiting as proof of work dumb waiting as proof of work. Technical Report UCAM-CL-TR-703, University of Cambridge (2007)

7. Dingledine, R., Mathewson, N., Syverson, P.: Tor: The next-generation onion routern. In: USENIX 2007: Proceedings of 13th USENIX Security Symposium. USENIX Association (2004)
8. Feamster, N., Balazinska, M., Harfst, G., Balakrishnan, H., Karger, D.: Infranet: Circumventing Web Censorship and Surveillance. In: Proceedings of the 11th USENIX Security Symposium, pp. 247–262. USENIX Association, Berkeley (2002)
9. Laurie, B., Clayton, R.: Proof-of-work proves not to work. In: WEIS 2004: The Third Workshop on the Economics of Information Security (2004)
10. Raghavan, B.: Staple project (2009), `http://sysnet.cs.williams.edu/staple/`
11. Rivest, R.L.: All-or-Nothing Encryption and the Package Transform. In: Biham, E. (ed.) FSE 1997. LNCS, vol. 1267, pp. 210–218. Springer, Heidelberg (1997)
12. Soghoian, C., Stamm, S.: Certified Lies: Detecting and Defeating Government Interception Attacks Against SSL (2010), `http://ssrn.com/abstract=1591033`
13. Stark, E., Hamburg, M., Boneh, D.: Symmetric Cryptography in Javascript. In: Proceedings of the 2009 Annual Computer Security Applications Conference, ACSAC 2009, pp. 373–381. IEEE Computer Society, Washington, DC, USA (2009)
14. Waldman, M., Mazières, D.: Tangler: a censorship-resistant publishing system based on document entanglements. In: Proceedings of the 8th ACM conference on Computer and Communications Security, CCS 2001, pp. 126–135. ACM, New York (2001)

Scrambling for Lightweight Censorship Resistance (Transcript of Discussion)

Rubin Xu

University of Cambridge, Cambridge, UK

Hello everyone, today I will talk about new ideas about censorship resistance. First of all, what threat models are we assuming, and what kind of censors are we talking about. In this paper we are assuming a passive global censor, that basically means there is some well-founded organization who would be able to sit at the backbone of some internet communication, possibly on the outgoing router of some internet infrastructure, and watch all communication going in and out of the domain. And what they do is, they will inspect the packet contents, possibly deep-packet inspection on the TCP session, etc, and detect any content which is in blacklist. If any of the blacklisted keywords is being detected in that TCP session, then the adversary will try to block the connection by various means. What the censor will not do is trying to actively modify the communication channel, it will only observe passively. One readily available example in the real world is the Great Firewall project of the Chinese government. Basically it observes all traffic goes in and out of China, uses deep-packet inspection techniques to detect any blacklist keywords, and if any of them is detected then it will inject a malformed packet to disrupt the TCP session, and cause the connection to reset.

Well there's actually more about the Great Firewall project itself, that not only does it do this passive monitoring as a passive censor, it also attacks endpoints by other means such as IP address blacklisting, or DNS poisoning. but we are not going to consider these two cases in our paper, because the IP blacklisting attacks on endpoints can be circumvented by several ways, for example by hosting your web service on IP address that is used by other famous websites, such as Google or Wikipedia, so the censors will not risk to block the whole set including the popular website as well. And also we could do a so-called fast flux hosting, which basically means that you can host mirrors of your website at different IP addresses, and you change the DNS record so fast that it becomes difficult to know how many IP addresses you are using to mirror your site, and hence be able to block the entire range of all possible IP addresses. So we're not considering these attacks on endpoints here, we're only considering a censor doing a passive monitoring of the communication and try to block it only after bad content is detected.

OK, naturally you will think, well let's encrypt the content. Well that's kind of OK, you can encrypt, though you have to encrypt the channel somehow to avoid being detected. But encryption itself is a complicated issue. First you have to distribute encryption key, which is often a weak point for attack. And

B. Christianson et al. (Eds.): Security Protocols 2011, LNCS 7114, pp. 303–312, 2011.

what's more, you have to distribute the software or the algorithm you use to do the encryption. This is also a problem because you want your website to be as accessible as possible, and you don't want to make people install some unfamiliar software kit which they may consider as dodgy, just to be able to view your website, for the sake of accessibility. So so far the only widely available crypto software that can do this kind of communication encryption is, as we all know, SSL, the TLS stack. It's good for many scenarios, apart from the fact that it's been based on the public key infrastructure, i.e. the Certificate Authority and the chain of trust. Well this whole PKI is basically not that safe anymore because, as Ross has pointed out two days ago, we have these large number of Certificate Authorities living inside your browser, and all of them are to be trusted. If any of them goes wrong, or be coerced by a government, then your entire chain of trust is broken. The recent Commodo incident suggests that, SSL is not always safe, because as long as one of the Certificate Authorities is broken into, or being coerced to reveal his private key to an adversary, then he will be able to issue fake or forged certificates which allows him to impersonate any website of his interest, and effectively perform a man-in-the-middle attack on SSL itself without your browser being alerted. That's going to be bad because your communication is effectively in plaintext to the adversary. As a matter of fact there are actually already commercially available hardware that can do SSL man-in-the-middle attacks in realtime, so SSL is not that safe now.

So, what is our solution to this problem? We claim that encrypting is sufficient but it's not always necessary, we can actually achieve censorship resistance by using something less than encryption. Our goal is to prevent the censor from seeing your communication content, and if you perform proper encryption, that is on top of the assumption that you have a perfect way of distributing encryption keys, then you can make it impossible for the censors to decrypt the communication, if he has no access to the key. In some sense we can achieve the same goal using scrambling as well, where scrambling is just a weaker form of encryption, a kind of transformation on the communication content. And how can we stop the censor from being able to see the communication? We just need to make descrambling beyond the capabilities of any censor we can imagine.

How can we do this? First of all we can make the descrambling as difficult as possible. In this case, the network's large volume of traffic is actually on our side. Remember, the censor is someone that sits at the backbone of the infrastructure, so he's going to need to check all the traffic that goes through, and if we try to make individual descrambling just somewhat difficult for them, then they will suffer a bad time in descrambling a million pieces of traffic at the same time. In that sense we will make it impossible for them to achieve successful descrambling as they have to do it on a very large scale. And in reality what we do is that not only do we scramble the content that you do not want the censor to see, but also we scramble some innocent content just to make sure that content is scrambled by itself is not revealing that the content is sensitive. This also increases the workload of the censor as well.

So, what can we do? Here are a few examples of scrambling functions. We may simply perform a mono-alphabetic substitution cipher to the content of our interest. Yes it's not perfect, as you can see the censor could just reverse this transformation easily, even on the scale of a million connections, because this operation is not very complex at all. What's more, the censor could perform a pre-computation of the censored keywords, scan for the transformed content in the traffic and try to block it instead, so there's actually no need for him to reverse this scrambling at all.

Also, we could apply a block cipher to the content, but now we are just using a fixed key which is known by everyone. We don't care about the secrecy of the key, we just want to perform some transformation on the plain text. And yes, similarly the adversary can either reverse this cipher, which he may have to use some special hardware to accelerate this operation on a million connections this time , or he could also just pre-compute the transformed blacklist as previously, and scan for the the transformed keywords instead.

Here is another interesting scrambling function, which is called the Package transform, or All or Nothing Encryption. What it actually does is it generates a random key, K_R, and in order to scramble some message X_0 to X_N, you encrypt individual message block using the random key K_R. The interesting part in that you actually transmit the K_R as well, but only in a scrambled form. The construction makes sure that no one will be able to obtain the actual encryption key K_R if he does not have access of all the transformed cipher text. This operation basically makes the message blocks into an inseparable big chunk of data so even if you just lose one bit of data, then you will not be able to infer anything about X_0 to X_N.

Ross Anderson: You can do slightly better than that I think because with this you've got the feature that you have to receive all the ciphertext and then decrypt a few blocks in order to see that it's a prohibitive content, but there are other transforms where you can force the adversary to do a cryptographic operation on each block, if they are aligned with a constant key, for example.

Reply: Yes, The original Rivest proposal has to do three runs of the block cipher around the entire thing and that is the most secure version.

Robert Watson: But the interesting thing is not the crypto, right, the interesting thing here is the state maintenance for the people who sit in the middle, and they have to maintain the state and all the traffic, whereas the previous ones are state free.

Reply: So they have to keep all this data, to be able to decrypt even one of them, and that's going to cause a heavy burden on the censors.

Ross Anderson: So there's any number of ways you can tweak the parameters with an appropriate choice of transform. You can force the censor to do as much work as the browser is able to do for a message.

Robert Watson: Or as much work as the server is supposed to do, I mean, the problem you always have with schemes like this is that you increase the burden on the client and the server, and if you have a billion websites all hitting the same servers, the servers are now doing a lot more work than they were doing before.

Reply: Actually this is just one example of all possible scrambling functions that we have. Yes, this one alone will create equal burden to the server and the censor, but as we can see later, by building up other scrambling functions on top the the package transform, we can create asymmetric workload between the server and the censor.

Omar Choudary: Will you talk also about how the website could be involved, let's say I'm talking to Wikipedia, or some website, will you also describe how the other website knows which kind of scrambling I'm using?

Reply: Yes. Actually it's a website that tells you what kind of scrambling he uses.

Omar Choudary: Well maybe the website is not doing any scrambling, I mean, what is the motivation for the website to use the scrambling. Yes, maybe it's a website that doesn't care about the fact that you are blocked or not, and the problem is on your state, you know. What if my state says, no, I don't like Wikipedia anymore. Wikipedia may not care since the other 249 countries or something are not blocked.

Joseph Bonneau: Well then somebody would get somebody on the outside to mirror it for you.

Omar Choudary: So the question is, do you have some kind of mechanism for this?

Joseph Bonneau: Yes, they have to set up a proxy. If the actual server doesn't care then you have to get a proxy that has access to it that will do what you want.

Ross Anderson: There's perhaps another consideration which is that if you send an active object that has to be executed in order to be read, then some kinds of surveillance operation may be very nervous about executing your content within their classified boxes.

Robert Watson: The effects of all this is to cause the censor to have to distribute their work, so the question is, can you continue to get scalable censorship from the censor network, or do you have to push it to the edges so it will scale, and therefore the solution is, you know, you put the censorship in the consumers devices, because that's the ultimate number of consumers, and it uses their electricity, and that kind of thing. You could also imagine if these censorships systems are sort of like Tor but backwards.

So having seen various examples of scrambling functions, now we describe what the kind of properties we want for a scrambling function. First of all we want it to be a one-way. Well that's quite a strong requirement. We basically assumes that if you have some scrambled content, y, then it will not be able to infer any information about underlying plaintext x, without computing the inverse of the scrambling, i.e. without descrambling y.

Frank Stajano: How can you do the unscrambling if it's one-way?

Reply: The one-wayness here is different from the hash properties of one-wayness.

Frank Stajano: What does one-way mean for you?

Reply: So it's basically you cannot deduce any information more efficiently than computing the inverse of it.

Jonathan Anderson: Right, so the function is reversible, but the sender cannot find a shorter path to reverse it.

Reply: Yes. The most efficient way of learning anything on the plain text is doing the reverse computation.

Frank Stajano: I have just a question on this one-way, I mean, there's no shortcuts on the provided inverse, it's obviously two-way.

Reply: Yes, it's not the traditional meaning of one-wayness.

And second we want it to be randomised. So we want this scrambling function to take a random nonce, S, such as it will produce a different result even for the same input as long as the nonce is different. This property is desirable in order to deter the pre-computation attack I described earlier. The censor would not be able to use the attack of a scrambled blacklist.

Robert Watson: Are you imagining applying these to objects or to streams? Well I'm wondering about the ability of at least the web server to pre-compute results, right, and if it's on a stream then the web server can't do that, but if it's on the object it can, and then you reveal the metadata.

Reply: Well I think we were working on streams, the raw content of TCP streams.

Robert Watson: Right, so sort of SSL like, but not SSL.

Reply: Yes.

So randomisation prevents pre-computation keyword attacks here.

And another desirable property of a scrambling function is that we want it to be as hard as possible to accelerate by various means. First of all, preferably you don't want it to be the case that there exists some hardware that can perform the inverse transformation with significant speed advantage. It's basically a way to stop the well-funded censor to be able to invest in specialised hardware to accelerate its descrambling process. Also we want this requirement that you have N piece of data with N piece of scrambled data, you have to spend a linear end times the work of descrambling one piece of data. This basically means that a scrambling function has to be free of some interesting properties such that you can actually combine the anti-scrambling process into something which is easier.

Frank Stajano: And you probably want to put a big omega instead of big theta, because you don't care, in fact you're happy if the adversary does more work.

Reply: Yes, well I guess it's quite hard for you to do so.

Frank Stajano: It shouldn't be the requirement if it's exactly N.

We want this function to be asymmetric and preferably adjustable. This asymmetric property is actually quite important. Remember as a web server, if you want to provide some scrambled content you have to evaluate S, but as a censor, if you want to descramble something you have to evaluate S^{-1}. Well you have to make sure that the S^{-1} is much harder than S, because otherwise then the web server has to do as much work as the censor does, which is undesirable. The idea is we want some exponential increase in the workload between descrambling and scrambling, and it would be better if this exponential increase is actually adjustable, so we could adjust how much work we are trying to force the censor to do in order to descramble the content.

Finally we want this scrambling function to be universal, compact and complex. Remember when I talked about the problems about encryption is that you have to distribute the software to perform the decryption, and we want our scrambling function to be universal, that means it can run on commercially available platform that you can use, and that you don't need to install some software just to do the decryption. And we want it to be compact such that the description of this scrambling function, or the descrambling function, can be actually transmitted on the fly to the user's device. JavaScript is actually a good candidate for this description of scrambling functions because, first of all, almost every browser has JavaScript support built-in. The language itself is also compact and complex as well.

In reality what we do as a framework is that we want to transfer the descrambling function implemented in JavaScript back to the client side so that the client's browser is able to execute these scrambling functions and gives you the descrambled content, so you don't install any extra software to do it. You just go your website as normal, and within a few seconds everything is descrambled and presented to you. One nice thing about this idea that you are transforming the descrambling function to the clients is each time the server can decide what descrambling function you are going to use, and because we are implementing all algorithms in JavaScript, we are forcing the censor to implement an entire JavaScript execution engine on their censorship hardware and force them to execute JavaScript each time they want to descramble some content. This is going to be very difficult for them to do because, well, JavaScript itself is quite a complex language: it's functional, very difficult to accelerate, and the fact that hardware acceleration of JavaScript is not an active area of research. This is exactly what we want, we don't want the censor to be at an advantage even if he has money to invest.

Robert Watson: In your thinking this will be used with TLS or without TLS?

Reply: Well it doesn't matter because it's actually the underlying content.

Robert Watson: Well I'm just wondering because if I was a censor I'd inject some JavaScript that censored your webpage when it rendered.

Reply: Exactly, so, I was assuming that the censor is not active and is not hijacking things on your JavaScript code.

Ross Anderson: If you want to make sure that the censor also has to run JavaScript then perhaps you're not looking for a single function, but you keep on changing the function, you have a family of functions of relatively compact description and you choose one at random.

Reply: Yes, that's a good point.

Here is the overall architecture of the framework. Firstly one makes the whole chunk of data inseparable, by applying the package transform that was described earlier. We can use Rivest's version or achieve the similar results with this cipher Bear, proposed by Ross. It's a class of block ciphers with arbitrarily long block length, is been constructed by composing a hash function, a fixed-length block cipher and a stream cipher in an unbalanced Feistel network style. We use it to construct a very long block cipher which operates on the entire traffic content, such that the censor has to collect the entire content before he can decrypt it, and that further increases the storage requirement of the censor.

After we apply the package transform on the content we will transfer it block by the block using an AJAX mechanism, such that we can do it asynchronously and whenever you receive the relevant blocks you can start doing further descrambling on it.

The actual scrambling function we are using is something like this. It is asymmetric CPU puzzle. It takes some plaintext and applies a block cipher to it, with the used encryption key revealed partially in the output. Because you've erased some bits of the encryption key, this forces the client to brute-force for these bits. The nice thing about this puzzle is that you can adjust how many bits you erase, i.e. how much work that you want the client side to do in order to descramble the message.

So this is one example of our scrambling functions that we can have, but it depends on the computation power you have in your client side, and nowadays you have these portable devices which are slower, and you also have these desktop computers which are much faster. The difference of computation power between these different clients can cause you problems, because either you adjust the security parameter too high such that portable devices will take a very long time to descramble the content, or you adjust the security parameters too low such that the censor may be able to descramble it as well. So that's one particular problem associated with the CPU puzzle. Actually we can use a memory-bound puzzle as a way to deter a censor as well. A memory-bound function employs some kind of trapdoor function, which is easy to compute one-way, but in order to reverse it the fastest way is to devote a large amount of memory as a lookup table as part of the algorithm. That's going to cause a lot of burden to the censor because if each individual memory-bound puzzle has to use say 16 megabytes of memory, then for the censor who has to descramble a million connection at the same time, he will have to have a million times 16 megabytes memory, which is very difficult to achieve nowadays. The nice thing about memory puzzles is that the difference between the low-end and high-end devices is much smaller, and censors cannot outperform the slower consumer devices significantly.

Robert Watson: It's the additive property of a time, right, if you only need that much memory instantaneously, then it's not a problem to do it in a middle, but if you're required to maintain that state over an extended period of time then it is a problem, because it all adds up based on the number of simultaneous connections or objects, or whatever it is, it's implicit in what you're saying.

Jonathan Anderson: And the are two kinds of puzzles that you've described here are also kind of two sides of the same coin in that you can do, you can brute-force the block cipher really fast if you're willing to have lots of storage, and so either of these can be traded off into CPU or memory respectively.

In face the CPU and memory puzzles are something that we borrow from the proof of work system. The proof of work system was originally intended to stop spammers to flood email service with lots of spams, but it didn't work well for that purpose because the spammers nowadays have control of large botnets, and effectively they can crack the puzzles in a distributed computation fashion. But for our global passive censor these techniques work well, because a censor is kind of a centralised device, and it does not have as much computation power as a large distributed system like a botnet has.

Finally we could introduce human factors into this scrambling function. We provide a CAPTCHA to the client, and the encryption key is just there, hidden in the CAPTCHA. The censor has to solve this CAPTCHA in order to obtain the key to descramble the contents. Well there exists CAPTCHA farms, but it is just an extra burden on the censors.

Having combined all the things together we have this proposed framework. The plaintext is firstly scrambled by the packaged transforms such as it becomes inseparable big chunk of data, and the big chunk of data is then split into different parts, each of which can be scrambled using one of the proposed scrambling functions, either memory-bound, CPU-bound or CAPTCHA-based. It can also subject to delay before transmission, in order to increase the storage burden of the censor. Together with this we have to transmit the loading page that can then do the descrambling and assemble the original message. Basically that's it.

Robert Watson: So your shuffle and delay set, you said that was to make more state, requires more state to be held in the network as you're processing, but that also means the client has to maintain, do incremental interpretation and stuff.

Reply: Well the client has to collect all his data packets.

Robert Watson: You turned it into object delivery as opposed to, you know, a stream that you can potentially process earlier, so in a jpeg you might start rendering before it entirely gets there, but in this model you have to wait for everything to get there?

Reply: Yes, in that sense the framework operates on sort-of objects.

Jonathan Anderson: But presumably you can also use this mechanism to use puzzles that take a long for stuff that you actually want to hide from the censor, puzzles that look like they take a long time, but can actually be solved very quickly for things that you might want to start pre-processing which the censor doesn't care about.

Sandy Clark: You can do a one track this way?

Jonathan Anderson: Well it depends, can you construct puzzles that look as time intensive as the ones that actually are.

Matt Blaze: If the censor can afford to devote some amount of computation, you know, the censor knows the ones that fail.

Joseph Bonneau: Well you can also, I mean, in the key search example you can have it, the likely first or second key you try is actually the correct one, you can't cheat in that way, if you're trying to make something and cheat that looks like it's expensive. And then it's interesting if you can make something that's even much more expensive than it looks like, right, and try and put an infinite loop somewhere in there, and assume that people will re-transmit.

Robert Watson: So you could of course just essentially have an algorithm that you will cut off all computation after a fixed time band, and even if it was hard to decode it was something you wanted to censor anyway.

Joseph Bonneau: Yes, but then you've won, right, oh well then you block it.

Robert Watson: Yes, then you block it, and if you can't make it cheaper for the uncensored material, the censored material, because then you could say, if this gets too expensive obviously it was censored.

Jonathan Anderson: Well I mean, I do kind of like the idea of having a very large search space for potential keys, but then you distribute through any stuff that you know the censors probably aren't going to bother to look at, a list of keys you could try first.

Robert Watson: That's the CAPTCHA model right, the CAPTCHA model is, I provided a key, and you know the shared secret, and then it's always based on the shared secret, and it's just weak crypto.

The Metaplace Security Model

Michael Roe

University of Hertfordshire, Hatfield, UK

Abstract. As part of an ongoing project on the security of online games and virtual reality applications, we joined the open beta test of *Metaplace*, to carry out our own analysis of Metaplace's security mechanisms, and to observe what went wrong in practise during the beta test.

The beta test version of Metaplace is particularly interesting because it went further than most online games in allowing "user generated content". For example, users were able to customize the game (or effectively, build their own game) by writing code that was run on the game server. This clearly has serious security implications, and Metaplace had its own unique security mechanisms to address the resulting issues. At the end of the beta test, Metaplace (then renamed *Island Life*) was changed to be more modest in the forms of user generated content that were permitted. The beta test was therefore a one-off opportunity to see if these mechanisms worked in practise.

We found that some well-known operating systems security issues reappeared in new forms in Metaplace: anyone who in the future would like to build a game with this degree of user-generated content in their game would do well to be aware of these issues.

The obvious competitor to Metaplace was Linden Lab's *Second Life*, which also permits advanced forms of user-generated content. Second Life's approach to security is significantly different from Metaplace, and there both advantages and disadvantages: we give a more detailed comparison later in the paper.

1 Introduction

Some online games support "user generated content": users are allowed to upload their own graphics and scripts that are incorporated into the game. In order to allow this while preventing various forms of mischief-making by users, the game platforms need to be, in effect, secure multiuser operating systems. These game platforms have a different architecture from more traditional operating systems, which causes some traditional operating system problems to appear in new forms.

During the open beta test of Metaplace (ending in December 2009), we built some applications on top of Metaplace, with a view to understanding its security properties. In this paper, I will first describe the security model that Metaplace used during its open beta test. I will then describe a number of issues with the architecture that we and other developers encountered; propose some changes to the architecture that would have avoided them; and finally, I will give some examples of why Metaplace's security model might be too strict, in that it makes

B. Christianson et al. (Eds.): Security Protocols 2011, LNCS 7114, pp. 313–326, 2011.

it very hard to implement some features that are very important in Metaplace's rival, Second Life.

2 Qualitative Approach

Initially, we considered making a quantitative comparison of Metaplace versus Second Life: what is the difference in the demographics of their users, what is the difference in the styles of game play, what is the difference in the security problems that were encountered, and so on. However, there are a number of factors that make quantitative comparison difficult.

Firstly, during the beta test, Metaplace's user demographics were constantly changing. The makers of the game were taking out targeted advertising (e.g. on other web sites) and seeing how good a response (in terms of new user registrations, etc.) they got from different types of potential user. As a result, there is no single answer to the question, "what kind of person played Metaplace?": it varied over time as the advertising was changed.

Secondly, Metaplace's beta test had far fewer active users than Second Life, which was out of beta test and in full production use. A system with fewer users is a less attractive target to attackers, and has fewer people with an interest in breaking its security. Some of Metaplace's gain over Second Life may have been partly due to its smaller user base. (After the beta test, Metaplace's user base rose to over half a million users, but as the advanced forms of user generated content had been removed by that point, this is also not a useful comparison).

Instead, we shall present qualitative results, giving some typical examples of the kind of user generated content that was built, and the kind of security problems that arose.

3 Social vs. Game-Like

In a taxonomy developed by Richard Bartle[1], text-based "Multi User Dungeons" were classified on a spectrum from "social" to "game-like". The Bartle taxonomy also applies to today's online graphical "virtual worlds". On this scale, both Metaplace and Second Life have been used to create social and game-like environments, but Metaplace users tended to create more game-like worlds than Second Life. An example of a game-like world built with Metaplace during its beta test was "Virek Online", an adventure game with a folk music sound-track by Daniel Fredriksson.

Metaplace's development was led by Raph Koster, who had also worked on the extremely successful multiplayer game *Ultima Online*. A significant number of Metaplace's beta testers had also played Ultima Online, and this probably affected many player's expectations of what Metaplace would be like: at the game-like end of the spectrum.

Part way through the beta test, a different group of users arrived in Metaplace in large numbers. They were what were euphemistically referred to as the "dating" crowd. In the Bartle taxonomy, "dating" (or looking for sex online) is on the more social end of the spectrum.

The dating crowd and the gamers wanted different features from the software (e.g. roughly speaking, adventure gamers preferred text-base chat, while daters wanted real-time voice communication), and raised slightly different security concerns. In particular, members of both of these groups expressed a wish to do what they were into without being unduly disturbed by encounters with the other group.

Later in this paper, I will make some comparisons between Metaplace and Second Life. It should be borne in mind that the two platforms tend to support different kinds of virtual world, with different requirements from the software platform.

4 The Metaplace Architecture

Metaplace lets every user have their own (very small) virtual world, which anyone (their friends, passing strangers, or an attacker) can visit.

Places. Each world is divided into one or more *places*, which are 2D or 3D co-ordinate systems. Moving between places, or between worlds, is a discontinuous jump, a "teleport". Movement within a place depends on what kind of "physics" has been defined for the place, but will typically be continuous movement through the co-ordinate system (e.g. getting your on-screen avatar to walk from A to B).

Superusers. For each world, users are divided into superusers and ordinary users. Only a world's superusers have access to content creation tools, such as the ability to upload code. People can visit your world without being given the superuser privilege that would enable them to upload code (although the attacker will probably have superuser rights in their own world).

State. The state associated with a player is specific to a single virtual world (although there are some exceptions to this, which we will describe later). If the player logs out of world A and logs in to world B, in world B they pick up the persistent state they last had in world B, with no state from world A being carried over. It is possible to be logged in to more than one world at once. If a player moves between "places" within the same world, the associated state moves with them.

Login. Login is single sign-on, with a trusted authentication server. Users only need to enter their password once, to authenticate to the AS, and then can enter any Metaplace world without needing to re-enter a password.

Object-oriented programming. From a programmer's perspective, a world is represented as a collection of objects that have state variables (known as *properties*) and which communicate by exchanging messages (known as *triggers*). Each player is represented by an object; the entire world and each place within it are also objects. Messages sent from the client to the server are known as *commands*: at the server, they are received by the player object for the user.

Commands can be invoked in two ways. The user can type them into the client's command line window, or the server can tell the client to send back a particular command when a certain UI action is taken (such as clicking on a button).

Scripts. One or more *scripts* can be attached to an object. Scripts are written in a modified version of the Lua[3] programming language. The extensions to Lua include:

- The `Define Properties()` block, in which the script's properties are (statically) declared. The Properties block may contain declarations for whether a property is *exposed*, whether it is *persistent*, and the property's type.
- The `Define Commands()` block, in which the script's commands are (statically) declared.
- The keyword `Trigger`, which introduces a function that handles a trigger sent to the object.
- The keyword `Command`, which introduces a function that handles a command sent to the object.
- The variable `self`, which (within the body of a handler for a trigger or command) evaluates to a Lua metatable containing the object's properties.

Behavior Tool. A configuration tool known as the Behavior Tool allows a world's superusers to attach scripts to objects, and examine and modify the values of *exposed* properties. Normal Lua variables are dynamically typed and don't need to be declared before use. The declaration of the type of a Metaplace property is for the benefit of tools (including the Behavior Tool) that use reflection; type safety isn't enforced.

If the player logs out and back in again, the properties of the player object that have not been made persistent are reset to their default values.

Concurrent programming. Scripts are non-blocking. If a script needs to do something that might block, such as wait for user input, the programming paradigm is for the handler to return control to the scheduler, and for another handler to be activated (by an incoming trigger or command) when the blocking action completes. Within a single object, at most one handler is running at any given time, so there is no need for locks to guard against concurrent access; Metaplace objects are like monitors[2]. If several scripts are listening for the same command or trigger, the scheduler runs all of them, in sequence.

Modules. Scripts (and other resources, such as bitmaps) can be organized into *modules*, which provide both version control and access control. A module can be exported from one world and imported into another; this is the main mechanism for moving resources from one world to another. Each script within a module has a permissions bit that marks it as "open source" or "closed source". This refers to whether the superusers of worlds importing the module have read access to the script, not the software license under which it is available. Scripts are run on the server (not the client) so it is not possible to gain access to closed source scripts with a modified client.

Scripts from different modules can be attached to the same object, so it is possible to have mutually suspicious subsystems[7] attached to the same object. It is possible to attach a script to an object even if the script is closed source and you can't read it, so (for example) an attacker can attach a closed source script they are interested in, and an attack script, to the same object.

It is common for scripts from the same module to be attached to different objects, and for these scripts to communicate with each other by sending triggers. For example, a combat system module (for games where the player fights monsters) could have a script that is attached to each player object and a script that is attached to each monster.

Every object has an `id` property, that contains a unique identifier for the object. `GetObjectById` takes this unique identifier and returns the object (or `nil`, if the identifier does not correspond to an existing object). If object A wishes to send object B a reference to object C, A can send B a trigger with the value of `c.id` as a parameter, and B can reconstruct the reference to C using `GetObjectById`.

The names of triggers are just strings, so object A can send object B a trigger with the name of another trigger as a parameter. (This is useful for implementing callbacks, for example).

Thin Client. The client software (written in Flash) is a "thin client" that does not contain any logic specific to a particular game or virtual world. All it does is receive graphics primitives sent to it by the server and render the result on screen; and send commands to the server when there in input from the user (e.g. the user presses a key or clicking the mouse on a screen element). The server tells the client which commands should be sent when there is user input (so these commands can be different for different games; as far as the client is concerned, the commands are just strings). From a security perspective, the client is untrusted. There is no attempt to make the client tamper-resistant, and it is assumed that an attacker might have their own modified client. The thin client architecture has a performance implication: there is a delay of at least one network round trip between the user pressing a key and the result appearing on screen. For some types of game, this delay is unacceptable, As a special case, "tool tips" (extra information that appears in a pop-up window when the user points the mouse an on-screen UI element) are handled locally by the client, so there isn't a large delay before the pop-up appears.

Instancing. Some multiplayer games have "instanced dungeons"–each player or group of players to enter an instanced dungeon gets a fresh, clean copy of it that has not been affected by previous interactions with other players. (Otherwise, in–for example–a fantasy game, the player would get to the dragon's lair and discover that the dragon had already been slain and its treasure taken by someone else. With instancing, each player gets a fresh copy). To implement instanced dungeons, Metaplace has an API call that allows a script to create a copy of a place and all the objects within it. This is rather like `fork()` in Unix. The internal state (values of variables etc.) of all the objects within the place is also copied, even if they are "closed source". Player characters within a place, and the associated real-world human beings who are playing the game, are not copied by this API call, for obvious reasons. (Typically, a place will be copied before any players enter it, so this problem doesn't arise).

Cross-world state. The basic picture is that worlds do not share state with each other. However, application developers sometimes need to share state across worlds. An example is the avatars[5] package from the Metaplace-provided module library. This gives the player's avatar a human appearance, and allows the player to customize their avatar's skin colour, hair colour, and clothing. Configuring your avatar takes a significant amount of time, and it would be unacceptable to expect users to redo it for each world that they visit. To get around this problem, the standard avatars module shares state across worlds, using a special API call. The scripts in this module are marked "closed source" (i.e. execute only). This is an instance of an issue often encountered in operating systems security, where it is found necessary to make a hole in the security model to get applications to work.

The state stored by the standard avatars module also includes the avatar clothing items that the player owns. These were purchased with tokens, which could be gained through game play or purchased online with a credit card. There was thus a financial incentive to try to tamper with this state.

If other application developers need to share state across worlds–but without adding a new API call–there are various ways to do it, including having a script make HTTP requests over the Internet to your own database server that is outside Metaplace.

5 Comparison with Second Life

In Second Life, all users share a single, extremely large virtual world: "the grid". There are a number of exceptions to this (under 18's have a separate virtual world, the "teen grid"), but this is the basic picture. In particular, it usually means that the attacker is sharing the grid with the victim and has the same ability to upload code. Many of the differences from Metaplace follow from this design decision:

- In Second Life, the world's "physics" is unchangable, and avatars are always based on a humanoid pattern. Metaplace gives users greater ability to change these. Metaplace can allow users to make these changes because they only affect that player's world, not everywhere.
- In Second Life, if a player creates a virtual item that has a program attached, they can take it anywhere on the grid, and run that program anywhere. In Metaplace, there are completely separate mechanisms for moving an object within a world, and moving it between worlds. Second Life gives players

greater flexibility in mixing and matching scripted objects, but has the disadvantage that an attacker can bring malicious code into the victim's area of the grid.

6 Threat Model

There are several possible scenarios:

1. The attacker only has user level access to the victim's world. The attacker might have a specially modified version of the client that doesn't follow the protocol specification.
2. The attacker writes a module that implements a useful and apparently benign function, but also contains a Trojan horse. The victim imports this module into their own world (believing it to be benign) and the attacker then makes use of user-level access to the victim's world to complete the attack. Metaplace doesn't try to defend against this attack. An analogy with traditional operating systems is that the kernel isn't protected against malicious device drivers.
3. The attacker imports a module into their own world (where they have superuser access), some scripts in the module are marked "closed source", and the attacker seeks to breach the confidentiality of the contents of those scripts in order to re-upload them. Bitmaps must of necessity be transmitted to the client, which is untrusted, in order to be shown on the user's screen, and so they are vulnerable to copying. But scripts run on the server, and so there is some hope of preventing them being copied. If a content-creators business model is to charge customers who import their module, then scripts seem a better prospect than graphics. But this business model would be undermined if users could copy scripts, re-upload them, and give away the copy for free. So this business model depends on the protection provided by the "closed source" flag. Games which do not support user-generated content–such as World of Warcraft–do not have this problem: customers pay to access the game server, and pay extra for additional items for their character. But as users cannot upload any new content, there is no possibility of items the game company sells being undercut by user generated copies of them being uploaded to their own servers.
4. The attacker imports a module with "closed source" scripts into their own world, the module shares some cross-world state with the victim's world, and the attacker seeks to interfere with the operation of the script in order to change the shared state, and hence affect the victim's world. This attack only makes sense if the script acts as a protected subsystem[6] that ensures the shared state satisfies some property. (If the scripts are all "open source", or the attacker is permitted to set the shared state to any value, this attack doesn't make sense). The attacker could either (a) violate the secrecy of the closed-source script or its properties, obtain any cryptographic keys or capabilities the script uses to gain access to the shared state, and use these to modify the state; or (b) trick the script into writing a bad value to the shared state.

7 Security Issues: Attacker with User-Level Access

7.1 State Transferred via the Client

For each user, the corresponding player object on the server is responsible for sending and receiving messages from the client. If an object wishes to engage in a UI dialogue with the user, it will typically send a trigger to the player object, which makes an API call, which causes messages to be sent over the Internet to the client (including a callback command). The client then displays a UI element on screen. If the user clicks the UI element, the client sends the associated command back to the server, where it is handled by a script attached to the player object, which sends a trigger to the object that made the original request. To make all of this work, the callback command given to the client will typically include a little bit of state, such as which object originally made the request, so the player object knows where to forward it and the receiving object knows what to do with it. But the client is untrusted, and an attacker with a modified client could put a different value in the callback (e.g. causing the reply to be forwarded to entirely the wrong object).

A common approach to defend against this was to have the script attached to the player object validate the parameters of the commands it receives, so that an attacker with a modified client can only change the parameters of the callback command to values that they could have sent by legitimate means.

It is very tempting for developers to implement the aforementioned UI protocol with a generic forwarder: a command that takes as parameter the id of an object, the name of a trigger, and additional parameters, and which sends the trigger to the object. However, doing this leads to a security breach: the attacker can use it to send any trigger to any object, with any parameters.

It is possible to use cryptographic techniques similar to those that are used to protect state in Web page URLs (e.g. put a MAC on callback commands that are sent from the server to the client, and have the generic forwarding command check the MAC and check for replays before forwarding on the enclosed trigger).

8 Security Issues: Attacker Imports a Module

8.1 Properties have Global Scope

In Metaplace, *properties* (that is, the variables that hold an object's current state) are all global in scope. If scripts from two different modules both declare the property `foo`, and those scripts are both attached to the same object, then the object has only one `foo` property that is shared between them. Before we even consider security, this makes it hard to write reliable code. The writer of a module doesn't know how users of that module might combine it with other modules, written by other people, that happen to use the same property; this might well result in the module not functioning correctly. Properties are global variables.

The reliability problem could be solved by adopting a naming convention (e.g. prefixing all variable names with the identifier of the module they are in), or the programming language could be modified so that each module gets a separate namespace for properties (e.g. make `self.foo` refer to property `foo` in the current module, and `self[1234].foo` refer to property `foo` in module 1234). Some properties need to be accessed from modules other than the one in which they were declared, so making all properties local to the module isn't an option.

But naming conventions don't solve the security issue: if you can guess the name of a property, you can access it. This has the unfortunate consequence that properties must have difficult to guess names to protect them from being accessed from outside the module in which they were declared.

8.2 Triggers Have Global Scope

Triggers also have global scope, and so suffer from similar problems to properties.

8.3 The Stylesheet Attack

A Metaplace *stylesheet* was–at one point in the evolving design–a virtual world equivalent of cascading stylesheets in HTML. For our purposes, the stylesheet API allows a script to examine other scripts. (i.e. it is a "reflection" API).

A script's properties can be queried with `stylesheet.properties`. This API performs a permissions check, and will only return a property if either the script declaring it is marked as "open source" or the property is made public with an `ExposeProperty` declaration. If it didn't do this check, giving a variable a hard to guess name wouldn't be effective. An attacker who had imported the module into their own world could use `stylesheet.properties` to discover the names of a script's properties, and then access them.

`stylesheet.triggers` returns the triggers that a script is listening for. Unlike `stylesheet.properties`, it does not perform a permissions check; in any case, there is no equivalent of `ExposeProperty` for triggers.

The outline of an attack is to import a module into your own world; use `stylesheet.properties` to discover the triggers a script is listening for; send that trigger with an unexpected parameter; as a result, cause it to modify cross-world state; and take advantage of the corrupted state in the victim's world, that imports the same module.

A classic trick to authenticate the caller of a function is for the function and its legitimate callers to share a secret; callers pass this secret value as an extra parameter, and the function returns without doing anything if it doesn't receive the right value.

This trick can't be used to authenticate Metaplace triggers. Remember that several scripts attached to the same object can be listening for the same trigger. If the attacker knows the name of the trigger, they can attach to the object their own script that listens for it; discover the correct value of the authentication parameter when a legitimate sender sends the trigger to the object; and then use that value to send spoofed messages to the object. This is a man-in-the-middle attack.

The fix for this problem is fairly obvious: there should be an `ExposeTrigger` declaration that does for properties what `ExposeProperty` does for properties.

9 Is Metaplace too Secure?

It would be difficult to make a quantitative comparison of the security of Metaplace and Second Life because there are several confounding factors:

- Software in beta test can be expected to be less reliable than the released product.
- In beta, Metaplace had fewer users than Second Life, which probably made it less attractive to attackers.
- Unlike Second Life, Metaplace did not have a cash out facility for converting its virtual currency back into real-world money. This makes it slightly harder for someone to make money out of an attack, and hence there is less incentive to attack it.
- Many online games have a significant "real money trading" black market in which virtual items are traded between players for real-world money. This happens even in games where it has been forbidden by the game company. During the beta test, Metaplace had not developed a significant real money trading market. (Though players had worked out that you can use "closed source" modules to sell Metaplace modules for real money: create a module that won't work unless it is given a valid license key, and sell license keys for real money outside the Metaplace infrastructure). So this route for turning an attack into profit was not viable in Metaplace.

However, qualitatively, the Metaplace beta was relatively free from malicious attacks. But was it *too* secure? In some cases, Metaplace's security mechanisms got in the way of implementing functionality that is considered fairly important in Second Life.

9.1 Cross-World State

Given that Metaplace's worlds are small (usually created by a single user), users will switch between them often; going to visit a friend involves a switch to their world. It turns out that applications occasionally need to have state that is shared between worlds. The standard avatars module is good example: a player's avatar will have the same appearance in all worlds that import that module.

Cross-world state can be made somewhat safer by either

- Using the "closed source" permission on scripts to hide from users of the script whatever capabilities or cryptographic keys it uses to modify the shared state. This is potentially vulnerable to the attacks described in section 8.

- Giving only a single (trusted) world the privilege to modify the module's state, and making the state read only in all other worlds. In the Metaplace beta, some changes to the state of the standard avatars module (e.g. buying new clothing items) could only be done in a special world ("The New You"), so the shared state didn't really need to be writable elsewhere.

  One problem with this approach is that it introduces a single world that users from different communities all have to visit. As Metaplace worlds are by default multi-user, this will be a point where users from conflicting communities come into contact with each other.

9.2 Neighbours

In Second Life, you often find areas of the grid where on the order of a dozen people all have online residences next to each other, on the same theme (e.g. feudal Japan, medieval Europe etc.) The community aspect is clearly important: a group of people can jointly share a themed region of the virtual space, and be neighbours to each other. In Metaplace, each user is marooned by themselves on a desert island. Some designers of Metaplace worlds have chosen graphics to make them actually look like desert islands; but whatever the theme or visual metaphor chosen by the world designer, the security model makes them as isolated as islands. The security model protects against bad neighbours by taking away the possibility of having good neighbours.

9.3 User-Generated Avatar Clothing

A popular style of play in Second Life is for people to choose clothing for their avatar (a type of play that is perhaps similar to dressing up dolls) or to design avatar clothing for use by others. The two are, of course, linked: Second Life has a large range of clothing items to choose from because lots of other players have designed them.

Metaplace did not have user-generated avatar clothing items. Some of the reasons for this were not to do with security. The clothing items in the standard avatars module were created by building 3D models of the avatar in 3DStudioMax; adding the clothing to the 3D models; pre-rendering 2D images of the avatar as seen from different directions; and then uploading the 2D images into Metaplace. Users did not have access to the 3D models, and so would find it hard to create new 2D renders for upload. More generally, there were simply no tools make it easy for users to do this.

The security model also got in the way. It would have been possible to make the standard avatars module extensible, so that a user could create a new clothing module, and the user-created clothing item would be available in worlds that imported the module. The effect of this would be that a user importing (and buying) the module would be able to wear the clothing item in their home world, but not elsewhere (unless the world they were visiting has also imported the module); and visitors to their world would also be able to wear it. But this is not what is required: users buying a virtual clothing item want to be able to wear it when they visit their friends, not just at home.

This is another example of Metaplace's lack of a mechanism for a form of cross-world state. In this case, it seems harder to fix. A general mechanism where user A could create a module, and user B could buy it and take it into user C's world would be a serious threat to the security model. (Consider the case where A and B are both the attacker, C is the victim, and the code in the module does something malicious).

One approach could have been to restrict user-generated clothing to bitmaps, with no accompanying code, on the grounds that bitmaps are guaranteed to be "safe". However, it is not clear that bitmaps are "safe". One policy that Metaplace can currently enforce is that an attacker cannot cause an obscene or offensive image to be displayed in a world without the consent of the world's superusers. In Second Life, a common form of attack is to display obscene or offensive images in places or contexts where they are not welcome, so this is an important protection.

9.4 Shops

In Second Life, there are virtual shopping malls where users can buy clothes for their avatar, virtual furniture for their online home, and so on. This is using Second Life to buy or sell things for use with Second Life. Any user can create such a shopping mall, and Second Life's security model doesn't present a problem: you just need a script that accepts a payment from a user and gives them an item in return. Shopping can be a social experience, so one advantage of a Second Life mall over a web site (for example) is you can go shopping with your friends, ask their opinion before buying something, and so on.

Metaplace did have one world where users could buy avatar clothing, "The New You". It was created by Metaplace staff, and relied on having privileged access to the state of the standard avatars module, and the payment system.

Metaplace modules weren't purchased using a world as the interface; instead, there was a simple interface build into the client where you could select a module and pay for it. This interface was rather hard to navigate, and would have got worse if the number of modules on sale had grown. Another advantage of Second Life's shopping malls is that items on sale can be arranged in the three dimensional virtual space like products in a real world department store, making it easier to navigate to the thing you want.

Metaplace's security model made it hard for users to create a shop for modules in a Metaplace world. A shop would need access to the shopper's account, in order to deduct the money to pay for the item. It would also need access to the shopper's home world, in order to add the purchased module to it. Both of these features have clear potential for misuse, and were not made available to ordinary world creators, just the Metaplace staff who built The New You.

10 Conclusions

- The Metaplace approach of many miniature virtual worlds, each of which can only be programmed by its superusers, was highly effective at preventing attacks, and enabled developers to build many kinds of games. It was a good answer to the question: if users are allowed to upload code, what prevents them from cheating at the game?
- A user importing a module into their world had to trust the module's author. There was no protection against malicious code hidden in apparently benign modules.
- Several types of play that are common in Second Life did not occur in Metaplace, in part because the security model prevented them. It was not possible for users to design avatar clothing for use by other players; it was not possible for players to build virtual shopping malls; groups of players couldn't build virtual villages where they each had a residence.
- Making all state specific to a single world, with no cross-world state, was too restrictive. Some applications–including the standard avatars module, which was imported by most Metaplace worlds–needed state which was specific to a user, and travelled with them when they moved between worlds. Cross-world state was provided on an ad-hoc basis for particular applications.
- The addition of cross-world state changes the threat model, and additional security mechanisms are then required.
- Making the cross-world state read-write in only one world, and read-only everywhere else, is a simple security solution that can be used if applications do not need write access from all worlds.
- It was almost possible to build protected subsystems that guard access to cross-world state.
- The main obstacles to building such protected subsystems are (a) Metaplace's version of the Lua language does not protect triggers and properties from being accessed by scripts outside the module in which they are defined, although it is possible to give them names that are cryptographically hard to guess; (b) Metaplace's stylesheet API fails to perform a permissions check, rendering hard to guess trigger names ineffective as a security measure.
- The inability to make triggers and properties local to a module also caused developers to have difficulty writing robust code, even in the absence of a malicious attacker.

Acknowledgements. I would like to thank Raph Koster and the other Metaplace staff who built the Metaplace platform; Tami Baribeau (Metaplace community manager); Peter Ludlow and the Alphaville Herald[4] staff for news reports on Metaplace; and the Metaplace beta testers for their newsgroup postings on issues with the platform.

References

1. Bartle, R.: Hearts, clubs, diamonds, spades: Players who suit MUDs
2. Hoare, C.A.: Monitors: An operating system structuring concept. Communications of the ACM 17(10) (October 1974)
3. Ierusalimschy, R., de Figueiredo, L.H., Celes, W.: Lua 5.1 Reference Manual. lua.org. (2006)
4. Ludlow, P., Wallace, M.: The Second Life Herald. The MIT Press (2007)
5. Morningstar, C., Randall Farmer, F.: The Lessons of Lucasfilm's Habitat. MIT Press (1991)
6. Saltzer, J.H.: Protection and the control of information sharing in Multics. Communications of the ACM 17(7) (July 1974)
7. Schroeder, M.D.: Cooperation of Mutually Suspicious Subsystems in a Computer Utility. PhD thesis, Massachusetts Institute of Technology (September 1972)

A Code Example

```
Define Properties()

  foo = 0
  ExposeProperty("foo")

end

Define Commands()

  MakeCommand("set_foo", "set the value of foo", "t:int")

end

Command set_foo(t)

  self.foo = t

end
```

The Metaplace Security Model (Transcript of Discussion)

Michael Roe

University of Hertfordshire, Hatfield, UK

OK, so I'm Michael Roe, my new organisational affiliation is the University of Hertfordshire, and this talk is going to be about the beta test of the Metaplace, which was an online game that was in test a year or so ago. This is a case study that is part of a larger project on the security of online games. I wasn't the one who developed this game, I just volunteered as a beta tester in the open beta so that I could see what their security problems were.

Joseph Bonneau: Is the game actually released?

Reply: It actually was released, but the version that was released as a final product ended up being quite different from what was in the beta test. Some of the security features I'm going to talk about were present in the beta but didn't make into the final released version.

OK, so I'm going to talk about user generated content. The idea here is that designing content is very expensive, you need to pay script writers, artists to draw the graphics, etc. It would be so much cheaper for game designers if you could get the users to do it themselves, and possibly it might even make the game more interesting as well. One of the things that makes a multi-player game more attractive (to the player) than a single player game, is that there are other people you can interact with. So part of the idea is that players might find a game more compelling if a lot of the content in the game was created by other players.

You can do this at several levels. The most basic way in which you can have user generated content is just put a chat system in the game, and let people talk to each other, and the messages that people send to each other are effectively user generated content. From a traditional computer security point of view, that's kind of safe because there's no malware problem there. You can get more advanced, and you can let people move furniture around: you can give players a set of graphics that have been created by professional designers, and let players rearrange them to make game levels, or something like that. Or if you want to be really advanced you could even let players write their own code and upload it to your server.

As I said, although chat is kind of safe in the conventional computer security sense, in a wider sense of "safe" it's not safe at all, because users might say all kinds of naughty or offensive things to each other. People who are designing games specifically aimed at children consider even chat not to be safe, for this reason.

B. Christianson et al. (Eds.): Security Protocols 2011, LNCS 7114, pp. 327–335, 2011.

Frank Stajano: So you said that they could get into trouble for letting this be a platform where people say things that are not allowed?

Reply: Yes, that's right. One of the "metagames" you can play on some of these games is to try and work out a way in which you can say a naughty word to another player. Children have great fun with this, the list of euphemisms gets bigger, and the list of words blocked by the chat system gets bigger and bigger.

Robert Watson: And with some games people only have a limited vocabulary of things they can actually say.

Reply: Yes. But as long as you've got two different things you can say, you can use this to encode an arbitrary message, in some sense the censors cannot win this game, but nevertheless they try.

Joseph Bonneau: Frank, in the games for really young kids, you don't want kids to be able to give away their real name or their real contact info outside of the game.

Robert Watson: This is basically the same problem Rubin was describing, the censorship problem.

Reply: Yes.

If you're going to let players write code and upload it into the game, then you certainly have a massive malware problem that you want to deal with. That's what made this interesting. In the beta test, Metaplace went for the maximum user generated content option. They let you write your own code, write your own graphics, change the physics of the game world, change how a character appears. You could change anything. And after the beta test it became much less interesting. They reverted to just letting players move the furniture around, which from a security researcher's point of view is not all that interesting, but from the point of view of somebody producing a product, being interesting to security researchers is not where you want to be.

While I'm doing these security experiments, the company producing the game was doing their own experiments as well. They were advertising to different communities and seeing how many of those people they could persuade to play it. And there's a problem with this if you try and do any statistics on what happens in the game: you've got a massive confounding variable in that you're seeing a very different demographic of players at different times.

These different groups sometimes don't mix well with each other. As a particularly severe example, you might, as previously mentioned, write a game for ten year olds and then try to attract those people in; or you could go for the sex chat room market and try to attract those people in. Doing either one of these would be fine and work technically, but if you're trying to be both at the same, or on alternate days, you rapidly discover you need some mechanism to keep these people apart from each other. And that's not quite a security problem in that you're not really assuming any malice; it's just people getting in each other's way. Nevertheless, you have to do something about it.

Frank Stajano: Once you've written the software you could run it on two separate servers at different addresses to keep the communities separate.

Reply: Yes, so you've realised that you've got to do that. You have to make sure that you don't have central points that everybody goes through where they end up interacting with each other.

So one question you might seriously ask is whether players really want to write their own code. Sure, they want to create their own game world, but do they really want to be presented with a compiler? Quite possibly not. Most players aren't programmers, or even if they are programmers, they might not want to be a game developer in their spare time. So you could imagine a system that lets users design games at a much high level of abstraction. Rather than giving them access to the compiler you could give them a much, much higher level interface. It might be easier from a player's point of view, and it's an open question whether that's an easier security primitive to defend.

Robert Watson: When you say a compiler, is it really the C compiler?

Reply: Well, it's a Lua compiler actually. A lot of games companies prefer to use Lua.

Frank Stajano: If you let the users change the world's physics, and Alice makes gravity go up, and Bob makes it goes sideways, when Alice walks in which way does she go?

Reply: In the Metaplace model, everybody gets their own miniature virtual world. Unlike Second Life (where you have a single massive three-dimensional space into which you put everybody), you create lots of miniature worlds which can have their own community. This partly helps the goal of keeping apart different communities who don't get on with each other, and it also helps with security goals in that if you upload code into a world and change its physics, you only change the physics of that particular local world, you don't change it everywhere else. So as Frank was saying, if Alice changes gravity in a way different to Bob, then it only changes in Alice's world. Bob is affected by Alice's gravity when Bob is in Alice's world, and Alice is affected by Bob's gravity when she's in Bob's world.

Frank Stajano: So out of every 100 players there are going to be five who can be bothered writing new physics and stuff, and each of these five have their own world, and the other 95 play in some of these five worlds?

Reply: There's another mechanism I'm coming to in a minute, which is that you can write modules, that encapsulate the code that other people import. So one person can implement some new form of gravity or whatever, and if lots of people like it they maybe they'll say, I would like that for my world, can I have that please, and import it and run it.

Frank Stajano: The bit I don't quite understand is, if everybody created their own world it would be, like each world has one person, so you have to have people who come to your world.

Reply: Yes, so you can visit other people's worlds.

Frank Stajano: If you come to someone else's world then you bring your own physics, then you screw everything up.

Reply: No, so you get the physics of the world you'll be going into, nothing comes with you.

Frank Stajano: So it is the case that there are going to be people who make a world and say, well you can come to my home if you like, but then it's my physics.

Reply: Yes.

Joseph Bonneau: But Mike, can you bring any new scripts with you into another person's world?

Reply: No. This is the critical decision where it's different from Second Life, that gets rid of a lot of the security problems you have in Second Life, that you can't bring script with you. So in Second Life you've got the problem that if you have a private island in Second Life anybody who comes to visit it brings with them whatever arbitrary code they feel like, which might have some serious security implications. Metaplace's great idea to stop these kinds of problems is to say that you can do arbitrary things in your own world but not in somebody else's.

Joseph Bonneau: So Metaplace sounds a lot like the strip on Las Vegas where a few people have built their own little worlds where the normal rules of physics don't apply, when you come in you have to accept their rules, play by the house rules, and someone will check your bag on the way out.

Reply: On the way in and out, yes.

Robert Watson: And there are lots of adversaries.

Reply: So the next thing is to say, when you see what it looks like from a programmer's point of view, everything in the world is represented as objects, with synchronous message passing between objects, and the locking policy is run until completion. An object has a queue of messages coming into it, and it takes one off the top, processes that message until it's finished, and then processes the next one. So effectively objects are monitors.

An object can have multiple scripts attached to it, and these scripts can belong to modules. Modules are used both for revision control and security. The idea is that when a module is updated, the worlds that use that module will get all of the scripts that are in that module updated atomically. If you want to change some kind of API between scripts you can make sure that the caller and callee gets updated at the same time.

Modules are also a security mechanism, in that modules can be made closed-source. This doesn't mean in the proprietary source code versus Linux/GPL sense, it's an access control. When the closed-source bit is set on a script, it means you can't pull up the source code in an editor, but it also has implications for other things like the reflection API, that mean the person who is using the module can't inspect its internal state.

So having said all that, what on earth could possibly go wrong? Well the first thing is you've got this thing called the object tool, which is like a graphical user interface for game level creation. It shows you the graphical representations of 3D objects, and you can move them around, and you can attach them to programs, and that's how you create a game. And a question you might wonder is, how on earth does this program get permission to configure the parameters of a closed-source program? The answer is that the object tool is unprivileged, and it sends a message to the closed-source program which says, the user would like to configure you now, and the closed-source program can pop up some UI directed at the user via a trusted path, into which they can input configuration parameters. And so you can do all this and make the object tool untrusted.

The second problem... Avatars are the graphical representation of the users; they're computer generated cartoon characters that represent you. If you've got lots of little worlds that you visit, you don't want to have to go through a character creation process where you define your appearance for every single one of little those worlds you visit. So what you really want to do is configure it once, and have the same appearance wherever you go, but to do this you need shared state. So Metaplace has an API that gives the avatars module shared state; but this is massive hole in the security model that breaks all the nice isolation properties that you were hoping to get.

Robert Watson: When you import a module it gets to download the state for the world where it happens to be executing, so there's no state there that's shared.

Reply: Right. So what this problem reveals is that you would like the avatars module to not just get state local to your world and specific to the avatars module, but global state across all worlds that is specific to that module. And the original architecture didn't really pay enough attention to this problem.

Omar Choudary: Before you go on, can you explain a bit more?

Reply: The attack is they create their own world, import the same module you're importing, write code in their world which does something nasty to that shared state, then login to your world which picks up the shared state that they have just put in, that they have corrupted in some way.

Omar Choudary: So you could make your avatar a red alien, with blue eyes, or something like that.

Matt Blaze: Yes, but avatars have code.

Reply: The shared state is only data, but this is all written in Lua, which is an interactive scripting language. So given the usual kinds of cross-site scripting and buffer overflow attacks, being able to push data through this hole could well end up as a remote code execution vulnerability.

Matt Blaze: It's data that's being executed in a non-trivial way.

Reply: Right

Joseph Bonneau: But is Lua is a memory safe language?

Reply: Yes, Lua is memory safe.[1]

Reply: Possible fixes. You could make avatar state read-write in one world and read-only everywhere else. There's one world you go into to set up your avatar and those changes are propagated everywhere else. During the Metaplace beta, this was how the UI was set up: they didn't really need write access from every world.

The second approach would be to use the closed-source flag to implement a reference monitor. So now the idea is that the avatars module has some secret that lets it modify this global shared state, and we're going to use the fact that the consumers of this module can't read its source code, to be able to implement a reference monitor that can't be bypassed.

So can you break this? Well it's all coded in Lua, which is very common in the gaming industry, it's used by World of Warcraft, and other games like that. It's perhaps not the best choice if you've decided you want to do language based security, and protect trusted subsystems from each other using it, because if you know the name of anything in Lua you can read it.

With this approach, what you're implicitly doing is you're saying, names of my variables are secrets that attacker does not know, and the reason the attacker cannot modify this state is because they don't know the name of it. A second piece of bad news is that Metaplace has a reflection API that lets you ask what variable names a module has. To make this secure, the reflection API needs to know about the security policy, and look at the closed-source bit, and if you're asking for its variables, and it's closed-source, then it doesn't tell you. And the bug that they actually had in there was, it's not just variables that need protecting this way, it's also triggers. A trigger is a function that gets executed to process a message when it arrives. The names of those end up needing to be secret as well, because if they're not you can forge messages, and hence do all the usual attacks on crypto protocols that we know and love.

Matt Blaze: Are these variable names human selected, by programmers, or are they post processed to make them unguessable?

---

[1] So buffer overflows shouldn't be a problem.

Reply: The way it was actually done in beta, they were selected by programmers. If you wanted to close this hole properly, you would put in an extra level of indirection, so the name of the variable as seen by the programmer was some kind of macro that expanded out to a 128-bit value that was generated by a cryptographically strong random number generator.

Robert Watson: This also means you could accidently write scripts that mess up other people's stuff as well, since you're dealing with a global name space.

Reply: So right, this is the other problem that happened.

Robert Watson: So it's not only insecure, it's not robust either.

Reply: There's an online transcript of a meeting with the developers as to what people didn't like about Metaplace, and the fact that you could accidently use somebody else's variable name, and cause bad things to happen if your module and their module are imported into the same world was a big gripe. For robustness reasons you want to do this anyway.

Robert Watson: Is there a Lua interpreter for each world, or is there one Lua interpreter run globally, and all the worlds are somehow divvied up inside that interpreter.

Reply: There is effectively one Lua interpreter for each object, so that each object has its own consistent state.

Robert Watson: How do you exchange data between the different Lua interpreters?

Reply: By message passing.

Robert Watson: And are the messages marshaled, then passed though C-land? Can I have an object reference in the message?

Reply: In the full version of the paper you can see there's an API called GetObjectById(), so what you can do is send the ID of an object in a message, and in the receiving object you can get this ID and you can say, "run time system please, get me a handle for this object", so you can pass references out that way.

Robert Watson: I was confused by your comment about, if the same variable name is used twice in the same world then it's a collision, but then that sort of implies that if they were used in different worlds there wasn't a collision.

Reply: The problem is if an object, within a particular world, has two mutually suspicious subsystems attached to it, and those mutually suspicious subsystems happen to use the same variable name. In particular, the attack you want to do on the avatars module, if you know the variable names, is you create a world where the standard avatars module is attached to a player object, but you also write your own piece of code that's also attached to the player object, which maliciously makes use of the same variable names in order to poke the state of the avatars module.

Joseph Bonneau: What is the possible attack? I mean, I can see how we could override variables and things, and change the physics of the world, but...

Reply: One of your business models might be, let people play a game for free, but you charge them extra for having particularly nice pieces of avatar clothing. So this gives you a direct mechanism by which the state of the avatars module you are trying to protect is translatable into money by the attacker. It lets them do something they're supposed to have to pay money for. They might also work out a way in which to take cash out. Because typically the thing you're really worried about with these games is, somebody has an attack which can create virtual coins or virtual objects in a world, which they can then convert into real US dollars, which they can take out with PayPal, and make off with the money. In Second Life there were a number of good examples of this being done. This was never actually managed in Metaplace, partly because the final link in the chain that would have let you cash out into real money never got implemented.

Bruce Christianson: But even if I can give you an artefact I have made, I could still cash out, because you would say, I will pay you a dollar in real life.

Reply: This is likely for games like World of Warcraft. They have a flourishing black market in game items.

Matt Blaze: How big is the user base?

Reply: Disappointingly small. I think about half a million after the beta test, when they'd made some changes.

Matt Blaze: And what's Second Life? The point is, is their security success due to their user failure?

Reply: Yes, you're right, this is a good one to point out. Part of the reason Metaplace didn't get such a rate of attacks during the beta test is that they were a much less attractive target for attackers, because there were far fewer uses to attack. So I'm making an unfair comparison here, in the same way that a naïve comparison between operating systems would be unfair, if there is orders of magnitude difference in the user population.

But nevertheless, some of the beta testers were determined attackers, so the fact that we didn't manage to do as many amusing attacks as we might have done against Second Life is kind of a data-point, but you're right, we can't really draw any good statistical inference from that.

Frank Stajano: Did they have an environment where artefacts were going to be exchanged for money in the secondary market, and things like that, where you actually had an incentive to cheat for making real cash?

Reply: They had in place a mechanism by which you could, on your credit card, buy virtual money, and use that virtual money to buy virtual artefacts. They didn't have the reverse path out which Second Life does have, where you can sell a virtual artefact, get virtual coins for it, and then turn that into US dollars. So they were a one-way sink for players' money.

Frank Stajano: But that depends on how popular the game is, because if it does become popular then the rich kids will say, OK, well I'll just give you $50 for the labour you're doing building me a good character, and you can get money out that way. But that only works if the game is popular enough.

In the first non beta appearance of the game, they called it Island Life. It was integrated with Facebook, and it's kind of a fairly obvious clone of Farmville. In the game, you're on a desert island, and all your friends, or all the attackers, are lost over the horizon. This is a visual metaphor for the problems that the security mechanism has. By preventing you having bad neighbours that do things that are malicious or annoying, you also can't have good neighbours. Second Life is full of collaborative builds, where groups of a dozen or so people have got together and made a themed village where they've all contributed a bit. And you can't really see that in Metaplace or it's later incarnations, because there isn't a mechanism that would let you do that. You can build small virtual worlds created by a single person, but the security mechanism has effectively cut off all collaborative building, which arguably was a great deal of the fun of Second Life. (Well the attacks are part of the good fun as well). It's a classic case of, yes, it worked, but it only worked at the expense of stopping a lot of the things that people really wanted to do. It was partly a success, but all the user generated code stuff was cut out at the end of the beta test and when they went finally live.

One-Way Cryptography

Sandy Clark, Travis Goodspeed, Perry Metzger,
Zachary Wasserman, Kevin Xu, and Matt Blaze

University of Pennsylvania, Philadelphia, PA, USA

1 A (Perhaps Typical) One-Way Protocol

In a forthcoming paper [2], we examine the security of the *APCO Project 25* ("P25")[3] two-way digital voice radio system. P25 is a suite of digital protocols and standards designed for use in narrowband short-range (VHF and UHF) land-mobile wireless two-way communications systems. The system is used by law enforcement, national security, public safety, and other government users in the United States and several other countries.

Because two-way radio traffic is easily intercepted, P25 includes a number of security features, including encryption of voice and data under a variety of cipher algorithms and keying schemes. It is regarded as being sufficiently secure to carry highly sensitive traffic, including confidential law enforcement criminal surveillance operations and to support classified national security investigations, and is extensively used for these purpose by the various U.S. federal agencies that conduct such activities.

A full review of the P25 protocols and security model is well beyond our scope (see our forthcoming paper). However, several protocol features will be relevant to us here:

- Radios can be loaded with one or more symmetric traffic keys that can be used to encrypt outgoing transmissions and decrypt incoming transmissions.
- Traffic keys are loaded into radios either manually (with special hardware) or upon request over the air (via a key distribution server). Keys can be set to expire or self-destruct under certain conditions.
- There are no "sessions"; each transmission is designed to be self-contained and decoded by any receiver (assuming it has the the correct key material if encrypted).
- Received cleartext voice transmissions are always decoded and played over the receiver speaker.
- Received encrypted voice transmissions are decoded if the correct key is present (a key identifier is included in the transmission).
- There is no authentication – the security model is designed to assure confidentiality only.
- The sender's radio unilaterally makes all security decisions about its transmissions. Radios can be configured to always send in the clear, always send encrypted, or to encrypt based on a user-selectable switch. In practice, most radios use the latter configuration.

B. Christianson et al. (Eds.): Security Protocols 2011, LNCS 7114, pp. 336–340, 2011.

We might observe that while P25 is used in "two-way" radio systems, the security protocol is, in fact, entirely *one-way.* That is, unlike most of the security protocols used today in communication systems, there is no "negotiation" with the receiver or, indeed, any round-trip between sender and receiver before the transmission commences. The sender effectively broadcasts blindly, in the hope that the desired receiver(s) have the key required to correctly decrypt and decode the transmission.

Our study found that "secure" P25 systems are, in practice, actually frightfully insecure. We found a number of fundamental weaknesses in the protocols that are beyond the scope of this paper, the most serious of which render P25 systems almost uniquely vulnerable to highly efficient and difficult to detect denial of service attacks. But protocol weaknesses aside, we also found evidence of an even more serious, and widespread, practical problem that we examine here: the "encrypted" radios are often actually transmitting in the clear, with their users none-the-wiser.

In particular, we found that unintended transmission of cleartext commonly occurs in practice, even among trained users engaging in sensitive communication. We sampled over-the-air P25 traffic from the secure two-way radio systems used by federal law enforcement agencies in several US metropolitan areas over a two year period and found, to our great surprise, that a significant fraction of the most sensitive "encrypted" voice transmissions sent over the air are actually sent in the clear, without apparent detection by the users. We typically captured 20-30 minutes per day per city of unintended cleartext on the federal law enforcement frequencies we monitored.

We saw no evidence that these unintended clear transmissions were caused by low-level protocol weaknesses being exploited by malicious active attacks (although we also found that the protocols are, in fact, vulnerable to such attacks). Instead, they were caused by the protocol's susceptibility to particular (and difficult to detect) user and configuration errors that, in combination, make it very difficult to ensure that the "secure" mode is actually being used and that make cleartext a de-facto default mode of operation even in systems that have encryption enabled.

Sensitive traffic was sent in the clear under three different scenarios:

- *Individual Error:* One or more users in the clear, but other users encrypted. In this scenario, all users clearly shared a common cryptographic key, since communication was able to occur unimpeded. But the users transmitting in the clear apparently accidentally switched their radios to transmit in the clear mode. Because the offending users still received the other users' encrypted traffic and because those users had no way to reliably tell that they were sometimes getting clear traffic, this situation typically remained undetected.
- *Group Error:* All users operated in the clear, but gave an indication that they believed they were operating in encrypted mode. In some cases, this involved one user explaining to another how to set the radio to encrypted mode, but actually described the procedure for setting it to clear mode.

In other cases, the users would simply announce that they had just rekeyed their radios to operate in encrypted mode (but were actually in the clear).
- *Keying Failure:* One or more users did not have the correct key, is unable to receive encrypted transmissions, and asks (in the clear) that everyone switch to clear mode for the duration of an operation so that all group members are able to participate.

Across all the agencies we monitored, the unintended cleartext we intercepted was roughly evenly split among the Individual and Group Error and the Keying Failure categories. In general, even when users knew they were operating in the clear (because they expressly switched to clear mode due to keying failure) and were engaged in sensitive operations, they made little effort to conceal the nature of their activity in their transmissions. Every system we monitored had P25 encryption capability, and, indeed, most of the traffic was apparently successfully encrypted most of the time. Yet we nevertheless were able to intercept literally hundreds of hours of very sensitive traffic sent in the clear over the course of the last two years.

We emphasize that we were analyzing "live" traffic of real users doing their day-to-day work, not synthetic user-behavior in a controlled laboratory environment. This approach has both limitations and benefits. On the one hand, we did not perform a controlled usability study such as the one seminally performed by Whitten and Tygar with PGP [4]. Such a study might allow us to isolate variables or compare the efficacy of different protocols or user interfaces with one another. On the other hand, we captured "real world" conditions – especially the motivation of the users to maintain security while getting their work done – which gives us a better representation of the system's true usability under field conditions [1].

2 One-Way Encryption Is Hard

What's going on here? How can such a simple solution to such a seemingly simple security problem go so wrong in practice?

Part of the answer may be that it isn't actually as simple a problem as it seems. As we note above, the P25 protocols do not fit the negotiated communication model under which most security protocols are designed (and to which our community devotes most of its attention). One-way protocols in which there is no negotiation or exchange between the transmitter and the receiver are actually rather unusual, and relatively little is known (or written in the literature) about robust designs principles for them.

Let us make a few observations that may serve as a basis for progress here.

2.1 One-Way Protocols Reverse the "safe" Assumption

The first goal for any communications system or protocol – secure or not – is usually that it enable the authorized parties to communicate, not that it prevent unauthorized interception, which is at best only a secondary requirement as far as its users are concerned. But as misplaced as these priorities may seem to us security specialists, it does not matter much in practice. We can still usually accomplish both reliable communication and reasonably reliable security.

But the reality that security is often only a secondary requirement has far more dangerous implications in one-way protocols than in conventional two-way protocols. The reason is that in a two-way protocol, the senders and receivers can *negotiate downward* from the *most* secure configuration, whereas in a one-way protocol, the sender can only guess about the receivers' capabilities.

That is, a reasonable (and indeed, standard) way to design a conventional two-way security protocol is for the initiator to ask the responder what its capabilities are, match those against its own, calculate the most "secure" set of overlapping capabilities, and proceed from there if the result is sufficiently secure to conform with policies of both. Done properly and carefully (something that is admittedly non-trivial), the parties communicate using the most secure techniques available to them, and either party has the opportunity to halt the exchange if there result is not sufficiently secure.

But we can do nothing of the sort in a one-way protocol. The sender aims to communicate with one or more remote receivers, the current capabilities and keys of which it can only assume. If the sender is very conservative and places a higher value on security than communication, it might choose to assume that the receiver has a fully secure configuration with properly matching keys. (Whether such senders exist in real systems is open to debate). But if the sender is chiefly motivated by the desire to get its message through, as most probably are, it must assume the *least* secure probable configuration by the receivers and transmit accordingly.

In the case of P25 systems, where receivers' keys can be frequently updated and out of sync with one another, this often means that the "safest" configuration for the transmitter is to use the clear, since that is guaranteed to work.

2.2 Error Detection and Recovery Is Important

A frequent unintended cleartext scenario we encountered was a single user transmitting in the clear as part of a group that was otherwise successfully using encryption. That is, the cleartext sender must have the current key being used with the rest of the group; if it did not, it would be unable to hear there. The only reason for the user to be transmitting in the clear is a simple error – its encryption switch being in the wrong position.

This is a potentially dangerous error, since the damage of transmitting sensitive information is done as soon as the push-to-talk button is pressed, but we might expect the cleartext transmissions to be quickly noticed by the receiving users, who could inform the offending user. And yet in the two years of transmissions we analyzed, this never once actually happened. The lone cleartext users would continue on sending sensitive data in transmission after transmission, despite sharing a key with other users who had their encryption functions correctly enabled.

The problem appears to be not only insufficient alerting of the sender that it is operating in the clear, but of the receivers that something they are hearing was sent in the clear.

We can imagine user interfaces that might do a better job of alerting users to insecure configurations and settings. For example, radios in encrypted mode might ignore clear received cleartext althogether, or might beep loudly when receiving a clear signal. But there are tradeoffs to consider when the system is to be used in a critical public safety application. How do we also ensure, for example, that emergency messages get through, even if they were sent in the clear?

3 Where Have We Seen This Before?

Although most security protocols are two-way, P25 radio systems are not unique. In fact, the problems in P25 remind us of perhaps the most "classic" application of encrypted communication, one which also shares the one-way property: electronic mail.

We hope we can be forgiven for observing that e-mail has not exactly been a shining example of our community's success in deploying encrypted communications systems. Despite PGP, GPG, and S-MIME's long availability, almost no one – much less your authors – actually uses e-mail encryption of any form routinely.

However, perhaps we can apply some of what we've learned from email to other one-way systems. Recall, for example, the call, from very early on, for a key distribution infrastructure. In some respects, a PKI or key distribution infrastructure can be thought if as making a one-way protocol partly into a two-way protocol, in which the infrastructure serves as a proxy for the receiver. We can say what we might about the problems with PKI, the presence of an online infrastructure does appear to have some benefits here.

Acknowledgements. We are grateful to Peter Sullivan for many helpful discussions on the practical requirements for public safety radio systems. Partial support for this work was provided by a grant from the National Science Foundation, CNS-0905434.

References

1. Brostoff, S., Angela Sasse, M.: Safe and sound: a safety-critical approach to security. In: Proceedings of the 2001 Workshop on New Security Paradigms, NSPW 2001, pp. 41–50. ACM, New York (2001)
2. Clark, S., Goodspeed, T., Metzger, P., Wasserman, Z., Xu, K., Blaze, M.: Why (Special Agent) Johnny (Still) Can't Encrypt: A Security Analysis of the APCO Project 25 Two-Way Radio System. In: Proc. USENIX Security Symposium (2011)
3. Telecommunications Industry Association. Project 25-DataOverview-NewTechStandards. Technical Report TIA-102.BAEA-A
4. Whitten, A., Tygar, J.D.: Why Johnny Can't Encrypt. In: Proceedings of the 8th USENIX Security Symposium (1999)

One-Way Cryptography (Transcript of Discussion)

Matt Blaze

University of Pennsylvania, Philadelphia, PA, USA

So what do I mean by one-way cryptography? We were actually given an example here on the projector: this message, "Protected for education use only, if you see this message call the Police." All of the security functions of this are decided on in advance by the people who configured the projector and sent it out into the world, and by the time the receiver of this message sees it, it's too late to change anything about the protocol, there's no interaction involved, the damage is done; everything that you need to do to secure this has to have been done in advance, there's no negotiation.

The motivating example for our work is a protocol called APCO Project 25: APCO is the Association of Public Safety Communications Officers, Project 25 is a digital radio protocol used for two-way radios, walkie talkies, car radios, and other land mobile communication systems. It's not widely used in the UK, although it is an international standard, but it's become the standard in the United States for low bandwidth voice and text two-way communication systems particularly for government and public safety users. It's widely fielded by the government, and all their new radio systems have to use P25 to replace the analogue narrowband FM systems that these agencies had used in the past. The federal government in the United States is probably the dominant user: it's used by all of the security services, the FBI, the Secret Service, Alcohol, Tobacco and Firearms agencies that you've never heard of, Emigration and Customs Enforcement, the Postal Inspector, and so on, for confidential surveillance operations, which are most of what they use their two-way radio systems for. Local Police and Fire agencies use P25 as well, although the penetration in local government is not as large, a lot of them are still using their analogue systems.

Joseph Bonneau: It is this purchasable by citizens?

Reply: Yes, it's not just for government, but there are mandates for government to switch over that don't apply to the private sector, so the equipment is priced for government buyers. The standards were under development starting in about 1991, I believe it was, products became available on the market around the turn of the century.

Ross Anderson: In central Cambridge there's an arrangement whereby the private security guards run by the University, the supermarkets, etc, have a

B. Christianson et al. (Eds.): Security Protocols 2011, LNCS 7114, pp. 341–358, 2011.

radio system that's compatible with the Police. Do you have that sort of thing in America?

Reply: One of the goals of the P25 standard is to get a common system that can allow for some interoperability, mostly between local Police and the federal government for major incidents, rather than routinely. To a large extent that hasn't yet happened, but it's one of the visions behind mandating that government users switch over to this standard. One of the properties of P25 is that it is intended to be a kind of compatible replacement for the analogue systems, backward compatibility particularly of channels and spectrum use is a primary requirement of the system: it uses the same narrowband analogue channels that the analogue systems have, it can be used with limited infrastructure, it doesn't require deploying anything like a cellular or mesh network, it can be used in all of the standard repeater style configurations, or point-to-point configurations that analogue radios can be used in, it's just a digital modulation scheme, and a vocoder. The standard includes security options for encryption, which is obviously important to the security services, particularly for confidentiality. So voice traffic can be encrypted, data traffic can be encrypted, and that's included in all of the products that have been available since 2000.

It uses entirely symmetric encryption, there's no public key involved, at least in the voice standards. The encryption can be based on standard algorithms, AES, DES, triple DES, there is a 40-bit RC4 option for export versions of the system, and there are options to use type 1 ciphers for classified traffic. So the model of key distribution is that every radio has to have symmetric traffic keys (that are going to be used to communicate with those it wishes to communicate with) installed in it before the communication happens. Keys can be loaded into radios in one of two ways. The simplest method is to load the key in a radio using a device called the key variable loader, which is a piece of hardware that physically attaches to the radio, and loads key material into it's crypto module. There's also an over-the-air key in protocol in which a key distribution centre can send keys to radios that can be configured with unique unit key encryption keys that can obtain current traffic keys from a key distribution centre. But again, it's all based on symmetric encryption, there's nothing particularly interesting about the key distribution model, it's very simple.

Keys can be set to expire or self-destruct under certain circumstances, so a key can be set to become invalid after some period of time, or to zeroise itself if the battery is removed from the radio, or a button sequence is pressed so that if somebody realises the radio is about to be stolen they can zeroise the keys out of it, although presumably that's a somewhat embarrassing thing for users to have happen to them. The central security model is that every transmission with these radios is an independent unit: there are no sessions, the sender selects the crypto mode and the key to be used when it transmits, the message is sent out either encrypted or in the clear, as the sender chose. If it's encrypted, it's encrypted using the algorithm and key that the sender's radio is configured with to send, and once it's sent out into the ether any receiver with the correct key material if it's encrypted, that's tuned to the same channel, can modulate and play the audio. If cleartext is sent and a radio is tuned to a particular channel, it's always played.

Now all of the encryption is for confidentiality, there's no authentication.

Frank Stajano: Can the receiver have a bank of, for example, 25 different keys and select the one that's appropriate.

Reply: Yes, there's a key identifier, and you look at the key identifier and check your index of what keys you have loaded in your crypto hardware, and if you have a matching key you use that to decrypt. If ciphertext is sent over the air the receiver will look at the key identifier, decide whether it has that key, if it has that key it will use that key to decrypt the over the air transmission and play it, if it doesn't have a key it will save the unit.

Jonathan Anderson: So I can call you as opposed to calling all the Police in the immediate vicinity?

Reply: Yes, there is a notion of talk groups, there is a notion of also point-to-point communication, but that's not enforced by the cryptography, except that the two sides have to have the same key, rather by sending some control bits that say whether this is a broadcast message, a talk group specific message, or a point-to-point message. In practice almost all the communication is just broadcast, not directed to any particular radio, and who receives it is simply determined by who has the key if it's encrypted, and who's tuned to the channel and within range. So it's very straightforward, completely analogous to the analogue systems that it's replacing.

All of the security decisions are being made by the sender at the time it's transmitting. There is no negotiation between sender and receiver, there is no key agreement protocol, you select your key and take your chances. Now the policy configuration is again up to the sender. A radio can be configured by the local administrator to always send in the clear, it can be configured to always send encrypted, or it can be configured to have a user selectable switch for clear and encrypted, and will make its determination based on the position of this selector switch. In practice that's almost always the configuration that radios use, radios have the capabilities of sending either in the clear or encrypted depending on this little crypto button, or crypto toggle switch.

James Malcolm: Is it a physical switch, or is it something on the screen?

Reply: It depends on the radio. So most of the walkie talkies have a rotating switch around the channel selector knob, there are ones with a push button that toggles between two positions. I think there are some radios that have it as a soft menu where you have to scroll through. So that seems to be up to the vendor. And almost all these radios are also configurable so that the switches themselves can be configured by the system administrator, and what their functions are, which has the effect that there's no standard manual that tells you what the switches do.

Jonathan Anderson: Do you ever see things like if you are customs and you want to talk to the FBI and the local Police, and they're all using different keys, do you ever see people having to change key?

Reply: Yes, there are menus that you can use on these radios to select what key you want to use, if you've got the optional user configurable encryption, you can also have a key selection function, there's also a thing where it will follow the last key it's received within a certain time, so that users can communicate in that way. And there are standards for this. All of the vendors are producing essentially the same user interface, the user interface is part of the standard, and certain properties of how this is supposed to work are part of the standards, because one of the goals is this interoperability across agencies, and across vendors. And this is a protocol that was designed over again, since the beginning of the 90s, and has multiple parties contributing to the requirements, and to the technical development of the standards, and so the standards are as easy to read and well designed as you would expect that process to produce.

Now, the security of this is entirely ad hoc. If there is a principle protocol design behind it, it's not obvious from looking at the standard; essentially they did what seemed like good ideas to the protocol designers, and hoped for the best. That's of course just great for those of us who like to write papers about security systems. We believe we're the first people to analyse it outside of the standards bodies, and we have a forthcoming paper that will look at some of the security properties of the protocols that we found. Interestingly, it is a terrible mess, although the crypto itself is not the worst part of the mess: there aren't any obvious blunders like exclusive or the key with every block, or something like that. They seem to be using properly configured initialisation variables, or at least not obviously misconfigured initialisation variables, and so forth, although there are some certificational weaknesses.

Omar Choudary: I'm not very familiar with how standards are done in the US but, aren't security forces involved in the standardisation bodies as well?

Reply: Wherever you learned how standards work, I'd love to go there; we don't have that in the US. The vendors and users are the dominant players.

Omar Choudary: So there are no experts.

Reply: A lot of the standards read as if the NSA and other government people were involved at the beginning and then stopped showing up for the meetings. So the terminology is very kind of acentric, and the details clearly don't leave behind the fingerprints of somebody who's done any protocol at all.

Frank Stajano: Well the situation is not as bad as it could be if you say that the vendors and users are involved.

Reply: Well the users for the requirements, and the vendors for how they'll be involved in it.

Joseph Bonneau: You said it was like a nine year standardisation process.

Reply: Well actually it's not done yet.

Joseph Bonneau: Well that's probably.... You know crypto people lose interest after ten minutes.

Reply: That's right. But we just started our ten minutes. So some of the problems, and we have a paper that will be out shortly which will go into the details of this[1], the crypto itself has some certification weaknesses, they're not the biggest problems, the biggest problems are the lack of authentication anywhere in the protocol. As we all know, even if you don't care about authentication as an end-user function, it can still be a lever for an adversary, particularly an active adversary. The protocol is particularly vulnerable to traffic analysis, because every unit has a unique ID that's sent out in the clear, even if the traffic itself is encrypted there is an option to protect the unit IDs with encryption, but none of the actual equipment appears to correctly implement that, and so its sent out in the clear no matter what, and no-one appears to have noticed that every piece of equipment has this particular bug. The other problem is that it's intended to replace analogue FM systems, we found denial-of-service attacks that give a 16 dB energy advantage to the attacker, which is the inverse of what you normally get in digital radio systems based on spread spectrum where you get an energy advantage with the sender, so these systems require you to use much less energy to effectively jam than an analogue FM system, and you can do it in a way that's incredibly hard to detect.

Joseph Bonneau: Are there any timestamps in the messages that are sent out? Could you replay these things forever.

Reply: Well since there's no authentication, there's no replay protection.

Joseph Bonneau: So there's no authentication, no MAC at all?

Reply: No authentication features are used in any place in this protocol.

Jonathan Anderson: So even if the Police surrounding this building are all using encryption, I can go on in the clear and say, he's running out the back door?

Sandy Clark: And they'll all hear it.

Reply: They'll all go around, presuming that they follow instructions. Or you can also replay encrypted messages.

Omar Choudary: But can they just not listen to cleartext?

---

[1] "Why (Special Agent) Johnny (Still) Can't Encrypt" Proceedings of the 20th Usenix Security Symposium, August 2011.

Reply: No, they can't. One of the requirements is that you have to always play unencrypted audio.

Joseph Bonneau: So what was the difference then between cleartext, encrypted and user configured?

Reply: Over the air there's no difference, your radio can be configured to only send an encrypted message, but that's only for sending, on the receive side you receive everything. Now there are supposed to be indications of your received crypto state, but from a usability point of view they're not effective.

Ross Anderson: So you can easily do a service-denial attack on President Obama, when he goes somewhere to campaign for re-election you simply jam P25 at the venue, and the Secret Service get an attack of the willies, and take him away at high speed.

Reply: They will say, you can't go here, that's right.

But there are other things you can do. Because it's so susceptible to traffic analysis, even if they're being encrypted, you can build a little FBI detector, and because the signals are narrowband you can easily direction-find them, and so on. So these are the properties of the protocol and the problems that you can see right way, but that's not what I'm actually here to talk about. What I'd like to talk about is the effects of this in practice. This has a large user base, it's a fielded system, what are the consequences?

Sigint[2] turns out not to just be for the NSA anymore, it turns out an academic budget is sufficient to set up a fairly sophisticated signals intelligence gathering mechanism, and that's of course exactly what we did. So we built a network of P25 interception stations and put them in three US cities within an array of inexpensive software controlled receivers, all available on the commercial market, all we did was network them together, and be systematic about it, and wrote some software to control them. And we configured these radios to systematically search the spectrum allocation used by the federal government for the security services, which are conveniently segregated into their own section of frequency bandwidth. So we were monitoring every P25 transmission within range in the frequency bands that are used to coordinate federal security services investigations. That's legal in the United States, we had lots of conversations with lawyers before we did this, and it's not merely legal by omitting a law to make it illegal, it's actually explicitly legal to monitor cleartext law enforcement communications in the United States.

Frank Stajano: I wanted to ask if you had a get out of jail free card, but it's not necessary?

Reply: No, it's just what the law says. It is not the case in every country, in the UK that is not the case, for example, so don't try this at home if your home is here.

[2] http://en.wikipedia.org/wiki/Signals_intelligence

Every agency that was targeted on our frequency lists that we looked at had crypto capability, and we kept this running as we were building this up for over a period of about two years. And what have we found? Well what we found was that in each of the cities we had our intercept station we got about thirty minutes of unintended, that is, not known to the sender, cleartext per day across the various federal agencies. All sensitive, confidential information, surveillance of organised crime figures, names of informants, plans for arrests, and particularly of how many were people with a wiretap plan reading out information about what the current state was, to let them know where their suspect was, installation of vehicle trackers, names of who the targets are, what their addresses are, about the most sensitive types of information you can imagine, and national security information that was clearly intended to be encrypted under the type 1 ciphers, such as executive protection for high ranking government officials, and the details there. And we found that this, every federal agency that uses radios that we could find, every one of the three letter agencies that has domestic operations occasionally sent out unintended cleartext in this form, except for the Postal Inspector for some reason is extremely good at keeping their crypto turned on, but nobody else is.

Robert Watson: Do you know if their devices are configured to use switchable encryption?

Reply: Almost everybody is configured to use the crypto switch, so yes.

Omar Choudary: Did you try to take the position of one of the real devices in order to take the keys, or something like that.

Reply: No, we didn't do anything, this was entirely passive monitoring, we didn't go and steal their radios, or anything like that, and we didn't do any of the active denial-of-service that we discovered either.

Joseph Bonneau: If the law says it's legal to listen to this, is it by extension legal to publish all the sensitive information you have?

Reply: Well there are still laws against things like obstruction of justice, so if you're tempted to do this, and then call people and let them know that they're under investigation, you can still get into trouble for that, so we're not telling anybody details of what we've found.

Joseph Bonneau: Would it be legal to set up a website that did?

Reply: I think you're finding the edge of the law here. What we have to go by ultimately is what would be harmful, and clearly that would be harmful, even if we don't like some of the laws they might be enforcing, when you get to the names of confidential informants and things like that, literally things that could get people killed.

Joseph Bonneau: I was just thinking that in a city like say Oakland, where there may be a lot of criminals, they should cooperate and build this interception station, and then just dump it all on the Web.

Reply: We did nothing that the criminals couldn't easily do; our resources were incredibly modest.

Jonathan Anderson: Well the only difference is that organised crime for all of their availability of money and such, they might not find it easy to hire a post-graduate programmer.

Reply: No, the only reason we had to do any software was to gather the data in order to get the thirty minutes a day number. If you just want to listen it's much, much easier, you can just buy a piece of equipment and configure it properly.

James Malcolm: But the thirty minutes a day is spread around all the criminals in the city?

Sandy Clark: Well not necessarily around all the criminals, but around all the investigations.

James Malcolm: And they don't probably cooperate that much?

Jonathan Anderson: The organised ones do.

Reply: So we actually found that, while we secured this thirty minutes a day on average, there was high variance, sometimes it was two hours, sometimes it was two minutes, we found that there were three categories, and roughly uniformly spread among the three categories, of reasons that we were able to derive that this was going on based on listening to the content. One was a single user error, one user in a group had their crypto switch sent to the clear, because you hear cleartext even if you're in encrypted mode, no-one notices, and that one user goes along their way revealing their one side of the message, you don't hear who they're communicating with, but you hear everything they say.

Another example was where everyone made the mistake, kind of a group delusion about how to turn the encryption on: you would often hear instructions being given out, make sure everybody has your encryption switch on, right, it's the 0 without the slash through it (which is actually the cleartext position). The 0 *with* the slash through it is the encrypted position; so sometimes there was a failure to read the instructions.

Sandy Clark: Wasn't there in particular that one case where we heard the same negative, negative, do not go into the clear.

Reply: Well, that's right, negative, nobody go into the clear, and we're going to send some sensitive information out, everybody needs to be encrypted just like me. And then another reason was that where they knew they were going in the clear, and they had to do it because one member of their group didn't have the proper key material, usually because the over the air routine protocol had expired their previous key, and not everybody had the currently operating key. So this is actually an interesting counter example to this cryptographic folk wisdom that says, change your keys frequently for more security, in fact that policy led them to have to go in the clear fairly often.

Robert Watson: That's sort of like the poor wisdom on password cycling.

Reply: Exactly; make sure that you have to write your password on your monitor and change it frequently.

Frank Stajano: There's this saying, which I think originated with David Wheeler, that all computer science problems can be solved by adding one more level of indirection. In this case I'm going to suggest the reverse, which is, there seems to be a disconnect with the idea of group, and what actually is a group. How about defining the group as the people who have that key, and that's the only way you can talk to the group.

Reply: But the purpose of these people's job is not to communicate in encrypted mode over the radio, but actually to conduct their investigation, so they can't really say, sorry George, you can't help us follow the suspect today because you don't have the key.

Frank Stajano: But if there's a purpose of having groups, and one group is the firefighters, and one group is the investigators, and so on, how about just defining the group as the people who have that key, if you want to be part of that group get the key?

Reply: That would be a way to do it, and changing keys frequently is not something we want to do, because that will run the risk of excluding group members.

Alf Zugenmaier: Are you sure that you didn't just get counter intelligence decoys?

Reply: It is entirely possible that they are so far ahead of us that there's this team of voice actors sitting in the office sending us enticing sounding fake messages just to confuse us; that is a weakness of our research methodology.

Sandy Clark: Then publishing in the newspaper a week or two later some about the details of the operation, yes.

Joseph Bonneau: It seems like the other problem is that there's no feedback. You have feedback about what you're transmitting on, which maybe they don't understand, but there's no feedback about what you've just received.

Reply: That's right.

Joseph Bonneau: So if you receive something that's in the cleartext, and there's an annoying beep right afterward then people would know.

Reply: Well they actually have that. There's a beep that can be configured to appear at the beginning of a received cleartext, but the same beep is used for other purposes in the radio, so your radio is beeping all the time anyway. So there are some serious usability issues that prevent you from reliably knowing what the state that you're receiving is, as well as the state you're transmitting from.

Alf Zugenmaier: So in select you would have to have a user interface that provides this comfort?

Reply: I've come up with all sorts of designs, the one I like the most is if you try to transmit in the clear, you can, but your radio becomes uncomfortably hot, something like that, but I'm not a usability designer, so I don't want to make the same kind of amateur user interface designs that the designers of the system itself have made.

Joseph Bonneau: So the thirty minutes per day statistic, what's this as a percentage then? How many minutes of successful ciphertext were transmitted, and intentional cleartext?

Reply: We didn't measure that, but we observed almost all of these channels seem to have a few hours a day of traffic on them, although that's highly variable as well. So less than 50% and more than 10%, is my completely wild estimate. But we don't really know, we just know that thirty minutes of highly sensitive information that could get people killed are revealed per day.

So let me look a little broader, what's going on here. In a broader sense this is a motivating example for something that maybe our community has ignored, which I'm calling one-way cryptography. Almost all of the protocols that we study are negotiated. We had Alice and we had Bob, and Alice and Bob conduct a negotiation before they communicate, but P25, although it's used for two-way radios, it's in fact an entirely one-way protocol. The sender hits every security parameter, and in fact even the parameter of whether security features are available here, and broadcasts away, by the time the message is received by the receiver, even if they do notice that it was sent in the clear, it's already been sent to the adversary, the damage is done, at least for that particular transmission. Now it's exacerbated by a usability issue that the next transmission is likely to also go out in the clear because the receiver may not be able to notice and warn the sender, but it's an entirely unilateral protocol.

Now we know not everything about designing crypto protocols but we have some good crypto protocols, and almost all of them involve negotiation between Alice and Bob as part of it. We actually have only the kind of discussion we've just had of making some equally ad hoc observations about what's wrong here, that the designers of the protocol in the first place were making. Well we can think of some things, we can throw some darts, but we don't really have anything to say, well clearly you should be using the Anderson-Gligor protocol for broadcasting your encryption, because that protocol doesn't actually exist for this one-way environment. So I think this is a corner of our field that a lot of our design advice just fails to apply to. So let's look at the protocols that we've discussed here, and we've discussed here at this workshop, at every other workshop, and at just about every other published and analysed crypto paper. We have our usual cast of characters, Alice, Bob, and a variety of different adversaries. Alice and Bob typically have equal say over the protocol, there's a bilateral negotiation that has the property that before anything sensitive happens either party has an opportunity to force the protocol to end, or to contribute to its security. If Bob isn't cooperating, Alice will never send anything, so both Alice and Bob can fix errors.

This leads us to a type of design in which where we have multiple security options we can do conservative security designs. We can, for example, start with the assumption that our receiver is going to have the most secure of the possible configurations, and negotiate downward from there, we make a default assumption that Bob is going to be able to handle every crypto option, and has every key we need, and if that turns out not to be true we can compromise, and if either party finds the results at the intersection between their capabilities to be unacceptable for security reasons, nothing happens.

Ross Anderson: But what's the largest number of participants you've seen in one of these sessions, 20, 50, 300?

Reply: Less than 20.

Sandy Clark: Except the one with the helicopters.

Reply: Yes, there are occasional large operations in which information is broadcast to everyone, but the average group is small.

Ross Anderson: If you're going to do some kind of group key negotiation protocol, a subject in which there were a tremendous amount of papers about 10 to 20 years ago, then the communication costs of that are high, even if you use public key crypto. And so in an environment like this, if you may on average have 15 participants, the best way to deal with unintended cleartext might be labelling rather than the protocol changes. So if someone produces cleartext in a conversation where everybody else is encrypted, the phone should perhaps overwrite what he says, this is cleartext, this is cleartext.

Reply: Right, that's absolutely, I can imagine other things you could do, you could imagine a protocol in which any receiver with correct key material could send a message to a sender that says, your last message was not encrypted, but I would have been able to decrypt it, turn your crypto on. We might imagine building such a capability into the protocol, although that may have other security implications when your security features are going to be influenced by messages you received as well. So, I don't know how to do this, but I know some things that might work.

Ross Anderson: Because there's another thing that occurs. If people could manually enter keys then you could fix at least the second case that you talked about, where one member of a group had an expired key so everybody went in the clear; you could just say, we will use the password beeblebrox, and everybody would type it in.

Reply: Well you could imagine, let's all meet in the parking lot and set our keys up. We might touch our radios together, or even enter a number on the keypad, but there's no capability to do that, you need a keyloader device.

Ross Anderson: Because of key escrow, right.

Reply: It's not true that it's because of key escrow, although the key variable loader device certainly looks an awful lot like the style of crypto you use in government designed systems.

Robert Watson: So this compares with PGP, right, I send you an encrypted email and if lucky you can read it.

Reply: Well hold that thought for just a moment. So we also have in our typical protocols by the way round trips that happen all the time, they're explicitly part of SEC whereas even though P25 has externally conversations going on in it, every message is essentially an isolated unit, and that's an important property from the user point of view of a system like this. And again, we don't really have a lot of advice to give on designing these.

Robert Watson: It has excluded a vocabulary of protocols like freshness and things.

Reply: Yes.

Alf Zugenmaier: Is there any advice you could give based on digital set-top boxes?

Reply: Well, hold that thought, again. So let me just point out that there are a couple of conservative design techniques that don't work in the one-way context, that we can't start with the most secure configuration possible, as we do in a typical two-way protocol where we negotiate downward and assume that we have mutual satisfaction, because we don't know what the receiver's capabilities are. In a one-way protocol there is this perverse incentive for the sender to choose the least secure configuration if their goal is primarily to ensure that their message will be received. You need to use only as much security as you are absolutely sure your receiver will have and no more than that because any more than that decreases the probability that your message will be properly received. And of course the goal of the users of these systems is to communicate properly, not to have the most secure communication. They want security, these are people who are in the security business, but they're also following someone around while driving a car, and they need to say, hey, he just turned left, and they really want that message to get received.

So one question is, can we get the benefits of negotiation, are there ways to relax the one-wayness of a protocol just enough to allow us to get the benefits of negotiation without breaking the essential one-wayness of the underlying application. Certainly anything where you do a key exchange at the beginning of every transmission is not going to work, but maybe we can relax this requirement in some way. Error detection and recovery matters an awful lot, once the cleartext is sent the damage might be done, the parties in a position to detect the failure aren't part of the protocol. So can we have an exception handling protocol? This is a one-way protocol unless a receiver detects that the security policy is being violated in which case the receiver now can become an active party and help you correct your error. Again, we can imagine ways to do that, but I'm not aware of any standard protocols that can analyse, that can give us any principled properties that we can say that they have.

Virgil Gligor: Can I guess?

Reply: Please, don't guess, tell us.

Virgil Gligor: So suppose that the sender sends plaintext and you as the receiver really want to communicate in ciphertext. So essentially what you do, you use authenticated encryption, and when you decrypt cleartext obviously you'll get an error, you obviously didn't decrypt with the right key. So basically that error would trigger the exception processing phase of your protocol in which the sender now knows that he should be in ciphertext.

Reply: Yes, but that might have the risk that that message won't get through.

Virgil Gligor: Why? The first message is decrypted incorrectly and the sender will re-transmit encrypted.

Reply: Well there's no retransmission involved, it's all real-time voice.

Robert Watson: There's also the related Kerberos issue, which is, if you don't share a password with the KDC, the KDC cannot reliably tell you that you don't share a password.

Frank Stajano: I'm not convinced of the need for this to work in a one-way cryptography way. Technically it has obviously the capability of talking two-ways, so what is your requirement for having it one-way, is it there is some kind of beauty, or is there some application the requirement that it be one-way?

Reply: Well, for example, you will have configurations in which the receivers may not have transmitting capability, or you may still be required to work when the transmitter is a high powered base station and the receivers are low powered walkie talkies where their transmitting range is smaller than the transmitter they're listening to. We don't want it to break if the receiver is out of range of the transmitter.

Joseph Bonneau: There's also the password safe in this case, where you're encrypting, and then it's not decrypted, and so five years in the future you may have forgotten some of the key material, and you have to fix it.

Reply: That's right, file encryption falls into the category of one-way encryption. You're encrypting to yourself in the future, and anything you do has to be fixed at the time of encryption.

Omar Choudary: What are the exact properties that you would like go back to in this one-way time protocol, because if you say that some receivers don't have the key but they must get the message, that means that you must send in cleartext.

Reply: That's right, there are contradictory requirements at work here, but they're not explicit requirements, so I think one of the first pieces of advice that we can give is, let's state what the security properties of this protocol are supposed to be, and figure out if they can be met at all.

Jonathan Anderson: So both in the radio case that you've described, and in the encrypting stuff for yourself five years down the road case, if the damage is already done I'm not convinced that there's actually a protocol thing to be done to fix this, but that it isn't just purely a usability problem. Because I mean, in the radio case, if the radio goes errggg every time you started to talk in the clear, or if you were doing a password vault, and you thought you were encrypting the password, but it turns out you weren't really encrypting, does it let you know, I mean, that's the sort of thing you want to stop the damage from being.

Reply: Well it's possible, but I'm not convinced that it is a possible protocol problem, you know, you're never going to be able to prevent the first clear, you know, if somebody blurts out, the name of the informant is Bill, and they send it out in the clear, obviously there's no way of undoing that.

Jonathan Anderson: But there are usability ways of discouraging that, so that it's harder to do it by accident.

Reply: Right. But among the ways of making this both usable and more secure would be to have this act as a one-way protocol, but allow receivers in some way to become active if they detect a problem.

Virgil Gligor: That's precisely what I suggested: I receive cleartext from you, and I use authenticated encryption, decryption will fail, which means obviously that I can now initiate an encrypted communication with you, and I am the initiator, I am the one-way, so we've switched roles.

Reply: We switch roles, right, and that may be a way to do it. I don't know of actual protocols that do that.

Virgil Gligor: Well this would work with existing applications.

Reply: Right, no, well we're designing it in an ad hoc way.

Virgil Gligor: Well it's not quite that hard, and I'll tell you why. Authenticated encryption has a one property, has one property that is very much ignored by most people, namely that if they give you the wrong key decryption won't work, so it's not just that you protect the integrity of the ciphertext, but also you if you decrypt anything with the wrong key it will fail.

Reply: Yes. I did mention a constraint in the P25 case, which is that they have to tolerate bit errors over the channel, though there are error detecting codes that operate below it.

Virgil Gligor: That's OK.

Reply: But there are some difficulties that they have, you want there to be no delay, you want every voice frame to go one at a time, and to be transferred in real time, you don't want it to only be transferred the day after you speak. So it may be hard to actually use any of the current authenticated encryption mechanisms, because you need a stream cipher, you need every bit to be available to the vocoder one after the other.

Dongting Yu: I think that when you say the more sensitive things, my intuition is that it might be more into the conversation, instead of the beginning, so there might be tricks you can do with the usability where, because now you get to the sensitive part before you change the conversation.

A second thing I wanted to say about the kind of feedback where you say, I don't have a key, I am a little concerned about ways of finding out if they are in a certain group by seeing if they have a certain key.

Reply: Yes, you can, although if that was the worst difficulty that this protocol had with traffic analysis, it would be far ahead of where it is. Here we have the problem that everybody is transmitting their identity in the clear all the time, even if they're in encrypted mode, so it's pretty hard to do worse than that. Also every receiver will act as an oracle if they're running the over the air routing protocol, you can send a message to a particular unit ID and they'll respond to it, so you can find out, even if they're not using their radios, which radios are nearby.

Sandy Clark: And where they are.

Reply: So let me just observe that we've been here before. We've mentioned a couple of examples of one-way protocols, and there's both good news and bad news, but the news is mostly bad. So the most prominent example to me is email encryption, as we all know that that is a solved problem, we all use encrypted email all the time. [laughter] This has not been our finest hour, and email exchange has a lot of the same properties as this, and we never figured how to do it in-spite of the fact that we've all tried, and as a community this has been probably the first widely used example of communication encryption that is widely deployed, and we never figured out how to actually build an infrastructure that made it properly work.

Omar Choudary: There was a proposal, I think Frank mentioned at some point that maybe if you transmit at midnight, you can propose a system where it doesn't quite get sent until after five minutes. But it's a different case because you can delay there, but in the case of, hey he's turning left, it's slightly different.

Reply: Right, and we don't even have the delayed think better of it email protocol, because it isn't likely to be implemented except by the state. So the other is broadcast video cable, set-top boxes, satellite television, but there we have a simpler problem, the sender, the goal of the sender in a satellite, or cable, or set-top box system, is not to ensure that everybody is able to see it, in fact it's specifically to exclude those who haven't paid. So the incentive structure that occurs with email and with the two-way radio system in which the sender is incented to downgrade their assumptions doesn't exist there, so even though direct broadcast video protocols are largely successful in keeping the encryption turned on at least even if they have other problems that members of the Cambridge and elsewhere community have structured.

Robert Watson: These are structurally as simple as a GPS and Galileo as well.

Reply: Right, if you had only one policy configuration this problem is much easier. So this doesn't, the lessons here seem to not to be that applicable, the successes seem not to be that applicable, and the failures are just depressing.

Robert Watson: The failures are applicable.

Reply: Yes, the failures are applicable, but not the successes. So that's all I've got.

Feng Hao: Is there any reason why a public key cryptography can't be used, you could use key transport to, as a one-way to transport the key.

Reply: I don't think there's any fundamental reason, there's no aversion to the use of public key cryptography, but there is a scalability issue that you can't have, you can't have sessions between two parties, so we do want every member of the group to get, to end up with the key without requiring some n^2 or even n two-way communication at the end of every session.

Virgil Gligor: There is a reason, we may go back to those previous mistakes.

Mike Roe: Web anonymity protocols like Tor might have a similar problem even though they're at some level non-interactive: it's the failure where you forget to ask for anonymity and you go to whatever website, and everything else works, and you don't notice.

Reply: Tor is ultimately a two-way protocol, it's being used to tunnel round trips, so I'm not sure first of all Tor counts as a great success yet.

Robert Watson: You seem to be distinguishing two-way and one-way protocols, and I almost wonder if the difference you're trying to get at is more synchronous and asynchronous, because in the case where maybe somebody calls back later and says, by the way you're not doing this right, it's not so much that you're expecting them to do it but if there's an opportunity you'd like them to do it, as opposed to a protocol that requires synchronous response with freshness, nonces, and things like that. I'm not quite sure of the state of play there, but it seems like there's some exploration to do.

Joseph Bonneau: I was going to say, even SSL, which is clearly two-way, has some one-way properties for web browsers: we haven't come up with an effective way to tell them whether they're viewing encrypted content or not.

Reply: Maybe it's a usability issue only, but it may actually be something that the protocol itself can contribute to.

Joseph Bonneau: You have the same thing with the radio. It knows whether it received encrypted or not, and they haven't found a good way to tell the user, and it's the same problem with the web browsers. So there's sort of a one-wayness on the receiver end about whether or not you know what you've received, and on the sender end whether or not you know that the receiver has received what you sent properly. They seem to be separate problems.

Sandy Clark: But neither one ends up really being one-way, there has to be some sort of feedback somewhere. One thing that we've been exploring but don't know whether or not it will work, is if you can create some sort of infrastructure that is outside of the actual devices themselves, maybe appearing somewhere else, or maybe a form of devices that provide some feedback.

Reply: Yes, you want infrastructure that steps in if there's a problem, but isn't required in order for the system to work.

Frank Stajano: The radio by itself is a broadcast, but if you did use the suggestion I made earlier of just using the key of the group as the name of the group, then you would basically be addressing who you want to talk to.

Sandy Clark: Like label it?

Virgil Gligor: Yes, so don't just have the group as an entity, and the key for the group as another entity, the group is the key.

Reply: Effectively that is what they do, except they didn't really design the system around that principle. The key does define the group of all receivers, and having the key allows them to receive and to transmit.

Robert Watson: It's a usability issue isn't it. You have these end-to-end user properties you want, and the question is how to split that functionality between the protocol, the features which will only accept messages, which is kind of policy as opposed to protocol, and the operation of a switch, and I think you can see different solutions in different models. The question I suppose is, is there missing protocol vocabulary, and also what is the best solution in the context of this system.

Reply: We could sit here and start designing a protocol, and 15 minutes later we come up with something better than what was done here. But that's not really the interesting part. To me, the interesting part is that there are at least two examples of important problems that appear to be unsolved because of sets of requirements, and sets of limitations on protocol designs for meeting those requirements. We've mostly ignored them, we're solving the problems that we know how to solve, in which Bob gets to send stuff back to Alice. And I think this is an unfortunate property that leaves out some real important applications.

Omar Choudary: So regarding the feedback, you don't necessarily need all of the receivers to be able to transmit back, you just need one of them.

Reply: And it doesn't have to be a particular one.

Omar Choudary: Exactly. And if you send cleartext, and you receive feedback like, hey, you are not using the key, doesn't it mean that you might get different feedback for each of the different receivers?

Reply: Yes, it's not obvious how to do this in a way that won't lead to some very poor interfaces.

Jonathan Anderson: But it sounds like these guys already have this human protocol in place, because one guy says, I'm going to go clear, and the other guys says, no, no, do not go clear, do not go clear. The only problem is that they aren't actually aware whether they're in clear or not.

Bruce Christianson: Even if we solve the case where they were in the clear, we don't have a handle on the case where they were using one group key but thought they were all using a different group key, but they happen to belong to both groups, and they have therefore lost control over who else was listening that might be in one group but not the other one that they thought it was. Frank's suggestion doesn't address that.

Robert Watson: This has already come up in the workshop at least once, when we talked about sensor nodes two days ago[3], i.e. you only want to respond if the right person is coming in, and therefore you can't do a two-way protocol.

Reply: Some of the requirements that we can derive from those that they seem to be trying to meet, are clearly contradictory. But that's life.

[3] Burmester, these proceedings.

How to Keep Bad Papers Out of Conferences (with Minimum Reviewer Effort)

Jonathan Anderson, Frank Stajano, and Robert N.M. Watson

University of Cambridge Computer Laboratory, Cambridge, UK
{firstname.lastname}@cl.cam.ac.uk

Abstract. Reviewing conference submissions is both labour-intensive and diffuse. A lack of focus leads to reviewers spending much of their scarce time on papers which will not be accepted, which can prevent them from identifying several classes of problems with papers that will be. We identify opportunities for automation in the review process and propose protocols which allow human reviewers to better focus their limited time and attention, making it easier to select only the best "genetic" material to incorporate into their conference's "DNA." Some of the protocols that we propose are difficult to "game" without uneconomic investment on the part of the attacker, and successfully attacking others requires attackers to provide a positive social benefit to the wider research community.

1 Introduction

One view of a Program Committee's role is the defence of sacrosanct publication venues—conferences, journals, workshops—from invading PhD students[1]. Committee members wish to admit worthy researchers as fellow-guardians of the state of the art. Unfortunately, most of their limited and valuable time is spent repelling hordes of unworthy submitters, trying to get published with minimal effort and literacy in the ancient lore of the discipline. A second view casts the Program Committee as an individual member of a species, attempting to select the mate that will most increase the genetic fitness of their offspring. In this case, the committee's goal is to encourage the survival of the discipline by populating it with strong researchers—promoting the *Darwinian fitness* of its publications [4]—and to stave off monoculture through the continual integration of fresh new problems and ideas.

Figure 1 shows the trend of some research communities built around publication venues—both security-centric and otherwise—to cite their own work more and more over time, to the exclusion of "outside" research[2]. Obviously, work

[1] Readers should note that, at the time of writing, two of this paper's authors were PhD students, tongues firmly placed in their cheeks.

[2] These graphs have been generated from data supplied by arnetminer.org [6,7], itself based on DBLP. Despite a manual cleanup by the authors of this paper, there are some inconsistencies (e.g. citations of a technical report from the previous year turn up as citations of the journal article version, from two years in the future).

B. Christianson et al. (Eds.): Security Protocols 2011, LNCS 7114, pp. 359–367, 2011.

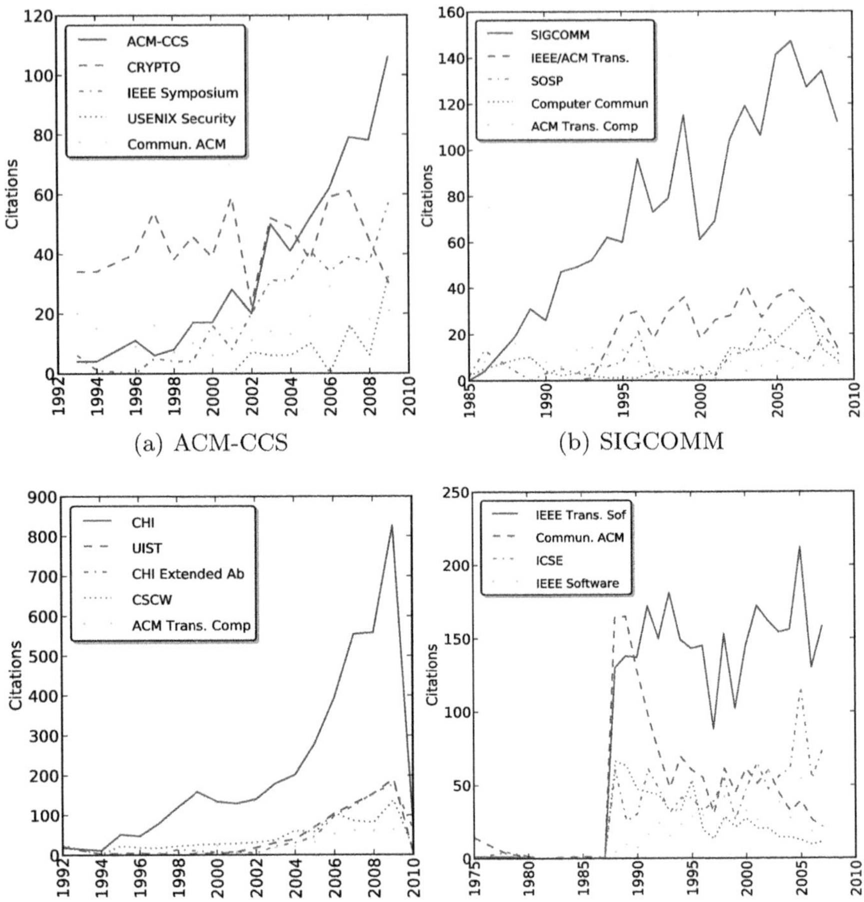

(a) ACM-CCS (b) SIGCOMM

(c) CHI (d) IEEE Trans. on Soft. Eng.

Fig. 1. Frequency with which papers at four conferences cite work from various venues

published at a particular conference will tend to cite other work from the same community—papers accepted by WiSec will be focussed on wireless security, and will thus tend to cite previous WiSec papers—but it is possible that some conferences may be growing quite introspective, delving deeper and deeper into the depths of known problems without continual exposure to the new "genetic material" (problems and ideas) that is essential for the health of any community. It is, of course, important for research communities to optimise existing solutions to existing problems, but if authors only submit "the kind of paper that always gets in," if new ideas and new problems are never explored, the overall health of the community may suffer. Offspring of such an unhealthy community are unlikely to be selected by discerning partners—in academic terms, their work will not be cited outside their own community.

In this work, we describe threats to the health of academic disciplines, including unscrupulous authors faking genetic fitness and established communities selecting only their own academic offspring (Section 2). We propose mitigating these problems via the judicious application of automation: reviewers can apply statistical techniques to measurable things in order to focus human attention on the subjective quality of conference submissions. We can remove some labourious work from reviewers' shoulders (Section 3.1): we can force attackers to step up their game, ultimately writing better papers or, if attempting to game the system, provide useful benefits to the wider research community (Section 3.2). We can look for authors attempting to socially engineer themselves into acceptance (Section 3.3), and we can promote diversity of ideas within conferences, reducing monocultures and increasing the health of the community (Section 3.4).

2 Threat Model

In our threat model, the attacker is the unscrupulous author of a submission. These authors may be seen as attempting to gain entry to the "ivory tower" of an academic discipline without first proving their worth through strong research. Alternatively, we may view the attacker as an individual attempting to "mate" with a conference without demonstrating "genetic" fitness or the likely fitness of potential offspring (research which successful publication might inspire).

The attacker can attempt to frustrate the proper functioning of the Program Committee by abusing citations or coasting on reputation. Citations are meant to be a signal that an author has read and understood the work of others. Unscrupulous authors, however, can tailor them to the program committee at little cost—citing what they've written, citing what they like, citing what will make them think the authors are very well versed in the literature, all without actually reading and understanding the work they reference. Established authors, who have previously published at a conference, can also send the kind of signals that they know will be well-received, whereas proving one's fitness to a new research community may require truly superior research in order to overcome that community's institutional resistance to change. Such attacks are successful today in part because it is much more time-consuming for the reviewer to verify a citation than for the attacker to insert one, and the reviewer has many citations which she might choose to review.

Furthermore, the attacker can submit "the kind of paper that always gets in to this conference", which has the twin effects of increasing the chances of unworthy research and reinforcing a vicious cycle of monoculture begetting monoculture. Such a cycle might, in the end, lead to the stagnation of the discipline.

Finally, we recognise that attackers, in current systems, can effectively carry out a Denial of Service attack on reviewers, distracting them with the necessity of refuting incorrect statements and correcting poor writing. This "busy work" may keep them from arguably more important tasks, such as shepherding good papers or detecting subtle flaws (such as incorrect proofs) in bad ones.

3 Mechanical Assistance

Reviewers' time is a scarce resource, which a conference review process should spend carefully. Assuming that semantically-meaningful content of submissions can be reliably extracted (e.g. submission requires latex sources as well as PDF files, or PDF-to-text is reliable), thre are several ways in which mechanical assistance can be provided to program committees. Such assistance will allow reviewers to focus their scarce attention on the aspects of the review process which cannot be automated—evaluating the quality of ideas and research.

3.1 Clustering Submissions

Today, some conferences ask authors to provide keywords that describe their work, as in Figure 2. Where employed, this scheme makes it easier for review tasks to be distributed among reviewers. Nonetheless, significant human effort is involved in sifting through e.g. all of the abstracts tagged "committment schemes." We propose that mechanical analysis of submissions' reference lists could augment this process.

We presume that submissions can be usefully classified by their citations: papers that cite similar work are likely to be about similar topics. Indeed, it has long been known that it is possible to mechanically classify academic publications into sub-fields via the citation graph without any special knowledge of the content of the literature [2]. Rather than asking reviewers to review a set of abstracts, then, reviewers might be asked to rank their interest in existing

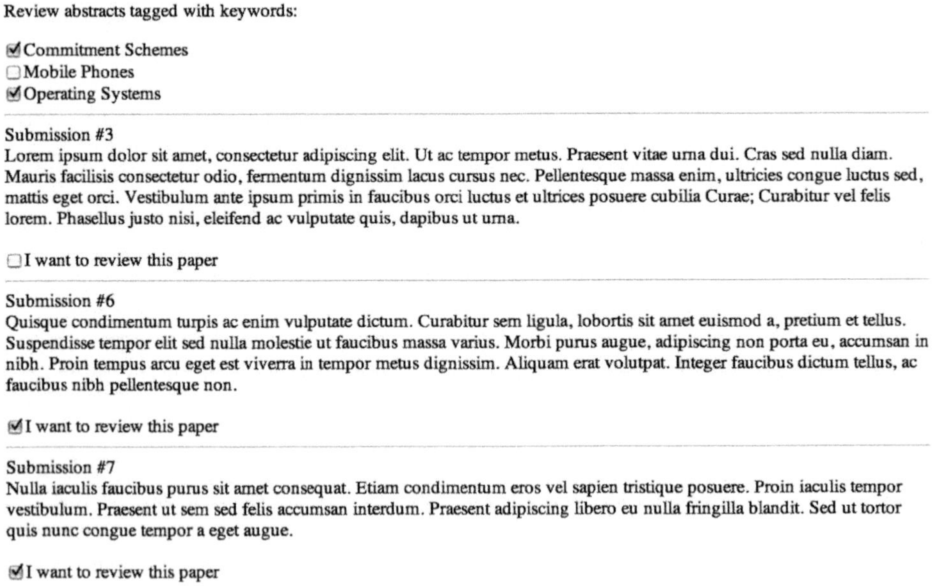
Review abstracts tagged with keywords:
Commitment Schemes
Mobile Phones
Operating Systems
Submission #3
Lorem ipsum dolor sit amet, consectetur adipiscing elit. Ut ac tempor metus. Praesent vitae urna dui. Cras sed nulla diam. Mauris facilisis consectetur odio, fermentum dignissim lacus cursus nec. Pellentesque massa enim, ultricies congue luctus sed, mattis eget orci. Vestibulum ante ipsum primis in faucibus orci luctus et ultrices posuere cubilia Curae; Curabitur vel felis lorem. Phasellus justo nisi, eleifend ac vulputate quis, dapibus ut urna.
I want to review this paper
Submission #6
Quisque condimentum turpis ac enim vulputate dictum. Curabitur sem ligula, lobortis sit amet euismod a, pretium et tellus. Suspendisse tempor elit sed nulla molestie ut faucibus massa varius. Morbi purus augue, adipiscing non porta eu, accumsan in nibh. Proin tempus arcu eget est viverra in tempor metus dignissim. Aliquam erat volutpat. Integer faucibus dictum tellus, ac faucibus nibh pellentesque non.
I want to review this paper
Submission #7
Nulla iaculis faucibus purus sit amet consequat. Etiam condimentum eros vel sapien tristique posuere. Proin iaculis tempor vestibulum. Praesent ut sem sed felis accumsan interdum. Praesent adipiscing libero eu nulla fringilla blandit. Sed ut tortor quis nunc congue tempor a eget augue.
I want to review this paper

Fig. 2. Selecting papers to review via author-supplied keywords and abstracts

classic papers which have been calculated to convey the most information about clustering via e.g. principal components analysis [3]. Such a list of papers, shown in Figure 3, might even be pre-populated with suggested selections based on the reviewer's authorship and citation records, greatly reducing the amount of work, but still providing reviewers with the opportunity to express disinterest in work that they did in the past but have since lost interest in.

Which of the following are you most familiar with:

- [x] "A new problem", Alice et al., *Security Protocols Workshop*, 1995.
- [ ] "First crack at Alice's problem", Bob and Sam, *Security Protocols Workshop*, 2005.
- [x] "A better solution than Bob and Sam's", Eve and Moriarty, *Security Protocols Workshop*, 2009.

Fig. 3. Selecting papers to review via citation clusters

Furthermore, the results of citation-based classification can be compared with author-supplied keywords. Submissions whose keywords do not match the automatic classification can then be flagged as "interesting", either because the authors are using keywords in a clueless manner, or because their research defies the existing keyword classification scheme. Which of the two is true must be determined by a human reviewer, but checking a small portion of the total submissions for "interestingness" could be a much better use of reviewers' time than trawling through vast oceans of submitted abstracts.

3.2 Signalling That Authors Possess What They Cite

A paper's citations are like a bird's plumage, enhancing the chances of the subject to be selected by a discriminating audience with a large field of suitors. Given the stakes, there are obvious motivations to exaggerate one's citations: it makes the authors appear literate, lending credibility to the submission; it may flatter members of the Program Committee; it may be seen as a prerequisite to working in the field ("you can't publish here unless you cite Smith's seminal work on Public Key Widgets"). Such behaviour dilutes the quality of the conference in the long run, however: it fills reference lists with meaningless data, reducing the amount of information per page of proceedings.

In order to discourage such behaviour, we propose an information signalling protocol. This protocol requires authors to signal that, at minimum, they have gone through the trouble of *finding* and *looking at* (though not necessarily reading thoroughly) everything that they cite. The protocol requires little reviewer effort and communications overhead, and can even be verified after publication by any third party who can read the bibliography. The protocol is in-band, relying on the annotation of citations, but authors cannot simply replay annotated citations from other papers.

Such a signalling protocol cannot *guarantee* that an author has, in fact, read and understood everything they cite. If we assume, however, that the "energy gap" between opening a PDF and actually skimming its conclusion is not large enough to overcome PhD students' genuine interest in learning, this should be a very useful signal.

In the reference list at the end of a submission, we require authors to annotate each citation with a single word within square brackets. This word is taken from the referenced document, a response to a challenge which is public but unique. This challenge, c_i (the challenge associated with reference i), is given by:

$$c_i = (n_i \bmod P, n_i \bmod N) \,|n_i = h\,(h_m\,(s)\,|h_m\,(i)\,|n_c) \tag{1}$$

where n_i is a nonce specific to a particular reference in a particular submission, P is the number of pages in the referenced document and N is a number small enough to be easily counted by humans (e.g. less than 50). $h_m\,(x)$, the "metadata hash" of paper x, is defined as:

$$h_m(p) = h\,(n_c|\text{authors}\,(p)\,|\,\text{conference}\,(p)\,|\,\text{year}\,(p)) \tag{2}$$

where n_c is a nonce generated by the conference (perhaps the filename of a supplied LaTeXclass), authors (p) is a comma-separated list of last names of the paper's authors (in the same order as on the paper itself), etc. Including $h_m\,(s)$, the metadata hash of the submission, ensures that authors cannot collaborate in generating hashes[3]. Furthermore, if the authors have a partial list of words in the referenced document, the only way to change the challenge to a "favourable" value is by changing the author list—a high price to pay.

Verifying the responses associated with references should be a relatively low-effort task: most citations can be automatically examined, assuming the PC software has access to a large corpus of literature. Any "cache misses" (whether due to not having access to literature or poor PDF-to-text conversion) can be probabilistically flagged for human review, and the outcome will be a more complete corpus with better textual equivalents.

Finally, attackers could collude to build a large corpus of relevant literature with high-quality PDF-to-text conversion, but if they did, would it be such a bad thing? Surely such a corpus would be of benefit to the research community, although copyright holders may not be pleased[4].

3.3 Checking That Authors Have Read What They Cite

A more difficult, and therefore more interesting, problem is checking that authors not only possess what they cite, but have read and understood it, critiquing it or allowing it to influence their own research. This is clearly the province of the experienced human reviewer, but mechanical assistance could be provided to reviewers to help them focus their energy where it would be most productive.

[3] That is, unless they collaborate to disseminate the relevant literature to researchers who haven't read it, which is surely a positive outcome!

[4] Of course, an wise publisher would use such a corpus to improve their own PDFs and citation graphs, again, a useful service to the research community.

Identifying Usage. To fully combat the problem of "token citations", reviewers could look at every reference in every submission and ask themselves, "can I see the influence of the referenced work on the submission?" In the real world, such analysis is impossible due to time constraints. Software tools could help reviewers, however, by displaying every place a reference is cited, including a few additional lines of context. Such a tool, especially if employed primarily for "interesting" references (see below) could help reviewers make cursory inspections and quickly judge whether or not the cited work has an influence on the submission.

Identifying Outliers. One class of "interesting" references which are trivial to identify is that of statistical outliers. Figure 4 shows the increasing age of references, most of which are outliers, at the ACM Conference on Computer and Communications Security. These outliers date back to some of the seminal papers in computer security, and may be important references whose lessons have greatly influenced authors' thinking. Unfortunately, they may also be token citations which merely provide an air of historical literacy. Sorting the wheat from the chaff clearly must be done by a human; identifying which references particularly need to be sorted can be done more effectively by computer.

Identifying PC Citations. Another class of "interesting" references are those which have been written by Program Committee members. Clearly, PC members are more likely to be cited than the average author; if their work were not valuable to the field, they would not be on the committee! Nonetheless, authors

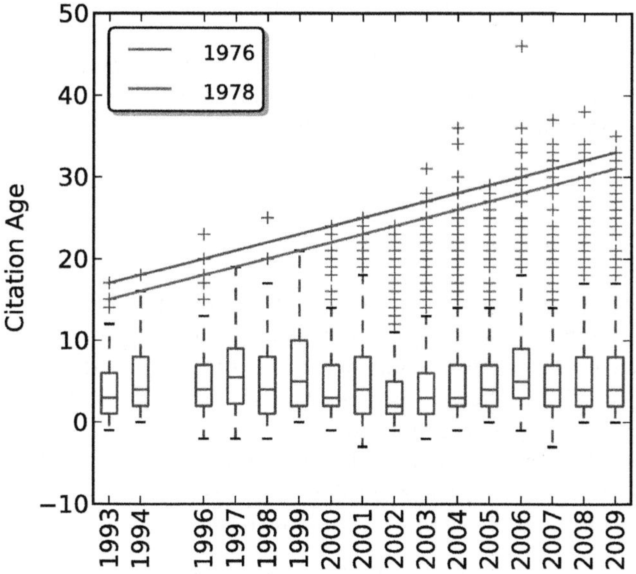

Fig. 4. Citation Age at ACM-CCS

may be tempted to pad long strings of citations with PC members in an effort to flatter them or "pay their dues." Such citations are therefore more interesting than many others, and thus can be probabalistically flagged for human review.

3.4 Encouraging Diversity

Human reviewers can often sort submissions very quickly into three bins: "definitely accept", "definitely reject" and "maybe." Much effort then goes into deciding which of the "maybe" papers deserve to be accepted, even though the number of papers to be accepted may be a small fraction of the "maybe" category. In such cases, automation can help provide two properties that we consider useful: focussing the most reviewer effort on a small number of to-be-accepted submissions and encouraging diversity within the conference.

From biospheres to computer security, monoculture is often recognised as a systemic weakness [1,5], but as stated above, we may be able to observe a worrisome trend towards monoculture in Figure 1. In order to encourage diversity, then, PC software could treat submissions preferentially that cite substantially different work from the papers that will definitely be accepted—if the reviewers have already accepted six papers on the finer points of zero-knowledge proof, perhaps one paper about a new real-world problem would be a breath of fresh air, an injection of new "genetic material," even if the sixteen zero-knowledge proof papers in the "maybe" bin are slightly better written.

One interesting property of this scheme is that, even though it is a statistical-classification–driven approach, it is very difficult to tactically adapt to: since its inputs are not "what got accepted last year", or even "what got submitted this year", but "what has been accepted this year", the kind of paper which will be most advantaged this year cannot be known until all of the first-pass reviews are in. The fact that social networks get an automated leg-up one year in no way implies that they will again next year: in fact, once they become a bandwagon, there will be pressure to get off the bandwagon and restore an interesting balance of work.

4 Future Work

We would like to conduct an experiment with a real program committee in which we ask each reviewer how much time they spent reviewing each submission, broken down into per-submission activities such as "reading up on things the submission cites", "convincing myself the idea works", "explaining why the idea doesn't work", "correcting grammar", etc.[5]

With more data, we would also like to explore the relationship between regular conference attendees and their publication records. Do authors who attend a conference every year tend to be more "introspective" than those who do not?

[5] Obviously, such data must be collected anonymously and could not be shared with the chair before aggregation, otherwise reviewers might experience some trepidation about honestly expressing how much or how little time they spend on each paper.

Does attending a conference encourage others to cite your work, even if that work was not published at the conference in question? Only data can tell.

5 Conclusion

Through the judicious application of mechanical assistance, we believe that the conference submission review process can be made more efficient, focusing the limited time and energy resources of reviewers on those problems which can only be solved by humans. Furthermore, mechanical assistance could encourage good "genetic hygene" in conferences, leading to overall better health in the future.

References

1. Geer, D.J.: Monopoly considered harmful. IEEE Security & Privacy 1(6), 14–17 (2003)
2. Kessler, M.: An experimental study of bibliographic coupling between technical papers. IEEE Transactions on Information Theory 9(1), 49–51 (1963)
3. Pearson, K.: On lines and planes of closest fit to systems of space. Philosophical Magazine 2(11), 559–572 (1901)
4. Simkin, M.V., Roychowdhury, V.P.: A Mathematical Theory of Citing. Journal of the American Society for Information Science and Technology 58(11) (2007)
5. Stamp, M.: Risks of monoculture. Communications of the ACM 47(3) (March 2004)
6. Tang, J., Zhang, D., Yao, L.: Social Network Extraction of Academic Researchers. In: Seventh IEEE International Conference on Data Mining (ICDM), pp. 292–301 (2007)
7. Tang, J., Zhang, J., Yao, L., Li, J., Zhang, L., Su, Z.: ArnetMiner: extraction and mining of academic social networks. In: ACM SIGKDD International Conference on Knowledge Discovery and Data Mining (KDD). ACM (August 2008)

How to Keep Bad Papers Out of Conferences (Transcript of Discussion)

Jonathan Anderson

University of Cambridge, Cambridge, UK

So the problem with social networks and the talks that I've given about those is they're not controversial enough; people just don't have enough opinions about social networks. So let's talk about something that absolutely everybody has an opinion on, which is keeping bad papers out of conferences. This is based on some thinking that Frank and Robert and I have been doing, and I promise that there will be lots of pictures. I know it's the last talk, but you have opinions, I have pictures, so let's all stay awake.

So what is the point of the review process? There are a couple of different ways you can look at the review process for conferences, journals, etc. Here is one perspective: the ancient lore of the discipline is locked away in, and people with festal gowns and Tudor bonnets guard this ancient lore. PhD students, people like me, can be allowed into the ivory tower if they bring a useful contribution, but it's so much easier just to gang up and try and storm the gate together. And so this is one view that you can have of the review process, that the Programme Committee are pouring hot oil on potential usurpers who'd like to get into a place where they don't belong.

Another perspective is to take a genetic view where you see the Programme Committee as a discerning animal saying, "I'd like to improve my genetic fitness," as it were, "so I need to choose suitors, which ones I'm going to allow come mate with me." So they say, "right now I'm really looking for somebody with a big beak, because that's the sort of idea that would make our conference more interesting," or, "oh what beautiful plumage." So you have this field of applicants, and they're all trying to demonstrate their fitness to the Programme Committee, and the idea is that your field will evolve over time as new genetic information is brought in.

In this view, you can look at a paper's lineage, where its inspiration came from, and then you can trace back where that thing's inspiration came from, and all together you have sort of a family tree. But if you come from a place that is susceptible to diseases that come from low genetic diversity, you know that sometimes, everybody is related to everybody, and you don't have as much genetic diversity in the input as you thought you did.

So an alternative name for this work could be, "how to maximise the genetic information of a conference by keeping papers out if they're either weak or exactly the same as what we already have while accepting papers if they're

B. Christianson et al. (Eds.): Security Protocols 2011, LNCS 7114, pp. 368–380, 2011.

really strong and/or contain fresh new material with minimal reviewer effort." But that title was a bit long so we didn't use that one.

Alf Zugenmaier: I think they're two different things. One is keeping bad papers out, the other one is what do you define a bad paper. Keeping bad papers out, depending on the conference organiser, can actually be keeping papers out where you would have not many participants, or you can have all kinds of definitions for bad, actually I think it's harder to find a good conference than it is within a good conference there might be good papers.

Bruce Christianson: I think here a bad paper is one that would be bad for the field.

Reply: Yes, so this is from the perspective of, we have a conference, and it has its kind of DNA, it has its lineage, and you're saying, "who's going to come along and meet within the species next," as it were, to produce new ideas, and to let the field evolve.

Matt Blaze: So we have this crazy system of reviewing papers to solve two problems, and I'm curious which one you're trying to solve, or both. As far as I can tell the two problems are, we want to avoid wasting everyone's time by forcing them to read bad papers, and thereby identify the papers that are worth reading, so we perform this editorial function. And the other function is divvying out brownie points to people who are using them to advance their career, in order to reward the good people. Which, or both, or none of these problems, are we talking about here?

Reply: So, I'm definitely interested in problem 2, and I'm interested in a spin of problem 1. I'm making the assumption that there are a bunch of people who are going to perform an editorial function, but I'm also interested in saving their time a little bit too, because they're busy people.

Matt Blaze: So the third problem is, being on a Programme Committee is increasingly sinking out all of our time.

Reply: Right, that's the third problem which I'm interested in. I don't want to imply that I think the "castle defense" model has no merit whatsoever, I really do think that part of the role of the PC should be to, as easily as possible, just dispense with the potential usurpers so that you can go onto a more thoughtful consideration of which of these potential suitors you want to pick.

So the motivation for this work came out of a conversation that I had last year with several security researchers in which somebody said, "I never read papers that are older than ten years because they have nothing useful to say today, but I still cite them because if you don't cite them you won't get into the conference." And I thought this was a little bit appalling.

Robert Watson: This came from a notable security researcher.

Reply: A notable security researcher. I was a little bit shocked, but apparently you should have seen the reaction of someone who was present who's been in the field for 40 years; he really thought that the work he did more than ten years ago was worth reading. So we started thinking a little bit about what can we do to measure if people are displaying "plumage" that they don't really have, faking it in order to get somewhere we think they shouldn't be.

So some of the attacks that we're interested in are "mating" with the conference, as it were, without actually demonstrating your genetic fitness. In nature it's very expensive to do some of these things: if you want to be a really, really red cardinal, you have to waste a whole lot of keratins that you could have been using developing your bone structure or whatever, but you're effectively saying, "I have so many of these keratins, I'll just throw them away on colouration, that proves how fit I am, mate with me." But if you can have fake keratins, and you can look fit even though you're really not, then you're subverting the whole process, and that's no good. And so this citation abuse is one thing that we identify where people say, "I have to cite it, but I don't actually read it, and I don't actually care," and that's a problem. Another problem is reputation coasting when people just continue doing the same old stuff, without bringing new things to the gene pool, that's also a bit of a problem.

Omar Choudary: I wanted to ask, what is the main rule in deciding the moral aspect about the fact that I'm not reading your paper, and even if the paper is very good, but then citing for the purpose of getting into the conference, but the main thing is having a good idea, why should that be reject? What is the main thing?

Robert Watson: Well, there is a crisis of objectivity here.

Reply: A crisis of objectivity, certainly. Part of the problem is just that you're actually reducing the information content of proceedings. Part of the reason that you read a paper is to see what papers they thought were important and relevant to this idea, and if they're just throwing a bunch of fluff in that doesn't actually matter then you're reducing the content of the proceedings.

Omar Choudary: But maybe you've read it originally, or know something about the paper, but you haven't *read* the paper carefully.

Bruce Christianson: If you can simulate having read the paper well enough though.

Robert Watson: Then you may as well have.

Reply: That's good enough.

Joseph Bonneau: Or maybe you just cherry-picked one statistic from a 200-page PhD thesis, and you're trying to give them credit, but you're not claiming you've read the whole thing.

Reply: Right, and so that can be fine too, and so we don't want to turn the review process over to computers algorithmically determining everything that happens. There are some things where a human judgement will clearly see whether you're doing things in a way that we consider good or bad; it's a value judgement, a moral judgement, that a computer isn't so good at making. But there are some things that are pretty flagrant abuse, and we'd like it if we could help a Programme Committee identify these things, quickly weed out things that deserve to be weeded out quickly, so they can spend more time on interesting things like shepherding work that's really neat but hasn't been written very well, and needs to be described better, or needs just one more element, or something like that.

So the second element, the reputation coasting thing, we're afraid that it might be possible for people who have been around for a while to send all the signals that they know that red bird wants to see, just because they are the signals that they've always sent and it's always worked out for them in the past, whereas somebody who's new to the discipline then has to have really, really amazing research to overcome this institutional inertia, so that's a bit of a problem.

So, is this something that we really need to worry about at all? Do we actually care? We used data from ArnetMiner.org, which was this semantic search thing that took DBLP information, lots of bibliographic information, and charted out a citation graph. There are lots of caveats with the data, like a 15–year-old paper citing a two–year-old paper, rather than the other way around, but still we're able to get some interesting trends out of it. Here's a graph from ACM-CCS, and these are the other conferences that get cited in CCS papers. And you can sort of see there's a trend here: it used to be a big deal to cite CRYPTO, but not so much anymore. So more and more, people in a conference are citing within the conference.

Matt Blaze: The first year for CCS was '92 or '93 I think.

Ross Anderson: We were both there, remember?

Matt Blaze: I don't remember that far back.
So we'd expect that it would have to go up?

Reply: That's true that we do expect it to go up, and that can be a healthy and fine thing, because as a conference grows more mature, and as you have lots of interesting researchers come to a place and say, "here are ideas that I have," then of course you're going to cite that in the future. And people who are gathered in a place like WiSec are people who are interested in wireless security, so of course they're going to cite a lot of papers from a wireless security conference, and that's not necessarily a bad thing. Over time, though, if you're not careful, if this is unchecked, it could lead to a sort of inbreeding where you have the same sort of paper that always gets in in this conference, and increasingly, people outside of your conference don't care what you have to say. So if, hypothetically speaking, the only thing that happened at CRYPTO anymore was people talking about secure multiparty computation schemes that nobody actually cares about, or will ever use in the real world—I'm not saying that's the case—then you'd expect to see this kind of trend on these graphs.

Ross Anderson: But it is: CRYPTO attendance is way, way off from 600 a decade ago to 300 and something now. It's full of theory; I find no papers at CRYPTO I can read, this is a real world phenomenon.

You can also expect a real world effect in that, as a conference matures, more previous papers are cited because there are more previous papers to cite. The total number of ACM papers is 20-something times N, where N is the number of years since 1993.

Reply: Right, that's true, and so CCS doesn't look so bad, but I'll move onto other graphs in a second.

Alf Zugenmaier: Shouldn't you be looking at the outgoing links, like how many other conferences are citing the idea to evaluate how attractive your "children" are for further "breeding."

Bruce Christianson: The issues are, is CRYPTO more attractive as a citation to a CRYPTO paper than it is to a paper chosen from one of these other vendors?

Ross Anderson: Exactly, so this is how search engines work, the more "off the main" links you have, the fitter your paper is.

Reply: Right, so part of the problem with this dataset—and you could tell which conferences the people writing this academic search engine cared about—is that there is lots of data about who people at ACM conferences cite, and almost nothing about who the people at the New Security Paradigms Workshop cite. So, unfortunately, there's just such a scattered distribution that we can only really talk about conferences citing within themselves vs. citing outside; we don't really have a lot of good data to be able to say if other conferences cite in, we can't compare apples to apples.

So, that was CCS. Let me show you a graph to demonstrate that this isn't just a security thing, here's SIGCOMM, where you can see a similar trend, and so, in terms of the top five things that get cited at this particular conference, you can see that SIGCOMM has gone way up; it's getting almost to the point where it's like, "why do you bother citing things that aren't from SIGCOMM? There can't possibly be anything useful in other venues to talk about." CHI has a similar effect; you could imagine the attitude at CHI perhaps being, "if there's good usability research it would have been published in CHI, otherwise it couldn't possibly have been good."

Sandy Clark: No, there's just no good usability research.

Ross Anderson: It may just be that CHI is big. But you have to be careful what you're looking for here. If what you want to beware of is an area that's becoming stale, that people are losing interest in. If you're a good research manager you should be able to spot such areas and steer your students away from them, and there are a number of signals you can use. It would be interesting if, perhaps if some bibliometric researcher was to do some serious work on all this, and use all the various signals that people in the search industry use to figure out what are the best signals for measuring academic fitness. But it's hugely controversial because we have these Research Assessment Exercises every few years, the rules are always being changed, and when they change there are always losers. Computer Science is often a loser because if they, for example, give greater weight to journals, then we write for-the-journal papers, so we have a problem. And what sort of things should we be trying to promote at the policy level. Left to itself, Academia will allow theory to hypertrophy, because that's easier; doing real systems work is hard work, it's easier to sit in the bath and invent theorems. Do you have a deliberate policy mechanism to favour systems over theory, and if so, how do you reflect it in mechanisms like this?

Reply: Right, so I do a bit, and we'll talk about that later, but I will just say two things now. One is that, this data is very inconclusive, there's lots of noise, and I've tried to fix it up a little bit, but I wasn't going to spend three months doing this. The second thing is that this is really from the perspective of, if I'm a conference chair, how can I make sure that my conference continues to have good genetic health, as opposed to, if I'm a person who wants to submit a paper, how do I know which conferences are healthy. That's a related issue certainly, and one worth looking at, but I won't talk about that today.

So what I am going to talk about is better reviewing through automation. There are things that only people can do, and I call these HB-hard problems, for Human-Brain–hard, the sort of thing that you actually want an expert in the field who knows all the literature to say, this is important, this is not important, and I'm not proposing that computers do that. But what we do think that we could do is use some automation to help reviewers focus on the stuff that only people can do, and maybe if some things fall through automated cracks along the way because they're hardly even worth the reviewer looking at, well that maybe wouldn't be a bad thing, because the reviewer could review things much quicker. So we're going to talk about how we can cluster submissions together to aid the review process and then talk about some metrics and algorithms which can be gamed, but if you game them then you've done a public service; there's a societal benefit. We're going to talk about how we might be able to detect social engineering, and if not to say this is definitely social engineering, at least to say, this is the sort of thing that maybe we want a person to make sure they look at and say, does this seem legitimate or not. Finally, we want to promote genetic diversity within a conference, so you want to avoid the situation where it becomes the same old, same old, and every paper is about the same thing, and it's always the same kind of thing over and over.

On the screen now, we can see what today's submission clustering process looks like. Authors declare key words that describe their papers, then reviewers say, I know something about these key words, and then maybe review a long list of abstracts that you like the look of and then express interesting in reviewing certain papers. This can work well, but is rather time consuming. Assuming, however, that we know something about the citations, because authors are required to submit LaTeX source files, then maybe instead of doing all the work they currently do, we can have reviewers just what's here on the screen now, choosing from a set of classic papers. I can say with a fair amount of certainty that if a set of papers all cite the statement of a problem, and three attempted solutions, those papers are all about the same topic. So somebody's who's very familiar with the statement of the problem, and maybe wrote one of the papers that tried to solve it, they're going to be familiar with it, and they might be in a really good position to review that paper. So instead of having to do some of the manual work that you need to do before, why don't we just say, which of these classic computer security papers are you most familiar with, and use that to do the clustering.

Ross Anderson: But this is a problem for people who have been around a few years, I'm sure that Matt and other older people get this.

Matt Blaze: Stop it, that's the second time you've done this!

Ross Anderson: By the time you have got a few papers that are widely cited, we find that the number of really spammy review requests that come from journals you've never heard of becomes a firehose, and all you can do is press the delete button on all of them.

Reply: So in fact, I think that I've said this wrong; the screen shouldn't say, "which of the following are you most familiar with," it should be, "which of the following do you most care about," so maybe you select the paper that is the thing that you've done a couple of years ago, which is really the research area you're trying to focus on now, and you don't select the work from 15 years ago which has been cited ten million times, and now you wish that it would go away, and people would stop bugging you.

Robert Watson: I think that Jon is also pre-supposing this is not an unsolicited review; you're on the Programme Committee, and wisely or not, agreed already to do something.

Reply: Right, you've already agreed to review ten papers.

Robert Watson: And more abstractly, you would want to be on the committee for a conference that uses these algorithms; this might be characteristic of the conference.

Reply: So if you tell your reviewers, instead of doing all of this pre-work before you can do the work, and then the post work, instead you can have this selection be the extent of the pre-review process. So a person who knows what they're talking about has to do the review, but maybe all of the accounting and paper pushing that goes around that process, maybe we can automate that.

Ross Anderson: Well the next time you do a sabbatical at Google, then maybe this is a nice little project for you. If you've got access to the code of Google Scholar, then you can presumably have an automatic system for assigning reviewers to papers, you could try out dozens of different algorithms.

Reply: I think that Google Scholar doesn't publish all their citation graph data in a form that you can crawl, but if you're inside Google then, yes, that should be no problem. And you could imagine, if ACM gave you a big data dump you could write an EasyChair module that would try this out. That's future work, but it would be cool.

Alf Zugenmaier: But how many clusters would you expect for a conference?

Reply: It depends; the Protocols Workshop, probably quite a few, because interests are wide and varied, and very eclectic. Frank, how many clusters would you expect for Wisec?

Frank Stajano: I don't know, there would be a big bunch of RFID things, more wideband things maybe a couple more.

Alf Zugenmaier: But based on citations, you're trying to automate, not on the keyword clustering but on the citations.

Robert Watson: The one thing I'd want to do as an attacker is to cite things so that I get the right programme committee member.

Reply: Right, and so we're going to try and cut down on that with something we do in a few slides.

Ross Anderson: But your signal quality is going to be very, very low if you look at citations like RSA, because everybody cites RSA all the time.

Reply: And we're going to deal with that in a minute.

Ross Anderson: So you would end up assigning me a paper to review if I and the paper's author were the only two people in the universe ever who cited some obscure thing in the Mongolian Yak Keeper's Gazette of 1934.

Reply: Right, so if I were writing this EasyChair module, I'd be doing a Principal Component Analysis that says which citations convey the most information, and get you the furthest away from the mean, and only those papers would be the ones that get listed in the screen that asks what papers you care about. So nobody is ticking the box to say, yes, I think that RSA is really important and relevant, and I want to review papers that cite it. But you might tick the box next to a paper about secure grouping algorithms and wireless sensor networks. If you check something from that cluster, then you're probably going to get a bunch of papers from that cluster, because that seems to be one of your research interests that you care about.

Joseph Bonneau: So it seems like you can basically do the collaborative filtering Netflix-style approach, which has been beaten to death in the last five years by the AI people where you represent every paper as some weighted vector of all the previous papers, and represent all the reviewers the same way, and then you match them.

Reply: So in fact, maybe we don't even have to have this step, or we could start with a pre-populated list of papers that we think you'd be interested in, just click OK, or if you like you can change some of the tickboxes and say, I don't care about that anymore, I want to move on with my life.

Ross Anderson: But come to think of it, you don't need Google Scholar's database, because at a typical conference you will find that there are a 100 paper authors and there are 20 reviewers, and let's assume that everybody's got an average of 50 papers, so that's a total of, not very much.

Reply: Right, so the other thing is, all you need is the citation graph of the *submissions*, and you can require that authors give you that, either because they've given you the LaTeXand you can look for `\cite` commands, so that you have the complete citation graph for all submissions, and that should be enough to do what we need. The graphs that I did earlier had to be drawn from a global view, which was kind of noisy, but this clustering is done from very clean data, and you could be fairly confident about it.

So the other thing about clustering is, you can still do the keyword thing, and sometimes the keywords are going to look very different from what you get in clustering, and by the Law of Excluded Middle, this is either bad or good. It's either bad, because people are just randomly throwing keywords out there, and they don't have a clue what they're doing, they couldn't be bothered to look at the list of keywords, or it's really good because somebody's doing new research that defies the traditional categories. Either way you can flag this up so a human is more likely to look at this aspect of this paper early in the process.

The next thing that we think about is possession. If citations are plumage, that you're trying to prove your genetic fitness. The bird on the screen has very beautiful plumage, but it doesn't matter because it's dead, it can't do anything useful, it's a dead parrot.

Bruce Christianson: It's on sabbatical.

Reply: No, he's just pining for the fjords.

So we'd like to stop you from exaggerating the quality of your plumage very inexpensively through annoying things like flattery, or this attitude where you say, "it's a pre-requisite, you can't really publish here unless you cite Smith's seminal work in Foo." That's no good, because this brings dilution; everybody has to have a huge reference list that's full of sound and fury, signifying nothing. So we have a protocol—it's a protocols workshop after all—where, every time you cite something, we would like you to put a word next to the citation that's generated from a challenge, and this challenge is a word on a page that comes from a hash of metadata about your submission, the thing you're citing, and some kind of nonce that the conference gives you; that might be, for instance, the file name of the LATEX class file. So you take the authors, the conference that it was published in, the year it was published, maybe that nonce again, that's how you get a metadata hash for a paper. And so this is an information signalling protocol, that demonstrates that, at the very least, you have acquired the PDF of the paper, and you have looked inside of that PDF. It doesn't prove you've read it, it doesn't prove you understand it, but if most of the work is in finding the PDF, then there is a chance that you've actually read it out of interest in learning something.

Alf Zugenmaier: So it requires you to have a PDF that has the same layout that you have.

Reply: Well, if you have canonical proceedings, journals and things, they're fanatical about having a specific format.

Alf Zugenmaier: If I go to the HTML version that the author has put up on her website?

Reply: Well, yes, that is a limitation, but we already have this idea of a canonical version and a particular layout and paper size.

Robert Watson: Your citation is supposed to refer to the specific one you read.

Bruce Christianson: This protocol is the death of self-archiving.

Joseph Bonneau: Why can't you do this automatically? You seem to want some sort of human interactivity here, but I don't understand why you can't write a script that will do it for you.

Reply: Right, so I'll get to that in a second. So the thing about possession is, what about collusion and cheating? What if you collude with a bunch of other people to create a really large repository of research papers, and better PDF-to-text conversion than the ACM and all these people have. So you build up this huge collection of research, and machine readable forms of it, and that's fine! If you're ready to go to all that work and create a *better* repository of academic information than we already have, then you've done a service to society.

Ross Anderson: And then people will stop citing all papers, at least nobody will cite the RSA paper anymore, because it's on paper.

Reply: Citing it purely for the sake of citing it, yes.

Robert Watson: This is a known problem for computer science;, so my wife is an historian, she can read papers from the 1950s, but in computer science you can't do that.

Bruce Christianson: That's right.

Reply: The only people who are unhappy in this brave new world are Springer, and I know it's going to be in the transcripts, but I don't really care if Springer is unhappy.

Bruce Christianson: Elsevier is going to be even more unhappy.

Reply: The next thing is, you go from possession to understanding. You'd really like to know that a person has read a paper, they've understood it, and they are either creating a critique of it, or they're allowing it to influence their own research, and that's the sort of thing that a computer can't tell. You need an expert human reviewer, this is an HB-hard problem, but maybe we can help focus the reviewers a little bit in order to make the most productive use of their time. So we can identify the usage, we can identify the outliers in the citations, we can identify citations of Programme Committee members, and we can say to the human, does this look reasonable. We can look at the usage of, for instance, gratuitous citations of Programme Committee members that have nothing to do with the work. So you can imagine software that says, here are the three places where I've cited reference number 1, and you can very quickly look at it and say, this work about transitive trust has nothing to do anything he's saying here, and very quickly dispense with people who are doing this gratuitous citation thing. All it is doing is bringing focus.

We can also statistically find outliers, so this graph shows CCS again, these two lines are years when seminal papers were produced, and you can see that over time, people are citing older and older papers, they're citing back to a fixed date almost, but 50% of the papers are still less than 10 years old, because "who would cite anything less than 10 years old unless it's a token." So what we'd really like to do is to identify, not to show citations, but say, this is one of those citations that either they're using it because they really know their literature, or they're just throwing it in because they think they need to.

The other thing, of course, is Programme Committee citations. Now there's a good reason to cite PC members: if they didn't have good research relevant to the conference that you're submitting to, then they probably wouldn't be on the Programme Committee. But on the other hand, if you're just trying to flatter their vanity, that's the sort of thing again that we want to draw attention to and ask, does this look like a proper citation, or are they just being sycophantic?

So we've talked a little bit about clustering, possession, understanding, the last thing I would like to talk about is diversity. When you're reviewing papers, you can very quickly sort things into definite yes, definite no, and a large maybe pile in the middle; that's a very quick pass. What we would like to do is introduce intentionally preferential treatment to some papers, based on statistics, to encourage people to have new genetic material, and to keep things fresh, to have a balance of what's going on. We'd like to break monoculture wherever possible. And the idea is that, if you've already accepted six papers to the Protocols Workshop on the finer points of zero knowledge proof, then out of the maybe bin, you could give a privileged position to papers that aren't about zero knowledge proof. Yes another paper about zero knowledge proof might be better written than some other thing, but the other thing talks about a new problem that we're not thinking about already in this workshop, so let's bring that in just to mix it up a little, have a breath of fresh air, add a bit of fresh genetic material. It will be for the health of the conference, because you always have to be rolling in new problems, new insights, from outside the discipline, otherwise you will have stagnation.

Now this diversity is classification driven, which means you theoretically could game it, but it's impossible to adapt because it's not about what papers got in last year, it's not even about what papers got submitted this year, it's about what papers have already been accepted *this* year, which means that, if you see a bandwagon developing, then in fact that's not a good place to be.

Bruce Christianson: You're already too late.

Matt Blaze: That bandwagon left.

Reply: So we've already had quite a few questions, but if you have more, and Bruce is happy to let you ask them, then I'm happy to take them.

Matt Blaze: So what I find when I'm on a PC or reviewing, the truly dreadful papers like the ones that are making stuff up about what they should be citing, have lots of other problems that make the reviewing process take time, but it doesn't uniquely take me more time than anyone else: you bat the paper away by pointing out that semantically it is not a valid paper, because it does not appear to solve a research problem, or your proofs don't have an actual end, or whatever. And the problem is not that I've been assigned the wrong paper, the problem is that this paper got submitted in the first place, but it's always going to be rejected, the process doesn't accept those papers, unless the PC is completely asleep. So I wonder which part of the problem you're actually solving.

Reply: So I'm not so much interested in the initial sort into three bins, yes, no, maybe. What I'm really interested in is that the maybe bin is pretty big, and the number of slots left in the yes bin is pretty small. And so you could spend your time reading each of the maybe bin papers very carefully, and going through them, and checking all of the logic, but if you had a little bit of assistance that said, maybe you should focus on these ones, and maybe if you're trying to tell if this paper from the maybe bin is good research or just trying to BS you, maybe a little bit of mechanical assistance could help you with things. "I'm not even going to bother to read this one carefully, because look at the weird, random things they're doing, they think that because they've cited Frank's work that they're going to get into WiSec."

Bruce Christianson: It's the same question as picking a cricket team: do you just pick the 11 best players and hope that something will happen, or do you pick the best team of 11 players? Do you say, well I've already got six fast bowlers, I don't need another fast bowler, I need someone who can keep wicket. And we do this have dilemma when we're on a Programme Committee of saying, all the good papers this year are on zero knowledge proof, but is that what the field needs?

Joseph Bonneau: What's the disincentive to put five random citations to Ross' Yak Gazette thing that nobody else will have? It will make your paper look really unique, and you just ignore the other citations.

Robert Watson: It ends up in the yak pile.

Ross Anderson: But it then ends up being read by me, this is where you can target a particular PC member. But remember that journals and conferences are very different: with a journal you're doing quality assurance of the paper, you're proof-reading it and red-penning it. With conferences, what you're typically trying to do is select the 20 best papers out of 100 that are submitted, so where mechanical assist may be best is in helping to accelerate the triage process, because you start off by saying, here are 10 wonderful papers that we're certainly going to accept, done, finish, here are 70 totally bloody awful papers that we're going to reject, done, finish, and the Programme Committee then spends the rest of its time selecting which 10 of the other 20 are to be accepted, and who's going to shepherd them.

Reply: And so it would be nice if you could have a little help with, "well this paper looks somewhat unique in what it cites, maybe we'll bump that up a little," unless the uniqueness is BS, and it should be obvious when the relevant PC member looks at it.

Ross Anderson: But it can be helpful. If you come to a workshop like this where we don't often see zero knowledge stuff, and somebody sends in a zero knowledge paper, you might have someone on the Program Committee who knows all about zero knowledge, and then if they're talking complete BS the expert on the subject can say, no this is hopeless, very much more rapidly than someone who doesn't work in that field.

Reply: So the goal is, through mechanical assistance, to save PC members time so that they can spend more time doing important things, which include shepherding papers that really need to be shepherded and just doing the rest of their life, other research, going home sometimes.

Robert Watson: There is a tension if you introduce bibliometrics into the situation: it can initially be helpful in the introspective sense, but there might be a broader societal sense in which a sudden focus on bibliometrics can be quite bad, so we should only give this to programmers and chairs, and not to administrators.

Reply: Right, and we certainly hope that the metrics that we use are the kind of metrics where you can game them if you want to, but if you do, you're going to have a net benefit to society.

Bruce Christianson: It encourages wholesome behaviour; that's the protocol that he wrote.

Reply: You can game it by being a very nice boy.

Postscript: Alice Reflects upon the State of the Art in Security Protocol Design*

Flo: What is it you want?
Alice: If I knew that, I wouldn't be sitting here crying in the toilet.

---

* Dialogue from the film "Alice Doesn't Live Here Anymore", Warner, 1974.

Author Index